HUMAN PRODUCTIVITY
ENHANCEMENT

HUMAN PRODUCTIVITY ENHANCEMENT

Organizations, Personnel, and
Decision Making

Volume 2

Edited by
Joseph Zeidner

PRAEGER

New York
Westport, Connecticut
London

Library of Congress Cataloging-in-Publication Data

Organization, personnel, and decision making.

(Human productivity enhancement; v. 2)
Bibliography: p.
Includes index.
1. Organizational effectiveness—Addresses, essays,
lectures. 2. Decision-making—Addresses, essays,
lectures. 3. Employee selection—Addresses, essays,
lectures. I. Zeidner, Joseph. II. Series.
HD57.H84 vol. 2   658.3'14 s   86–528
[HD58.9]   [658.3]
ISBN 0–275–92163–8 (alk. paper)

Library of Congress Catalog Card Number: 86–528
ISBN: 0–275–92163–8

First published in 1987

Praeger Publishers, 521 Fifth Avenue, New York, NY 10175
A division of Greenwood Press, Inc.

Printed in the United States of America

∞

The paper used in this book complies with the Permanent
Paper Standard issued by the National Information Standards
Organization (Z39.48–1984).

10 9 8 7 6 5 4 3 2 1

PREFACE

In the fall of 1982 I joined The George Washington University faculty after a long association with the Army Research Institute for the Behavioral and Social Sciences, whose antecedents go back to the entry of the United States into World War I. In preparing for my new teaching responsibilities, I systematically examined a number of current behaviorally oriented books concerned with organizational performance. I was surprised to find a high degree of similarity among them in structure, content, references, and emphases. Although the areas covered were significant and warranted continued attention, they were very different from those research areas that were being most actively pursued in major governmental and military laboratories. A much broader range of issues was being investigated than those reflected in traditional organizational behavior texts. Rather than embracing the conventional social, organizational, and motivational issues, the newer laboratory approaches emphasized such areas as information engineering, computers and training, and knowledge-based expert systems.

I decided, then, to develop and edit this book, *Human Productivity Enhancement*, and the other volume in this series because I saw the need to bridge the gap between the extensive body of literature on human behavior in organizations and the ongoing personnel, training, and human factors research that holds great promise for affecting performance and productivity. This work was made possible by an Army Research Institute Contract (MBA 903-83-M-5893) to The George Washington University titled "Human Performance and Productivity."

A first step was to determine those current human performance and productivity research topics in the governmental laboratories that would have theoretical, methodological, or applied interest to the behavioral science community as a whole. An analysis was conducted of the research programs of the Army Research Institute, the Naval Personnel Research and Development Center, and the Air Force Human Resources Laboratory, the human factors program of the National Aeronautics and Space Administration, and the Office of Naval Research psychology program. A literature search was made of recent relevant books and articles. Telephone interviews were conducted with leading scientists to obtain their viewpoints. From this review and analysis, a tentative list of topics was compiled. Visits were then made to each of the laboratories mentioned above, as well as to NASA's Johnson Space Center in Houston, Texas, and Ames Research Center, Moffett Field, California, and to selected industrial research facilities. At each of these sites, leaders and senior scientists were interviewed to obtain corroboration of potential content and to solicit recommendations for possible contributors to the volumes.

The areas that were finally selected were organized into five parts:

Training introduces the concept of cost-effective measurement of training and then examines training technologies and applications in computer-based learning, flight simulation, team training, job performance aiding, and biofeedback and performance.

Human factors in systems design examines human factors concerns in user-computer interaction and software development. It also considers new human roles in automated systems and means for designing intelligent interfaces in such systems. Techniques are developed for determining personnel requirements in systems development, along with techniques for measuring human workload.

Organizational effectiveness analyzes various organizational techniques for improving performance from a systems perspective. A new approach to leadership research is examined and an historical account of sociotechnical systems is given. Productivity in organizations is defined and a variety of productivity improvement programs is evaluated.

Knowledge representation and decision making considers theories and practices in the interrelated areas of knowledge representation, expert systems, and cognitive decision making.

Personnel selection and utilization describes the link between cognitive psychology and individual difference psychology in the measurement of human abilities. It also reviews current issues in selection, classification, and allocation, along with detailing a major research program that has the potential for resolving significant technical problems.

Another step was to identify for each topic leading government scientists and experts in universities and industry who were familiar with ongoing work both in and out of the government laboratories. The scientists finally selected for each topic are the chapter authors of these volumes. Instructed to provide a comprehensive, coherent, self-contained view of their topics, they were given the difficult challenge of informing and appealing to the specialist, the professional reader, and the graduate student. Their statements were to be at the cutting edge of their fields and to reflect the state of the art. I believe that the authors achieved the goal of providing significant reviews of their topics, while at the same time expressing their own points of view.

I wish to acknowledge my sincere appreciation to all those who have made this project possible. I am indebted to the reviewers of the chapters from The George Washington University: Karen Hamel, James Mosel, Lynn Offerman, Charles Rice, and Samuel Shifflet. I am also indebted to the reviewers who are Army Research Institute alumni: Abraham Birnbaum, Arthur Drucker, Frank Harris, and Cecil Johnson. I am particularly grateful for the advice and close supportive efforts of Edgar Johnson, the technical director of the Army Research Institute; and to James Tweedale, technical director of the Personnel Research and Development Center; and Earl Alluisi, chief scientist of the Air Force Human Resources Laboratories, for their scientific assistance and the cooperation of their staffs. Also, I was assisted greatly by key members of these laboratories, including Jerrold Levine, Eugene Ramras, and Robert Sasmor, as well as other scientists at ONR and at NASA's Johnson Space Center and Ames Research Center.

In addition, I am grateful to The George Washington University for providing the proper work environment and especially for the encouragement of Henry Solomon, dean of the Graduate School of Arts and Sciences. It is impossible to credit adequately Frank Zajaczkowski for his contributions to the preparation of the manuscripts and the many hours he spent editing the final version. I am also indebted to Gillian Norton for her valuable assistance in typing, proofing, and keeping in touch with the contributors. Finally, I thank my wife, Dorothy, for her support, encouragement, and patience.

CONTENTS

INTRODUCTION
JOSEPH ZEIDNER

Over the last several years the public has become aware of the importance of increasing human productivity by considering the design of a hardware system from the point of view of the potential user. But the design of a hardware system must be considered within the broader context of the job and the organization, which is a more appropriate framework for research on ways to enhance human productivity. Only in this way will the total system then incorporate the various perspectives offered by manpower and personnel, organizational structure and process, training, and systems design.

In planning new behavioral science research, scientists have an obvious need to know what has been happening in all major areas of relevant research, such as academic, industrial, space, and military research and development. However, in attempting to review the state of the art or to probe topics in depth, scientists frequently find that they do not know where or how to obtain definitive material on major military and government behavioral research findings. This is because only a small fraction of the research is reported in refereed professional journals or presented at meetings of professional societies.

Yet, despite this dearth of available information, the total military and space output of research findings and products is vast. A half-dozen major military behavioral science organizations support the U.S. Army, Navy, and Air Force; another half-dozen military organizations are involved in administering contract research. (Two major behavioral laboratories support NASA exclusively.) Indeed, the U.S. Department of Defense is the largest employer of research psychologists in the world, with 750 in-house scientists the majority of whom are psychologists. They conduct basic exploratory and advanced research and development on the acquisition, development, training, and utilization of personnel in military systems to improve organizational effectiveness. Annual expenditures of more than $300 million on in-house and contract efforts ensure comprehensive scope of research efforts that exert a major influence on the field of psychology.

Unfortunately, the essence of this research has not undergone sufficient integration to be maximally useful to managers, scientists, or students interested in historical, methodological, theoretical, or applied summations. Although emanating from military and space settings, the basic scientific orientation of this research has substantial impact on some of the major issues of concern in contemporary society and, in turn, has universal appeal and usefulness to the world of work at large.

The two volumes in the series describe and evaluate research areas and applications that have as their goal enhancement of productivity. Four specific outcomes are targeted:

1. A consolidation of theory, research, and application of human performance findings of the governmental laboratories and their integration within the extant body of literature.
2. An examination of the relationship between human productivity and performance from a systems perspective, incorporating new concepts and research findings that emphasize the technological environment of information engineering, to highlight the criticality of computer-based aids for enhancing selection, training, systems design, and decision making.
3. A projection of future human productivity and performance and operations research needs and applications of findings.
4. A uniquely comprehensive coverage on improving performance in the work place—unique because the multidisciplinary nature of the research would normally be found only in many diverse books and periodicals. Its coverage ranges through a wide array of topical issues confronting the behavioral scientist today.

I have attempted to summarize major ongoing and planned research, technology and issues from the perspective of behavioral scientists in the military laboratories that has promise for improved performance and productivity in the work place. This summary is provided under several broad groupings.

TRAINING

A 1982 study by the Defense Science Board describes new directions in training technology and appears to be very influential in setting the training research agenda for the 1980s (Defense Science Board, 1982). To increase the ability to evaluate and capitalize on new training technology, the five major recommendations of the board with the highest priorities have been singled out. These recommendations represent the most critical and implementable steps that might be taken to improve training and to ensure that systems are operated and maintained to their full design potential.

1. Establish a performance measurement R&D program to develop criterion methodology and equipment for use at all levels of training; set up demonstration projects for new training technology to collect data on performance and cost-effectiveness. Since training requirements continue to increase in scope and complexity, the traditional approach to training performance measurement is inadequate and fragmented. A systematic program is needed to obtain performance data, to evaluate and support training acquisition and management, and to appraise the potential of new training technology.

2. Increase exploration and use of current and advanced technology devices (such as arcade-like games) to motivate and teach functional skills. New training technologies may be applied to teach basic skills (language, computation) and job performance (functional) skills while reducing reliance on bulky and frequently ineffective printed matter.

3. Increase support and use of voice recognition and synthesis (including speech storage), interactive display technology, personal microprocessor training aids, and application value of Very High Speed Integrated Circuits (VHIC) to training. These technologies are necessary for a dramatic improvement in the state of the art of training. Work must be accelerated in these areas to facilitate progress in classroom and unit operational training.

4. Develop and incorporate embedded training and performance measurement and recording capabilities in systems. Emerging systems with internal microprocessors and computers afford the opportunity for incorporation of embedded training and performance measurement. This capability should be considered early in systems development.

5. Future acquisitions of training equipment should use transportable software and be user-friendly in delivering instructions. Systems that utilize computer-specific software complicate operations and training and increase costs. More generalized software that is designed for the nontechnical (noncomputer-trained) operator and maintainer will increase operational capability, reduce training scope and complexity, and therefore reduce training costs.

Several other points are worthy of note. Microprocessor-based, interactive videodisc systems have revolutionized the instructional industry. Software, including courseware development, is the dominant cost factor for computer-based instructional systems. Advanced software techniques promise gains in software/courseware production efficiency, but they have not yet been applied. Systems based on digital technology can be used to provide more effective training and performance measurement with little additional cost. Satellite communications capacity exists that may be used for remote training, maintenance, technical manual updating, and maintenance teleconferencing.

Individual, basic skill training has already benefited from advances in some areas of training technology. This technology will be equally applicable for teaching advanced skills. The ability to couple computer-based devices with digital communications and picture outputs will provide the possibility of improved initial and refresher training devices, including picture outputs, and should be exploited as quickly as possible.

Another issue is that of effective simulation to create, as closely as possible, realism within the training environment. Because of this, team performance and training should emerge as a major focus of interest, supplementing the traditional orientation of the individual's processes and activities.

SYSTEMS DESIGN AND COGNITIVE PROCESSES

Decision making is one critical function that will change radically as distributed information networks evolve. No longer are information systems being automated using larger, centralized processors and a hierarchical structured approach that encompasses all functions. A continuing problem with these systems is the mass of data that inundates decision makers. Decision makers have few aids available to help them make effective use of the overwhelming data. Most information systems in use today rarely take advantage of natural language or user-oriented dialogues; nor are there decision support techniques within these systems that emphasize cognitive compatibility and friendly interfaces. For even though user-friendly interfaces and languages are often proposed, the distinguishing characteristics necessary for a friendly interface have not been well defined or evaluated. Other required user support tools include graphics, means of organizing and presenting information, and development aids for procedural, computational, perceptual, and cognitive tasks (Modrick 1982).

Incorporating automation to support operators in their use of cognitive and perceptual skills will continue to be increasingly important in the person-systems interface. However, currently the functions required for these skills are not performed well by computer-based data processing techniques. On the other hand, repetitive tasks that require high reaction and search speeds, including accuracy, are performed very well by the computer and should be automated. What is needed, then, are principles for apportioning activities between users and computers that are appropriate—that is, those best suited to the computer and those best suited to the user. The activities that individuals and computers perform well together are those interdependent components of tasks and functions within a system that simply cannot be allocated automatically.

The limiting factor in systems development to date has been the inadequacy of hardware and software systems for organizing and processing information. However, the increasing transferability and flexibility of software should add capabilities in future years. The extension of automation into the cognitive domain has several research implications, including near-real-time knowledge representation of hierarchically structured data bases and special techniques to encompass tasks that require mixed initiatives and interactive context-dependent dialogues between the user and the computer.

Another broad area of promising new research involves the merger of artificial intelligence (AI) and cognitive psychology. The principal objective of such research is to develop systems concepts that will provide smarter systems through automation of some human functions. AI is expected to increase productivity, reduce personnel needs, and permit more effective utilization of individuals. Current limitations in software architectures and in specifying psychological behaviors impede implementation of complex cognitive functions. However, sufficient progress has been made in emulating human perceptual and cognitive processing functions to justify seeking additional advances in the design of more intelligent systems. Research is needed to determine which intelligent functions can be built into systems, which capabilities are worthwhile, and which applications presently constrain, condition, and determine design requirements. We must also be able to narrow the scope of information processing by selectively filtering data in accordance with an adaptive, goal-directed strategy.

Evolving technology in the development of intelligent terminals and interactive displays will bring about a marked increase in person-computer interactions. Pictorial and graphic representation will transform sensed data in the external environment and filter the data to remove unwanted information or selectively enhance important information. Such displayed environments will consist principally of emergent situations. The user will perform semistructured tasks that emphasize recognizing and diagnosing situations in terms of the action they require. Recent advances in hardware and software have provided capabilities in interactive graphics, dynamic presentation, analytic aids, and symbology to make sophisticated and adaptive interaction possible. For instance, some types of graphics interact strongly on the basis of the user's experience with computers in the subject area concerned.

Another key factor in the use of graphics is the extent to which they are compatible with the user's way of thinking. Knowing the user's mode of thinking may simplify the process of graphic design in systems. An increase in user-computer interactions also can be expected because of new speech recognition and synthesis techniques that provide ways to reduce visual demands and hard activation of controls. Speech recognition also provides faster control input, whereas speech synthesis permits the user a "heads-up" capability. Speech synthesis is currently more advanced than speech recognition; in fact, commercial systems are already available for various military applications.

The application of computers is ever accelerating, along with the use of specialized data processing systems, general management information systems, special microsystems, and chip technology applications. The application areas for these technologies are diverse, from food processors to vehicle ignitions. It seems likely that soon virtually all new equipment will be computer-based. What is needed are guidelines for integrating the individual into computer-based systems that include person-computer interfaces designed on the basis of an individual's capabilities. Certainly, the accelerated development and application of artificial intelligence techniques will permit significant advances in this area.

Increased personnel costs and the declining availability of skills require a reduction in both the number and skill levels of personnel needed to field systems properly. An additional need is thereby imposed on human factors design engineers for their input into the concept phase of systems development. Concentrated efforts will be needed to simplify rather than complicate equipment—to use technology to better prepare individuals to operate and maintain it and to better match hardware to the people available. Research is underway to assess the manpower, personnel, and training implications of a new system before it is built. Such research uses a nearest-equivalent piece of existing hardware to test the ability of personnel with available skills to perform the actions proposed for a candidate system. This technique permits identification of necessary changes that will simplify or reduce operator or maintainer skill requirements. Much more work remains to be done to develop this technique before it can reach its full potential.

MANPOWER AND PERSONNEL

Each year the military and the civilian sectors recruit, select, classify, train, and assign thousands of new individuals to their work force. The system devised for running the work force is necessarily broad and complex. Preceding the recruitment process itself are projections of personnel requirements, identification of requisite personnel resources, and the plan for allocation to meet specific requirements. Then individuals are recruited, selected, classified, and often assigned to training tracks to optimize the fit between requirements and capabilities. Programs for retaining effective individuals and for providing career development are devised to protect the enormous investment in training and experience that an effective individual represents.

One major effort in this area is the Army Research Institute's seven-year research program to relate preaccession personnel measurements based on results of Armed Services Vocational Aptitude Batteries (ASVAB) to actual individual performance on the job. A comprehensive research effort of this kind is necessary because the current classification system has not been validated against individual performance for specific Military Occupation Specialties (MOS) with

Armywide applicability. Performance data obtained by tracking individuals from initial recruitment through successive tours will be used to develop a longitudinal data base, which in turn will lead not only to Army models for selecting and allocating individuals more cost-effectively but may have important implications for criterion-related validity studies in the civilian sector and case law under Title VII of the Civil Rights Act of 1964, as well as its interpetations and enforcements.

An additional applied outcome that can be addressed within the ASVAB validation framework is a more realistic evaluation of the value of adaptive testing and goal programming techniques applied to ability testing and the allocation of jobs. Methodologically, a more comprehensive examination of the appropriateness of validity generalization or transportability can be expected. Also, this program can serve as a vehicle for exploratory efforts that seek to bring the psychology of individual differences closer to classic psychology through convergence with cognitive psychology.

The demographics of the civilian population have been changing rapidly, with serious implications for the available labor pool for the military, industry, and academia. Trends include such areas as unemployment, growth, immigration, technology, occupational supply and demand, education and training, standard and nonstandard recruitment age groups, compensation and benefits, households and families, working conditions and attitudes, women in the labor force, migration pattern, and unionization (Futures Group 1983). Specific issues related to these changes include person-machine mix, career development, separation, skills development, readiness, and family-worker support.

The ongoing trends in the labor force include decreases in the number of 18-to 21- and 22- to 34-year-olds and increases in the numbers of blacks and Hispanics; growth in employment benefits as a percentage of total compensation; an increase in participation and retention of women in the labor force; an increase in demand for mathematical and literacy skills and in technical and maintenance jobs, but a decrease in low-skilled jobs; an increase in female-headed households; an increase in participative management and in worker individuality; high unemployment among low-skilled and low-literacy workers; population increases in the South and West; an increase in white-collar unionization and more compulsory arbitration in lieu of the right to strike; the growth of white-collar occupations; increased competition for skilled blue-collar workers; and high demands for engineering, computer science, and medical technology specialists.

The most important change anticipated in the labor force over the next two decades will be the age structure shift of the U.S. population. The 18- to 21-year-old group will decline from 12.3 percent of the labor force in 1980 to 9.5 percent in 1990. A decline will also occur among 22- to 34-year-olds, accelerating by 2000. The 35- to 54-year-old group will increase from 35.7 percent of the work force in 1980 to 41.5 percent in 1990 and 51.5 percent in 2000.

Implications for the work place over the next two decades are becoming quite clear: It will be increasingly difficult to recruit 18- to 21-year-olds. Competition from all sectors of the economy may become intense; pay and benefits and training opportunities may require drastic changes if qualified candidates are available. Still, an older labor force will mean an increase in both work experience and educational levels and should lead to a decrease in unemployment or underemployment.

Women, with or without familial commitments to children, and even mothers with children under 6, have become members of the labor force in increasing numbers. By the end of the 1970s, 50 percent of all women had entered the labor force. The projected figure is 60 percent by 1990. Women have begun to view work in terms of lifetime employment much as men do now; they compete with men for both compensation and career advancement opportunities. The fact that working women have gained tremendously in social acceptability is only part of the reason for the increase. In other cases, two or more salaries in the household may have become a standard requirement. In addition, divorce is on the rise, significantly increasing the number of female-headed households. Since working women are changing their career expectations and requirements, employers may well have to modify their policies and procedures.

Compensation and benefits are expected to change radically during the next decade. As a result of the changing age structure and changing social values, the following are expected to be important shifts: Overall compensation for new entrants into the labor force will increase as their numbers decrease, creating increased dissatisfaction within the baby-boom generation already at work; and employers will increase employee benefits as a percentage of compensation to keep pace with inflation (nontaxed benefits) and to help solve the growing problems of employee dissatisfaction and lack of motivation. Many employers will offer "cafeteria-style" benefits, allowing employees to choose fringe benefits best suited to their lifestyles and needs.

One of the most likely issues of the next decade will be that of equal pay for comparable work. Even though current laws require equal pay for equal work, they have not achieved their desired result because the pay scales for traditional female jobs have not increased comparably with traditional male jobs. One argument might suggest that the intrinsic value of the job must be assessed to determine its "true" value in comparison with other jobs, and in this light compensation should be geared toward equal pay for jobs of equal worth. Although it would be difficult to implement, this system could well create a major change in the entire job market.

The revolution in the communications and computer industries caused by the advent of the microprocessor will have a profound impact on the types of skills required of future workers. Service industries will see rapid advances in automation, as will the manufacturing sector, thereby displacing low-skilled workers. The new jobs created by increased automation will require both literacy and mathematical skills, making retraining difficult for many displaced workers.

Research should examine the entire area of technological change and its impact on skill requirements. To understand future labor requirements, a systematic investigation is needed to determine the relationship between skill types and new planned systems and the degree to which the necessary skills will be available in the civilian labor pool. Alternatively, research should look at the need to change the new systems to accommodate the expected skill and performance levels of both recruits and current members of the military.

DEVELOPMENT OF COHESIVE TEAMS

One critical concern is how to get the best leadership at all organizational levels. A leader development system needs to be designed that will produce leaders who can build cohesive, disciplined, high-performing units. The changing demands of leadership roles that occur because of technological advances and a rapidly changing environment require responsive leadership to accomplish the decision-making requirements of the future. While much good work is underway using conventional methods, the use of microprocessors, video-discs, interactive displays, and telecommunications can significantly enhance flexibility and realism in simulations used for leader training.

Time is a crucial resource; we do not have enough of it. Modern technology, coupled with current methods, promises better use of the precious training time we do have. Development and implementation of realistic simulations designed expressly for leader training are much needed, along with simulators and associated courseware. These simulators need not be complex or expensive. In a microcomputer-based management game an individual or a team plays against the machine, which provides not only a realistic environment but also data on the execution of the player's decisions. The end-to-end development cost could be small, and development time is relatively short.

Although microcomputer games are proven training tools, simple paper simulation might be equally effective. Using paper displays, a game may simulate a manager's decision and display environment, carrying the manager through a sequence of operational events and decisions to ensure a complete understanding of systems characteristics and rules of operation. Development time is a few weeks, and development cost is quite low.

Regardless of the approach, team training remains perhaps the most vital kind of training for leaders. Investments should be made now in implementing on-the-shelf technology to enhance ongoing training efforts. Many scientists are convinced that great possibilities exist for enhancement in the future. New methods and devices will be required to meet this need. Trainers have witnessed a fascinating parade of initial attempts at simulation and, of course, computer-aided instruction for a wide variety of subjects and topics. Such efforts should be organized, integrated, and intensified. An automated, embedded capability built into the console of team stations should be extended to alter existing systems and new systems.

Future use should be made of exportable training packages built around portable microelectronics. Ideally, training packages would not need to rely on specifically trained instructor personnel or special equipment, although for effective implementation, a greater understanding of performance measurement, evaluation, and training strategies would be required. Effective design of such packages would profit from a better means of characterizing users and their needs. In conjunction with these developments, emphasis should be given to developing an integrated system for the feedback of performance data from operational units as a basis for upgrading training programs.

Measurement of unit effectiveness and cohesion, which embraces all aspects of human behavior in a work setting—selection/classification, training, total systems performance—is a fundamental concern of all human performance research. Because objective measurement of individual and collective performance is the quintessential dependent variable against which experimental alternatives are measured, this program must be broadly based, addressing technology-aided techniques for objectively assessing improved individual competence for job tasks, team performance and its contribution to total system effectiveness, and, with more precision that ever before, cohesive unit performance.

ORGANIZATION OF VOLUMES

This summary of current research served as the basis for organizing the volumes around five major areas that correspond to the major functions in systems development of designing the system, running the system, specifying systems processes and decision aids, training systems personnel, and developing cohesive teams for systems operation. The five areas are presented in two volumes to reflect better the human factors versus the industrial and organizational interests of readers rather than specific sequences of events in systems development.

REFERENCES

Defense Science Board. 1982. "Summer Study Panel on Training and Training Technology." Washington, D.C.: Office of the Undersecretary of Defense for Research and Engineering.

The Futures Group. 1983. "Trends in the U.S. Labor Market and Their Implications for Future Army Manpower Planning." Paper prepared for Army Research Institute, February.

Modrick, John A. 1982. "A Projection of Research Needs of the Army of the Year 2000." Paper prepared for Army Research Institute, July.

HUMAN PRODUCTIVITY ENHANCEMENT

I ORGANIZATIONAL EFFECTIVENESS

The decline in U.S. productivity during the last decade, however measured, has been the subject of a great deal of concern among governmental policymakers, industrial and labor leaders, workers, and scientists. The causes attributed to the decline in productivity are numerous, complex, and interrelated. But no matter what the causes, both labor and management are now actively working for ways of improving productivity.

One area of universal concern is personnel costs. Usually, the first response to "excessive" costs is to impose personnel freezes, reductions in force, and budgeting constraints. Managers feel that fat can be cut in this area without much impact on organizational performance, especially since estimates indicate that workers are only about 50 percent "productive." Such actions, however, invariably reduce organizational performance and result in reduced morale and undesirably high employee turnover.

Everyone acknowledges that people are the key to productivity and that they want to do a good job. At the same time, workers are rarely used to their full potential. Good management practices help motivate workers to perform better, but such increased effort needs to be directed toward achieving organizational goals. The worker, although more efficient ("doing things right"), may not be more effective ("doing the right things"). Efforts to improve organizational productivity are seen as involving both efficiency and effectiveness to varying degrees, depending on the situation. Of course, overall organizational productivity includes all structural elements beyond the individual.

A very large number of behavioral techniques and approaches have been successfully used to improve productivity within a given organization. However, the transportability of these techniques to other organizations has not been as successful, and a variety of contingencies or moderators are invoked to explain the limited generalizability of results. Currently, we lack an adequate conceptual framework to use in matching organizational characteristics with the underlying dimensions of the techniques employed to achieve maximum, predictive effectiveness.

One study examined 11 psychological approaches used in 207 field experiments aimed at improving productivity (Katzell and Guzzo, 1983). In 87 percent of the cases, there was improvement in at least one concrete measure of productivity. The intervention programs that were most often successful were training, goal setting, financial compensation, participative supervision, and sociotechnical systems design. Worker output measures (quantity, quality, cost-effectiveness) were more consistently improved than variables related to personnel costs (attendance, turnover). The psychological intervention programs not only improved employee productivity but had a favorable impact on quality of work life at the same time. Because they are the subject of separate chapters in this section, two types of intervention programs are considered in greater detail below.

Managerial leadership is generally considered a major factor in organizational behavior because of its putative effect on individuals, groups, and organizational outcomes. Some regard leadership as a special case of social influence. But progress has been very slow in understanding why leaders exert influence in certain situations while not in others. Research has not produced particularly robust and reliable findings in this regard. Typical readings in this area include topics on theories of leadership, demands of the leadership role, leadership selection and training, normative models of leader decision-making styles, attribution analyses framework for leaders, and organizational substitutes for leadership.

The sociotechnical systems approach to job design concerns the interface between the technological system and the social system. In practice, this involves the redesign of technological work processes and the formation of autonomous, self-regulating teams. A widely publicized use of the sociotechnical systems approach was the "successful" Volvo project in Sweden in the late 1970s, where the conventional continuous assembly line was changed so that work remained stationary to reflect more natural modules of work. A number of companies in the United States have also tried this approach, stressing design and job structuring goals and an optimum variety of tasks, a meaningful pattern and wholeness of tasks, introduction on the job of elements that engender recognition and respect from others, opportunity to meet standards of quantity and quality of work, and implementing quality of work life and industrial democracy objectives. With gathering societal support for the improvement of quality of work life, and with the rapid introduction of automation, it seems likely that the sociotechnical systems approach will assume greater importance in the future.

In the first chapter of this section, a new leadership theory is formulated in which leadership is viewed as an attribute of a system. The second chapter reviews the current literature on psychological approaches to productivity improvement. The final chapter provides a review of sociotechnical systems theory and applications, and future.

In Chapter 1, T. O. Jacobs and Elliott Jaques present their theory of leadership in formal organizations. At the outset, the authors find that most current theories of leadership are directed only at the lowest organizational levels and employ methodologies that capture the near-immediate time frames exclusively. The consequence is that narrow, interpersonal perspectives are stressed and cause and effect linkages with longer durations are not discovered. The authors reject the four traditional approaches to the study of leadership phenomena: trait, behavior, situational variables, and power/influence. The broader view taken by the authors is an organizational perspective based on general systems theory (or later variations), particularly on Jaques's general theory of bureaucratic organizations. A key assertion in Jaques's theory is that organizations have one particular structure of work strata that is both discrete and discontinuous if the organization exists in its requisite form. In the requisite form, each stratum has its own unique critical tasks to perform and adds value to each of the other strata by performing them. The critical tasks themselves have time spans or horizons (the maximum time allowed for accomplishing the task), which can be used to index the strata. In large organizations, seven work strata are identified along with their associated time spans (three months to ten or more years) and the general functions they serve.

The leaders in each stratum must interpret their own environment and reduce uncertainty by defining adaptive change to the next lower stratum. The role of leadership is to ensure that the uncertainty reduction process is accomplished, the short-term versus long-term balance is judicious, and appropriate resourcing of adaptive change is effected. Thus, leadership is more properly viewed as an attribute of a system than of an individual. Effective leadership at senior levels depends on the extent that leaders' frames of reference or "cognitive maps" accurately represent the relevant external reality. These maps permit leaders to act proactively in the causal stream of events, structuring and energizing their organizations to be adaptive. An effectively adapting system must maintain sufficient energy reserve to mediate change. Leaders balance current systems output and future needs, ensuring that neither efficiency nor adaptability is compromised. Jacobs and Jaques conclude that executive selection techniques must focus on ability and willingness to form complex cognitive maps of organizations as key variables. Also, they stress that development of executives should include the process of "guided discovery." Understanding of leadership is best served by identifying organization end states that act as causes themselves to produce future desired outcomes.

In Chapter 2, Cynthia M. Pavett, Laurie A. Broedling, and Kent H. Huff examine psychological approaches to productivity improvement. Their aim is to integrate the current literature with previous reviews of worker productivity programs. After analyzing salient factors that influence the operational definition of productivity, they view productivity as any aspect of work output (quantity, quality, values) or any aspect of input or cost expended (labor and material costs) to achieve output. Productivity improvement is seen as an increase in output or decrease in input without an offsetting change in the other component. Using the same criteria developed by past reviewers, 31 field experiments conducted after 1981 were placed into one of eight intervention categories and then critically evaluated. They found that while the productivity-related literature produced between 1981 and 1984 is prodigious, only a handful of studies describes the results of productivity enhancement and meets the strict criteria for inclusion in this review. The literature provides much advice about increasing performance but little empirical evidence for the advice. The behaviorally based studies included in this review significantly improve productivity in organizations. Although comparisons among the types of interventions are difficult to make because of contextual factors, four of the eight types were judged to have significant effects on productivity. A popular and traditional approach to productivity enhancement is to provide training and instruction to workers and supervisors. Results indicate that training and instruction efforts can be large and substantial, provided that they are focused on relevant job tasks and of sufficient duration. Appraisal and feedback interventions involve assessing employee job performance and providing guidance through feedback, coaching, or counseling. The majority of field experiments in this area used behavior modification techniques. While performance improvements were significant, little evidence is provided on how long improvements last.

In goal-setting interventions, goals are generally set at high but achievable levels for important tasks. While goal setting can improve performance and productivity, it is often difficult to separate its effects from feedback effects. Financial compensation interventions attempt to link performance to some type of monetary incentive and generally have good results. However, the duration of performance contingent reward systems effects are not known. In this review, work design, supervisory methods, and work schedule interventions were not as successful. Only one study dealt with the area of recruitment techniques. The authors discuss limitations in criterion specification, assessment of cause and effect relationship, generalizability, and issues involved in implementation. They make a number of suggestions for new directions in productivity research and conclude that emphasis should be given to those interventions that enhance quality and durability rather than those that enhance quantity. Quality concerns of business are evidenced by the increase in the use of statistical quality control methods; psychology approaches to quality issues need equal attention.

The body of knowledge about sociotechnical systems, Kenyon B. De Greene writes in Chapter 3, concerns both theory and applications work, which have evolved over the last 35 years. The term "sociotechnical systems" was first used by researchers at the Tavistock Institute in 1951 to describe the type of analysis and design of industrial-production systems that focuses on the match between social and technological subsystems. A sociotechnical work system must be viewed not only as the outcome of interaction between the two subsystems but also in terms of the organizations in which it is embedded. De Greene points out that the Tavistock researchers contributed to the development of two of the most important social themes of contemporary work organizations—quality of work life and industrial democracy. Attitudes toward work, benefits, and behavior on the job have changed greatly in the past two decades. Commitment has decreased and alienation has become widespread, especially among American and British assembly workers. Despite high relative pay and benefits, productivity and quality of output are declining. One idea to spur productivity is to improve the quality of work life through better technology-work-systems matches or alternative design ideas such as the high degree of participation by Japanese workers in decision making and methods of arriving at group consensus.

Applications of industrial democracy have involved such features as greater worker decision making and control at the work-systems level, design of all space (parking, driving, office) on an egalitarian basis, and participation through elected representatives at all levels of corporate management. The classical sociotechnical systems approach, holistic in concept, is limited by the context in which it is applied and by interfaces with other approaches. Variables that can affect sociotechnical design include poor management support, hostility of unions, and poor human factors design. The author believes that the factory of the future will not be totally revolutionary because considerable automation has already been accomplished. It is likely to combine the efficiency of mass production with the person-based flexibility of batch production. The work force will consist largely of small numbers of professional systems managers. Most of the command, control, communication, and coordination (C^4) will be performed automatically in the cybernetic factory of the future, linked to humans through intelligent interfaces (I^2). C^4I^2 systems design can provide a holistic view of total factory function and operation. De Greene concludes with a discussion of "getting from here to there" and says that the major challenge will be the management of complexity, and complexity is best managed by seeing the whole.

REFERENCE

Katzell, R. A., & Guzzo, R. A. (1983). Psychological approach to productivity improvement. *American Psychologist, 38,* 468–472.

1

LEADERSHIP IN COMPLEX SYSTEMS

T. O. Jacobs and Elliott Jaques

A vast leadership research literature exists, as is evidenced by the number of citations in the recent revision (Bass, 1981) of Stogdill's earlier, 1974 review, *Handbook of Leadership: A Survey of Theory and Research*. However, most of these efforts and most of the current theories address leadership only at the lowest organizational levels. Where work has been done at higher levels, it has generally used—uncritically, it would seem—very similar methodologies. Unfortunately, these have generally been attempts to link measured attributes of managers to their measured success (for example, by salary growth or by ratings by superiors or subordinates) or to the measured effectiveness of their group/organization. Where the work has been done by psychologists, the main focus has been on behavior, searching for direct causal links and seeking to explain their absence through recourse to moderator variables, intervening variables, and the like. In these and most other cases, the time horizon of the research has been relatively short, that is, a cross-sectional design has been used or a longitudinal design has been pursued over a period of one or two years. Longitudinal designs beyond this near-immediate time frame are quite rare. The consequence is that cause and effect linkages with longer durations have been rendered invisible by methodology.

That methodology and research focus may have precluded discovery of causal mechanisms at higher organizational levels was given a great deal of implicit attention by Hunt and Larson (1979) and specifically by Luthans in that volume. Dansereau, Alutto, and Yammarino (1984) addressed the same issue in a systematic differ-

7

ential examination of methodologies appropriate to specific theoretical issues by level. While these two treatments are morphologically dissimilar, the base issue is the same: A test of theory must be based on a theory and on the proper questions derived from the theory. Without these, tests may be meaningless. Worse, the research is blind, not providing insight to support leadership theories. One thesis of this chapter is that current leadership theories are too limited by their historical focus on interpersonal behavior to enable derivation of appropriate questions. A concomitant purpose is to suggest appropriate directions by offering the beginnings of a more general theory.

TRADITIONAL POSITIONS

Yukl (1981) has provided an excellent overview of current traditional positions. As he describes them, there are four major approaches to the study of leadership phenomena: power/influence, trait (or leader attributes), behavior, and situational. In each of these four areas of research, the vast majority of available empirical studies focus on leadership and leadership effects at the lower operating levels of formal organizations.

The power/influence research has followed at least two lines, stemming, in Nagel's (1968) view, from work by Lasswell and Kaplan (1950). The first of these was characterized by a fundamental interest in power differentiation, power dynamics, and the impact of use of power within organizations and systems. Social exchange theory and transactional leadership theory are functionally related to this body of thought, as is game theory. Exemplars within this broad thrust are French and Raven (1959), Etzioni (1961), Homans (1958), and Blau (1964). Hollander and Julian (1969) developed a transactional theory of influence development (idiosyncracy credit) using principles of an exchange variety; Jacobs (1971) suggested a broader integration of the leadership literature that explicitly uses exchange theory. Graen (Graen & Cashman, 1975) and Dansereau (Dansereau, Graen, & Haga, 1975) have since provided very substantial extensions of leadership theory (vertical dyad linkage) using exchange principles. The second major line of power/influence research includes primarily social-psychological thought as exemplified by Cartwright (1959, 1965), among others, and a focus on the internal dynamics of groups.

In both lines of thought, most of the data-based research, at least that done by psychologists, has been at the level of the individual or the individual collectivity, and not at the substantially higher level of aggregation required to understand causal linkages between leader/ manager performance and organizational outcomes.

In comparison with power/influence research, trait research is ancient. Enough work had been done on leader attributes to permit a review as early as 1933 (Smith & Krueger, 1933). Much of the research included in that study and in Stogdill's (1948) review was psychometrically oriented, that is, focused on identifying consistent characteristics of the individual that were predictive of future performance. Within the past three decades, trait research methodology has broadened from extensive use of narrowly construed paper-and-pencil self-report measures to include such other methodologies as assessment centers, projective tests, and situational tests. It should be noted that trait research has thus converged with behavioral approaches; no current body of theory relying solely on trait constructs is in use. Perhaps the strongest criticism of trait approaches is just that. No convincing identification of cause and effect linkages between traits and group/organization performance exists within a coherent current theory. Thus, while some consistencies do appear even in the current literature, the work itself is more descriptive than prescriptive, and even then is more relevant to personality theory than to organization theory. Further, most of the work is cross-sectional, that is, correlational, and therefore is lacking in methodological capacity to identify long-term cause and effect linkages between the measured constructs and organizational performance.

Efforts to relate salient leader behavior to relevant criteria can be found in the very early literature. However, systematic behavioral approaches originated in World War II with the British Army War Office Selection Boards (WOSBs) and the Office of Strategic Services (OSS) situational testing. They were given programmatic focus by the efforts of Stogdill (Stogdill & Shartle, 1948; Shartle & Stogdill, 1953; Stogdill & Coons, 1957; Halpin & Winter, 1957; Shartle, 1963) at Ohio State University and of Katz and Kahn (Katz, Maccoby, Gurin, & Floor, 1951; Katz & Kahn, 1952; Kahn, 1960; Katz, 1963) at the University of Michigan. In terms of total volume, most of the leadership research in the preceding three decades has been behavioral in nature (including the contingency or situational approaches described below).

However, measurement and the focus of theory still have been at the level of the individual or the collectivity, in the main. Relatively little quantitative effort has been expended in study of the more senior levels, particularly with regard to the possible impact of executive behavior on long-term organizational performance. Examples of exceptions now appearing are Mintzberg's (1973) research on the nature of managerial work, Kotter's (1982) descriptive study of executives, an essentially phenomenological study of decision-making processes of a small number of executives by Isenberg (1985), and Levinson's series of studies of higher level leadership culminating in his recent work on chief executive officers (1984). A notable long-term study using assessment center technology is Bray's (Bray, Campbell, & Grant, 1979) follow-up of initial assessments of 274 Bell System recruits. Most of the current understanding of effective leadership practices at lower organizational levels has come from behavioral research. However, the major contributions to theory building have come from situational and contingency approaches, as discussed below.

Situational and contingency approaches originated with reviews by Stogdill (1948) and Gibb (1947), both of whom concluded that leader effectiveness rests on situational determinants, whether the leader attribute studied is a trait or a behavior. The logic of both situational and contingency theories is that leadership is a functional process. Knowledge of the function that needs to be served in any given situation and at any given time allows one to infer the required leader behavior, if the cause and effect linkages between leader behavior and desired outcomes are known. In the original situational theories the logic was simplistic. It was uncritically assumed that leaders were effective if they were authentic in the role behaviors demanded by the situation. Contingency theories are more complex, in that they generally define criteria of leader effectiveness and then seek methodologically to relate leader behavior to them, examining the manner in which explicit intervening or moderator variables govern the obtained relationships. Perhaps the best known contingency theory was developed by Fiedler (1967). Examples of relatively mature situational theories are provided by House (1971), Osborn, Hunt, and Jauch (1980), and Yukl (1971). These have the potential for becoming quite complex, particularly those of Osborn, Hunt, and Jauch and of Yukl. Situational and contingency theories have major promise, in that their architecture offers the potential for going beyond the focus on interpersonal leadership that up to now has characterized the field. However, this promise has yet to be realized in reported research.

Several problems remain to be solved before leadership theory achieves full maturity. First, it must demonstrate utility beyond purely descriptive purposes. Korman's (1966) criticism of nearly two decades ago, in which he noted little evidence for improvement in leader effectiveness following training based on structure/consideration constructs, remains pertinent. While a substantial number of studies in his review of that literature showed cross-sectional relationships between leader behavior and various dependent variables, the results of efforts to improve on dependent variables by training on those leader behavior variables were uniformly disappointing. Perhaps, in view of Miller's (1973a, b) work on structuring and destructuring—increasing and decreasing the structure of open systems—this should not be a surprise. From a systems perspective, the complexity of the internal and external environments determines the degree of structure needed, and failure to control for complexity should obscure any systematic relationships that might otherwise be demonstrable. In this view, leader behavior is a systems mechanism to adjust the operating characteristics of the system itself, to make its utilization of energy more appropriate to the task and external environment with which it must deal.

Lack of predictive utility raises questions about the theory itself, of course, even considering the possibility that the studies cited were too simplistic, that is, did not reflect the greater maturity of contingency/situational approaches by controlling situational variables. Two exceptions are the result of work with Fiedler's LEADER-MATCH (Fiedler, Mahar, & Chemers, 1977) and with leader training that Graen (1984) developed using vertical dyad linkage (VDL) concepts based on social exchange theory. Graen found that VDL-based training for leaders resulted in substantial group productivity improvements. The reasons for this improvement probably lie in improved leader sensitivity to the actual motivators of subordinate behavior and improved skill in management of work place contingencies. While results from use of LEADERMATCH are not uniformly positive, they are mostly so. Again, the dynamics underlying improvement in group performance are not totally clear. However, analysis of the content of LEADERMATCH suggests an interesting hypothesis.

The LEADERMATCH theory is that the relevant personal characteristics of the leader are not amenable to change, but that relevant aspects of the situation are. LEADERMATCH thus attempts to sensitize the leader to his or her own relevant personal characteristics and to methods for changing the relevant characteristics of the situation to make it more favorable. While this approach does not deal with the issue of attaining a leadership position, the suggested methods of situational change appear subjectively quite useful. LEADERMATCH probably results in improved leader skill at understanding and managing situational contingencies. If these speculations are correct, there is a common thread: Improved skill at understanding and modifying situational contingencies will increase leader effectiveness. A corollary is that a focus on leader behavior divorced from situational factors may not increase effectiveness.

While generalization from two examples is obviously risky, there are other reasons (for example, theoretical issues concerning time span of work) to suspect that the dynamics of leader influence may be found to rest more in indirect mechanisms activated by modification of situational contingencies than in direct means (for example, interpersonal interaction) and that the indirect nature of leader influence is more pronounced at more senior levels.

A second major area of needed improvement in leadership theory lies in the dependent variables of interest. This, of course, is the criterion problem with which scientists have wrestled for some time (Campbell, Bownas, Peterson, & Dunnette, 1974). However, this problem appears particularly burdensome for leadership and organizational research because uncertainty about what dependent variables are appropriate increases as one moves from production-oriented work groups to the level of the organization (or corporation) as a whole. Indeed, at the level of the whole organization, there are conceptual issues about how organizational effectiveness should be assessed (Seashore, et al., 1982a). And even if these conceptual issues did not exist, there would still be a major obstacle confronting research at executive levels. The elapsed time between the initiation of a causal event and the observation of the dependent event may span a period of years in some cases, and these may be the more critical events for purposes of leadership theory construction. In the most complex cases, there may be both uncertainty about the proper dependent variables to observe and the time frame over which they should be observed. An example is provided by research that modeled the demise of the *Literary Digest* (Hall, 1976) and found that the managers in charge evidently had not understood the systems variables or the interdependencies among them, thereby causing the magazine to collapse.

The framework advanced in this chapter will take the form of a situational theory. It proposes that the critical tasks required of leaders differ across organizational levels, with the tasks at higher levels systematically requiring greater conceptual effort, specifically the capacity to deal with more uncertain and more abstract constructs. Effectiveness at any given level within an organization is thus dependent on the capacity to learn the role behaviors demanded by the tasks at that level. The theory itself thus has implications for organizations—information systems, for example—and for leader development. Perhaps more significant, it will provide a systematic view of leadership beyond the first one or two levels of formal organizations, the focus for most research thus far.

LEADERSHIP—A BROADER FOCUS

One problem with theory development has been a lack of consensus on what leadership is, as evidenced by the very large number of definitions Stogdill found (1974). In general, however, this variety has been characterized by a focus on interpersonal behavior, within a collective context, with regard to goals made collective through some process and based on some means whereby influence can be generated. Some specify constraints (Stewart, 1976) and yet others specify contingencies (Fielder, 1967). Yukl's (1981) conclusion is appropriate, "The operational definition of leadership will depend to a great extent on the purpose of the researchers . . . [but] leadership research should be designed to provide information relevant to the entire range of definitions, so that over time it will be possible to compare the utility of different conceptualizations and arrive at some consensus on the matter" (p. 5). In the present view, this useful direction can be pursued only with a broader construct of leadership than has generally been used thus far.

That broader construct, a view of leadership as a systematic discretionary process within an organizational context for specific organizational purposes, was given focus in the mid-1960s (Katz & Kahn, 1966) and became a major tool for integrating leader behavior and organizational performance in the 1970s (Osborn, Hunt, & Jauch, 1980). Specifically, this view is that leadership is "influence over and above that typically invested in the role" (Hunt, Osborn, & Martin, 1981, p. 11), that is, something beyond what is mandated by rules, regulations, and procedures. By inference, this "something" is discretionary, that is, the result of a decision by an actor to do something, and is aimed at getting something done that needs doing. This perspective ties leadership to problem management and problem solving as critical aspects of the role.

This broader view is based on a perspective of organizations as systems, from either general systems theory or one of the later variations, such as living systems (Miller, 1978) or open systems (Katz & Kahn, 1978). Systems theory is a powerful tool for developing a more general theory of leadership with relevance at all levels of organizations, whether complex or not, drawing attention to such generalized phenomena as boundary management, subsystems interdependency, information acquisition and use, and exchange with the external environment across systems or subsystems boundary. Viewed as open systems, organizations are entities, acting within an environment that is generally competitive and sometimes hostile. They are dependent on the external environment for resources (information, matter, and energy) and must maintain no less than parity between resources acquisition and resources utilization or eventually die. Parity permits a state of organizational homeostasis. The most fundamental organizational issue is continued survival, and the key leadership task at any given level is to contribute to survival by whatever means is appropriate for the level of system or subsystem at which leadership is being exerted. Leadership is not the unique property of a given role incumbent, because the survival issue is collective (system or subsystem), not an individual issue. (Leadership will normally be ascribed to heads of systems or subsystems because of consistencies in the allocation of slack and fixed energy within systems and subsystems, but it clearly is not necessary that one be a head in order to lead.)

When viewed as open systems, theoretically organizations should be found to have similar kinds of general problems, for example, co-ordination of interdependent subsystems (Georgopoulos & Cooke, 1979), movement of information markers across boundaries (Miller, 1978), and evaluation of interdependent processes, particularly between reciprocally interdependent subsystems requiring information exchange (Thompson, 1967). These problem types fall into very broad categories relating to organizational adaptation, transformation process efficiency/effectiveness, and organizational maintenance. These categories, in turn, provide direction toward a systematic approach to leadership that is quite general. The conceptual task is to derive from them useful formulations amenable to test in real organizations.

Organization theory has become progressively more complex over time. Most theorists view organizations as open systems, but sometimes with a caveat. Seashore et al. (1982a) compare and contrast a natural systems model, a goal model, and a decision process model that describes how organizations employ information resources to maintain systems integrity while attaining organizational goals. In its pure form, each model is insufficient to deal with the complexity of organizational behavior; however, the three together were thought to be "nicely complementary, referring to different but interdependent facets of organizational behavior" (p. 6).

> Drawing upon a little optimism . . . one can assert that for most organizations, most of the time, there must be a state of compatibility among the three domains of effectiveness that have been described. Systemic integrity must exist in sufficient degree of balance among the component factors; goals must be attained to some sufficient degree—particularly those describable as system outputs of kinds that sustain resource input transactions; decisions and control processes must be sufficiently appropriate and workable to deal with the problems relating to goal structures, systemic maintenance and the maintenance of a sufficiently efficient goal-oriented input-throughput-output system. (p. 7)

In general, the view one takes of organizations is dependent to some extent on the phenomena of interest. By the same token, leadership is dependent on the organizational view.

A general theory of bureaucratic organizations has been proposed by Jaques (1976). A key assertion in this theory is that organizations

TABLE 1.1. Functional Domains in the Requisite Organization

Stratum	Time Span	Functional Domain
VII (Corporation)	20 years	Systems Domain—Operates in a nearly unbounded world environment, identifies feasible futures, develops consensus on specific futures to create, and builds required resource bases to create whole systems that can function in the environment. Conditions environment to be "friendly" to systems created. Creates a corporate culture and value system compatible with social values and culture to serve as a basis for organizational policies and climate.
VI (Group)	10 years	
V (Company)	5 years	Organizational Domain—Individuals at stratum V operate bounded open systems thus created, assisted by individuals at stratum IV in managing adaptation of those systems within the environment by modification/maintenance/fine tuning of internal processes and climate and by oversight of subsystems.
IV (Division)	2 years	
III (Department)	1 year	Production Domain—Runs face-to-face (mutual recognition or mutual knowledge) subsystems units, or groups engaged in specific differentiated functions but interdependent with other units or groups, limited by context and boundaries set within the larger system.
II (Section); I (Shop floor)	3 months	

have one particular structure of work strata that is both discrete and discontinuous if the organization exists in its requisite form. In the requisite form, each stratum has its own unique critical tasks to perform and adds value to each other stratum by performing them. The critical tasks themselves have time spans or horizons (the maximum time allowed for accomplishment), which can be used to index the strata. Work strata, typical terms by which they are named, and their associated time spans are shown in Table 1.1, together with the general functions they serve. The significance of this theory as a vehicle for the development of a general theory of leadership is that the key problem-solving tasks of leaders are clearly those associated with the critical tasks of their level and the critical functions those tasks serve. In these terms, and the earlier formulations pertaining to discretionary use of influence, leadership consists of discretionary action directed toward dealing with unanticipated events that otherwise would influence outcomes of critical tasks at the actor's level. In Miller's (1976b) terms, "leadership operates 'at the margin'; its role is to compensate for the inappropriateness of other components of process structure for dealing with the problem at hand" (p. 18).

Very broadly, and for present purposes, leadership at any given level is a discretionary process of giving purpose to an aggregate expenditure of energy and mobilizing energy to achieve the defined purpose in relation to critical tasks relevant to systems adaptation, effectiveness, maintenance, and/or efficiency. The specific form leadership takes will vary from level to level within an organization, within the generic of problem solving and energizing adaptive action.

CRITICAL TASKS BY LEVEL

This approach differs from the conventional practice of first recording leader behavior and then of inferring its class or purpose. Instead, it first suggests a general model of organizational functioning and then the leader/manager/executive behavior requisite to that functioning, by level. It thus is the beginning of a theory linking leader function to specific organizational functions by level (Jaques, 1986).

A variety of quite important implications flow from the notion that there are critical tasks at each organizational level and that effective leaders address these tasks. A first task has to do with assessing leader effectiveness. Proper assessment will require identification of the correct dependent variables and these may well differ from stratum to stratum. A second has to do with the selection of leaders/ managers/executives. Jaques's general theory suggests that there is a predictable growth over time of capability to perform at more senior organizational levels, based on maturational processes associated with growth of cognitive power. Capability defines the extent and complexity of the context within which an individual can operate and the ultimate level of organization at which an individual can operate, given that complexity increases with organizational level. However, selection is a process that usually is accomplished at entry level, before capability has matured. This, in turn, has implications for development of leaders/managers/executives. If there is predictable growth of capability over time, it seems likely that there may be some sequences of growth experience that are useful for producing executive ability and, unfortunately, others that may systematically deny individuals the growth opportunity needed to achieve their full potential.

The nature of the critical tasks at each level is suggested by analysis of current organizations with reference to the general theory and by time spans found to be associated with incumbents at the various levels. Table 1.1 shows one possible grouping of the seven strata of requisite organization into three broader domains. As thus conceptualized, these major domains are characterized by major shifts in complexity and abstraction of the critical tasks. It should be noted that these three domains correspond to conceptual divisions of hierarchies as made by others (for example, Katz & Kahn, 1966), but with greater differentiation of function internally and more pointed reference to actual organization structures and correspondingly differentiated tasks. Stamp (1981), for example, has described the particular features of rules and regulations at each stratum and how people handle them. Jaques, Gibson, & Isaac (1978) have provided one approach to a theoretical explanation of the nature of the discontinuities pointed out by Stamp.

Systems and Subsystems

To understand the function of leadership in such organizations, particularly as it relates to control systems and information systems, it is essential to identify the level that constitutes a true open system operating in an unbounded environment and the levels that constitute subsystems operating within the boundaries of the open system. According to Jaques's theory, it is only at stratum V that one finds an open system in the full sense of the term. This is the level of the full-scale, profit-and-loss account trading subsidiaries of large corporations.

The levels below stratum V, from I through IV, are all subsystems contained within the boundary constraints set by stratum V. These subsystems are increasingly constrained at progressively lower levels within the organization, and these constraints decrease openness as they increase rationality. When work at these levels does reach out into the surrounding environment of the total system, it is within rules set by the system and regulations that limit the environment within which the subsystem may operate and its options in that environment.

At the upper end, the roles at strata VI and VII operate within the relatively unbounded environment. These levels are the strategic or corporate levels of functioning, whose incumbents are concerned with the establishment, fielding, or modification of stratum V systems, overseeing and resourcing these systems, and sustaining conditions within the external environment favorable for the resourcing and operations of these systems. Figure 1.1 shows conceptually the positioning of a stratum V open system within the environment, with higher strata superimposed, and the nesting of increasingly constrained subsystems within the open system. The particular significance of time for these systems and subsystems has been discussed by Jaques (1976).

FIGURE 1.1. Stratum Structure.

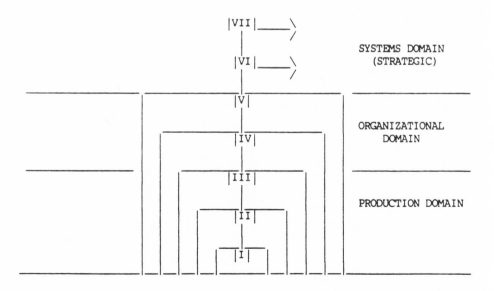

The Production Domain

At the production level, the superordinate operates a section or department that is a bounded subsystem performing either a service function, a production function, or a marketing function. The personnel strength of the first-level section will generally not exceed 60 (all members must be able to know each other) and that of the second-level department will not exceed 350 (all members must be able at least to recognize one another). The important superordinate production functions are defining tasks, setting goals, monitoring progress, and maintaining an even pace in the flow of work. In Thompson's (1967) terms, these are core organizational elements that achieve efficiency through rational processes, that is, the pace regulated or buffered to eliminate surges. Although total rationality can only be approximated, and may not even be desirable, the leadership task is to achieve the right approximation by defining what is to be done, protecting the doing process from turbulence, and maintaining stable integration of people, machines, and resources. The processes performed at this level are almost always direct and concrete in the sense of people working with their hands (or tools or machines) on tangible materials.

Stratum I—This is the level at which an organization's production work is usually done. It thus is the basic level at which the transformation operations are conducted in systems. Incumbents work by the immediate process of operation upon objects, guided by rules and procedures at the "touch and feel" level. A high level of certainty usually exists about what is to be done, based on task specificity, job descriptions, control measures, work rules, and other means of standardization. A central issue at this level is the pacing of work by the individual so as to complete tasks by the required completion time, within the energy resources available.

Stratum II—This is the first level of management. Incumbents work through the flexible use of rules (deductive context), given a set of incompletely specified goals or means. Ambiguity is reduced by "filling in" of the objectives and needs of each concrete situation. This stratum must accomplish some uncertainty reduction in defining tasks for stratum I, in part by balancing out surges in workload and requirements (buffering to increase rationality at stratum I). A central issue at this level is maintaining the output capability of the work group by balancing the requirements for individual development against the requirement for immediate production.

Stratum III—This is the second level of management, in which an incumbent will have several subordinate section leaders or foremen. The work remains concrete in the sense that tasks are still specifically given. However, at this level, they take the form of objectives over time, and buffering of lower levels may take the form of anticipating variation in tasks and work load over time in the accomplishment of objectives. Extrapolative skills are required to ensure that current operations will, over time, meet objectives. A central issue at this level is balancing improvement of the system to meet current quotas or goals against the improvements deemed necessary to meet future predicted requirements.

Two consistencies can be noted, one across all strata and one across strata within the production domain. The consistency across all strata is the "central issue" at each stratum. In each case, a decision is required to balance immediate gain against future gain. At higher strata, the "time of future balance" between the two conflicting opportunity costs is more distant.

The consistencies across the production strata are the concreteness of objectives and tasks and the need to work with individual people (or machines) within groups as the means of production. Stratum II groups are "mutual knowledge" groups, so characterized because managers should have knowledge of their subordinates as individuals, together with their strengths, weaknesses, and personal goals. In exchange terms, personal knowledge is a necessary basis for trust. Where manager and subordinate have positive regard for one another, increased personal knowledge of one another increases trust, perhaps in part because it constitutes an investment that then tends to be protected, and forms a basis for the differentiation of reward structures required by Graen's role-making processes. By the same token, stratum III groups are "mutual recognition" groups, too large for systematic mutual knowledge but small enough that members, and leaders, recognize one another as "belonging to one another." Jaques suggests that stratum III groups become less effective when their size increases beyond the limit at which this is possible. (It should be noted that the lower limit is not fixed, but rather is contingent on other factors, among which are turbulence, proximity of members, and technology.)

Production leadership is thus influence exerted in face-to-face interaction, based largely on interpersonal skills and the emergence of influence potential within an interpersonal and group context.

The current leadership literature is focused predominantly on the lower end of this domain and leadership processes appropriate to it.

The Organizational Domain

At the organizational level, the stratum V superordinate operates a bounded open system: a major company or a division of such a company. Because of the complexity of the process, it is no longer possible to work directly with individual people or machines as at the production level, except in rare instances in which the direct output occurs at stratum III. (Basic research is one example.) Again to use Thompson's concepts, the organizational domain is a buffer between the turbulence of the external environment and the rationality of the production elements and subsystems. Perhaps the most important functions of the operational level are to provide rational environments for subsystems by decreasing both uncertainty and equivocality (Daft & Lengel, 1984), to coordinate the actions of the interdependent subsystems, and to monitor and maintain the transactions between the whole system and the external environment.

Stratum IV—This is the first level of general management. The work at this level is no longer concerned with the concrete realities of the production process, except in those cases in which the complexity of the task puts the lowest level of production at stratum II or III. The significant change at this level from the next lower level is that direct scanning of subordinate operations is no longer possible, either because of the geographic distribution of subordinate units or because of their number and complexity. Stratum IV general managers are responsible for coordinating the vertical integration of several production units, making milestone plans for achieving production or other goals, keeping their production technology current, and recommending capital investment to transform technology where that is needed to maintain competitiveness. They are also more responsible for the maintenance of collateral relationships than managers at lower levels. A central concern at this level is whether existing subunits and subunit technology (and their integration) are the best for the transformation processes for which the manager is accountable.

Stratum V—This is the highest level of general management, corresponding to the president of a full-scale independent company or subsidiary of a larger corporation. Stratum V managers are responsible for the adaptation of their organizations within the external environment. They thus are within-systems change managers. They are responsible for vertical and horizontal integration of the total system, management of collateral interdependencies of subordinate stratum IV subsystems, and the formation of pricing and marketing strategies. This is the first level at which integration of product development, production, and sales occurs, and thus is the level at which strategic investment decisions are made that would change the vertical integration of the company or its future ventures. It is also the level at which policy is made that governs the internal climate of the organization. The basic criteria are profit and loss, for the short run, and product development, marketing, and production strategies in relation to cash flow and future investment needs, in the long run.

The consistencies at the organizational level lie in the need to manage organizational processes and the adaptation of the organization as a system to its environment, in competition with other systems within the same environment. In broad concept, decisions at the organizational level determine, among other things

- The product lines to be produced and the timing of changes
- The production technology to be used and the timing of changes
- The structure of the production subunits
- The methods for coordinating interdependency among production subunits
- Quantity and quality standards for production subunits
- Control systems, information systems, and measurement systems

In addition to decisions that govern production subsystems, decisions are made at the organizational level that determine integration of product development, production, and sales (for manufacturing organizations) or their analogs (for other types of organizations). Decisions of these types determine, among other things

- What constitutes effectiveness at the organizational level
- Methods for assessing effectiveness
- Resources allocations to the various major functions at the organizational level, for example, development, production, sales
- Strategies for acquiring and using relevant information from the environment

- Strategies for managing organizational change in the face of anticipated environmental change to maintain effectiveness and competitive advantage

The Systems Domain

Here managers operate at the level of either executive vice president or chief executive officer of a corporation with more than one independent operating company subordinated to a corporate headquarters. At this level it is no longer useful to work with the separate parts of individual companies. Rather, the concern is with developing new subordinate business units and conditioning the external environment to be both favorable to existing business units and receptive to new ones. Managers at both stratum VI and stratum VII are intensively involved with national and international networking because they are responsible for "reading" the external environment and seeing the stratum V systems in the context of that environment.

Stratum VI—Managers at this level validate the profit and loss objectives of subordinate companies within the context of the corporation as a whole and the environment. They formulate development objectives both for the corporation (new businesses either to develop or acquire) and for subordinate companies within the context of corporate objectives. Through networking and the use of corporate information sources they provide subordinate companies a far richer understanding of the external environment than normally would be obtained by that company on its own. The actions of stratum VII corporations have major impact on future developments in that environment, so access to understanding of where the corporation as a whole is going, provided by stratum VI executive vice presidents, enables the stratum V manager to provide substantially more certain guidance to her or his own company and to be far more efficient in the acquisition of useful outside information.

Stratum VII—The CEO's primary responsibility is the development, construction, and fielding of new business units. The CEO opens avenues for stratum VI managers, validates their judgment that their business units are the viable ones for the world in which they operate, uses them for systematic environmental scanning, and creates opportunities for them by forming coalitions that result in creation of resources bases necessary for the development or acquisition of new businesses. The theory suggests that these CEOs are also responsible for ensuring that their business units "fit" the societies within which they are embedded, largely by ensuring that the corporate culture and value system are "like" the culture and value system of the encompassing society, which, in turn, increases the acceptance of the business unit by the society.

The consistencies at the systems level stem from the location of the corporate headquarters, essentially outside their subordinate systems and within the external environment—political, economic, social, technological, and intellectual (ideas). The primary business at the systems level thus lies in two areas. One is interaction with this external environment, both impacting on it and getting and interpreting information from it to produce a more rational (stable) environment within which subordinate companies can operate. The second is creating critical resource masses, that is, fiscal, raw materials, personnel, technology, and favorable public and/or political opinion, for future ventures.

Skill Requirements by Level

If the critical tasks of managers and leaders vary by level, then it is also reasonable to assert that critical skill requirements also vary by level. This notion, of course, is not new. Executive development programs depend on the assumption that executive skills can be systematically honed through guided experience in some combination of educational and occupational exposures. Most organizations have systematic developmental tracks for executive development. Unfortunately, very little systematic information is available about the logic used to develop these tracks, the assumed underlying growth dimensions, and the extent to which any given growth experience produces increments of executive (or other) ability within these dimensions (or others). And without systematic information of this nature, there is little assurance that any given formulation is capable of either replication or generalization or, for that matter, evaluation.

There is little research on which to draw for systematic formulations of growth dimensions and variation in performances within dimensions across organizational levels. Katz and Kahn (1966) speculated about three broad skill areas (technical, interpersonal, and conceptual) within which variation across organizational levels could be expected to occur. Lower level requirements were more heavily biased toward the technical, with higher levels biased toward the conceptual. However, they did not provide systematic skill identification within dimension by level.

One of the earliest systematic formulations of growth dimensions and skills by level within dimensions was provided by Clement and Ayres (1976). Nine dimensions were identified, which varied across five organizational levels. The nine dimensions were communication, human relations, counseling, supervision, technical, management science, decision making, planning, and ethics. The levels were labeled first-line, low, middle, top, and executive. The nine dimensions can be located without difficulty into the more general Katz and Kahn dimensions, as follows:

Conceptual: Decision making, planning, ethics
Interpersonal: Communication, human relations, counseling, supervision
Technical: Technical, management science

In addition, the five levels can be located without difficulty into the three general domains described above, as follows:

Executive: Executive
Organizational: Middle, top
Production: First-line, low

The Clement and Ayers model has been used extensively for identifying specific leadership skills by level within the Army. The Jaques model has also been used extensively for the conceptual structuring of large industrial organizations and is presently used as the theoretical base for major experimentation in both the Army and a large multinational corporation. The integration of these two permits the general specification of leadership skill requirements by levels, as thus far identified, within the broader categories of conceptual, interpersonal, and technical.

Postulates—Discretion and Frame of Reference

In the following sections a general specification of this nature will be provided, with the following underlying postulate: Leadership is a *discretionary* function, that is, it is outside the application of established process structure (Miller, 1973b; Hunt, Osborn, & Martin, 1981), though establishing process structure generally is a leadership function. (Note that defining leadership as a discretionary function by fiat requires that leadership theory focus on contingencies.)

This discretionary postulate has already been discussed at substantial length. It clearly leads to the assertion that leadership is, among other things, one outcome of an interpretative process that reduces uncertainty about what to do, by whatever means is necessary, and that thus maintains the integration (coordination, control, momentum, interdependence) required to do what must be done within a defined organization. It is not exclusively the property of managers, though it tends to be regarded as such, for example, a boundary spanning unit has a leadership function within the thrust of this postulate. Thus, managerial role relationships are merely one particular subset of a larger set that may, for example, include subsystems interdependencies.

The exercise of leadership requires a *frame of reference*, which is a tool for understanding information flows relevant to discretionary requirements and is sufficient for that purpose. (Note that this postulate by fiat places an emphasis on cognitive aspects of leader performance.) Hunt (1983, p. 142) states that cognitive science "treats thinking as the manipulation of an internal representation of an external environment." He illustrates by making an analogy to computer problem solving, in which the effectiveness of the process is determined by the extent to which the internal representation captures the key aspects of the external world, the efficiency of the program for manipulating the internal representation, and the power of the elementary operating processes. The parallels in humans are representations, strategies for manipulating the representations, and the elementary operations themselves.

It would seem reasonable to postulate that a process of this nature underlies the thinking operations used to understand (interpret) the complex patterns of events, particularly external environmental events, that typically are encountered at higher echelons of formal organizations. This interpretive process is at the heart of the conceptual skill area. Nadler and Tushman (1983) summarized issues of complexity, control, and the need for an implicit model of the organization: Given its "inherent complexity and enigmatic nature, one needs tools to help unravel the mysteries, paradoxes, and apparent contradictions that present themselves in the everyday life of organizations. One kind of tool is the conceptual framework or model. A model is a theory which indicates which factors (in an organization, for example) are most critical or important. It also indicates how these factors are related, or which factors or combination of factors cause other factors to change. In a sense, then, a model is a road map that can be used to make sense of the terrain of organizational behavior" (p. 112).

This model, or theory, is what Hunt called a representation and is here called a frame of reference. It is a tool that enables one to understand the flow of events that constitute experience. Viewed from the perspective of the actor, the stream of events at any one moment is cross-sectional. Some of the events have no antecedents, that is, are noise. Other events have immediate antecedents, and still others have distant antecedents. To the extent there is noise and/or events with antecedents that cannot be inferred through use of the model, or frame of reference, the stream may not make sense, that is, may lack a discernible pattern. As Watkins (1981, p. 10) notes, "Perception involves the active construction or synthesis of a model of the world rather than the passive reception of pictures of the world." When the frame of reference is inadequate for the task, that is, lacks the capacity for sufficient complexity to match the complexity of the picture that must be constructed, the perceiver will be unable to determine what the data stream means. In contrast, to the extent one has a model, or frame of reference, with internal complexity sufficiently great to allow discernment of whatever patterns exist in a given data stream cross section, the situation will have meaning and that meaning can then be a basis for decisions concerning subsequent required action.

The total map, in theory, consists of the factors, elements, and events that are salient for the actor, together with their interrelationships, causal or otherwise. By "mapping" these factors and their dynamic interrelationships, the frame of reference enables the actor to understand how a given situation came to be and how to influence it further. Discretionary control of a situation can exist only through understanding the causal mechanisms through such a frame of reference.

A frame of reference of the requisite complexity is thus a requirement for discretionary action at any given organizational level. However, the complexity of the event stream that an actor must be able to interpret generally increases at higher echelons, for at least three reasons: First, the number of elements that are interdependent increases, and the complexity of their interdependence increases as a power function of the number of interdependent elements, if one can roughly equate number of linkages with degree of complexity. Second, the variance of the timing of antecedent events increases with hierarchical levels, so that the problem of differentiating the separate threads of consequent events in the total stream becomes more difficult. There are simply more threads, and thus more intermingled events within any one cross section of time. Further, at least some of the threads extend over substantially longer periods of time, which means the search for causal antecedents is more complex and thus requires more "computing (cognitive) power" and more comprehensive maps. Third, at higher levels, managers are increasingly dealing with the external environment, which contains events produced by purposeful strategies of other managers at the same or higher levels. To the extent that these are complex strategies and, further, that competitors make efforts to conceal or disguise their strategies, the complexity of event patterns should increase very substantially, and the difficulty of pattern perception should increase proportionately.

Production Domain Leadership Skill Requirements (Strata II and III)

Because the work at this level deals with production processes, leadership here is concerned with the integration of people, materials, equipment, and tasks. Discretion is generally limited by the body of technology, rules, and control measures established at these levels and by the degree of rationality they produce. This, in turn, varies with the nature of the production process itself and, perhaps more specifically, with the complexity and scale of the process.

The fundamental requirement is for an understanding of the technology employed and how to keep it going, on the one hand, and the people employed and how to keep them going, on the other hand. The existing leadership literature clearly shows these two foci, which is not surprising given that most research has focused on small face-to-face groups, whether in the laboratory or in the context of real formal organizations, and has produced contingency theories of leadership that deal with leader behavior in relation to subordinates with respect to task functions. This is, of course, congruent with the Katz and Kahn generalizations and with the integrative view of the present writers (see below). Skill and frame of reference requirements at this level have a concrete quality and would be of the types shown in Table 1.2, drawing from Clement and Ayers (1976).

These skill requirements are not an exhaustive set; Clement and Ayers provide a far more elaborate matrix of skill requirements by level. However, those selected for presentation above illustrate the production level, which encompasses Jaques's strata I through III, his mutual knowledge and mutual recognition levels. Reflection on the existing leadership literature shows that this is where the focus has been, with minor exceptions. While that focus is by no means unimportant, it seems fair to conclude that a much broader scope is required, a scope that has until now been the province of the organizational theorists.

Organizational Domain Leadership Skill Requirements (Strata IV and V)

Organizational leadership is much more complex than that required by the production domain. There is substantial evidence that organizational leadership requires interpersonal skills no less polished than in the production domain, but in addition requires much broader conceptual skills. McCall and Lombardo (1983) built 40 case histories, 20 each of successful and unsuccessful executives in Fortune 500 companies, and compared them to determine why the unsuccessful executives had failed to achieve their expected potential. Among the "fatal flaws" they found were insensitivity to others (an abrasive, intimidating, bullying style) and interpersonal abrasiveness (coldness, aloofness, or arrogance) as the second and third in a list of ten reasons for "derailment."

The interpersonal skills requirement probably stems from three broad requirements for this domain: to build and maintain consensus on objectives (purpose) within the organization, to develop subordinate capabilities, and to begin the development of information networks that are essential for executive effectiveness at the strategic level (Kotter, 1982). Since Bray (Bray, Campbell, & Grant, 1979) also found interpersonal skills to be of major importance in his six-

TABLE 1.2. Skill Requirements by Level

PRODUCTION LEVEL	ORGANIZATIONAL LEVEL	SYSTEMS LEVEL
Conceptual	**Conceptual**	**Conceptual**
Planning -- Establishes intermediate general objectives and organizes short-term programs; schedules work, maintenance, and short-term production goals.	Planning -- Develops plans, makes forecasts; analyzes organizational progress within long time frames; defines and interprets policy; allocates resources.	Planning -- Develops a flexible change posture; interprets ambiguity; originates structure; synthesizes economic principles; synthesizes social and cultural influences.
Decision making -- Makes decisions on operational procedures carries out decisions, dealing with structured content; follows standardized procedures and decision-making processes with regard to specific work unit functioning; and assigns workers and groups of workers to specific jobs.	Decision Making -- Establishes an effective decision-making climate; decides whether to seek to obtain capital resources.	Decision making -- Synthesizes abstract content; plans decisions within long-term perspective; chooses whether or not to procure resources.
Ethics -- Focuses on product improvement and service quality; deals with client complaints.	Ethics -- Is responsible for reputation of products/ services; is responsive to social and community needs; is concerned with public relations.	Ethics -- Articulates appropriate organizational value system; focuses on company integrity and reputation; formulates plans for maintaining the good will of the organization; develops ethical framework consistent with corporate goals and policies; synthesizes and responds to environmental issues.
Interpersonal	**Interpersonal**	**Interpersonal**
Communication -- Employs organizational feedback techniques; provides interpersonal and performance feedback; provides daily production information.	Communication -- Establishes information networks; facilitates organizational communication.	Communication -- Communicates extraorganizationally with Government officials, pressure groups, and so on; represents the organization's viewpoint to the public; relies on organizational channels for internal communication.
Human Relations -- Works to create a supportive work atmosphere; "maps" interpersonal relations within small work group and between work groups; and maintains equity within the workforce.	Human Relations -- Creates a supportive environment and an effective working climate within the organization.	Human Relations -- Develops the organization's relations with those outside the organization.
Counseling -- Establishes yardsticks to evaluate individual and group performance; provides unit performance feedback.	Counseling -- Evaluates performance appraisal systems; identifies colleagues who have personal problems that might adversely affect organizational well-being.	Counseling -- Establishes conducive climate.
Supervision -- Focuses on efficiency of operation; performs "linking pin" tasks; establishes procedural and quality control checks; reviews production results; organizes use of equipment and develops workforce cohesion; assigns individuals to tasks; orients and trains new people; assures safe operation of equipment.	Supervision -- Reinforces the motivational climate; coordinates sub-unit objectives; establishes organizational structure;	Supervision -- Focuses on executive development programs; develops an effective motivational climate; maintains total organizational perspective.
Technical	**Technical**	**Technical**
Technical -- Comprehends advanced technology; selects procedures, techniques and methods related to specific task or subject area.	Technical -- Relies on technical experts for technology.	Technical -- Relies on technical experts.
Management Science -- Develops performance standards and performance appraisal methods; maintains inventories; differentiates results from one production period to another.	Management Science -- Sets three- to seven-year objectives; develops management techniques; reviews budget proposals; develops performance appraisal systems.	Management Science -- Formulates and approves executive development programs.

year follow-up of management processes, and since managers at all levels have immediate subordinates, it may be assumed that these skills are instrumental in management success and progression at all levels.

The conceptual skills requirement in the organizational domain stems, as at the production level, from the need to understand causality. As noted earlier, the complexity at the organizational level far exceeds that at the production level, in part because the time frames are longer. As at the production level, the manager stands in a data stream, receiving and selecting some data elements and missing or rejecting others. Those the manager receives are the result of both chance and antecedent events. Further, the timing of antecedent events runs the gamut from the immediate past to points in time considerably more remote. The frame of reference used to map and interpret the meaning of the data stream must therefore enable the following, at a minimum: separation of spurious from meaningful data, attribution of meaningful data to causes, and determination that data are missing, given the information in hand and the frame of reference that specifies the total probable information set, together with identification of the probable sources for obtaining the missing elements. Again, to draw on Clement and Ayres, the types of skills required are shown in column 2 of Table 1.2.

The empirical research at this level has increased substantially over the last few years. Much of it has been behaviorally focused, however, and very little exists that relates organizational outcomes to leadership and management actions. In addition, the volume of work is small, and the differentiation between the organizational and systems levels, as defined here, has not been clearly drawn.

That complexity differentiates across levels seems hardly in doubt, however. Streufert and Streufert (1981) cite evidence from their own previous work that more complex executives perform better in complex decision making (that is, decision making in a fluid and multifaceted environment) than those who are less complex. Complexity is defined in their work as the capacity to differentiate and integrate informational dimensions. (This is also a useful way to regard frames of reference, differentiation being the number of elements that can be encompassed within such a "map" and integration being the extent to which they can be fitted together to form a composite model.) The salience of the complexity variable is also underscored by Watkins (1981) and Nadler and Tushman (1983).

The requirement for appropriate frames of reference, though logically compelling, has not been the subject of research—either to verify the construct or to determine the elements of such a construct by level. However, two interesting studies permit inferences to be drawn. In the first, Hall (1976) relates the demise of the *Saturday Evening Post* and the Curtis Publishing Company. The growth and performance curves for the *Post* were very similar to those of *Look* and *Life*. Initial crisis occurred as each reported its largest revenue and highest circulation, and each continued growth until decisions were made to reduce circulation in order to cut production costs. Hall used a computer simulation to model significant variables relating to systems dynamics in all three cases, in the following categories: accounting information flows, measures of performance, managed variables, and relations of the firm with its environment. The total set of relevant variables is too extensive to describe here. Operation of this model revealed the presence of a complex positive feedback loop.

- Circulation promotion money produced *growth* in readership
- *Growth* reduced the *cost of advertising* (cost per 1,000 readers)
- *Lower advertising costs* stimulated *sale of advertising pages*
- *More advertising pages* caused *growth of content pages*
- *Growth in magazine size* caused more trial subscription readers to become regular readers, *increasing readership*
- *Increased readership* (growth) further decreased the price of advertising

However, the cost of producing and distributing a thicker magazine to an increasing readership drove up the total cost of operating the firm at a rate faster than the increase in total revenues, and the profit margin declined accordingly. Hall tried three commonsense or intuitive remedies that management might have applied: increase the subscription rate, increase advertising costs, and decrease circulation promotion expenditure. Because none of these addressed the positive feedback loop, all three had only transient effects. The winning strategy was "counterintuitive." When a constant advertising rate was imposed, there was a very small but constant growth each year in readers and revenues, with steadily increasing profits.

This analysis permits several interesting observations. First, the terms "intuitive" and "counterintuitive," which are frequently used by both senior level managers and those who do research with them, have no meaning apart from the model or prior experience that leads to those judgments. For Hall, the winning strategy was "intuitive" only *after* it was found and its dynamics understood. Second, the "intuitive" solutions—some of which management had actually tried when the *Post* was seen to be in trouble—were simplistic in their directness, while the "counterintuitive" one was not. Management essentially looked for short and direct cause and effect linkages, that is, looked for the solution in the near vicinity of the problem. The winning strategy was a complex, indirect linkage. Third, had this simulation been available to management, discovery of the winning strategy would undoubtedly have been possible. However, its utility would not have been derived from its exercise to make a choice between available alternatives, as in decision analysis, but rather in aiding management to "map" correctly the critical variables with which they had to deal. Used in this manner, it would have been a decision support system in the true sense of the current use of that term.

Phillips (1982) also reported using a decision support system with a company that had to decide whether to invest in new product development or to maintain a well-established current product line in the face of substantial uncertainty about the competitive environment. That decision support systems can be used well for resolving such difficulties is not an unusual finding. However, the interesting aspect of this report is that the use of the decision support system enabled company executives to discover interdependencies within the decision matrix that they had not realized were there, and to discover that a given potential regulatory concern had no relevance. Thus, their "maps" had been incorrectly drawn, as had been the "maps" of the executives of the Curtis Publishing Company. In the first of these two cases, use of an incorrect map may very well have been the cause of a company's failure, and in the second might have impacted severely on a company's competitive edge. If these are not isolated events, it seems reasonable to assert that development and validation of a correct map is one of the important growth objectives for executives.

A final set of conceptual skill requirements stems from the requirement at the organizational level to integrate the major business elements of the total system, which are new product development, production, and selling. It is necessary to identify desired and/or necessary interdependencies and establish information and control systems to cause these interdependencies to occur. In theory, the way organizations manage information for decision purposes, and where decisions of what type are made within the organization, should be major determiners of organizational effectiveness. Experimental confirmation of these and similar assertions has been found repeatedly. However, a general theory relating information to organizational effectiveness *by level* has not yet emerged, though general systems theory would seem to offer a profitable base from which to start the development of such a theory.

Two studies by Olmstead (Olmstead, Christensen, & Lackey, 1973; Olmstead, Elder, & Forsyth, 1978) contribute substantially toward such theory building. The first used a closed-play organizational simulation (a battalion command post exercise) to test whether the quality of organizational processes that dealt with information use would relate to overall organizational effectiveness. The second used free-play organizational simulation (battalion-level command post exercise using computer-based battle simulation to determine outcomes). For each study, seven organizational processes using information or influencing information use were identified, based on Schein's adaptive coping cycle: sensing information (both internally and externally), communicating information to users, making decisions, communicating decisions, implementing decisions, stabilizing the internal environment as needed following decision implementation, and getting feedback on the effectiveness of the implementation. In each study, effectiveness of organizational process performance correlated .7 with criteria of organizational effectiveness.

While neither of these studies offers a basis for judging cause and effect relationships, one further observation from the first study, which used ad hoc groups, is illuminating. The groups were subjected to steadily increasing information loads over time, as might be expected to occur in actual practice with an increasing pace of events. Olmstead split his sample of groups at the median on performance and then examined their decision-making performance. What he found was that high performing groups with increasing information load made more decisions at a lower hierarchical level and thus maintained high overall performance under high load to a much greater extent than the groups performing less well. These latter groups attempted to maintain centralized decision making and usually lost control of the problem as a result of inability to cope with the pace of imposed events.

From these, as well as from much more work that could have been cited, it appears evident that the key requirements for this level consist of understanding the organizational processes by which a general manager integrates the elements of an organization, gives them direction and purpose, uses resources, and mediates between the organization and constituencies in the environment to ensure a flow of future resources. Information acquisition and use within the organization are critical to the other performances. And an appropriate frame of reference, or cognitive map, is apparently essentially for effective performance, though little effort has been spent thus far explicating this construct or investigating how it is acquired.

Systems Level Leadership Skill Requirements (Strata VI and VII)

Relatively little has been published about leadership at the systems level. As Jaques defines it, this is the level of corporate executives who are outside the relatively well-defined boundaries of companies falling under corporate umbrellas. Some descriptive work has been done, notably by Mintzberg (1973), Kotter (1982), and Isenberg (1985). However, it is difficult to determine what domain, organization or systems, or both, they are writing about. (Kotter's descriptions, for example, would appear to span managers working at strata IV through VI.) Unpublished work (Burke, n.d.; Klauss et al., 1981) has also been done within two government agencies to identify executive competencies, and Burke cites other unpublished work. Finally, parts of the work at this level have been addressed extensively by various theorists, for example, strategic planning by Ackoff (1981). Difficulties stem from the paucity of work done, the mixing of subjects across levels (at least four and possibly all of the first five authors just cited probably pulled from both the organizational level and the systems level without differentiation), and a methodological focus on behavior without an adequate theoretical basis for determining what data to collect.

Some of the skill requirements can be inferred nonetheless. The time horizon of executives at this level extends beyond ten years. Ackoff implicitly recognizes the implications of such extended time horizons in his differentiation of analysis and synthesis as modes of dealing with the future. Most futures work is in fact trend extrapolation of one sort or another; trend extrapolation methods are good for a time horizon of perhaps as much as seven years, but no longer. Beyond that time extent, the probable error brackets are so broad that the utility of the extrapolation is less than its cost. If it can be assumed that one of the critical leadership tasks in formal organizations is making decisions that determine directions taken by either people within groups, groups themselves, or whole organizations, then a logic emerges.

It seems useful to consider that there is an interaction between time horizon and the nature of the direction-taking decisions that constitute this part of leadership. At the production level, the decisions are within a maximum time frame of one to one and one-half years and have to do with the application of resources to production functions as established within a more or less rational context. Analytic methodologies are excellent and are the methodologies of choice for these decisions. At the organizational level, the decisions have to do with time frames of three to seven years, which are required to formulate and execute major programs, particularly the kinds of programs required to bring a new product to market or to make major capital investment. The critical decision thus is not how current production will be managed, but rather what production will be undertaken, when, in response to what market forces, and within what context. And uncertainty is considerably higher than at the production level. Analytic methodologies may well be sufficient for these kinds of decisions, though Ackoff would probably assert that they are not the best.

At the systems level, however, the time horizons, 10 to 20 years or more, are too extended for analytic methodologies. The problem of building nuclear power plants in the United States illustrates what happens when time frames become too extended. When capital projects are stretched beyond 10 to 12 years, they become too uncertain and unwieldy to manage. The critical work at the systems level thus is not based on analytical methods but rather, Ackoff asserts, on synthesis—integrative approaches for first determining futures that are both desirable and feasible and then undertaking to make the preferred futures happen. Importantly, the work at this level is largely conceptual and political. Its conceptual nature stems from the fact that the desired future outcome is necessarily intangible when first conceived. It *becomes* conceptually possible only because it *is* conceived, and the conception itself must be shared by enough others to constitute a critical mass if it is to have a chance of being made tangible. The interpersonal skill requirements stem from the need to build this critical mass, through persuasion. The philosophy thus cannot be reactive, adjusting to anticipated trends, but rather must be proactive, working toward creating a future context that will allow the desired future state of affairs to be made real. Clement and Ayers (1976) reached similar conclusions, though they also confused the organizational and systems domains. Drawing on their work selectively, column 3 of Table 1.2 shows the types of skills found at this level.

If an appropriate frame of reference, or cognitive map, is a requirement at the organizational level, then it must be even more so at the considerably more complex systems level. Organizations are structures for coordinating effort and for processing information to reduce uncertainty (Galbraith, 1973) in order to produce a rational production environment (Thompson, 1967). The formulation thus far presented suggests that uncertainty reduction may well be the highest priority task at the executive level and that the required methods are probably different from those required at lower levels because the uncertainty may be greater and more difficult to reduce.

The reason for the particular quality of uncertainty at the systems level is that the leader is faced with an unbounded external environment with which he or she must cope without the aid of a structure provided by a superordinate manager. Leaders must structure this unbounded and dynamic world for themselves, deciding what is irrelevant and therefore not to be attended to, what is relevant for themselves and their corporate colleagues, and what is relevant for their subordinate subsidiary CEOs. It is in this last respect that a leader helps to create an orderly, selective environment for those subordinates.

Daft and Lengel (1984) define uncertainty as an insufficiency of information and introduce another concept, equivocality, to deal with the situation wherein information is available but lacks clear meaning. The equivocality concept follows from Weick's (1979) conceptualization of problems that lack structure because alternatives cannot be identified, data cannot be obtained or evaluated, and outcomes of various actions are unpredictable.

Equivocality cannot be managed in the same way as uncertainty. Uncertainty, thus defined as insufficiency of data, can be reduced through the collection of more data, and that can be done by a single individual using relatively mechanical (prescribed) means. (In present terms, this is probably the modal operation at the production level.) However, equivocality cannot be reduced in this manner, because equivocal data have uncertain meanings. More equivocal data would not produce more clarity. So equivocal situations and data must be dealt with in a different way.

Daft and Weick (1983) suggest a view of organizations as interpretation systems, that is, systems for finding out about and knowing the environment. In essence, strategic level managers (executives in our terms) formulate the organization's interpretation of the environment, even though there may be other boundary spanners. The upper-level managers bring together and interpret information for the system as a whole—or for the collection of systems if one can assume corporate level functioning. The interpretation process enables organizations to render unequivocal those situations about which they have only equivocal information. It is in essence a rapid cycling of interpretations among the executives experienced in those situations and is a process that "gets them on the same sheet of music." It may not be the right sheet of music, but the unequivocal understanding of the situation that emerges nonetheless permits action to be taken.

But humans are the information processors Daft and Weick are talking about, and there is a limit to the complexity humans can deal with. However, before exploring executive capability for complexity reduction, it seems useful to formulate a more highly differentiated concept of uncertainty. If uncertainty is made the overarching concept, then one may specify various sources of uncertainty:

Insufficiency of information—There is not enough information. Uncertainty thus can be resolved through acquisition of more information in mechanical (prescribed) ways. This type of uncertainty would characterize situations wherein cause and effect linkages are relatively well known, are *not* characterized by equifinality, and wherein operational issues (probably) are routinized.

Equivocality of information—Information exists, but it may have more than one meaning (interpretation), that is, it leads equally well to mutually exclusive interpretations. This type of uncertainty cannot be reduced by more information of the same type but can be by the interpretation process suggested by Daft and Weick. This type of uncertainty would characterize situations where cause and effect linkages are either known or knowable but *are* characterized by equifinality, and the operational issues (probably) are not routinized.

Ambiguity of information—Information exists but is of inadequate quality for decision making. Ambiguity could exist for any of four reasons: The information is sufficiently "fuzzy" that it is not possible to be certain what it actually is; it is spurious and thus lacking meaningful antecedents; it is a part of a complex pattern of events that has meaning, but not enough of the pattern is available to be discerned; or it is a complex pattern that *could* be discerned and is not because the perceiver lacks the cognitive map needed to organize the existing detail. In general, this type of uncertainty would characterize situations in which cause and effect linkages may *at that time* be either unknown or unknowable, and the measurement operations necessary to get relevant information may be either unknown or imperfect.

This analysis of uncertainty sources is similar to that found in Miles (1980), who addresses in some depth the importance of managerial understanding of the external environment through uncertainty reduction. Following the earlier logic concerning requisite frames of reference as tools for uncertainty reduction, it seems reasonable to conclude that executive capability must be based at least in part on having cognitive maps of sufficient complexity (adequacy of representation) to permit understanding of the environment through recognition of the nature of the uncertainty at hand and application of the appropriate methods for reducing it. Referring again to Ackoff's argument about analytic and integrative methodologies, in relation to the necessity for correct attribution of causality, it seems reasonable to hypothesize the following uncertainty type/uncertainty reduction means relationships:

Insufficiency of information—Analytic methods are sufficient. Cognitive maps need be capable of dealing only with conjunctive cause and effect chains.

Equivocality of information—Analytic methods are sufficient, but cognitive maps probably need to be capable of dealing with disjunctive cause and effect chains.

Ambiguity of information—If in fact the situation is knowable, the cognitive maps available for knowing it are not complete. Integrative methods will be required to build the cognitive maps and measurement methods for knowing the situation.

There is some support for these hypotheses. Anderson (1983) researched available records of the decision-making process used by the president and the Executive Committee (EXCOM) during the Cuban missile crisis and found that this process was very different from decision making in the sense conveyed by decision analysis. Instead of facing an array of competing alternatives in order to choose the best one, the EXCOM faced a series of "yes-no" choices from within an array of noncompeting courses of action. Rather than identifying an explicit set of goals as the first step, the EXCOM identified most of the eventual goals as they proceeded. And, finally, action resulted not from advocated choice among competing alternatives but rather from avoidance of alternatives to which objections had been raised. There was full recognition that each of the actions taken probably would not solve the problem, but at the same time the clear expectation was that they would *not make it worse.* Anderson comments that this kind of approach is typical of the complex situations faced by senior (executive) decision makers, where the logical complement of success is not always failure and the causal texture linking means to ends is equivocal.

Isenberg's (1985) work with six senior managers resulted in similar observations. His description of their approach to work—*how they thought about* what they were doing—is quite consistent with what Anderson found with the EXCOM. Isenberg reported that they did little decision making in the sense of choosing between well-defined alternatives but rather focused more on keeping options open and creating new alternatives. When decisions were made, it was not through the use of external analytic tools but rather through nonlinear thinking, guided by hunch and "gut feel." His executives described this intuitive approach as a skill that develops through experience and enables seeking out holes in the data, in part by organizing problems into a network with overarching issues that can be addressed as one structure that can then guide subsequent processes of problem management. This process required tolerance of apparent inconsistency, as well as the capacity to perceive and understand novelty. The latter required paying attention to the sense of surprise and using analogical reasoning to understand ambiguous or novel situations.

These accounts are representative of other descriptions of executive decision behavior. However, the argument thus far presented suggests that the phenomena being described do not really constitute "decision making" at all, at least in the conventional sense of the term. In both of the above descriptions, it seems clear that executive behavior was focused on gaining an understanding of—"mapping"—

the dynamic decision context. There was a sense of patience in dealing with a perplexing situation. Actions taken by the EXCOM seemed purposefully designed in some cases more to produce a deeper understanding of the situation than to solve it. (How the situation changes as a result of a given action provides further understanding of its nature and its dynamic interdependencies.)

Isenberg's analogy is empirical patient care, which is diagnosis through treatment, with the course of treatment adjusted over time according to the patient's reaction. Where the pathology is complex and the need for treatment is immediate, this may well be the best course of action. In present terms, it is a way of "mapping" complexity produced by *equivocal* data, which is probably a stratum IV problem. The use of this kind of strategy in dealing with problems made complex by *both equivocal and ambiguous* data, a stratum VII problem, is illustrated rather well by Anderson's description of actions by the EXCOM, which carefully avoided any move judged likely to make the situation worse while grappling empirically with the problem of finding a combination of actions that would work. These observations are also consistent with Kotter's description of executive approaches to problem situations and with some of Mintzberg's.

The focus on cognitive (conceptual) skills taken thus far at the systems level is clearly too narrow. As was noted earlier with regard to leadership at the organizational level, interpersonal skills are also quite important at that level, and it seems without question that they are important at the systems level also. The intention here is not to be exhaustive but rather to focus on critical tasks thus far underemphasized, with a view toward suggesting elements of a more general theory of leadership in formal organizations. Under the assumption that cognitive aspects of leadership have not received sufficient attention, those aspects have been given and will continue to receive attention here that is perhaps greater than otherwise might have been warranted.

The emphasis in the systems domain, viewed in this light, then, clearly is on the complexity of the executive's cognitive map in relation to the complexity of the external environment that must be interpreted through its use. Operation of the law of requisite variety would prevent a complex external environment from being patterned successfully by a simple internal representation.

However, as was noted earlier, human capacity for dealing with complexity is limited. A question then exists as to how complexity at the corporate level is handled, given human limitations. It would appear that there are two answers. One is that complexity sometimes is not handled well at all, though the time lag between fatal mistake and demise of the firm may be so long for very large corporations that this cause and effect link is not often established. (Also, given that equifinality applies to most corporate lines of action, really fatal mistakes may be difficult to make, each mistake being subject to subsequent corrective actions that prevent it from being fatal.) The second is that some organizations apparently evolve a corporate mechanism that supplements individual capability.

Jaques postulates that the CEO and the executive vice presidents of a corporation should have a working relationship that is different from that of the relationship between the stratum V manager and his or her subordinate managers. In the latter case, a clear line organization exists, and the relationship is usually directive in nature. In the corporate case, the CEO and EVPs form a more collegial working group in which relationships are less directive and in which clear line relationships are deliberately deemphasized. The utility of this collegium as an uncertainty reducing mechanism would seem to be quite high. Weick's (1979) concept of enactment specifies a "cycling" of information about uncertain situations among experienced observers or judges. The enactment process is one of interpreting or determining what meaning the information has. In point of fact, it might also be viewed as the construction of a representation (or model) of the uncertain situation, which then permits testing. It seems likely that this is the EXCOM process Anderson described.

If we can assume that the construction of this representation requires differentiation of data streams with respect to their antecedent causal events, and enhancement of signal to noise ratios so that any existing patterns become apparent, then the reason for the collegium's unique mode of operation is apparent. In a group with strong authority relationships, there is an inevitable tendency for group members to conform to the views of the highest status member. Thus, in an uncertain situation, not much enhancement of signal to noise ratios is to be expected from a low status member. In a group with strong suppression of conventional authority relationships, the capacity of each individual to contribute to enhancement of signal to noise ratios would be higher. If it is further supposed that individual members of a collegium have areas of individual specialized knowledge, "map segments," so that they jointly can operate a more complex representation than is possible individually, then it would in theory be possible for a corporate collegium to deal with more highly complex external environments than could individuals. If we can assume that this external environment is competitive, and that the complexity of the competitive strategy generated by a given corporation influences its competitive position, then it seems reasonable to specify the proper formation and operation of a collegium as a method of choice for dealing with the complexity of the level VII world.

But the importance of the capacity to deal with complexity exists whether or not the mechanism is a collegium. Since managers at strata VI and VII are in a far better position to sense environmental complexity than managers at stratum V and below, it seems reasonable to conclude that the principal focus of systems leadership is the process of reducing uncertainty about ("mapping") the external world and envisioning both desirable and attainable futures through the use of the resulting representations. How well this is done determines how well management then can resource and structure (mobilize) the organization. In turn, the excellence with which the organization is structured and the complexity of its strategy influence its capacity to achieve the envisioned futures.

AN INTEGRATING VIEW

This chapter opened with substantial criticism of the narrowness of current leadership theory. To avoid being subject to the same criticism, it seems now useful to specify characteristics of what would be judged a good theory and to examine current formulations in view of these specifications. At a minimum, it would seem necessary to encompass all organizational levels with the same basic set of constructs, that is, provide the basis for understanding effective leadership at any level without recourse to such artificialities as differentiating between leadership and management. A good theory should also provide a basis for rationalizing the growth of leadership capability across levels. And, finally, it should permit the integration of the currently disparate fields of leader behavior and organizational behavior. Of course, beyond these lie all the other formal attributes that characterize goodness, such as capacity to generate testable hypotheses and to guide the search for new information.

Basic Constructs

It is not possible within the scope of this chapter to provide a comprehensive set of basic constructs. However, at least three major sets of variables are made implicitly necessary by the preceding discussion—organizational adaptation requirements, environmental complexity by level, and issues of information acquisition and use.

From an open systems perspective, organizational adaptation to changing environmental requirements is a basic requirement for continued survival. This requirement stems from the view that organizations are input-transformation-output systems, competing with one another for finite resources. The issue is whether the organization does what it needs to do sufficiently well, as determined by external resources, to ensure resource continuity in that competitive environment. In a changing environment, "doing what it needs to do" will generally require continuing organizational change, that is, adaptation. The nature and rate of the required adaptation are a function of resources availability, the nature of external constituencies, and the nature and rate of change in their expectations, as well as variables internal to the organization.

The capacity to adapt depends on the availability of slack resources (energy reserve) within the organization. The amount of slack needed for adaptation depends on the magnitude of the change required and the organization's basic technology, among other things. The form taken by slack may vary, depending on what the organization's critical resources are; money, time, and capable human resources, including leaders, are examples. The use of slack to effect change takes the form of allocating resources to do something different; examples are to develop a new product, revise a product mix, or create a concept for a reorganization.

All of these examples are results of decision outcomes, as would be most other examples as well. In the sense of the term as used in this chapter, they are also leadership outcomes. One of the most critical leadership tasks in formal organizations, according to this perspective, is thus to create and use slack to mediate successful adaptation. Leadership roles accordingly are generally far less structured than staff roles, so that more energy (slack) will be immediately available in leadership positions for adaptive problem solving and decision making. The nature of the adaptation required and the time frame within which it must occur are determined by organizational level. At higher levels, the adaptation process probably needs to be more proactive and to be envisioned within successively longer time frames. It will also be mediated by different mechanisms.

An interesting insight into the relationship between leader behavior and organizational adaptation is provided by methodological work Miller (1973a, b) did with leader behavior description questionnaires. Using a pool of approximately 160 items from 9 frequently referenced standard instruments, he developed a consolidated list of 73 items. Responses to these items were then subjected to successive principal components factor analyses with varimax rotations, initially limiting the number of factors to 2 and increasing successively to 12. By so doing, he was able to replicate many of the factor structures found in the leadership literature. Higher order factor analysis yielded two factors, which were defined by the primary factors (from the 12 factor solution) of

consideration, power-equalization, and abdicating

production emphasis, directive-controlling, and inflexible

He then interpreted these findings in an open systems framework. A central organizational task is to cope with environmental variation. (That is the essence of adaptation, as discussed above.) It copes best (efficiency and effectiveness) when internal structure (process and organization) is optimum for the acquisition and use of information needed for coping. That optimum occurs when the complexity of the internal sensing mechanisms can encompass or at least match the complexity of the environment to be sensed. Highly structured rules systems enable organizations to deal efficiently with the information they are programmed by the rules to receive, but at the expense of being able to register and understand information not covered by the rules. Complete programming closes a system, that is, makes it rational or totally predictable. A decrease in programming makes it more open and able to deal with unanticipated environmental variation at the cost of some degree of predictability. This is roughly analogous to stability and flexibility, which are to some extent mutually exclusive and which must be balanced by effectively coping systems. An important part of leadership consists of acts that modify existing structure to achieve an appropriate balance, which then sets internal structure in relation to the complexity of the external environment. Since the required balance may change from time to time, effective leadership requires continuing parallel sensing of both internal structure and external complexity, and adjustment of internal structure as external complexity is sensed to change.

To relate Miller's concepts to Thompson's, the degree to which a subsystem or element should approach complete rationality (or closed status) is dependent on environmental complexity and the economies to be achieved by rationality (costs/benefits trade-offs of operational predictability). As was noted earlier, efficient use of resources requires a subsystems environment with a high degree of rationality. The question of how rational the subsystems environment should be is determined by technology, the extent of vertical and horizontal integration, and personnel skill levels, among other things. Following Miller's logic, if the subsystems environment is too rational (overdetermined), then it will lack the capacity to deal with the full range of environmental variation with which it should deal. If it is not sufficiently rational (underdetermined), then it will be inefficient. In a mass production technology, the economies are large and the opportunity costs low in most cases, so that high rationality attained through highly controlled operations is a likely choice. In a craft technology with a complex environment, the economies would probably be small and the opportunity costs potentially high, so that low rationality attained through low control might be a better choice. The choice in either case would be determined by information acquisition and utilization needs, on the one hand, and the cost of system slack, on the other hand. The general rule is that more slack is needed with more complex, dynamic, and otherwise uncertain situations. However, it will also generally create an opportunity cost by decreasing efficiency.

Two important utilities emerge from using this approach to understand the literature with its focus on the production level. First, it is a macroview that enables relating leadership at this level to that at other levels on the same conceptual dimensions, those provided by open systems theory. Second, it relates the leader behavior research, which has a very strong empirical bent, to the larger body of organization theory, much of which has a strong bent in the direction of seeking an understanding of purpose and function.

The structuring-destructuring action of managers at each level is in principle the same as that of managers at other levels, but in practice each will focus on different kinds of structuring, because complexity is different from level to level as is information needed to resolve complexity. In the production domain, structure is the organization of roles and authority relationships that mediate interpersonal and intergroup coordination in relation to task accomplishment. It includes the control/information/rules systems that govern work and work flow. In the organizational domain, structure deals with vertical integration of subsystems in the production process and with horizontal integration of functional area subordinate managers, on the one hand, and organizational processes, on the other hand. In the systems domain, structure deals with the vertical and horizontal integration of strategic business units as they stand in relation to the external environment, on the one hand, and with optimum internal business unit organizational structure, on the other hand. These differences are summarized in Table 1.3.

Each lower stratum has less uncertainty to resolve because each has been given successively more structure by higher levels of the organization. By the same token the accumulated structure leaves progressively decreased capacity for resolving uncertainty because there are progressively fewer discretionary resources (slack) available for that purpose.

Given that complexity is greater at the higher levels, Table 1.4 shows probable relationships among the nature of the interdependencies that must be coordinated by level, the focus of each level, the frames of reference needed for "mapping" relevant environments, and the "richness" of information needed to reduce uncertainty.

TABLE 1.3. Structure and Limitations Imposed by Structure

Domain	Structure	Structure Limits
Systems	Organization structure Vertical integration of strategic business units	Richness of corporate futures
Organization	Process structure Vertical and horizontal integration of subunits	Richness of current options Organizational responsiveness
Production	Work system Technology Operating procedures Job descriptions	Product flexibility

TABLE 1.4. Adaptation Interrelationships

Level	Nature of Level	Nature of Interdependence	Focus	Frame of Reference	Uncertainty Reduction Technique	Required Information Richness
7	CEO		Strategic direction business mix	Model of environment within which system fits	Collegium—enactment with other experts	
6	Executive VP	Reciprocal	Profit/loss objectives; vertical integration balance		Synthesis	High
5	President	Reciprocal/serial	Product mix vs. price/consumer trends; Profit/loss	Model of system within environment	Decision support system—computer-based or "mapped" by subordinate staff analysis	Moderate to High
4	General manager	Serial/reciprocal	Volume/cost trends			
3	Unit manager	Pooled/serial	Production units vs. revenue cost			
2	First-line manager	Pooled	Performance/ability	Model of Internal production process	Analytic projection linear programming	Low
1	Direct output		Pace/quality			

Interpersonal Organizational Systems

49

"Richness" is defined as the potential information-carrying capacity of data (Daft & Lengel, 1983). Communication media range in richness from face-to-face (rich) to phone calls, to letters, to written documents, and finally to numeric documents (low). Daft and Lengel assert that situations with greater uncertainty require information of greater richness for understanding, and that organizational success is related to the capacity to process information of the appropriate richness. In theory, this means not only that the nature of the information necessary for decision making will differ from level to level but also that the design of the organization will need to reflect information processing requirements. Both possibilities have strong implications for the design of management information systems.

To summarize, the constructs are driven basically by the requirement for organizational adaptation to dynamic environments, which is in turn driven by the need to compete for finite resources, on the one hand, and to use resources efficiently, on the other hand. Adaptation requires both slack resources (the reserves needed to make a change) and information (the basis for knowing what change is needed). In general, leaders are the source of determinations about what changes are needed, and thus are both the "holders" of slack and the "getters and interpreters" of information—the boundary spanners. The nature of the information needed varies by level because the critical tasks are different from level to level and the complexity of the environments that must be mapped increases with level. Effective choice of correct adaptive action then should require "richer" information at higher organizational levels, executives capable of getting it, and cognitive maps suitable for interpreting it.

Executive Development

If the present viewpoint is correct, the heart of the leadership role is getting and using information to reduce uncertainty (increase certainty) about what to do. There are, of course, other necessary role attributes as has frequently been noted (such as interpersonal interaction skills). And, as Jacobs (1971) has shown, superordinate behavior in general probably should be interpreted from within an exchange perspective. That is, each leader should *add value* to the subordinate group or unit. However, for present purposes, the focus will remain on uncertainty reduction as a key attribute that has thus far received less attention than it requires.

Since executive development is a logical progression over time, good theory should provide the basis for understanding the nature of this progression and how to manage it. In the present view, executive development is a process of acquiring successively more complex cognitive maps and other necessary "equipment" over time. As the tools required for successful operation at a higher level are accumulated, the executive becomes "ready" to transition to that level. And the primary tool is a cognitive map that enables its owner to understand the complexity of the level, that is, "map" its patterns accurately in order to make correct attributions of causality. This latter, of course, also enables the owner to set in motion desired causal chains.

The process by which these progressively more complex cognitive maps are constructed must then itself be of central interest. If the Anderson and Isenberg descriptions are veridical, and others like them, then the process of "mapping" is not necessarily easy, and "maps" are not necessarily correct. It follows that there must be a "learning how to learn" skill, the opportunity to learn, and the capacity to learn. None of these areas has been adequately explored.

In theory, the "learning how to learn" skill is at least a second-order skill. First-order skills are direct, such as learning to ride a bicycle. However, some kinds of learning are themselves learned. Practice in learning lists of nonsense syllables will produce improvement in the learning of successive lists. This might be called second-order learning. Beyond that, there is phenomenologically the capacity to reflect on experience, thereby developing what is essentially new knowledge without concurrent direct experience. Schon (1983) describes processes of reflection on action and reflection in action; they are processes that lead to a reflective articulation of the meaning of a given set of events or pattern of stimuli. It seems likely that these are either similar or identical to the processes Ackoff described as synthesis.

It seems reasonable to postulate that there is a progression of learning by which executive ability is eventually produced. Peterson and Rumsey (1981) describe four generic skills that emerge repeatedly from research on occupational and life tasks; problem solving, communication, critical inquiry, and valuing/self-knowledge. Of particular interest in the present context is the hierarchical arrangement they postulate for these generic skills. They are not assumed to be equivalent; rather, problem solving is considered to be an overarching skill that subsumes communication, critical inquiry, and valuing. Critical inquiry, in turn, is assumed to subsume analysis and synthesis. This model is not too different from the present one, if it can be assumed that analysis and synthesis skills probably develop at different rates and that valuing is synonymous with reflection.

Given a generic basis for development of capacity across levels, the actual process by which "maps" are constructed must also be of central interest. If these "maps" are actually representations (models) of external realities, it would appear, first, that they must be developed at least in part through experience and, second, that their development would be aided by the use of guided discovery methods. The reasons for these suppositions are straightforward. Experience must be a necessary ingredient of map building because a primary eventual use of the representation is its exercise in the interpretation of complexity in the external reality it represents. This must be a process of playing "what if" with the model to see if a given set of assumptions would produce an outcome like that noted in the external reality. If it does, then causality can be inferred, that is, the situation now has meaning and the necessary next actions become apparent. The process of playing "what if" is a part of the overall capability. Guided discovery, for example, through mentoring, would materially aid mapmaking, by facilitating differentiation of actual causal linkages from those that are possible but not real. Because the causal linkages operate over longer time periods at higher levels, it is likely that guided discovery is more valuable at higher levels. (A corollary might also be that guided discovery will materially hasten the development of the map required at a given level, but make more difficult the transition from level to level. This would explain the apparent life span of mentoring relationships. In organizations where mentoring occurs, the life span of such a relationship might correspond to the time required to transition a stratum.)

But regardless of the nature of the processes used in constructing "maps," evidence now exists in support of the stratified systems theory postulate of an underlying dimension of capability, or "cognitive power," which can be assessed. Stamp (1985) cites data that were derived from a ten-year follow-up of assessments given 100 executives of a large multinational corporation in 1975, using the Career Path Appreciation (CPA). This is a relatively short (one and a half to two hours) structured interview that includes a concept formation task. Assessment is based on a substantial number of factors, including the trials required to form the concept, the approach to concept formation, the use of negative information, and responses to structured interview questions. According to stratified systems theory, this assessment enables prediction of the ultimate level of future performance and, with a maturational assumption, the intervening levels as well. In this particular data set, 84 of the original 100 assessees were still with the company in 1984. The CPA prediction of level of work that would be attained by that time correlated .65 with the level of work actually attained at that time.

To summarize, executives require a constellation of capabilities not here addressed. The central focus for present purposes is development of capability to interpret complexity and thereby to provide greater certainty for subordinates or subordinate units. Executive development is the process of building cognitive maps that are the tools used for this purpose. It seems likely that cognitive map development must be experience-based, and that it may be facilitated by guided discovery methods (mentoring). Considerably more work is needed to clarify the issues in this area.

Leader Behavior and Organizational Behavior

There is a huge literature on leader behavior. When leader behavior questionnaires are factored, a two-factor solution generally takes the form of structuring and showing consideration. However, Korman's (1966) critique of leader behavior description work leaves a concern for any utility beyond that of mere description. That is, while correlational analysis shows relationships between dimensions of leader behavior and dependent variables, training that modifies behavior does not seem to have much impact on these same dependent variables.

Kerr and Jermier (1978) suggest that the utility of the leadership function is itself situationally determined. For example, if existing situational structure reduces uncertainty enough to rationalize work, leader initiating structure should not be needed. This hypothesis was tested by Pierce, Dunham, and Cummings (1982) in a study of the relative amounts of dependent variable variance explained by four different types of structure (job, technology, work unit, and leader) in 19 different work units. Structure stemming from the job and technology emerged as primary predictors of dependent variables taken as a group; leader initiating structure was consistently weak or nonsignificant as a predictor, except when structure from the other sources was weak.

Smith, Carson, & Alexander (1984) obtained similar findings from a 20-year longitudinal study of leader succession. The organizations in this study were churches, and the leaders were their ministers. Policy was that ministers would be moved about every six years, so the data base encompassed about three successions of leaders. It was possible to examine the effect of succession on a given church, holding reputation of minister (some were "high track" and some were not) constant. The contribution of minister "track" to organizational performance was quite small in comparison to the contribution of the initial states of relevant variables. The variance contributions of each were on the order of 10 percent and 50 percent, respectively.

These findings raise serious questions about leadership roles as currently conceptualized and in particular about the variance contributed by leaders to organizational performance. From the perspective of social exchange theory, the finding that leader structuring has marginal utility is not surprising. Exchange theory postulates that supervision results in both costs and benefits to subordinates (Jacobs, 1971; Hollander, 1956); subordinate attitudes about supervision are determined by perceptions about the net gains resulting from supervision. Where leader structure does not add value, that is, by reducing uncertainty, it has a net negative gain, and should show negative associations with dependent variables.

This strongly suggests a functional role for leaders, even in face-to-face relationships, that is contrary to the conventional stereotypes in both the popular and scientific literature. Given that structure is required to rationalize work, supervision may well be more effective even at the production level if that structure is imposed indirectly through modification of situational structure that then can exert situational demands on the individual. This contrasts with conventional views of the utility of directive supervision and with the interpersonal leadership focus of most of the current literature.

In summary, the real issue in leadership and management effectiveness at any level is whether the organization does what it needs to do, with an expenditure of resources that will enable it to remain viable. A leader at any given level, and especially at the more senior levels, may get the same end result by a variety of means. It thus is an error to attempt to establish one-to-one relationships between specific behaviors and specific outcomes in complex systems. They are not likely to be found. A corollary is that focusing exclusively on the behavior of individual leaders per se is likely to be a dead end. If the management objective is to create greater clarity for subordinates and subordinate units, presumably so that their energies may be more efficiently used for the good of all, then the key outcome is that clarity. Given that equifinality is characteristic of complex systems, it is reasonable to postulate that such clarity can come from a variety of sources. Thus, leadership is probably best regarded as an attribute of a system that essentially adds value to the resources possessed by the system, rather than an attribute of an individual. If resources are scarce, this "value adding" is of even greater importance, and one of the most important ways it happens is through the construction of maps that are adequate as a context for the work of subordinates. By the same token, structure that does not add value is a cost because it uses resources without gain. It seems likely that an understanding of leadership in formal organizations would be substantially better served by deemphasis on leader behavior and a stronger emphasis on identifying organizational end states that will act as causes in themselves to produce future desired outcomes.

SUMMARY

The purpose of this chapter has been to present a theoretical position about leadership in formal (bureaucratic) organizations as opposed to a broad systematic review. As such, it is built on a set of working hypotheses intended to be internally consistent, which hopefully will stimulate further research. Some of these hypotheses have already been tested, with support ranging from mixed to quite positive.

The orientation is taken from open systems theory, exchange theory, and a general theory of bureaucratic organizational structure (Jaques, 1978). Bureaucratic organizations are viewed as entities that compete with one another for resources. Organizational failure is the penalty for sustained noncompetitiveness. There are two requirements for high competitive status. The first is a requisite organizational structure. It specifically allocates not more than five organizational strata to operating companies (strategic business units) and, except for the very largest multinationals, not more than two additional strata to corporate headquarters organizations, for a total of seven. Each stratum has specific critical tasks that are not shared by other strata. The most crucial task each stratum must perform is interpreting or understanding the complexity of the environments with which it must deal in order to provide clarity about them to the next lower stratum. This clarity (uncertainty reduction) "adds value" to the productive efforts of that next stratum by defining adaptive changes that must be made to remain competitive. The specific requisite organizational form produces what in most cases will be optimum "value added" from stratum to stratum. This in turn should result, all other things equal, in some approximation to an optimum balance between short-term efficiency and long-term effectiveness.

The role of leadership is to ensure that the uncertainty reduction process is accurate, the short-term/long-term balance is judicious, and the appropriate resourcing of adaptive change is effected. A major thrust of the chapter is to broaden the concept of leadership beyond the narrow interpersonal perspective with which it has been saddled until the very recent past and to suggest an integration across all organizational levels. One resulting perspective is that leadership may perhaps be more properly viewed as an attribute of a system rather than of an individual. Especially in the organizational and systems domains, managers and executives must operate largely through indirect means that embed leadership functions in structure, technology, information systems, personnel systems, and control mechanisms. The effectiveness with which they do so depends on the extent to which their frames of reference, or cognitive "maps," accurately represent the relevant external reality. These "maps" are models with dynamic properties, probably much like decision support systems, which are useful in understanding cause and effect relationships to the extent they are accurate. Accurate representation depends, in turn, on having sufficient complexity to encompass the causal relationships in that external reality and sufficient experience of the right sort to produce veridicality in the model. Effective leadership at senior levels thus depends on an adequate cognitive map, which enables understanding and interpretation of complexity at those levels to subordinate levels. Even more important, such maps, when veridical, permit executives to act proactively on the causal stream of events, in part by structuring their organizations so as to cause them to be adaptive. If leadership at any level can be thought generically to be giving purpose (in part by giving understanding of

TABLE 1.5. Leadership Purposing and Energizing

Leadership	Purpose	What Is Structured	What Is Energized
Systems 10 years +	Desired futures	Strategic business units in relation to one another and the external entities to which they must relate	Strategic business units (SBU)
Organizational 2-9 years	Where the company is going: Objectives Product mix	Organizational process Subunit integration Technology transformation	Divisions and departments in SBUs
Inter-personal 3 months–2 years	What is to be done: Tasks Output rates	The production process Task role interrelationships	People and groups of people

complexity) and energizing action, the relationships across domains would appear to be that shown in Table 1.5.

At all levels what is energized can be thought to be either systems or subsystems. Systems and subsystems are energy economies. (Individual members of the work force can also usefully be considered energy economies.) Their energies are either programmed or remain in reserve, available for future use. Rules, regulations, and procedures program energy, which thus becomes "fixed." That which is discretionary is "slack." A leadership skill required at all levels is the capacity to balance fixed and slack energy in order to balance current requirements against future need. Efficiency is increased as fixed energy increases, that is, more systems resources are allocated to programmed production functions, as for example, in a simple, stable environment. However, increased programming decreases adaptability because adaptation to environmental and other change requires slack. Thus, an effectively adapting system either must maintain sufficient slack to mediate change or must have the capacity for reprogramming in response to sensed changes in the dynamic nature of the environment. Perhaps the most central function of leaders who control the discretionary resources is continuous monitoring of the balance between current output and future need, accompanied by reprogramming of systems resources as required to ensure that neither efficiency nor adaptability are compromised. Such a system has the capacity to learn, and leaders are the most important, single determiners of whether their systems can learn. Systems that cannot learn probably are uniformly destined to eventual failure.

The conclusions drawn here have important implications for executive selection and development. Selection must heavily emphasize both the capacity and the inclination to develop the complex maps and the associated complex understanding of organizations and their environments necessary for effective executive performance. And development must heavily emphasize the process of guided discovery thought necessary as a part of the map building. Much work needs to be done to make explicit the nature of these processes. It is hoped this will be one of the significant future directions in which research will proceed.

GLOSSARY

Bureaucratic systems are the managerial employment hierarchies widely employed in industrial societies to get work done. They include industrial and commercial employment systems; federal and local civil service, health, education, and social service institutions; and the armed forces. They do not include, for example, church organizations, political organizations, university academic departments, entrepreneurs, and partnerships.

Organizational strata are the bands defining the horizontal structuring of managerial levels by means of which the work gets done and which generate the familiar hierarchical pyramid. These strata are not to be confused with pay graded systems, which usually contain far more levels than are needed for managerial structure. Strata will be specified as stratum I, stratum II, and so on. Strata are divided into three domains: production, organizational, and strategic, from lowest to highest.

Managerial leadership roles are those in which a superordinate is held accountable for the performance of subordinate persons or organizational elements and must produce performance beyond the minimum levels ensured by the formal employment contract and the authority that derives from formal position.

Level of capability is the level of work an individual is capable of carrying in a particular position. It depends both on the person's potential and the match between position requirements and personal knowledge, skill, interests, and temperament. Levels will be specified as level 1, level 2, and so on, each level of capability corresponding to the potential to work at stratum I, II, and so on.

REFERENCES

Ackoff, R. L. (1981). *Creating the corporate future: Plan or be planned for.* New York: Wiley.

Anderson, P. A. (1983). Decision making by objection and the Cuban missile crisis. *Administrative Science Quarterly, 28,* 201-222.

Bass, B. A. (1981). *Stogdill's handbook of leadership: A survey of theory and research.* New York: Free Press.

Blau, P. M. (1964). *Exchange and power in social life.* New York: Wiley.

Bray, D. W., Campbell, R. J., & Grant, D. L. (1979). *Formative years in business: A long-term AT&T study of managerial lives.* New York: Krieger.

Burke, W. W., & Myers, R. A. (1981). *Determining managerial effectiveness among senior executives in NASA.* Final Draft Report. National Aeronautics and Space Administration (Tech. Rep. Contract No. NASW-3456). New York: Columbia University.

Campbell, J. P., Bownas, D. A., Peterson, N. G., & Dunnette, M. D. (1974, July). *The measurement of organizational effectiveness: A review of relevant research and opinion* (Tech. Rep. No. 75-1). San Diego, CA: Navy Personnel Research and Development Center.

Cartwright, D. (1959). A field theoretical conception of power. In D. Cartright (Ed.), *Studies in social power.* Ann Arbor: University of Michigan, Research Center for Group Dynamics.

Cartwright, D. (1965). Influence, leadership, control. In J. G. March (Ed.), *Handbook of organizations.* Chicago: Rand McNally.

Clement, S. D., & Ayres, D. B. (1976, October). *A matrix of organizational leadership dimensions* (Monograph No. 8). Ft. Benjamin Harrison, IN: U.S. Army Administration Center.

Daft, R., & Lengel, R. (1984, November). *A proposed integration among organizational information requirements, media richness and structural design.* Office of Naval Research (Tech. Rep. No. DG-10). College Station, TX: Texas A&M University.

Daft, R. L., & Weick, K. E. (1983, September). *Toward a model of organizations as interpretation systems.* Office of Naval Research (Tech. Rep. No. DG-04). College Station, TX: Texas A&M University.

Dansereau, F., Alutto, J. A., & Yammarino, F. J. (1984). *Theory testing in organizational behavior.* Englewood Cliffs, N.J.: Prentice-Hall.

Dansereau, F., Jr., Graen, G., & Haga, W. J. (1975). A vertical dyad linkage approach to leadership within formal organizations: A longitudinal investigation of the role making process. *Organizational Behavior and Human Performance, 13*, 46–78.

Etzioni, A. (1961). *A comparative analysis of complex organizations.* New York: Free Press.

Fiedler, F. E. (1967). *A theory of leadership effectiveness.* New York: McGraw-Hill.

Fiedler, F. E., Mahar, L., & Chemers, M. M. (1977). *Leader Match IV: Programmed instruction in leadership for the U.S. Army.* Seattle: University of Washington.

French, J. R. P., Jr., & Raven, B. (1959). The bases of social power. In D. Cartwright (Ed.), *Studies in social power.* Ann Arbor: University of Michigan, Research Center for Group Dynamics.

Galbraith, J. (1973). *Designing complex organizations.* Reading, MA: Addison-Wesley.

Georgopoulos, B. S., & Cooke, R. A. *Conceptual-theoretical framework for the organizational study of hospital emergency services* (Working Paper 801). Ann Arbor, MI: Institute for Social Research.

Gibb, C. A. (1947). The principles and traits of leadership. *Journal of Abnormal and Social Psychology, 42*, 267–284.

Graen, G. B. (1984, February). *A strong inference investigation of the job characteristics and dual attachments models of job design* (Research Note No. 84-37). Alexandria, VA: U.S. Army Research Institute.

Graen, G., & Cashman, J. F. (1975). A role making model of leadership in formal organizations: A developmental approach. In J. G. Hunt & L. L. Larson (Eds.), *Leadership frontiers.* Kent, OH: Kent State University Press.

Hall, R. I. (1976). A system pathology of an organization: The rise and fall of the old *Saturday Evening Post. Administrative Science Quarterly, 21*, 185-211.

Halpin, A. W., & Winer, B. J. (1957). A factorial study of the leader behavior descriptions. In R. M. Stogdill & A. E. Coons (Eds.), *Leader behavior: Its description and measurement.* Columbus: Ohio State University.

Hollander, E. P. (1956, July). *Variables Underlying Sociometric Status: 1. A Theoretical Model of Idiosyncratic Behavior and Status* (Navy Technical Report 4-56). Pittsburgh: Carnegie Institute of Technology.

Hollander, E. P., & Julian, J. W. (1969). Contemporary trends in the analysis of leadership processes. *Psychological Bulletin, 71*, 387-397.

Homans, G. C. (1958). Social behavior as exchange. *American Journal of Sociology, 63*, 597-606.

House, R. J. (1971). A path goal theory of leader effectiveness. *Administrative Science Quarterly, 16*, 321-339.

Hunt, E. (1983). On the nature of intelligence. *Science, 219*, 141-146.

Hunt, J. G., & Larson, L. L. (Eds.). (1979). *Crosscurrents in leadership.* Carbondale: Southern Illinois University Press.

Hunt, J. G., Osborn, R. N., and Martin H. J. (1981). *A multiple influence model of leadership* (Tech. Rep. 520). Alexandria, VA: U.S. Army Research Institute.

Isenberg, D. J. (1985). Some hows and whats of managerial thinking: Implications for future army leaders. In J. G. Hunt & J. D. Blair (Eds.), *Leadership on the future battlefield.* New York: Pergamon Press.

Jacobs, T. O. (1971). *Leadership and exchange in formal organizations.* Alexandria, VA: Human Resources Research Organization.

Jaques, E. (1976). *A general theory of bureaucracy.* Exeter, NH: Heinemann.

Jaques, E. (1986). Stratification of cognitive power. *Journal of Applied Behavioral Science.* Forthcoming.

Jaques, E., Gibson, R. O., & Isaac, D. J. (1978). *Levels of abstraction in logic and human action.* London: Heinemann.

Kahn, R. L. (1960). Psychologists in administration. 3. Productivity and job satisfaction. *Personnel Psychology, 13*, 275-287.

Katz, D. (1963). Survey Research Center: An overview of the human relations program. In H. Guetzkow (Ed.), *Groups, leadership and men: Research in human relations.* New York: Russell & Russell.

Katz, D., & Kahn, R. L. (1952). Human organization and worker motivation. In L. R. Tripp (Ed.), *Industrial Productivity*, (pp. 146-171). Madison, WI: Industrial Relations Research Association.

Katz, D., & Kahn, R. L. (1966, 2nd ed. 1978). *The social psychology of organizations.* New York: Wiley.

Katz, D., Maccoby, N., Gurin, G., & Floor, L. (1951). *Productivity, supervision and morale among railroad workers.* Ann Arbor: University of Michigan, Survey Research Center.

Kerr, S., & Jermier, J. M. (1978). Substitutes for leadership: Their meaning and measurement. *Organizational Behavior and Human Performance, 22*, 375-403.

Klauss, R., et al. (1981, July). *Senior executive service competencies: A superior managers' model.* Washington, DC: U.S. Office of Personnel Management.

Korman, A. K. (1966). "Consideration," "initiating structure," and organizational criteria: A review. *Personnel Psychology, 19*, 349-361.

Kotter, J. P. (1982). *The General Managers.* New York: Free Press.

Lasswell, H. D., & Kaplan, A. (1950). *Power and society: A framework for political inquiry.* New Haven, CT: Yale University Press.

Levinson, H. (1984). *CEO.* Cambridge, MA: Harvard University Press.

McCall, M. W., Jr., & Lombardo, M. M. (1983, January). *Off the track: Why and how successful executives get derailed* (Tech. Rep. No. 21). Greensboro, NC: Center for Creative Leadership.

Miles, R. H. (1980). *Macro organizational behavior.* Santa Monica, CA: Goodyear.

Miller, J. A. (1973a). *A hierarchical structure of leadership behaviors* (Tech. Rep. No. 66). Rochester, NY: University of Rochester Management Research Center.

Miller, J. A. (1973b). *Structuring/destructuring: Leadership in open systems* (Tech. Rep. No. 64). Rochester, NY: University of Rochester Management Research Center.

Miller, J. G. (1978). *Living systems.* New York: McGraw-Hill.

Mintzberg, H. (1973). *The nature of managerial work.* New York: Harper & Row.

Nadler, D. A., & Tushman, M. L. (1983). A general diagnostic model for organizational behavior: Applying a congruence perspective. In J. R. Hackman, E. E. Lawler III, & L. W. Porter (Eds.), (pp. 112-124). *Perspectives on behavior in organizations.* New York: McGraw-Hill.

Nagel, J. H. (1968). Some questions about the concept of power. *Behavioral Science, 13*, 129-137.

Olmstead, J. A., Christensen, H. E., & Lackey, L. L. (1973, August). *Components of organizational competence: Test of a conceptual framework* (Tech. Rept. No. 73-19). Alexandria, VA: Human Resources Research Organization.

Olmstead, J. A., Elder, B. L., & Forsyth, J. M. (1978, October). *Organizational process and combat readiness: Feasibility of training organizational effectiveness staff officers to assess command group performance* (Tech. Rept. No. 468). Alexandria, VA: U.S. Army Research Institute.

Osborn, R. N., Hunt, J. G., & Jauch, L. R. (1980). *Organization theory: An integrated approach.* New York: Wiley.

Peterson, G. W., & Rumsey, M. G. (1981). *A methodology for measuring officer job competence.* Paper presented at American Psychological Association annual meeting, Los Angeles.

Phillips, L. D. (1982). Requisite decision modelling: A case study. *Journal of Operations Research Society, 33*, 303-311.

Pierce, J. L., Dunham, R. B., & Cummings, L. L. (1982). *Sources of environmental structuring and participant responses* (ONR TR 1-1-11). Madison: Graduate School of Business, University of Wisconsin-Madison.

Schon, D. A. (1983). *The reflective practitioner.* New York: Basic Books.

Seashore, S. E., Cammann, C., Fichman, M., Ford, L., Ross G., & Rousseau, D. (1982a). Organizational effectiveness: Development and validation of integrated models. Report I: Development of an integrated multivariate model of organizational effectiveness (Research Note No. 83-23). Alexandria, VA: U.S. Army Research Institute.

Seashore, S. E., Fichman, M., Fakhouri, J., Ford, L., Rousseau, D., & Sutton, R. I. (1982b). Organizational effectiveness: Development and validation of integrated models. Report II: Empirical studies of organizational effectiveness using multivariate models (Research Note No. 83-24). Alexandria, VA: U.S. Army Research Institute.

Shartle, C. L. (1963). Studies in naval leadership. Part I. In H. Guetzhow (Ed.), *Groups, leadership and men: Research in human relations* (pp. 119-133). New York: Russell & Russell.

Shartle, C. L., & Stogdill, R. M. (1953). *Studies in naval leadership: Methods, results, and applications.* Columbus: Ohio State University, Personnel Research Board.

Smith, H. L., & Krueger, L. M. (1933). A brief summary of literature on leadership. *Bulletin of the School of Education, 9*, 3-80.

Smith, J. E., Carson, K. P., & Alexander, R. A. (1984). Leadership: It can make a difference. *Academy of Management Journal, 27,* 765-776.

Stamp, G. (1985). *A brief history of the time-frame progression curves.* Uxbridge, Middlesex, England: Brunel Institute of Organisation and Social Studies.

Stamp, G. (1981). Levels and types of managerial capability. *Journal of Management Studies, 18*, 111-124.

Stewart, R. (1976). To understand the manager's job: Consider demands, constraints, choices. *Organizational Dynamics, 4*, 22-32.

Stogdill, R. M. (1948). Personal factors associated with leadership: A survey of the literature. *Journal of Psychology, 25*, 35–72.

Stogdill, R. M. (1974). *Handbook of leadership: A survey of theory and research.* New York: Free Press.

Stogdill, R., & Coons, A. F. (1957). *Leader behavior: Its description and Measurement* (Monograph No. 88). Columbus: Ohio State University, Bureau of Business Research.

Stogdill, R. M., & Shartle, C. L. (1948). Methods for determining patterns of leadership behavior in relation to organization structure and objectives. *Journal of Applied Psychology, 32*, 286–291.

Streufert, S., & Steufert, S. C. (1981, August). *Stress and information search in complex decision making: Effects of load and time urgency.* (Tech. Rep. No. 4). Hershey, PA: Milton S. Hershey Medical Center, Office of Naval Research.

Thompson, J. D. (1967). *Organizations in action.* New York: McGraw-Hill.

Watkins, P. R. (1981, December). A measurement approach to cognitive complexity and perception of information: Implications for information systems design. In C. Ross, (Ed.), *Proceedings of the Second International Conference on Information Systems* (pp. 7–20). Cambridge, MA.

Weick, K. E. (1979). *The social psychology of organizing.* Reading, MA: Addison-Wesley.

Yukl, G. A. (1971). Toward a behavioral theory of leadership. *Organizational Behavior and Human Performance, 6*, 414–440.

Yukl, G. A. (1981). *Leadership in organizations.* Englewood Cliffs, NJ: Prentice-Hall.

2

PRODUCTIVITY IN ORGANIZATIONS

Cynthia M. Pavett, Laurie A. Broedling, and Kent H. Huff

The predominant theme of this book is productivity and how to improve it. The diverse nature of the chapters that make up this work clearly show that productivity enhancement is a multidisciplinary endeavor. Behavioral scientists, as well as economists, engineers, accountants, management scientists, statisticians, and others, have been concerned with productivity-related issues for many years. Interest in worker performance dates back to the early 1900s, when psychologists were studying ways to improve performance by reducing fatigue and creating the proper person-job fit. Later studies in the work place (for example, Roethlisberger & Dickson, 1939) examined not only worker performance but also psychological constructs, such as satisfaction and the impact of group norms. Since these early endeavors, behavioral scientists have continued to study human behavior on the job. Additionally, organizational psychologists have actively experimented with the application of theory to work-related problems. In the recent past, productivity enhancement has become a major concern in the workplace. The application of behavioral science theory and principles to the problem of productivity is the main topic of this chapter.

Specifically, this chapter examines programs that were used to enhance productivity through the effective use of human resources. This chapter integrates the current literature with previous reviews of worker productivity programs (Guzzo & Bondy, 1983; Katzell, Bienstock, & Faerstein, 1977) and critically evaluates the merits of these programs. Based on a critical assessment of the literature, gaps in knowledge are identified, and suggestions are made for future research. This chapter was compiled with both the practitioner and researcher in mind.

In reviewing the literature on behavioral science applications to productivity enhancement, it is apparent that a comprehensive literature review in and of itself would fill two volumes. Numerous books either deal exclusively with the topic of productivity and the behavioral sciences (such as Guzzo & Bondy, 1983), have sections devoted to the topic (for example, Dunnette & Fleishman, 1982), or have behaviorally based prescriptions for productivity enhancement (see, for instance, Kanter, 1983; Locke & Latham, 1984). The material contained in research reports and journal articles ranges from theories about what might work to very scientific assessments of what did work. The academic and technical journals are replete with lab experiments, case studies, and cross-sectional correlational studies that examine the merits of a particular theory for enhancing performance. In addition, there are several productivity information centers and services (Work in America Institute, American Productivity Center, National Technical Information Service) and resource guides (for example, Clawson & Meares, 1983) that provide unpublished and published information about productivity programs being conducted in both the private and public sectors.

Due to the overwhelming amount of information on productivity enhancement, a comprehensive review of all forms of literature is well beyond the scope of this chapter. Hence, the objective of the literature review section was to present the reader with a select group of programs that met six different criteria. These selection criteria were based on those used in previous reviews of psychological approaches to enhancing productivity (Guzzo & Bondy, 1983; Katzell, Bienstock, & Faerstein, 1977). The selection criteria are as follows:

1. The report that documents or describes the program was published and was available for public distribution. Journal articles, unclassified technical reports, and books served as the major information sources.
2. For purposes of comparability with previous literature reviews, only those programs conducted in the United States were reviewed. Furthermore, because Guzzo and Bondy (1983) presented a comprehensive listing of productivity experiments up to 1981, only those studies published after their cutoff point were

considered for inclusion. Noteworthy studies conducted prior to 1981 that had been omitted by Guzzo and Bondy were also reviewed.

3. The treatment involved the use of behavioral science principles and/or theories to enhance productivity or performance. While the behavioral science application need not be the primary emphasis of a particular study, its impact on performance had to be assessable.

4. The studies reviewed were field experiments rather than lab experiments, case studies, or correlational studies. Field experiments represent what is actually being done in ongoing organizations. This form of research involves some degree of scientific rigor and an assessment of program outcomes. Hence, confining the present review to this methodological approach combines the realism of case studies with some of the rigor of a lab experiment while overcoming the common problems associated with case, lab, or correlational studies.

5. Only studies that used at least one "hard" measure for evaluating productivity programs were included. Studies that used attitudes, affective reactions, or subjective performance as the basis for evaluating the efficacy of a program were not reviewed. The criterion variable had to be some quantifiable product or service-related measure.

6. As a logical extension to the preceding two criteria, only those studies that had been systematically evaluated were included here. Since the objective of the present review was to evaluate the merits of various programs, systematic summative evaluation of those programs was crucial for inclusion.

THE MEANING OF PRODUCTIVITY

Behavioral scientists, like economists, accountants, engineers, and managers, have difficulty agreeing on an operational definition of productivity. While the most widely used definition of productivity examines the ratio of inputs to outputs, there is no universally accepted specification of meaning for these two terms. For example, input can be measured as hours of human labor, total number of workers, capital expenditure, time, plant, or equipment that are used to produce a product or service. Output can be conceptualized as the quantity of goods or services produced, the quality of goods or services, the utility of these products, cost savings, shipments, sales, or value added. Implicit in these examples is the notion that productivity cannot be determined by human output alone (Muckler, 1982).

The behavioral scientist's main intent in productivity enhancement programs is to affect the individual's effort, motivation, or performance. Hence, when defining productivity, psychologists tend to focus mainly on the human element. However, other factors, such as technology, the external environment, and organizational function, need to be considered along with the human element. These other factors both affect and partially dictate the operational definition of productivity.

In a very simple sense, organizations can be viewed as microeconomic systems. According to this systems model, organizations are in constant interaction with their environment. Resources are taken from the environment and used as inputs to the organization. Inputs are transformed to produce outputs that go back into the environment. This elementary three-step description of an organization suggests that both inputs and the transformation process need to be examined when attempting to quantify or assess quality of the output.

Technology

The transformation process that is used to convert inputs to outputs dictates, in part, the limits on the firm's productivity. The equipment, tools, knowledge, and skill that go into the transformation process are referred to as technology. This broad definition intentionally encompasses more than just the type of equipment used by an organization since equipment may be only a small part of the transformation process. For example, small batch or unit production technologies (Woodward, 1965) are dependent more on worker skill for productivity than on equipment. The throughput process in organizations such as universities, R&D firms, and other adaptive organizations (Katz & Kahn, 1978) is predicated on the knowledge component of the technology definition.

Most definitions of technology imply that the characteristics of human resources must be considered along with degree of automation and work flow rigidity. For example, Mintzberg (1979) conceptualized technology as the degree of regulation and sophistication of the transformation process. A highly regulated system requires minimal worker input because the system controls the work. In an organization with a low degree of regulation, the transformation process depends on people rather than equipment. Hence, the knowledge, skills, and training of the human resources are critical components of the technology. Sophistication refers to the complexity of the technical system. Here, again, characteristics of the individuals within the production subsystem are important. These workers must either operate and manage a sophisticated system or provide the majority of labor to compensate for a simple technology. The education, training, aptitude, and motivation of an individual operating within the highly sophisticated technological subsystem is an important element in the productivity formula. Workers must be able and willing to utilize effectively and efficiently the available technology. In organizations using the simple technology, the quality and quantity of human input are critical. People really are the technology.

The quantity of the technology used by the firm will dictate, in part, the quality and quantity of its productivity. For example, an office with two personal computers and attending printers can produce significantly more "personalized" form letters than a comparable office with two typewriters. A university that hires only proven researchers will probably produce higher quality and more research reports than will a university that does not use this selection criterion. A new steel mill will likely produce more steel at a lower price than will a mill that is 60 years old. If a plant utilized a paced assembly line, then no matter how hard the worker tries, the quantity of goods produced will be dependent on the pace of the line. Skilled researchers without computer facilities would have a difficult time publishing several research articles per year. Personal computers and printers without skilled operators would produce low-quality letters. Both people and equipment contribute to productivity and are an integral part of the definition of technology. Characteristics of both people and equipment define productivity limits.

Structure

In addition to the predominant technology employed by the firm, organizational structure also affects both aggregate and individual level productivity. Structure and technology are interrelated concepts. Numerous researchers (Aldrich, 1972; Blau, Falbe, McKinley, & Tracy, 1976; Hickson, Pugh, & Pheysey, 1969; Marsh & Mannari, 1981; Thompson, 1967; Woodward, 1965) have sought to define the causal link between technology and structure. Woodward (1965) initially demonstrated her "technological imperative," concluding that technology determined structure in successful firms. The strength of her findings was attenuated by Pugh, Hickson, Henings, and Turner (1969), who found that size rather than technology was the main determinant of structure. More recent research and theorizing (Aldrich, 1972; Marsh & Mannari, 1981; Mintzberg, 1979), however, have been consistent with Woodward's hypothesis that organizational efficiency and effectiveness are predicated on a proper match between technology and structure. Technology acts as a mediating factor between the relationship of various aspects of structure and organizational effectiveness. Organizational structure, when combined with the predominant technology, can contribute to the overall productivity of the firm as well as the performance of individual members.

The term "organizational structure" is extremely broad, its definition depending on the particular school of thought that one is currently reading. When conceptualizing about the influence of organizational structure on productivity, several structural characteristics seem to be especially relevant. For example, productivity is dependent on the administrative component of the organization when inputs are defined as total direct and indirect labor hours. Vertical span, standardization, procedural specification, degree of specialization, span of control, autonomy, formalization, and the quality and amount of differentiation can definitely help or hinder productivity. These characteristics were drawn from a number of different theories that have attempted to operationally define structure. These variables control, in part, the level of productivity. Hence, structural variables need to be recognized and acknowledged when defining, measuring, or designing programs to improve productivity.

Environment

According to Mintzberg (1979), environmental conditions have a somewhat greater influence on the structure of the organization than do things like technology and size. The ability of an organization to respond to its environment is critical for both survival and performance (Burns & Stalker, 1961). In dynamic environments, organizations are pushed toward an organic structure. Successful firms change to meet these demands. Organizations that operate in relatively stable environments do not need to be as malleable as those whose market and technological environments are characterized by uncertainty and change. These organizations tend toward a mechanistic structure. Both types of organizations are open systems that interact with the environment. As such, the productivity of both mechanistic and organic organizations is dependent on the conditions in the external environment. However, the degree to which the organization and its performance are influenced by the environment varies from firm to firm.

While there is no shortage of definitions for the term "environment," there is a common element running through the definitions. All definitions consider the environment to be some set of factors outside the organization itself (Robbins, 1983) that influence the performance of the organization. The specific factors that make up the environment range from broad concepts like the economy, political conditions, social milieu, and the legal structure to very specific factors such as a particular labor union, relevant regulatory agencies, and the firm's suppliers, customers, and competitors. An organization and its performance are most influenced by the factors that are directly relevant to the accomplishment of organizational objectives. The relevant domain (Thompson, 1967) of the organization dictates the salience and specificity of the various environmental characteristics. Relevant domain refers to the nitch the organization has carved in both product and consumer arenas. If the domain is changed, the set of environmental influences on the firm also changes. Given the definition of productivity, conditions outside the firm unequivocally influence both the input and output components of the formula. Hence, explicit and implicit consideration should be given to this set of factors when examining productivity or changes in productivity.

People: Productivity and Performance

The effort, ability, motivation, and individual performance of people contribute to productivity. While the term "productivity" frequently appears in the industrial/organizational psychology literature, its meaning is often vague or confused with other terms like performance or production (Tuttle, 1983). The conceptual or operational distinction between performance and productivity is worth noting.

Productivity is generally an impersonal measure that considers tangible inputs and outcomes. It is intended to be an objective measure even though the decision of how to define input and outputs may sometimes be quite subjective. Performance can take productivity into consideration, but it is a broader assessment of behavior than is productivity. Performance may consider the means that are taken to achieve the desired end as well as possible constraints on desired behavior. For example, in a retail organization a common productivity measure consists of dollar sales per unit of labor. Performance may take sales per labor hour into consideration. Such factors as length of time spent per customer, length of time before customer is approached, employee friendliness, customer satisfaction, cyclical sales, and shopper fluctuations could also be part of the performance measure. Technically speaking, performance measures and evaluations tend to be more subjective in nature than are productivity measures. They involve more judgment calls than productivity measures in both definition and evaluation. Both performance and productivity measures may also include attendance behaviors, such as absenteeism, turnover, and tardiness. Organizational psychologists frequently examine behavioral indicators like psychological commitment as barometers of performance. Such behaviors as strikes, slowdowns, grievances, or substance abuse are included in this category.

For purposes of this chapter, performance was considered a valid surrogate for productivity when it was defined in objective, quantifiable terms that related directly to the product or service. For example, length of work cycle, number of defects, quality of service, or number of customers approached were considered valid indicators of or substitutes for productivity. Attitudes or psychological commitment variables were not included as criteria on which to judge the effect of a productivity enhancement program.

Working Definition of Productivity

In summary, the objective of this section was to examine some of the salient factors that influence the operational definition of productivity and to discuss some of the complexities involved in selecting productivity measures. Researchers have used a myriad of different measures as indicators of productivity. These measures range from the individual to the organizational level of analysis. They include objective assessments of outputs and cost savings, as well as turnover, absenteeism, and attitudinal changes. The present authors, like the "hard-nosed administrators, managers or practitioners" described by Pennings (1984, p. 129), choose to define productivity by using "hard" indicators. Similar to Katzell, Bienstock, and Faerstein (1977, p. 39) productivity is defined as any aspect of work output (quantity, quality, value) or any aspect of input or cost expended to achieve output (labor, material costs). Productivity improvement is viewed as an increase in output or a decrease in input without an offsetting change in the other component (p. 39). The vast majority of the studies reviewed to date measure only one aspect of the productivity ratio. Since this is common practice, researchers must assume that changes in one component truly reflect changes in productivity. In addition, there is an implicit assumption in the literature that increases in individual level performance aggregate to enhance the organization as a whole. We also will make these two assumptions. Given the definition selected, studies that use attitudes or indirect indicators of productivity (such as absenteeism or turnover) as the main criterion have not been included here.

PRODUCTIVITY ENHANCEMENT EXPERIMENTS: A REVIEW

Previous reviews of the recent behavioral science literature, which described productivity enhancement experiments, indicated that these programs can be categorized in a meaningful fashion. In their review of the literature published between 1971 and 1975, Katzell et al. (1977) proposed a 14-category taxonomy for classifying productivity interventions. This classification schema served as the organizing framework for subsequent reviews that used a 13-category system (Guzzo & Bondy, 1983) and an 11-category system (Katzell & Guzzo, 1983). The latter review of the literature was essentially a summary of the work of both Katzell et al., and Guzzo and Bondy. It contained a survey of productivity experiments conducted between 1971 and 1981. For purposes of comparison across reviews, this 11-category taxonomy is used in this chapter as the organizing framework for reporting intervention programs. Table 2.1 provides a sum-

TABLE 2.1. Typology of Productivity Improvement Programs

Category	Emphasis Is on Enhanced Performance Through	Examples
Recruitment and selection	Changing recruitment, selection, or placement programs	Realistic job previews and revised selection testing
Training and instruction	Education in various skill areas	Management training seminars; team building, and on-the-job training
Appraisal and feedback	Assessing an individual's performance and providing him or her with individual guidance	Management by objectives (MBO), appraisal interview, and self-monitoring of performance
Goal setting	Specification of goals for key performance areas	Goal-setting programs that do not necessarily use goal-oriented performance appraisals
Financial compensation	Money	Performance-based group or individual incentives, profit-sharing, gain-sharing, and Scanlon Plan
Work redesign	Enhancing the quality of work performed by individuals or groups	Job enrichment and job enlargement
Supervisory methods	Altering the supervisor's style; primary concern is with increasing subordinate participation	Leadership training, representative committees, labor-management committees, and quality control circles
Organizational structure	Changing patterns of responsibility, authority, or working relationships	Changing the chain of command, and improving the integration of specialized functions
Decision-making techniques	Changing the patterns of teamwork that are used to analyze work-related problems and recommend solutions	Any alteration in the decision-making process, the Delphi technique, and nominal group technique
Work schedules	Flexible or nontraditional working hours	Flexitime, 4/40, job sharing, and the use of time off as a reward
Sociotechnical systems redesign	Revising the patterns of human and technological resource utilization	Improvements in the fit between the technical and social organization via changes in both systems

Sources: Katzell, R. A., & Guzzo, R. A. "Psychological Approaches to Productivity Improvement," *American Psychologist*, April 1983, pp. 468–472; and Guzzo, R. A., and Bondy, J. S., *A Guide to Worker Productivity Experiments in the United States 1976–81*, Pergamon Press, 1983.

mary of the 11 categories, their main emphasis, and examples of programs that may be included in each category.

The productivity-related literature produced during the 1981–84 time period is prodigious. Yet only a few reports describe the results of productivity enhancement programs and meet the criteria specified at the beginning of the chapter. Compared with past reviews of the literature, the present endeavor encompasses a shorter period— two and a half years versus five years—hence reducing the selection pool of research articles. In addition, economic considerations may have contributed to the lack of published material on productivity programs. Specifically, the recession of the early 1980s may have limited the resources available for organizational change and experimentation. Both business organizations and funding agencies may have curtailed funding for research grants or investments into new personnel programs because of budget limitations. In short, researchers and practitioners may not have been conducting as many productivity experiments as they had during earlier time periods.

Most organizations are concerned with productivity. A substantial amount of informal experimentation with productivity enhancement techniques does exist. However, the informal programs are rarely documented, or if they are methodically assessed, the results are not released for publication. From a researcher's perspective, lack of documentation and secrecy of results are a travesty. It limits both the researcher's and the practitioner's knowledge and results in similar lessons being learned over and over again. The literature is replete with advice about increasing performance but seems to have very little empirical evidence about what actually works. No literature search is totally exhaustive, and hence apology is due to those individuals whose published work may have been unknowingly overlooked.

With the above limitations in mind, the following sections describe the work that has been done in the last few years in the ten different content areas previously described. First presented is a brief description of the published studies that had used the particular intervention under consideration. A study that was exceptionally well done is presented in some detail, including information about the subjects, organization, nature of the intervention, definition of productivity, criteria, numerical results, limitations, and a brief analysis. In each content area, an attempt was made to draw some practical suggestions or implications from the studies found.

Recruitment, Selection, and Placement

While the literature is replete with selection-related studies, there is a notable absence of selection experiments. Specifically, there are hundreds of studies that are correlational in nature and hence do not utilize pre- and postintervention measures or experimental and control groups. The reader of these reports cannot ascertain if productivity was enhanced as a result of a change in selection or recruitment procedures. Traditional validation studies do provide information on the efficacy of the selection criteria for predicting future performance but, by their very nature, they do not assess impact on productivity. An exception to this generalization are the realistic job preview studies that have utilized quasi-experimental designs to assess impact of the intervention on worker performance. During the time period under consideration, only one study fits this review's criteria for inclusion into the recruitment, selection, and placement category. This one study, by Dean and Wanous (1984), examines the impact of realistic job previews on attitudes and behaviors.

The Dean and Wanous study was a field experiment conducted in a large bank. Subjects—249 tellers—were hired and randomly assigned to a job preview group to begin training. The experiment was designed to examine the effects of three types of job previews (realistic specific, general realistic, no preview) on expectations, attitudes, job performance, and turnover. Realistic specific job previews consisted of providing the applicant with a booklet containing specific information on six different topics, such as pay and career opportunities. This information was obtained from interviews with and surveys from existing tellers and managers. The objective of the booklet was to provide the prospective employee with specific information that was not all positive. A general realistic job preview condition also utilized booklets but gave very general information. Last, the authors utilized a control group or no preview condition.

Job performance, which was used as one of the criterion variables, was measured in terms of quality. Using bank records, supervisors calculated the ratio of number of days without errors to number of days scheduled. In addition to performance, attitudes and turnover were assessed. With the exception of turnover, which was monitored for 43 weeks, postintervention measures were taken after five weeks on the job.

Results indicated that neither job performance nor initial attitudes were affected by the type of job preview. While turnover was not affected by the type of intervention, the rate at which tellers left the organization differed among the groups. Specifically, among those who left the bank, the people in the specific and general job preview groups tended to leave during the three-week training period. The individuals from the control groups who left the bank did so during the first 20 weeks after training. Realistic job previews did lower initial expectations about various aspects of job satisfaction.

From a research standpoint the above results are not what one would hope for. However, in terms of organizational efficiency, these results do have cost-savings implications. The authors pointed out that gross cost estimates for replacing a teller varied according to when the teller quit. Replacement costs during training were estimated to be $950, whereas replacement costs for a teller who leaves after 23 weeks totaled $2,800. While these cost estimates should be used with caution, they do illustrate the fact that early turnover costs less than later turnover.

The authors offer several explanations for their lack of performance results. First, the booklet may have had insufficient information about how to do one's job. Second, the three-week training program many have eliminated any effects that the preview may have had. Third, performance was assessed after only five weeks on the job. According to the authors, it takes at least four weeks to attain any degree of competence. Hence, individual performance may not have reached the competence level. Last, previous research had found that realistic job previews were more effective for high complexity than for low complexity jobs.

Given the limitations of the above study, the use of realistic job previews as a productivity enhancement strategy cannot be discounted. Attention needs to be given to both the design of the study (its measurement techniques, time lapses, possible confounding variables) and the design of the realistic job preview itself. The Dean and Wanous study has provided some information on one of the design aspects of realistic job previews. Their work, however, is only a start in an area that shows some promise.

Training and Instruction

A traditional approach to productivity enhancement is to provide training and instruction to workers/supervisors to improve their job performance. In fact, this approach is one of the more popular types of productivity interventions employed, especially with a new and in-experienced work force or where changes in job technology or procedures have occurred. Table 2.2 shows those studies that met our criteria for inclusion in this category.

The Scandura and Graen (1984) study has been selected as the exemplar for this category. This study was part of a larger research effort (Graen, Novak, & Sommerkamp, 1982) that found that training supervisors in how to improve leader-member relationships resulted in improved productivity and job satisfaction. Scandura and Graen (1984) provided leadership training to managers to improve the leader-member exchange (LMX) relationships. Based on the LMX model, it was hypothesized that the leadership training intervention would have a greater positive effect on productivity for workers who were initially low on LMX than those who were high.

The subjects were 83 workers in one department at a large government installation in the Midwest. The work was an office/clerical task involving the processing of paper forms using modern computer-assisted technology. Workers had the same job titles and descriptions and completed each case using the same equipment and procedures. The productivity data were obtained from computerized performance reports of weekly output. The criterion measure of quantity was defined as the total number of cases completed by an individual in a week divided by the total number of labor hours worked on the cases. Quality was assessed as the total number of errors per week divided by the total number of cases reviewed that week in the quality review process. Performance was monitored for a 26-week period with weeks 1 through 14 forming the before condition and weeks 15 through 26 the after.

For the 26 subjects in the experimental group, managers received 12 hours of training on the leader-member exchange model, active listening, exchanging mutual expectations, exchanging resources, and practicing one-on-one sessions. The objectives of the training were to

TABLE 2.2. Training and Instruction

Reference	Sample	Intervention(s)	Productivity Criteria	Results
Graen, Novak, & Sommerkamp, 1982	106 clerical workers from a case processing unit at public service organization	Supervisory training to improve leader-member relationships	(1) Quality equaled the total number of cases completed weekly divided by total hours worked on these cases for the week (2) Quality equaled the total number of errors detected weekly by total number of cases completed that week	(1) Significant gain in output measure (2) Decrease in quality
Meyer & Raich, 1983	122 sales associates from 14 stores matched for size, location market characteristics, etc.	Training of supervisors in behavior modeling techniques to improve interpersonal skills who in turn trained their subordinate sales staff	(1) Average commission per hour (2) Turnover	(1) Average earnings increased by 7% in the experimental group and decreased by 3% in the control group (2) Turnover was 15% less in experimental group
Scandura & Graen, 1984	83 computer processing employees of a large service organization	Leadership training of managers to improve leader-member relationships	Same as Graen, Novak, & Sommerkamp, 1982	(1) 19% improvement in productivity (2) Projected annual cost savings of $5 million (3) No decrement in quality

get each manager to analyze thoroughly and to be prepared to act on major positive and negative components of his or her relationship with each subordinate in a series of one-on-one conversations that were to last 20 to 30 minutes. For the 57 subjects in the control group, managers participated in three two-hour sessions of general input on job enrichment, performance evaluation, decision making, and communication.

Results showed that those employees low on LMX scores showed significant quantity performance improvements over those with high LMX scores with a nonsignificant effect on quality for initial LMX status crossed with treatment and control and from before to after. The effect of leadership intervention can be pervasive, but it appears that employees having poor quality exchanges initially are most affected by the intervention. Productivity improved 19 percent, with an estimated annual cost savings of more than $5 million without any loss of quality.

The studies shown in Table 2.2 demonstrate that training and instruction can have a potent effect on worker productivity and that this effect can be substantiated by objective bottom-line measures. However, at least two conditions for this effect to occur must be met: (1) the training must be of sufficient duration to change behaviors in the desired direction and (2) it must be focused on relevant job tasks or on relevant moderating variables influencing those tasks. With the expensive investment in time and money most training programs require, it is incumbent on those who propose training and instruction as a means of productivity enhancement to also provide evidence of its effectiveness. Assessment should use "hard" objective data rather than opinions of participants on the merit of the training.

Appraisal and Feedback

The majority of field experiments in the area of appraisal and feedback utilized the principles of organizational behavior modification (O.B. Mod). Studies by Anderson et al. (1982), Brown, Willis, and Reid (1981), Chhokar and Wallin (1984), Kunz et al. (1982), Maher (1982), Newly and Robinson (1982), and Wikoff, Anderson, and Crowell (1983) examined the impact of behavioral charting on the occurrence of specific task-related behaviors. Some of these studies used other O.B. Mod techniques, such as token reinforcement, supervisory praise, and goal setting in addition to behavioral charting. The charting, supervisory praise, and token reinforcements are forms of feedback that should influence behavior. In general, these combined studies did demonstrate that feedback has positive effects on the specific behaviors assessed in each study. These studies are summarized in Table 2.3.

Previous laboratory and survey research has provided a fair amount of information about the characteristics of feedback and how they influence performance. This research was used as the basis for Pritchard et al. (1981) study of the impact of impersonal, comparative, and personal feedback on the performance of data entry clerks. In addition, the authors sought to investigate the relative efficacy of feedback plus goal setting.

The field experiment was conducted among four different groups of individuals who worked in the credit card and payment processing center of a large oil company. Of the 189 clerks who participated in the study, 114 received both experimental treatments. These subjects worked in two different sections within the organization. The intervention/experiment lasted for six months in the remittance control section and nine months in the data input section.

Three major measures served as both the productivity criteria and the foundation for the feedback reports that were given to employees. Data on computer-recorded sorting error rates, a combined encoding rate (which consisted of three types of encoding weighted by difficulty), and encoding error rates were collected for two months prior to the intervention. These three measures were also included as a part of the feedback reports.

Feedback reports and methods of delivering the feedback were varied to create three experimental conditions that according to theory should differentially affect performance. The first condition was providing impersonal feedback in the form of the computerized performance reports. These reports contained additional information such as how much time was spent keying as opposed to formatting. A comparative feedback condition was created by giving the individual a performance ranking within the immediate work group on each of the performance indices. A personal feedback condition involved the reports being reviewed by the supervisor, who distributed them personally to the employee. Last, goal-setting conditions were applied to these feedback conditions in the second phase of the research study.

TABLE 2.3. Feedback and Appraisal

Reference	Sample	Intervention(s)	Productivity Criteria	Results
Anderson, Crowell, Sponsel, Aartie, & Brence, 1982	104 room attendants at a hotel	(1) Feedback checklist delineating 70 quality-related performance criteria (2) Token reinforcement for desired behaviors	Performance level on the 70 criteria expressed as points	(1) Increase in performance over baseline period for both interventions
Brown, Willis, & Reid, 1981	25 staff members in a residential facility for the handicapped	(1) Supervisory verbal performance feedback (2) Verbal feedback with praise	Degree to which subjects engage in three productivity-related target behaviors (1) Off-task behavior (2) Direct care stimulation (3) Social interaction with patients	(1) Off task behaviors decreased from 24 to 6% (2) Direct care increased from 15 to 37% of the observed behaviors (3) Social interactions increased from 8 to 14%
Chhokar & Wallin, 1984	58 male shop workers	(1) Safety performance feedback presented via charts and posters (2) Goal setting on safety behaviors (3) Training on safety	(1) Percentage of employees performing their jobs in a completely safe manner	(1) A combination of feedback, goal setting, and training produced significantly higher results than baseline or other experimental conditions
Kunz, Lutzker, Cuvo, Eddleman, Lutzker, Megson, & Gulley, 1982	13 staff members in a day-care center	(1) Behavioral charting (2) Supervisory feedback	Number of: (1) Diaper checks (2) Diaper changes (3) Times changes and checks were recorded	(1) Checks and changes increased from 88 to 100% (2) Recordings increased from 50% to 87%
Maher, 1982	15 school teachers	Performance charts	(1) Percentage of instructional programs planned (2) Percentage of evaluations recorded	(1) Planning increased from 9 to 87% (2) Recordings increased from 15 to 95%
Newley & Robinson, 1983	21 drugstore employees	(1) Performance charts (2) Performance-contingent nonmonetary rewards	(1) Cash register averages/shortages (2) Punctuality (3) Checkout proficiency	(1) Cash register discrepancies fell from 1.5 to .55% (2) Punctuality increased from 65 to 91% (3) Proficiency went from 71 to 92%
Pritchard, Bigby, Beiting, Coverdale, & Morgan, 1981	189 data entry clerks from a large oil company	(1) Performance feedback (2) Feedback plus goal setting	(1) Sorting error rates (2) Encoding rate (output) (3) Encoding error rate	(1) Error rates decreased an average of 11% (2) Encoding rates increased an average of 6%
Wikoff, Anderson, & Crowell, 1983	104 blue-collar workers and 10 managers in a furniture manufacturing company	(1) Performance charts (2) Supervisor-administered praise	(1) Average daily work output defined as a percentage of standard	(1) Output increased an average of 6% for both charts and praise

In general, the overall effects of feedback on performance were quite positive. The authors presented two sets of analyses—one set used only those subjects who were present for the entire experiment; the other set used data from newly hired individuals who replaced experimental subjects. The second analysis controlled for the learning curve of the new employees. Both analyses indicated that encoding rates (output) increased by 5 to 10 percent, with an average increase of 6.4 percent. Sorting and encoding error rates dropped by an average of 11 percent. More than half of the decreases were in the 15 to 28 percent range. Comparisons between the different feedback conditions found that impersonal feedback was as effective as personal feedback. There were no major differences between the performance data of the comparative and the absolute feedback conditions. Goal setting plus feedback was compared with the effects of feedback alone. In two of the nine comparisons, the goal-setting plus feedback conditions produced significantly higher performance levels. Interestingly, the authors noted that the treatment effects were strongest among employees who were initially low performers. These results were consistent over the duration of the study.

This study was grounded in the feedback and goal-setting literature. It used many of the principles of effective feedback to design the experiment and the feedback system. For example, the system that was implemented provided frequent, objective, and specific feedback. The system was also designed to allow individuals to see changes in the criteria that were directly tied to their efforts. In addition to the use of theory in the feedback area, the authors utilized some common principles of goal setting.

While the above laboratory experiment was done very well, the generalizability and durability of the results are questioned. Both the principles of goal setting and feedback are relatively easy to implement in a setting where job performance is quantifiable. The principles of both theories advocate objectivity, personalization of data, and responsive measurement techniques. These characteristics are sorely lacking in most jobs. The authors do not indicate if the systems they created remained after the data collection stopped. They do state, however, that the experiment lasted up to nine months and that the results were not influenced by time. There is no evidence that the increase in productivity lasted beyond the duration of the study. Last, one could fault the study for its lack of a control group.

In general, though, this feedback investigation was conducted in a very scientific and pragmatic manner.

Goal Setting

Goal setting is a thoroughly researched area of inquiry. During the past ten years, a fair number of laboratory and field experiments, case studies, and correlational studies have appeared in the literature. During the time of this review, four studies were found that met our criteria. As indicated in Table 2.4, three of the four included feedback into the productivity enhancement program. Crawford, White, and Magnusson (1983) used individual feedback reports as a basis for examining goal progress, whereas Ivancevich and McMahon (1982) examined the relative impact of goal setting plus different forms of feedback. The Crawford et al. investigation also examined the influence of assigned versus participative goals, finding no significant performance differences between the two interventions. All of the studies in Table 2.4, except that of Kim (1984), directed goal-setting efforts at such outcome measures as performance standards, costs, or number of truck trips.

In an innovative twist on the goal-setting process, Kim designed his study to examine both outcome and behavioral goals. Four separate branches of a retail organization provided the 93 salespersons for the study. All of the involved supervisors received training on the effectiveness of goal setting and feedback, along with instructions on how to use the forms that were developed for the study. The author had developed a behavior goal-setting form and an outcome goal-setting/feedback form. These two forms differed in their emphasis on behaviors versus outcomes.

Three experimental conditions were created: behavior goal setting/feedback, outcome goal setting/feedback, and both behavior and outcome goal setting/feedback. The goal-setting process involved both the supervisor and the subordinate. A fourth group served as the control. Performance was measured by computing the average hourly dollar sales per employee. At the end of each day, the supervisor recorded the total amount of sales made by each employee. These data were obtained from computerized online cash registers. The total was divided by the number of hours the employee had

TABLE 2.4. Goal-Setting Interventions

Reference	Sample	Intervention(s)	Productivity Criteria	Results
Crawford, White, & Magnusson, 1983	241 production workers at an engineer rework division of a naval air rework facility	(1) Goal setting (2) Individual feedback reports (3) Discussions of goal progress	(1) Performance efficiency using established standards	(1) The goal-setting group's performance was significantly higher than the control group (2) Performance increased by 5% (3) Performance of the low performers increased more than that of the high performers
Ivancevich & McMahon, 1982	209 engineers at six different locations	(1) Goal setting (2) Supervisory feedback plus goal setting (3) Self-generated feedback plus goal setting (4) Co-worker feedback plus goal setting	(1) Control costs (2) Quality control citations (3) Unexcused overtime (4) Supervisory evaluations	(1) Control costs and control citations were significantly better for the goal-setting than non-goal-setting groups (2) Performance at controlling costs and unexcused overtime was better for the feedback group than nonfeedback groups
Kim, 1984	93 salespersons in a retail organization	(1) Goal setting on either performance-related behaviors or performance outcomes (2) Feedback	(1) Average hourly dollar sales per employee divided by the number of hours worked	(1) Group with feedback and goal setting on both behaviors and outcomes showed the best results
Latham & Saari, 1982	74 logging truck drivers	(1) Assignment of goals	(1) Number of trips per truck per week	(1) Goal-setting groups had significantly higher number of trips per truck than control group

worked. Baseline performance data were collected for two weeks prior to the intervention.

In addition to the performance criterion, the author collected survey information about perceived role conflict: role ambiguity, satisfaction, expectancy, and instrumentality. At the end of this 12-week study, it was found that goal setting and feedback did not influence these perceptual measures as had been expected.

However, the results indicated that the three experimental groups performed significantly better than did the control group. Since the average retail price for merchandise in the three departments was not constant, selling performance was standardized through z-transformation. Numerically, the behavior and outcome goal-setting/feedback group produced the highest adjusted mean (.225); the outcome goal-setting/feedback group the second highest (.131); and the behavior goal-setting/feedback group the lowest (.017). When compared with a control group average of -.275, all three experimental groups showed positive performance. The author points out that the estimated monthly sales increases for one department that used behavior plus outcome goal setting/feedback was about $50,000.

This study should be the first in a series that examines behavioral goal setting as compared with traditional outcome goal setting. While the results may not be generalizable to different organizational settings, the basic idea has a lot of promise. The study's implementation of the goal-setting program seemed to be done with a fair amount of preplanning and supervisory participation. The program seemed to be accepted by the employees, who demonstrated public commitment to the program. Kim speculates that employee commitment placed pressure on the supervisors to support and maintain the program, hence contributing to its success.

On a research basis, the study could be faulted for its inability to separate goal setting from feedback effects, lack of consideration for extraneous influences on client purchasing behavior, and lack of random assignment to groups. However, these issues are minor when compared with the information provided by the study.

Financial Compensation

Programs that use financial compensation seek to increase productivity by appealing to the employee's vested (or enlightened) self-interest. These interventions are designed to change the compensation systems of the organization to produce a change in the employee's perception of the link between performance and monetary rewards. By creating a perceived causal relationship between high performance and gratification of self-interest needs, the organization seeks to elicit increases in productivity. Incentive systems can be designed to reinforce individual, group, or organization level performance.

Individual level incentive systems were successfully used to enhance productivity in four studies that are summarized in Table 2.5. As can be seen from the table, only one study (Schuster, 1984) used an organization-wide gain-sharing plan. Of the five studies, three were conducted in military organizations. One of these three studies (Nebeker, Neuberger, & Hulton, 1983) provides the reader with a detailed description of how financial compensation was used as an incentive and what happened as a result of instituting a performance contingent reward system.

Performance contingent reward systems have been successfully used for relatively simple tasks, such as trapping (Saari & Latham, 1982), data entry (Berger, 1983), and keypunching (Acton, 1984). The principles and theory behind this type of intervention program was extended to relatively complex tasks by Nebeker, Neuberger, and Hulton (1983). Specifically, 10 small purchase buyers and 12 supply clerks in a naval shipyard supply department served as subjects to examine the generalizability of a performance contingent reward system for improving productivity.

Prior to implementing or defining the reward system, performance standards and criteria were developed specifically for the study. Productivity was defined as the number of requisitions processed divided by labor hours expended. Labor hours were adjusted for employee experience, overtime cost, and sick/vacation leave costs. Number of requisitions processed involved several different tasks that were used as input to develop time-based standards for both supply clerks and small purchase buyers. Development of these standards was fairly complex and utilized multiple sources. In addition to the input/output criterion, backlog counts, procurement, and average lead time were used to assess the impact of the intervention. Baseline data on these measures were collected for 83 workdays prior to implementation. Standard performance was defined as the seventieth percentile of the preintervention performance level.

TABLE 2.5. Financial Compensation Interventions

Reference	Sample	Intervention(s)	Productivity Criteria	Results
Acton, 1984; Oliver & van Rijn, 1983	853 Army Material Development & Readiness Command employees performing various jobs	Financial incentives	(1) Varied according to job (2) Person-hours saved	(1) 74,000 hours saved (2) At least $188,000 net savings
Berger, 1983	44 data transcribers at the Air Force logistics center	Incentive pay for above standard performers	(1) Keystrokes per hour (2) Turnover (3) Overtime and backlog	(1) 28% increase in productivity (2) $69,000 savings (3) Turnover dropped from 100 to 43% (4) Eliminated overtime and reduced backlog
Mohr, Riedel, & Crawford in press	508 production workers and their supervisors at a naval shipyard	Incentive pay, feedback	(1) Labor hours expanded (2) Rework hours (3) Schedule slippage	(1) 18% improvement in the last four months (2) No decrease in quality or schedule slippage (3) Cost savings to organization of more than $60,000 thus far
Nebeker, Neuberger, & Hulton, 1983	10 purchasing agents and 21 supply clerks at a naval shipyard	Incentive pay, feedback	(1) Number of requisitions processed and labor hours expended (2) Overtime	(1) 26% increase in productivity (2) 94% decrease in overtime (3) 43% and 52% decrease in lead time and backlog
Saari & Latham, 1982	12 mountain beaver trappers	Variable ratio and continuous monetary reinforcement	(1) Number of rodents trapped per hour	(1) Overall performance increased by 78% from .52 to .93 rodents per hour
Schuster, 1984	890 union production/repair workers in two divisions of an aircraft repair facility	Scanlon Plan (1) Bonus plan (2) Committees (3) Suggestion system (4) Structural changes	(1) Quantity of units produced and hours worked	(1) Statistically significant increases in the time series analyses for productivity data (2) Plan paid consistent bonuses

Incentive awards were paid for performance over and above the standard. Monetarily, the employee earned 30 percent of their hourly wage rate for every hour saved by performing above standard. These incentive payments were accumulated over a two-week period. If the total amount exceeded $25, a request was submitted for payment. When the amount was under $25, it was carried forward to the next biweekly report. This process resulted in at least a four-week lag between performance and rewards. To help offset the negative impact of this time delay, an individual level feedback report was given to each employee. The weekly report provided detailed information on performance and earned incentives.

During the 17-week experimental period, overall production efficiency increased by 26 percent. This increase was due to a 13.5 percent increase in the number of requisitions processed, along with a 9.6 percent decrease in total adjusted labor hours. Overtime labor hours went from 11.7 to .71, or a 94 percent decrease. Workload backlog for the buyers was cut 51.7 percent, and procurement lead time in days dropped by 42.6 percent. When comparing the costs of the program with the savings accrued through increased productivity and decreased overtime, a $14,124 net cost savings was incurred during the trial period. Postintervention attitude survey results indicated that 73 percent of the participants and 83 percent of the managers were in favor of continuing the program.

The success of this program was due to several different factors. First, past research and theory served as the foundation for this field experiment. Vroom's (1964) expectancy theory provided the theoretical underpinnings, while the experience of Nebeker, who was the principal investigator, facilitated the implementation. Care was taken to define exact measures of productivity, delineate performance standards, provide detailed feedback, and construct the incentive award program. The report also implied that the incentive program had top-level management support, thus facilitating the implementation and acceptance of the intervention.

While the above program appeared to be a resounding success, the results should be tempered by both the small sample size and the relatively short duration of the study. In addition, the authors used both incentives and feedback to enhance productivity. The separate effects of these two strategies are impossible to determine. However, the authors attributed the productivity increases to the performance contingent reward system. Developing standards and quantifying productivity are two prerequisites for an individual level incentive system. Simple jobs are much more amenable to quantification than are complex jobs. While the study was progressive in its application of the performance contingent rewards to jobs that were more complex than data entry, clerical tasks are still considered relatively simple. The potency of performance contingent effects on productivity are strengthened by an ongoing study by Mohr, Riedel, and Crawford (in press) that is examining incentive rewards at the group level and involving greater task complexity. Table 2.5 summarizes their preliminary findings. Financial compensation systems appear to offer a robust methodology for enhancing productivity, provided the prerequisite conditions described above are met.

Job Redesign

Hundreds of correlational and laboratory studies have examined the influence of job design on perceptions, attitudes, and job behaviors. During the time period under review, however, only two field studies were found that met the criteria. They are shown in Table 2.6.

Griffin (1983) investigated the effects of objective task changes and informational cues from supervisors on employee task perceptions, affective responses, and productivity. The test sites were two very similar manufacturing plants of one division of a large multinational organization. Essentially the same in both plants, the jobs involved the operation of turret lathes, mills, and numerical control machines. The eight operating departments within each of the two plants were virtually identical in structure and methods of operation. Both had had recent upgrades in their production facilities to avoid technological obsolescence.

The total sample size was 351, with 169 from plant A and 182 from plant B. Because of the limited number of female workers—a total of seven at both plants—they were excluded from analysis. The average age was 33 years, and most had a high school degree. Analyses of differences between the two samples showed that plant A employees had lived in the city where they were employed a fewer number of years, had a higher hourly wage, and were more productive over the past year than were employees of plant B. These differences were statistically significant.

The experimental design employed a 2 × 2 factorial. The experimental conditions were the presence or absence of informational

TABLE 2.6. Job Redesign

Reference	Sample	Intervention(s)	Productivity Criteria	Results
Griffin, 1983	351 machine shop workers at two manufacturing plants	(1) Objectives task redesign (2) Supervisory informational cues	Average individual unit output Company-generated standards	Significant increases in productivity
Umstot & Rosenbach, 1983	73 vehicle operators and maintenance workers at two Air Force bases	Job enrichment based on workers' suggestions: greater task variability, communication patterns, etc.	Vehicles deadlined for maintenance, repair cost, direct labor percentage, reenlistment rates	No change in productive output

cures from supervisors and the presence or absence of objective task changes. In the supervisory cue treatment, supervisors were trained to offer consciously and systematically verbal cues to employees on specific task attributes. They were asked to provide at least five such cues each day to their workers. In the objective task treatment, task changes were introduced to restructure the jobs to provide more task variety, greater autonomy for deciding who did the work, responsibility for machine tolerance checks, feedback about worker productivity output and quality, greater personal identification with the work completed, and an understanding of how these parts fit into the finished product.

Four categories of outcome variables were measured: core task attributes, interpersonal attributes, affective reactions, and productivity. Productivity was assessed using company reports on individual worker unit output that were used to pay weekly production bonuses for units produced exceeding production standards. Productivity, which was measured as average daily output, was calculated for the three-month period prior to the intervention and for the three-month period after the change. Productivity standards were expressed as level of output based on 100 units per day.

Results indicated that both the objective task attributes and the supervisory cues influenced the perception of core task attributes, interpersonal task attributes, and affective reactions to task attributes of workers. Objective task changes were found to influence productivity, which went from 94 to 103 and 96 to 106 for the groups experiencing objective task redesign, but no relationship between productivity and supervisory cues was found. In contrast, Umstot and Rosenbach's (1983) study of job enrichment in the vehicle operations and maintenance shops at two Air Force bases found no significant changes in employee satisfaction or productivity as a result of job redesign.

The critical features for achieving positive outcomes using job redesign appear to lie in the nature of the task changes made, that is, whether the changes are perceived by the workers as cosmetic/superficial or substantially improving the way they accomplish their job tasks. With respect to the relationship between job redesign and productivity, it appears that the criterion measure used must be sensitive to individual unit output as opposed to global organizational measures. While satisfaction and productivity may be significantly related, this relationship depends on the job structure and the reward system. Satisfaction does not lead to greater productivity, but rather greater performance leads to greater rewards, which in turn creates more satisfaction. In most cases, the better performer accrues more rewards than the poor performer and as a result is more satisfied. Task changes that help the worker perform better (especially when this performance is rewarded) will most likely show positive productivity increases using job redesign techniques.

Supervisory Methods

Supervisory methods are often the cornerstone for the success or failure of a variety of intervention programs. Changes in supervisory style are often a critical component of programs, such as training, management by objectives, or new feedback systems. However, it is difficult to assess the sole influence of the supervisor on work productivity when combining changes in supervisory style with other types of interventions. Three reports of changes in supervisory style, which is defined as a change in the degree of influence or participation in decisions that a supervisor accords to subordinates (Katzell & Guzzo, 1983), have been found in the literature. Reed (1984) reports a major, multiintervention program that is currently taking place in the U.S. Copyright Office. The major component of this program seems to be an increase in employee participation and a change in the degree of consultative management. As indicated in Table 2.7, several positive results have been accomplished in this program. An article about productivity and teamwork by Allender (1984) is included here, even though it did not technically meet the selection criteria set forth in the preceding section. While the information provided in the article implies that the intervention was a somewhat controlled experiment, there is no explicit evidence to support this implication. The numerical and anecdotal information in the article, however, warrants inclusion because of the implications for productivity.

Numerous quality control circles have been implemented as a means to increase productivity. The underlying principles of these programs is worker participation in the identification and solution of operational problems. By their very nature, quality control circles (QCCs) necessitate a change in supervisory methods to allow for employee participation. While QCCs are only one form of participation, they are gaining in popularity. Both public and private sector organizations are currently using them. Research on QCCs, their effectiveness for producing suggestions, and their impact on member

TABLE 2.7. Supervisory Method Interventions

Reference	Sample	Intervention(s)	Productivity Criteria	Results
Allender, 1984	Unspecified number of individuals from Hewlett-Packard	(1) Formation of teams that solve problems and make suggestions	Varied	Of the 65 teams: (1) 4 teams reduced labor costs by over 15% (2) 7 teams reduced defect rates by 66% (3) 1 team solved a vendor problem resulting in savings of thousands of dollars
Atwater & Sander, 1983	550 blue-collar workers at Naval Material Commands	(1) Quality control circles (2) Training	(1) Sick leave (2) Promotions (3) Awards (4) Beneficial suggestions (5) Accidents (6) Attitudes	No differences between the experimental and control groups were found
Reed, 1984	520 employees of the U.S. Copyright Office	(1) Supervisory training (2) Increase on worker participation (3) Elimination of overtime	Changes in (1) Staff level (2) Work completed (3) Number of receipts processed	(1) Staff level decreased 19% (2) Work level increased 15% (3) Receipts increased 23%

attitudes has just begun (see Griffin & Wayne, 1984). However, there is very little information on the relative efficacy of this intervention for enhancing performance. One notable exception is the work of Atwater and Sander (1983), who conducted an assessment of QCCs in a public sector organization.

Participants in the study were 550 males who were predominantly blue-collar workers employed by six naval material commands. Three industrial activities were selected to be QCC organizations. These organizations agreed to implement QCCs on a one-year basis. An industrial organization and a personnel activity organization provided subjects to serve as one of the control groups. Within the experimental organizations, membership in the QCCs was on a volunteer basis, resulting in 144 members. Control group subjects were randomly selected from both the QCC organizations ($N = 148$) and from the departments that had no QCCs ($N = 80$). This nonequivalent control group quasi-experimental design study was primarily focused on assessing the impact of QCCs on organizational attitudes, cognitive evaluations, and affective responses. Pre- and postintervention measures of variables, such as job satisfaction, job involvement, organizational commitment, role stress, motivation, and supervisor behavior, were assessed. Archival data on sick leave, promotions, awards, beneficial suggestions, and accidents were also used to examine the impact of QCCs. While these types of organizational indicators are not direct measures of productivity, they have been accepted by other authors (for example, Guzzo & Bondy, 1983) as valid for evaluating productivity enhancement programs.

Participating organizations agreed to implement QCCs on a one-year trial basis. Before the study was initiated, top management of the QCC organizations selected a QCC facilitator from those who volunteered for the position. The facilitator received one week of training and then began orienting management and the supervisors in the QCC process. The facilitator then gave a presentation to potential QCC members and provided training to QCC leaders and members. Member training lasted eight hours and was conducted one hour a week for eight weeks.

Results for the attitudinal evaluation were based on a much reduced sample of individuals—62 QCC members and 269 controls. Over the one year period that the QCCs were in operation, no significant changes occurred within the QCC groups on the 31 attitudinal constructs assessed in the study. The responses of QCC members did not differ significantly from those of the control group on either the pre- or postintervention assessments. Results for the productivity-related indicators of sick leave, promotions, awards, beneficial suggestions, and accidents indicated that QCCs had no significant impact on the participants. Follow-up interviews indicated that many employees perceived positive outcomes of QCCs especially in the areas of communication and cooperation. Documentation indicated that the QCCs were effective in identifying and solving problems.

While the results of this study are not encouraging, they should be tempered by several serious constraints. First the study itself lasted approximately ten months and the QCCs were in operation for only eight months. Given the time it takes for a change to become institutionalized and the time lag between QCC initiation and suggestion implementation, the duration of the study was less than optimal. Second, numerous QCC members worked in departments and groups with non-QCC members, thus confounding the perceived impact of QCCs on the work environment. Third, in all QCC situations, participants agreed to try out their program for about a year and thus realized that it was only a temporary situation. It is difficult to become committed to a program that is transient. Fourth, clear indicators were not available to judge the degree of either participant or top-level management commitment to the program. Hence, the lack of impact could be attributable to the temporary nature of the intervention and its attending lack of commitment.

Griffin and Wayne's (1984) research showed that employee perception of the organization's commitment to the QCC program affected the effectiveness of the QCC. Fifth, while QCC training was provided, the report does not detail its content. Thus, it is difficult to evaluate the effect that the training may have had on the success of the program. Sixth, QCCs were instituted not because they were judged to be an appropriate solution but because of an organizational interest in using them. It is always possible that QCCs were the right solution for the wrong problems or the wrong solution for changing attitudes/behaviors in this specific environment. The researchers may have been using an inappropriate yardstick to assess the impact of QCCs. Last, the effectiveness of QCCs on productivity and member attitudinal disposition toward QCCs are mediated by a host of situational and social psychological variables (Griffin & Wayne, 1984). Hence, implementation and evaluation of future QCC programs should consider not only the QCC but also its context.

Work Rescheduling

Alternative work schedules are currently being used by thousands of organizations. However, evaluative information about their influence on productivity is scant. Table 2.8 summarizes the three studies that critically assessed the influences of work rescheduling on objective productivity indicators.

Greene (1984) has been chosen as the exemplar in this category. This field experiment was conducted in three plants of a manufacturer of business and electronic equipment. All three plants were located in medium-sized cities and were virtually identical in terms of organization, product, functions performed, union representation, and production volume. Subjects consisted of 420 operative personnel and 35 supervisors in the eastern plant, 513 operative personnel and 46 supervisors in the midwestern plant, and 497 operative personnel and 44 supervisors in the southwestern plant, for a total of 1,555 employees. Subjects were "matched" in terms of type of work performed, job or management level, pay, tenure, years of experience in the trade, and gender.

The eastern plant was selected to install the flexitime work schedule as one treatment condition. This schedule was composed of 11 working hours per day. The core, or fixed, period in which all employees were required to be at their work stations was five hours. Around this core, workers were free to set their own starting and stopping times to achieve a eight-hour day for five days a week. The midwestern plant installed the 4–40 schedule as a second treatment condition. Under this schedule, workers were required to work ten-hour shifts for four days to achieve the 40 hours per week with the fifth day off. Starting and stopping times were the same for all workers in this plant. The southeastern plant served as the control, with no changes in its conventional eight-hour-day, five-day work week, with all workers beginning and stopping at the same time.

The criterion measures included employee flexibility, work group relations, quality of supervision, satisfaction with work, absenteeism, tardiness, productivity, and lost-time accidents. Affective measures were obtained by means of a questionnaire. Productivity was measured using company reports for units produced. Production quality was assessed by the number of defects and rejects and hours required for rework due to errors in production. Absenteeism, tardiness, and lost-time accidents were assessed using company records. Baseline

TABLE 2.8. Work Rescheduling

Reference	Sample	Intervention(s)	Product Criteria	Results
Narayanan & Nath, 1982a	3,000 workers in a division of a large corporation dealing in high-tech products	Flexitime schedule with 12 working hours with 4.5 core hours	Self-ratings of individual and supervisor ratings of work groups	No change in reported productivity
Narayanan & Nath, 1982b	173 nonexempt employees (secretaries, technicians, and draftsmen) from a large multinational corporation dealing in high-tech products	Flexitime schedule with 11 working hours with 4.5 core hours	(1) Supervisor ratings of work group productivity (2) Absenteeism	(1) No changes in productivity (2) Absenteeism was reduced by one-third for experimental group
Greene, 1984	1,500 employees and supervisors of three plants manufacturing business and electronic equipment	**Plant A** (1) Flexitime schedule with 12 working hours with 5 core hours **Plant B** (2) 4–40 schedule 4 10-hour days per week **Plant C** (3) Conventional schedule with 8-hour/5-day week	Company reports of plant unit output, rework hours and rejects: absenteeism, tardiness, and lost-time accident rates	Flexitime was superior to 4–40 schedule on all productivity measures except absenteeism but not significantly greater than the convention plant. Rework hours and reject measures showed 8.5% decrease with flexitime, 10.2% increase with the 4–40 schedule, and 2% decrease in the conventional plant. These differences were significant for the flexitime schedule

measures were assessed three months prior to implementation of the treatment and 12 months after its implementation.

Results showed that the flexitime schedule was clearly superior to the 4–40 schedule in terms of productivity, both in output and quality, employee flexibility, work group relations, satisfaction with work, tardiness, and lost-time accidents. However, the productivity gains of the flexitime over the 4--40 schedule were not significantly greater than the production output achieved at the control plant. With respect to quality improvement, flexitime was superior to either the 4–40 condition or the comparison control, with an 8.55 percent decrease in rework hours and rejects under flexitime and a 10.23 percent increase in the 4–40 condition and a 2 percent decline in the comparison plant.

Work rescheduling schemes appear to offer significant gains in the quality of work life for employees. However, these affective gains are not being reflected in changes in the "hard" productivity measures. It may be that the productivity measures employed thus far are too global and not sufficiently sensitive to changes in individual productivity. Research in this area is still in a primitive state and clearly requires studies of a more rigorous nature to understand the relationships of alternative work schedules on productivity.

PROGRAM EFFECTS AND INTEGRATION
WITH PAST REVIEWS

The preceding section presented a summary of the productivity enhancement experience published during the 1981–84 time period. This review did not cover all of the 11 categories of psychological approaches to improving productivity that were delineated by Katzell and Guzzo (1983). Sociotechnical systems applications were omitted because they are discussed elsewhere in this book. Neither organizational structure nor decision-making programs were presented. The review of the literature failed to uncover any experiments that either fell into these categories or met the specified criteria for inclusion. However, the 31 experiments that were mentioned or reviewed in detail provide a wealth of information about the behavioral sciences and productivity enhancement.

Comparative Evaluation

Of the studies under review, 22 reported positive results on the output component of productivity. An additional three studies yielded positive results when using cost savings, earnings, or hours saved as the measure of productivity. Five studies used quality as a secondary criterion, and three of these found that the productivity enhancement program positively affected quality.

When examining the data in Table 2.8 it is obvious that the various programs have differential effects on the criterion; criterion definition varies among studies, the number of studies varies from category to category, and the number of criteria used to assess productivity varies among studies. Hence, the comparative analysis that is offered here is fairly subjective and elementary. Following the lead of Katzell and Guzzo (1983), a summary of the success rate of the various programs is presented in Table 2.9. Also included are the summary statistics from Katzell and Guzzo's review of the 1971–81 literature.

TABLE 2.9. Summary Productivity Experiments, 1971–84

	1971–81		1981–84	
Program	No. of Studies	Percentage Successful	No. of Studies	Percentage Successful
Recruitment and selection	0		1	0
Training and instruction	50	92	3	100
Appraisal and feedback	28	93	6	100
Goal setting	22	95	4	100
Financial compensation	20	90	6	100
Work redesign	25	88	2	50
Supervisory methods	25	92	3	33
Organizational structure	6	100	0	—
Decision-making techniques	4	100	0	—
Work schedule	18	61	3	33
Sociotechnical systems	19	95	not reviewed	

Source: Adapted from Katzell and Guzzo (1983).

As can be seen from Table 2.9, the training, feedback, goal setting, and financial compensation categories appeared to be the most successful. Within the feedback and financial incentive categories, performance change was frequently reported in percentages. On the average, the four studies in the feedback area, which reported percentage change, resulted in a 19.2 percent increase in the desired behavior. The four studies in the financial compensation area, which reported percentage change, resulted in an average 37.5 percent increase in productivity. These two categories of psychological interventions appear to be the most successful for enhancing performance. This judgment is based on the nature of the data presented in the studies, as well as the format used to present the data. For example, some studies used reduction in input as the criterion. These studies could not be compared with studies that used increase in output as the productivity measure. The format used to report the data, which was contained in several studies, precluded an assessment of percentage change. Most of the studies in the feedback and appraisal section were directed at changing very specific performance-related behaviors. The interventions were designed to induce the criterion behavior and hence were successful. The same general observation can be made for the financial compensation programs. Incentives were paid for specific behaviors; these behaviors were used as the criteria and increases resulted.

In contrast, other types of interventions, such as work rescheduling, training and instruction, supervisory methods, job redesign, and recruitment, utilized broadly based changes that should theoretically impact on productivity. The majority of the studies in these categories used fairly specific measures of productivity. However, the change itself was not directly tied to eliciting the specific performance behavior. An exception to this generalization are the goal-setting interventions. These programs were generally successful at demonstrating that goal setting was better than no change at all. However, the criteria that were used often encompassed several different types of behavior. For example, numerous behaviors would be necessary to achieve the objective of reducing control costs (Ivancevich & McMahon, 1982), increasing standard performance (Crawford, et al., 1983), or increasing sales (Kim, 1984). So while the intervention was directly tied to the criterion, subjects set goals for performance areas that involved a multitude of behaviors.

All of the interventions were conducted on a diverse range of subjects. Service workers as well as production workers were included in the studies. While data entry clerks are a relatively easy sample to use because of the ease of designing hard performance measures, they were not the predominant target of any one intervention. Engineers, purchasing agents, secretaries, and supervisors were represented in the studies. In general, the interventions were directed at the employees rather than management. The particular sample used, however, did not seem to contribute differentially to the success of the various programs.

Of the studies reviewed for the 1981–84 time period, three demonstrated a rather interesting result that should be mentioned. Specifically, Crawford et al. (1983), Pritchard et al. (1981), and Scandura and Graen (1984) found that their intervention had the greatest impact on those individuals who had an initial low level of the criterion. For example, the leadership training used by Scandura and Graen involved leader-member exchange. The training produced the best results for those subordinates who reported a low level of preintervention leader exchange. Feedback and goal-setting interventions produced the best results for low as opposed to high performances in both the Crawford et al. and Pritchard et al. studies. While other studies did not directly examine the differential effects of their interventions, it would be interesting to reanalyze the data to see if the above conclusions are generalizable.

Past Research Reviews

The article by Katzell and Guzzo (1983) presented a brief summary of the reviews done by Katzell et al. (1977) and Guzzo and Bondy (1983). This summary uncovered 207 experiments conducted between 1971 and 1981. The present review included two studies published in 1981, with the remaining 29 appearing between 1982 and 1984. As can be seen from Table 2.9, the summary statistics are similar to those of Katzell and Guzzo. However, given the relatively small number of studies reported in this review, it is difficult to make any generalizations about trends over time. Katzell and Guzzo noted that studies of the productivity effects of appraisal, goal setting, and financial compensation increase from 1971–75 to 1976–81. Our time-limited review corroborates this observation.

Meaningful interpretation of the data presented in Table 2.9 is limited by its crude nature. State-of-the art meta-analyses (for example, Hunter & Schmidt, 1983) are needed to assess the relative efficacy of the various programs for enhancing productivity (Hunter, Schmidt, & Jackson, 1982). Meta-analysis, which is discussed briefly in a following section, provides a statistical method to analyze data across studies and to examine the impact of various situational parameters on each criterion. However, the present sample size of 31 studies is too small to conduct these types of analyses.

In a follow-up study to the 1983 Katzell and Guzzo report, Guzzo, Jette, and Katzell (1985) conducted a meta-analysis on 98 of the 207 experiments described. Results showed that, on the whole, the psychologically based interventions raised productivity by one-half standard deviation. While the strength of the productivity increase varied by a number of contextual factors and the operational definition of productivity, the specific type of intervention program also contributed differentially to productivity increases. Specifically, the most powerful programs appeared to be those in the training and goal-setting categories, followed by work redesign, appraisal, and feedback. Surprisingly, financial compensation programs did not produce a statistically significant impact on productivity. This was attributed to the lack of impact of the large variance in results between financial compensation programs. Some of the programs produced very favorable results; others produced none.

The above results, with the notable exception of financial compensation, are very similar to the crude analyses presented in Table 2.9. Specifically, the present review found that training, feedback, goal setting, and financial compensation appeared to have the greatest impact on productivity for the limited number of studies that were reported between 1981 and 1984. In their analysis of only four intervention programs—financial compensation, goal setting, participation, and job enrichment—Locke et al. (1980) found that financial compensation had the greatest impact on employee performance. Their review and relatively simple analyses were based on experiments conducted prior to 1979 and as early as 1948. Hence, the relative efficacy of the various intervention programs, while dependent on the context of the intervention, also vary according to the analysis applied. It seems safe to say, however, that published reports of training, feedback, goal setting, and financial compensation programs produced positive productivity results.

Taken as a whole, the combined reviews show that various psychologically based interventions are effective for enhancing productivity. Katzell and Guzzo's review showed that 86 percent of the studies using output as the criterion yielded positive results. Guzzo et al. refined this statistic to show an increase of one-half standard deviation. In the present review, 75 percent of the studies yielded at least one positive productivity result. While these statistics should be viewed with caution because of the tendency not to publish negative findings, they do have a clear message: The behavioral sciences can be useful for enhancing productivity.

ISSUES, IMPLICATIONS, AND SUGGESTED DIRECTIONS

Psychological research on productivity enhancement over the past 13 years has produced very encouraging results. Yet both the research itself and the application of theory to practical organizational problems raise a number of issues that serve as both limitations and stepping-stones. Research results need to be interpreted with caution because of things like criterion problems and assumptions about causation. While these types of limitations detract from the strength of the study, they can provide information for improving future studies and implementation methodologies.

Research Issues

Criterion Specification

Behavioral scientists are typically in a double bind when conducting productivity research. Their unit of analysis is traditionally the individual. Yet, in all but the most simple jobs, individual level productivity is difficult to quantify. Ideally, individual productivity should be measured by using hard data that reflect the input/output definition. However, the use of such hard criteria is often impractical or impossible. This is especially true in specific cases. For example, volumes have been written about managerial performance and the difficulties associated with its assessment. The same statements could be made about productivity. In addition, many organizations lack information systems that are sensitive to individual or group level performance variations.

In those instances where hard criteria are used or developed specifically for the research endeavor, one must be aware of alternative explanations for changes in those criteria. For example, sales performance (Kim, 1984) can be more dependent on external influences that on the motivation or ability of the sales employee. The number of trips taken per truck (Latham & Saari, 1982) as a productivity measure could be influenced by mechanical difficulties, weather, or the speed of the truck loaders. While the measurement system needs to be sensitive enough to assess individual level contributions, it must also focus on behaviors that are controlled by the individual, not the environment.

Developing quantifiable performance systems can potentially produce unintended consequences. People generally perform up to the standards by which they are measured. Those behaviors that are measured can become the only behaviors that an individual engages in. However, as noted by Katz and Kahn (1978), organizational functioning depends to a large degree on behaviors that cannot be prescribed or required in advance for a given job. According to Smith, Organ, and Near (1983), these behaviors refer to day-to-day spontaneous practical gestures of individual accommodation to the work needs of others. These citizenship behaviors go beyond formal role requirements and are not easily enforced by threat of sanctions. They are not easily governed by individual incentive systems because they are difficult to measure. Yet these citizenship behaviors lubricate the social machinery of the organization, even though they do not directly inhere in the usual definition of task performance. Helping a co-worker with a work-related problem, accepting orders without complaining, tolerating temporary impositions, making timely and constructive statements about the work unit to outsiders, promoting a work climate that is tolerable or enjoyable, and conserving organizational resources are examples of citizenship behaviors (Bateman & Organ, 1983). Hence, strictly defining prescribed "productive" behaviors may eliminate cooperative behaviors that contribute to overall productivity. Interestingly, these cooperative behaviors have been viewed as something distinctly separate from productivity (Rothlisberger & Dickson, 1964). The formal structure of the organization was considered as the main determinant of productivity. Cooperation was viewed as a product of the informal organization. Yet, over the long run, efficiency and cooperation were considered interdependent at the organizational level of analysis.

In those instances where incentive systems are tied to either group or individual measures of performance, caution must be exercised to develop a "manipulation-safe" system. Several organizational productivity programs have failed because workers devised a method to make the productivity look good while actual productivity remained at its preintervention level.

On a practical level, measuring productivity can present administrative problems and elicit negative affective reactions. Numerous productivity projects have been abandoned because of the administrative burden of monitoring individual level performance or making performance observations. Flamholtz (1983) notes that employee reactions to the development of productivity measures or programs may contribute to the demise of the program. The mere title "productivity improvement" program may have negative connotations. Individuals personalize the perceived implicit message that they are considered unproductive. Resistance to the program and the attending measurement system is a natural response to a perceived insult. Developing and implementing productivity measures for research purposes suffer from the same problems encountered when implementing a performance standard system. They can engender fear, suspicion, and sabotage, especially when the organizational climate is less than optimal.

While there is obviously no one best method for generating productivity criteria, the literature offers several suggestions that could enhance the researcher's or practitioner's endeavors in productivity measurement. First, multiple measures of performance/productivity are superior to a single measure. The majority of the studies that were reviewed employed more than one performance measure. Often times only a subset of these measures was influenced by the intervention under investigation. It seems foolish to believe that programs like changing the job design, implementing QCCs, and conducting training programs should impact on only one narrowly defined behavior such as the output component of productivity. Notable exceptions to this generalization are, of course, the organizational behavior modification programs.

Assessment of Cause and Effect Relationships

Organizations are dynamic, and establishing causal links between interventions and outcomes is tenuous at best. A true field experiment necessitates a static situation where data can be collected, the experiment conducted, and results obtained without the intrusion of the outside world. If such an organization could be found, then one would have to worry about external validity. Hackman (1984) maintains, and we agree, that the field experiment model may be inappropriate for productivity enhancement research.

In spite of the limitations of the field experiment model, the studies that were reviewed suggested cause and effect links. These links typically involved attributing a unitary cause to productive behavior. Several studies identified a cluster of interventions that were viewed as the cause for increased productivity. For example, goal setting was considered the cause for an increase in truck driver performance (Latham & Saari, 1982). Given the organizational situation described in the article, the performance increase could have been attributed to a host of other variables like the citizenship behavior that seemed to coincide with the implementation of the goal setting. A cluster of interventions—leadership training, subordinate-supervisor discussions, and listening training—was seen as the cause for increased performance in the Scandura and Graen (1984) study. Were these interventions the sole reason for the change in behavior? Do control groups adequately control for extraneous influences? These questions are difficult to answer, but the point is that it is assumed the interventions caused the effect. Too often we search for simple—single, if possible—explanations for productivity.

This search for simplicity may cause more harm than good. It simplifies research efforts, yet it may obfuscate the real causes for productivity. According to Hackman (1984), searching for unitary causes of productive behavior makes it harder, not easier, to learn about organizational conditions that foster productivity. Rather than searching for a critical mass of favorable conditions, researchers attempt to isolate the one or two or three best interventions. Narrowing the focus of independent variables eases the research process but may lead to spurious cause and effect relationships that overlook obvious causal factors. Most behavioral science interventions are not precise enough to impact on only one behavior.

Most programs affect several kinds of behaviors, behavioral outcomes, and attitudes. Hence, several behaviors, behavioral outcomes, or productive behaviors should be assessed. For example, the goal-setting study of Kim (1984) used both behavioral outcomes (productivity) and facilitating behaviors to examine the efficacy of the program. Using several different behaviors or outcomes as criteria can provide the researcher with specific information about how the intervention is influencing the individual.

The present review focused on productivity programs that employed hard measures of performance. As such, the studies that assessed change via attitudinal measures and indirect indicators were ignored. Often times hard criteria are impossible to obtain. Hence, many excellent programs have been evaluated solely on the basis of self-report measures. Substantial progress has been made over the past two decades in the area of evaluating change via self-reports (Golembiewski, Billingsly, & Yeager, 1976). Recent research evidence (see Armenakis, Buckley, & Bedeian, 1984) indicates that one can statistically tease out the real change (alpha) in attitudes from concept redefinition (gamma) and scale recalibration (beta) change. Attitudes or self-reports can serve as an additional variable when examining the impact of a productivity program. Assessing attitudinal change or changes in perception may compensate for insensitive or inappropriate productivity criteria. There have been numerous studies (see Atwater & Sander, 1983) that resulted in no change in the productivity criteria. However, the individuals participating in the study liked the new system, perceived positive changes, and wanted to continue with the change program. While it seems difficult to reconcile these two conflicting results, one may hypothesize that the change effort theoretically was not designed to influence output as measured in the study. The point is that self-reports should be used in addition to the hard criteria. While the present review did not utilize studies without hard criteria, both researchers and practitioners can benefit from the outcomes of the organizational interventions that were assessed by changes in self-report data.

On a practical level, the research studies implied that existing productivity measures were easier to use than were measures that had been developed specifically for the research study. Existing measurement systems were more comfortable for the employees than were new systems that were introduced just prior to the change program. Resistance to change is natural. Conducting multiple changes, especially when they involve changing the measuring stick called performance, can produce resistance and confounded results. When implementing new performance systems, one obviously should assess the impact of the system itself on behavior before examining any other change program.

Sample Size and Generalizability

The above studies are very diverse in their sample size and the types of jobs involved. Hence, caution must be exercised in generalizing their results. For example, in the study conducted by Nebeker, Neuberger, and Hulton (1983), results were extremely positive and encouraging for the whole area of financial incentives. However, given the sample size of 22, enthusiasm for these results is somewhat dampened. As can be seen from skimming the summary tables, the majority of people involved in the intervention held nonmanagerial jobs that were relatively easy to quantify. Only a few of the employees held service jobs and data entry clerks seemed to be very popular with researchers. Again, it may be difficult, if not impossible, to generalize from one type of sample to the next.

Implementation Issues

Only a few authors reported on the process of implementing change in the organization. Of those reports that discussed these issues, many focused on basic elements of organizational development, while others discussed the lack of theoretical guidelines for program implementation. For example, problems were found in those programs that failed to gain top-level management support or managerial commitment in general. The Atwater and Sander (1983) study is a good example of this problem. Researchers and workers did not perceive that the supervisors did not support the QCC program. While this lack of support could have been due to the temporary nature of the change program, it more than likely had a detrimental effect on the success of the experiment. Organizational theorists strongly advocate participation of the affected employees in the change process. The aftermath of the study by Latham and Saari (1982) exemplifies the negative consequences of ignoring employee input. Truck drivers had voluntarily participated in a successful goal-setting program. After the experiment was completed, management decided to implement goal setting on a formal basis. Employees were not consulted about this decision and went on strike because of it.

The majority of the research studies were just that—research studies. None seemed to involve a complete version of action research/organizational development. There was a lack of reported organizational analysis to precede the implementation of a change program. Most changes were instituted on a short-term experimental basis and very few authors indicated that the program was anything more than an experiment. Some programs lasted only a few weeks (or did the researcher quit gathering data after only a few weeks?) and others lasted several years. Since there is no clear specification about how long a program should be online before its results can accurately be assessed, the timing of program evaluation varies greatly among studies. The issue here is that temporary solutions seem to be implemented before problems are adequately diagnosed. Science may be advancing but the same may not hold true for the application of science.

In their study on goal setting, Crawford, White, and Magnusson (1983) presented a detailed discussion of the implementation problems that they encountered. The goal-setting literature and research, while copious, failed to provide practical guidelines about training, defining goal difficulty, setting guidelines for goal specificity, overcoming employee fear of goal ratcheting, goal equity, feedback, and how to deal with poor performance. This list of failures is not uncommon when going from theory to practice. The motivational literature provides a lot of information about the process of motivation, yet fails to answer a host of practical questions about installing financial compensation systems. Each intervention category will provide its own laundry list of implementation problems. Some problems are generic to change; others are specific to a particular theory or class of programs.

In summary, the programs that appeared to be unsuccessful violated one or more of the basic organizational development tenets. It appears that gaining managerial commitment, getting top-level management support, conducting organizational diagnosis, and eliciting the participation of the employees will maximize the success of the intervention. Both the practitioner and the researcher will be treading on new ground no matter what intervention is implemented. Every organizational behavior program has unanswered questions. Even the answered questions or recommended operating procedures may not be appropriate from situation to situation. Hence, there will be uncertainty when attempting to enhance productivity with behavioral science principles. Theory, research, and common sense are always useful guides for reducing uncertainty.

New Directions in Productivity Research: Some Suggestions

By choice, the field experiment was the predominant research methodology in the productivity studies. Compared with the methods of gathering data and examining theory, the field experiment has a lot of merit. However, present research methodologies and theoretical foundations may not be optimal for studying organizational phenomenon. Hackman's (1984) commentary on this topic concludes by stating that the theory and method of experiment on social psychology were not designed for research or organizational issues. He argues convincingly that theory and method will have to be tailored to the special circumstances of the social system in which the research is conducted and to which the results are intended to apply. The following discussion uses Hackman's provocative propositions as a basis for encouraging researchers/practitioners to "fundamentally rethink how we do psychological research on productivity questions" (p. 208).

Research Approach

Rather than using the traditional experimental models from psychology and sociology, Hackman recommends using naturalistic observation. Rather than introducing a change, the researcher should study change as it is occurring. Organizations that are in the state of change would provide a meaningful setting for examining, via observation and inquiry, the relationship between the performing unit and the organizational context. This examination could yield insights into how changes in organizational conditions affect performance. Multiple settings or performance situations could be used to conduct comparative analyses. In these comparisons, multiple methodologies should be used to ensure accurate performance assessment. Comparative analyses can also aid in identifying those conditions that influence performance.

Organizational members, in collaboration with the researcher, should develop innovative methodologies to learn about the factors that influence productivity. Hackman maintains that collaboration between organizational representatives and researchers could produce a research system that is relevant to real organizational concerns and provides the researcher with a learning experience. As a suggestion to counter the tendency to look for unitary causes for productivity, case studies are recommended. In spite of their limitations, case studies can be extremely useful for identifying a critical mass of conditions that foster productivity. Rather than using simple causal modeling as the basis for research, or trying to tease out the separate effects of various interventions, case studies describe a set of circumstances about productivity. If case studies could be presented in such a way as to invite disconfirmation and test alternative hypotheses, then they might contribute to the understanding of productivity.

Models

Hackman also calls into question the theoretical models that serve as the foundation for organizational change. Contingency models, which are common in organizational psychology, are based on the assumption that variation between a predictor (goal difficulty) and a criterion (performance) depends on some moderator variable (goal specificity). Hackman maintains that contingency models are proposed partly because a researcher's findings on a universalistic (nonmoderated) model did not conform with past research. However, variations in findings across studies or samples is often the natural statistical result of small sample size, restriction of range on variables, and/or unreliable measures (Hunter, Schmidt, & Jackson, 1982). When theories are built on this type of variation, they will not hold up when properly tested. Moving away from contingency models and cause and effect relationships necessitates a reconceptualization of the organizational behavior model. New models of behavior should emphasize the contexts and conditions that support productive behaviors.

By their nature, the models would be complex because they should be built on the fact that productive behavior takes place within social systems. If, however, these models could be used to identify key conditions conducive to productivity, then this information would be useful for both business policymakers and researchers.

Values

As a part of the context and conditions examined by researchers, managerial values and assumptions should be scrutinized. Most research studies do not examine what Hackman calls "management's unexplored forbidden land." However, the values that are held and the assumptions that are made about people may be critical components of the productivity formula. Sensitive issues like standard organizational practices, policies, philosophies, and values, the authority structure, the core technology, and managerial value systems should be studied. Hackman offers several suggestions for studying these issues. First, one can watch unexpected or unintended change on authority structure, technologies, or human resource strategies. When these changes do occur, the researcher should be prepared to exploit the learning opportunity. Second, much can be learned from seeking out organizations that do things differently from standard corporate practice. These organizations could be compared with similar others that use standard procedures. Third, researchers can prepare themselves for the rare opportunity to create nontraditional organizational forms and document the results of the creation.

If psychologists are truly going to make a contribution to productivity, Hackman asserts that they must not only question managerial and organizational values but also be willing to question their own values. Psychologists should make explicit the values on which their work is based. The utility of a psychological intervention should be assessed in light of the stated values. Psychologists should also be cautious about unintentionally impeding the goal they seek. For example, the goal of productivity enhancement could be blocked by the installation of a nonresponsive and/or complex personnel system. The objective of the system may have been to increase productivity, but the system may impede the organization's ability to respond to a changing environment.

The best-selling book *In Search of Excellence* by Peters and Waterman (1982) exemplifies several of the alternative approaches to examining organizations. For the most part, the book presents a series of case studies that were compiled from multiple information sources, such as observation, interviews, and archival data. These data were gathered from a number of performance situations and used to make comparative analyses. Rather than seeking a unitary cause for organizational excellence, the authors identified a series of conditions that led to success. While Peters and Waterman's approach lacks scientific rigor, it serves as an excellent vehicle for managerial discussions about organizational values and philosophies. The book also presents several interesting conclusions that could be used as a basis for traditional or nontraditional research.

Analytical Suggestions

Given the existing research paradigms, evaluation of productivity programs would be enhanced by using both utility analysis (Hunter & Schmidt, 1982; Schmidt & Hunter, 1983) and meta-analysis (Hunter, Schmidt, & Jackson, 1982). Simply put, utility analysis can assess the economic impact of organizational programs. This analysis translates performance criteria into economic terms. Utility analyses have been used, especially in the area of selection, to demonstrate that psychological interventions do have economic value. Meta-analysis is a series of techniques that permits quantitative evaluation across research studies. These analyses take into account sampling errors, restriction of range, and other types of methodological artifacts. Meta-analyses have been previously used to analyze selection studies (see Schmidt & Hunter, 1981). Recently, meta-analyses have been applied to a wide variety of psychologically based programs and techniques.

Both analytical techniques provide information over and above that supplied by traditional methodologies. Economic and aggregate evaluations of productivity enhancement programs are invaluable to both the organization and the researcher. Given adequate numbers of investigations, meta-analysis should be conducted to judge efficacy of a particular intervention for changing the criterion of interest. If aggregate data reaffirm the viability of the technique across settings, then utility analysis could be conducted to judge cost effectiveness. Hunter and Schmidt (1983) suggest that the utility of several concurrent programs, such as goal setting, feedback, and training, is the sum of the utility of the individual programs. The potential here is enormous. First, however, one must use these analytical techniques and apply the results. Current trends indicate the increasing popularity of utility and meta-analysis. These trends should continue.

When examining productivity programs, researchers should be sensitive to the level of analysis issues. Future efforts could be directed at how changes at one level of analysis influence a different level (Thomas & Brief, 1984). Little is known about how individual level performance, for example, impacts on corporate performance. If workers increase their performance output by 10 percent, what does this mean for the productivity of their department? Much work is needed in this area of interlevel productivity assessment and the relationship among levels.

Quality, Not Quantity

Hage (1984), in his essay on organizational productivity, proposes a rethinking of the concept of productivity. His central argument is that in our postindustrial society the meaning of productivity has changed. Yet our measurement and conceptualization have not changed. In the industrial age the emphasis was on efficiency, producing large numbers of things at low cost. Consumers were willing to accept a certain percentage of faulty products as long as they could get what they wanted at a relatively low price. However, consumers are now becoming concerned with obtaining products or services that contain special attributes. Emphasis has switched from buying low-cost volume goods to goods that are durable and of high quality. In our service-dominated society, which is labor-intensive, quantity is not always a relevant yardstick for assessing productivity. Quality of services, he argues, should be a relevant criterion.

Hage's commentary on productivity assessment using quality measures focuses on the product line or profit center level of analysis. He maintains that "managers must strive to reduce the size of demand for their products" by building quality into the product. If the average life of a product is increased by producing quality goods and if maintenance costs are held constant, then one is reducing the size of the market. This logical outcome seems to contradict the stated goals of most organizations. However, while volume of sales and production may drop, this drop should be offset by the savings incurred by producing quality goods. An emphasis on quality should help reduce waste, rejects, and scrap orders. Quality services should help eliminate the costs of rework and administration.

The message contained here for psychologists and practitioners in the productivity enhancement area is that our concerns should be with the future trends, not the past. Special attention should be given to those interventions, experiments, or methods that enhance quality or durability rather than focusing solely on quantity. Ideally, it would be enlightening to study the process of quality improvement, the set of conditions that contribute to quality, the attributes of interventions that are conducive to quality, and the antecedents of quality. Measuring this abstract thing called "quality" may be difficult. One may have to rely on consumer estimations and subjective judgment. However, developing measures of quality may not present more difficulties than are now present with quantity measures.

Quality is an important issue for the majority of organizations that compete on an international market, as evidenced by the recent increase in the use of statistical quality control methods. Psychological interventions may make an equal if not greater contribution to quality than the statistical methods, especially in the service sector. Quality should be one of the criterion for assessing productivity programs. About one-fourth of the productivity experiments reviewed over the last 13 years used quality as a criterion. During the next several years, our emphasis should shift to quality issues to meet the concerns of the business community.

General Limitations

The present review of the productivity enhancement experiments is by no means complete. Its focus was on published studies, a focus that in and of itself imposes serious constraints. Programs are frequently implemented without ever being evaluated or written up. If evaluation is done, often times the data are not released by the organization. Program failures, while evaluated, may not be published.

The focus here was on experiments that utilized behavioral science principles. However, changes in human resource utilization may accompany changes in personnel practices that are not directly tied to the behavioral sciences. New methods of management may be a by-product of policy or strategy changes. These indirect or by-product results were not reported here.

In spite of the obvious limitations, the present review supports the use of psychology as a tool of improving worker performance and/or productivity. Like any science, the focus, measurement tools, and methodologies could be enhanced.

SUMMARY

The main topic of this chapter is the application of behavioral science principles to increasing productivity within organizational settings. Given the complexities of defining and measuring productivity, this chapter also devotes a fair amount of attention to the factors that impact on productivity. When attempting to operationalize productivity, consideration must be given not only to the human element but also to technology, structure, the firm's relevant environment, and the reasons for gathering productivity data. For purposes of reviewing the behavioral science literature on productivity enhancement, the present chapter narrowly defines productivity improvement as an increase in objectively measured output or a decrease in objectively measured input without an offsetting change in the other component.

Using selection criteria developed by past researchers, the chapter reviews the literature and selected 31 studies that represented 8 of Katzell & Guzzo's (1983) 11 intervention categories. All of the studies were field experiments conducted in the United States after 1981. Within each of the intervention categories—recruitment and selection, training and instruction, appraisal and feedback, goal setting, financial compensation, work redesign, supervisory methods, and work schedules—an exemplary study was selected, discussed, and evaluated.

Based on the information obtained in this review of the literature along with the results of previous reviews, behavioral science–based interventions have a positive impact on productivity. Comparisons among the various types of interventions are difficult to make, as the effects of any intervention are dependent on both method of implementation and contextual factors. However, both crude and relatively sophisticated analyses indicate that training, feedback, goal setting, and financial compensation programs have a favorable impact on various measures of productivity.

The last part of the chapter deals with both practical and ethical considerations involved in implementing productivity programs and conducting productivity-related research. Issues such as criterion specification, cause and effect relationships, sample size, and the implementation process are discussed from the perspective of the combined wisdom of past research studies. Suggestions and challenges are presented on these issues.

It is obvious that the behavioral sciences do make a bottom-line contribution to organizational efficiency. However, the assessment of the relative efficacy of various programs and the evaluations of the contribution could use improvement. The research approach, method of analysis, criterion specification, and emphasis on quantity should be called into question by future organizational researchers and practitioners.

REFERENCES

Acton, M. B. (1984). Reshape: A strategy for increasing productivity. *Defense Management Journal, 1*, 37-40.

Aldrich, H. E. (1972). Technology and organization structure: A re-examination of the findings of the Aston group. *Administrative Science Quarterly, 17*(1), 26-43.

Allender, M. C. (1984). Productivity enhancement: A new teamwork approach. *National Productivity Review, 4*, 181-189.

Anderson, C. D., Crowell, C. R., Sponsel, S. S., Aarlie, M., & Brence, J. (1982). Behavior management in the public accommodations industry: A three-project demonstration. *Organizational Behavior Management, 4*, 33-36.

Armenakis, A. A., Buckley, M. R., & Bedeian, A. G. (1984, August). *Research conditions affecting the measurement of change: A laboratory investigation.* Paper presented at the 44th meeting of the Academy of Management, Boston.

Atwater, L., & Sander, S. (1983). *Quality circles (QCs) in navy organizations: An evaluation* (NPRDC TR 83-05). San Diego, CA: Navy Personnel Research and Development Center.

Bateman, T. S., & Organ, D. W. (1983). Job satisfaction and the good soldier: The relationship between affect and employee "citizenship." *Academy of Management Journal, 26*(4), 587-595.

Berger, C. C. (1983). *Sacramento Air Logistics Center Data Transcribers Productivity Based Incentive Award System* (Final Study). McClellan Air Force Base, CA: Sacramento Air Logistics Center.

Blau, P. M., Falbe, C. M., McKinley, W., & Tracy, P. K. (1976). Technology and organization in manufacturing. *Administrative Science Quarterly, 26*(1), 21-30.

Brown, K. M., Willis, B. S., & Reid, D. H. (1981). Differential effects of supervision verbal feedback and feedback plus approval on institutional staff performance. *Journal of Organizational Behavior Management, 3*(1).

Burns, T., & Stalker, G. M. (1961). *The management of innovation.* London: Tavistock.

Chhokar, J. S., & Wallin, J. A. (1984). A field study of the effect of feedback frequency on performance. *Journal of Applied Psychology, 69*(3), 524-530.

Clawson, L., & Mears, C. L. (1983). Productivity information: A key to competitiveness. *National Productivity Review, 3*, 15-25.

Crawford, K. S., White, M. A., & Magnusson, P. A. (1983). *The impact of goal setting and feedback on the productivity of navy industrial workers* (NPRDC TR 83-4). San Diego, CA: Navy Personnel Research and Development Center.

Dean, R. A., & Wanous, J. P. (1984). Effects of realistic job previews on hiring bank tellers. *Journal of Applied Psychology, 69*(1), 61-68.

Dunnette, M. D., & Fleishman, E. A. (Eds.). (1982). *Human capability assessment*. Hillsdale, NJ: Erlbaum Associates.

Flamholtz, E. G. (1983, August). Comments for L. Broedling (Chair), *Productivity enhancement in the military using behavioral science approaches*. Symposium conducted at the 91st meeting of the American Psychological Association, Anaheim, CA.

Golembiewski, R. T., Billingsly, K., & Yeager, S. (1976). Measuring change and persistence in human affairs: Types of change generated by OD designs. *Journal of Applied Behavioral Science, 12*, 133-157.

Graen, G., Novak, M. A., & Sommerkamp, P. (1982). The effects of leader-member exchange and job design on productivity and satisfaction: Testing a dual attachment model. *Organizational Behavior and Human Performance, 30*, 109-131.

Greene, C. N. (1984). Effects of alternative work schedules: A field experiment. *Proceedings of the 44th annual meeting of the Academy of Management*, Boston.

Griffin, R. W. (1983). Objective and social sources of information in task redesign: A field experiment. *Administrative Science Quarterly, 28*, 184-200.

Griffin, R. W., & Wayne, S. J. (1984). A field study of effective and less-effective quality circles. *Proceedings of the 44th annual meeting of the Academy of Management*, Boston.

Guzzo, R. A., & Bondy, J. S. (1983). *A guide to worker productivity experiments in the United States 1976-81*. New York: Pergamon Press.

Guzzo, R. A., Jette, R. D., & Katzell, R. A. (1985). The effects of psychologically based intervention programs on worker productivity: A meta-analysis. *Personnel Psychology 38*, p. 275-292.

Hackman, J. R. (1984). Psychological contributions to organizational productivity: A commentary. In A. P. Brief (Ed.), *Productivity research in the behavioral and social sciences.* New York: Praeger.

Hage, J. (1984). Organizational theory and the concept of productivity. In A. B. Brief (Ed.), *Productivity research in the behavioral and social sciences.* New York: Praeger.

Hickson, D. J., Pugh, D. S., & Pheysey, D. (1969). Operations technology and organizational structure. *Administrative Science Quarterly, 14*(3), 378-397.

Hunter, J. E., & Schmidt, F. L. (1983). Quantifying the effects of psychological interventions on employee job performance and work-force productivity. *American Psychologist, 38*, 473-478.

Hunter, J. E., & Schmidt, F. L. (1982). Fitting people to jobs: The impact of personnel selection on national productivity. In E. A. Fleishman (Ed.), *Human performance and productivity.* Hillsdale, NJ: Erlbaum Associates.

Hunter, J. E., Schmidt, F. L., & Jackson, G. (1982). *Meta-Analysis: Cumulating research findings across studies.* Beverly Hills, CA: Sage Publications.

Ivancevich, J. M., & McMahon, J. T. (1982). The effects of goal setting, external feedback, and self-generated feedback on outcome variables: A field experiment. *Academy of Management Journal, 25*(2), 359-372.

Kanter, R. M. (1983). *The change masters: Innovations for productivity in the American corporation.* New York: Simon & Schuster.

Katz, D., & Kahn, R. L. (1978). *The social psychology of organizations* (2nd ed.). New York: Wiley.

Katzell, R. A., Bienstock, P., & Faerstein, P. H. (1977). *A guide to worker productivity experiments in the United States—1971-1975.* New York: New York University Press.

Katzell, R. A., & Guzzo, R. A. (1983). Psychological approaches to productivity improvement. *American Psychologist, 38*, 468-472.

Kim, J. S. (1984). Effect of behavior plus outcome goal setting and feedback on employee satisfaction and performance. *Academy of Management Journal, 27*(1), 139-149.

Kunz, G. G. R., Lutzker, J. R., Cuvo, A. J., Eddleman, J., Lutzker, S. Z., Megson, D., & Gulley, B. (1982). Evaluating strategies to improve careprovider performance on health and developmental tasks in an infant care facility. *Journal of Applied Behavioral Analysis, 4*, 521-531.

Latham, G. P., & Saari, L. M. (1982). The importance of union acceptance for productivity improvement through goal setting. *Personnel Psychology, 35*, 781-787.

Locke, E. A., Feren, D. B., McCalb, V. M., Shaw, K. N., & Denny, A. T. (1980). The relative effectiveness of four methods of motivating employee performance. In D. D. Duncan, M. M. Gruneberg, & D. Wallis (Eds.), *Changes in working life*. New York: Wiley.

Locke, E. A., & Latham, G. P. (1984). *Goal Setting: A motivational technique that works!* Englewood Cliffs, N.J.: Prentice Hall.

Maher, C. A. (1982). Performance feedback to improve the planning and evaluation of instructional programs. *Journal of Organizational Behavior Management, 3*(4), 33-40.

Marsh, R. M., & Mannari, H. (1981). Technology and size as determinants of the organizational structure of Japanese factories. *Administrative Science Quarterly, 26*, 33-57.

Meyer, H. H., & Raich, M. S. (1983). An objective evaluation of a behavior modeling training program. *Personnel Psychology, 36*, 755-761.

Mintzberg, H. (1979). *The structuring of organizations*. Englewood Cliffs, NJ: Prentice-Hall.

Mohr, D. A., Riedel, J. R., & Crawford, K. S. [in press]. *A trial of a group wage incentive system for production workers at Pearl Harbor Naval Shipyard*. San Diego, CA: Navy Personnel Research and Development Center.

Muckler, F. A. (1982). Evaluating productivity. In M. D. Dunnette & E. A. Fleishman (Eds.), *Human performance and productivity: Vol. 1. Human capacity assessment*. Hillsdale, NJ: Erlbaum Associates.

Narayanan, V. K., & Nath, R. (1982a). Hierarchical level and the impact of flex-time. *Industrial Relations, 21* (2), 216-229.

Narayanan, V. K., & Nath, R. (1982b). A field test of the attitudinal and behavioral consequences of flextime. *Journal of Applied Psychology, 7,* 214-218.

Nebeker, D. M., Neuberger, B. M., & Hulton, V. N. (1983). *Productivity improvement in a purchasing division: Evaluation of a performance contingent reward system (PCRS)* (NPRDC TR 83-34). San Diego, CA: Navy Personnel Research and Development Center.

Newley, T. J., & Robinson, P. W. (1983). Effects of grouped and individual feedback and reinforcement on retail employee performances. *Journal of Organizational Behavior Management, 5* (2), 54-68.

Oliver, L. W., & Van Rijin, P. (1983, August). Productivity improvement efforts in Army organizations: An overview. In L. Broedling (Chair), *Productivity enhancement in the military using behavioral science approaches.* Symposium conducted at the 91st meeting of the American Psychological Association, Anaheim, CA.

Pennings, J. M. (1984). Productivity: Same old and new issues. In A. P. Brief (Ed.), *Productivity research in the behavioral and social sciences* (pp. 107-142). New York: Praeger.

Peters, T. J., & Waterman, R. H. Jr. (1982). *In search of excellence.* New York: Warner Books.

Pritchard, R. D., Bigby, D. G., Beiting, M., Coverdale, J., & Morgan, C. (1981). *Enhancing productivity through feedback and goal setting* (AFHRL-TR-81-7). Brooks Air Force Base, TX: Air Force Human Resources Laboratory.

Pugh, D. S., Hickson, D. J., Hennings, C. K., & Turner, C. (1969). The context of organizational structures. *Administrative Science Quarterly, 14,* 91-114.

Reed, G. B. (1984). Public-sector productivity: A success story. *National Productivity Review, 4,* 155-162.

Robbins, S. P. (1983). *Organizational behavior: Concepts, controversies, and applications* (2nd ed.) (pp. 481-489). Englewood Cliffs, NJ: Prentice-Hall.

Roethlisberger, F. J., & Dickson, W. J. (1939). *Management and the worker.* Cambridge, MA: Harvard University Press.

Roethlisberger, F. J., & Dickson, W. J. (1964). *Management and the worker.* New York: Wiley.

Saari, L. M., & Latham, G. P. (1982). Employee reactions to continuous and variable ratio reinforcement schedules involving a monetary incentive. *Journal of Applied Psychology, 67*(4), 506-508.

Scandura, T. A., & Graen, G. B. (1984). Moderating effects of initial leadership-member exchange states on the effects of a leadership intervention. *Journal of Applied Psychology, 69*(3), 428-436.

Schmidt, F. L., & Hunter, J. E. (1981). Employment testing: Old theories and new research findings. *American Psychologist, 36*, 1128-1137.

Schmidt, F. L., & Hunter, J. E. (1983). Individual differences in productivity: An empirical test of estimates derived from studies of selection procedure utility. *Journal of Applied Psychology, 68*(3), 407-414.

Schuster, M. (1984). The Scanlon Plan: A longitudinal analysis. *Journal of Applied Behavioral Science, 20* (1), 23-28.

Smith, C. A., Organ, D. W., & Near, J. P. (1983). Organizational citizenship behavior: Its nature and antecedents. *Journal of Applied Psychology, 68* (4), 653-663.

Thomas, A., & Brief, A. P. (1984). Unexplored issues in productivity research. In A. P. Brief (Ed.), *Productivity research in the behavioral and social sciences* (pp. 285-301). New York: Praeger.

Thompson, J. D. (1967). *Organizations in action.* New York: McGraw-Hill.

Tuttle, T. C. (1983). Organizational productivity. *American Psychologist, 38*, 479-486.

Umstot, D., & Rosenbach, W. (1983, August). *The effects of job enrichments on worker satisfaction and performance: A controlled field experiment.* Paper presented at the 43rd meeting of the Academy of Management, Dallas.

Vroom, V. H. (1964). *Work and motivation.* New York: Wiley.

Wikoff, M., Anderson, D. C., & Crowell, C. R. (1983). Behavior management in a factory setting: Increasing work efficiency. *Journal of Organizational Behavior Management, 4*, 92-127.

Woodward, J. (1965). *Industrial organization: Theory and practice*. London: Oxford University Press.

3

SOCIOTECHNICAL SYSTEMS

Kenyon B. De Greene

The term "sociotechnical system" was coined in 1951 to describe features of the theory and design of industrial-production systems. The term, however, now has a far broader significance.

Sociotechnical systems can be identified at several qualitatively emergent, hierarchical levels. The lowest level, that of the work system, has received the greatest attention. Sociotechnical systems principles have been developed in the context of and applied to industrial-production, transportation, public service, and military systems. Causal or independent-variable factors have included kinds and amounts of mechanization and automation of the technological or technical subsystem and group structural, task structural, motivational, and cognitive aspects of the social subsystem. Productivity, efficient use of resources, output quality, and minimization of externalities or undesirable side effects can be considered the main effect or dependent-variable factors. Intervening variables include morale, job satisfaction, psychosomatic disorders, job turnover, absenteeism, theft, breakage, vandalism, sabotage, and so forth. Of course, this categorization of factors is a simplication of real-world systems in which all factors are tied together by feedback loops.

Sociotechnical systems can next be identified at the level of the business, service, or governmental organization. The factors just mentioned apply here too. However, information systems assume prominence over physical production systems, and the formidable problems of professional and managerial productivity arise.

The highest level of sociotechnical system identified in this chapter is that of the society. However, the society can be variously viewed as part of the external environment of the organization, which can be characterized in input-output terms of labor, technology, capital, and externalities; as a national society; as an international society; and as world civilization. At this level the concern is with the life cycles of products and technology, with economic cycles, and with the positive and negative impacts of technology.

The evolution of physical, biological, and social systems overall has been in the direction of greater complexity, where complexity can be defined in terms of number of systems elements, variety of systems elements, and interactions among systems elements. Systems co-evolve with their environments. Systems-environment interactions lead to the emergence of qualitatively different structures in which elements of the old structure may become subordinate subsystems of the new system. Organizational complexity is abetted by the large scale of today's organizations and by accelerated social and technological change. The increasing complexity of organizational environments has been aptly described in a seminal article by Emery and Trist (1965). The concept of the most complex of the four environments identified, the turbulent-field environment, provides a key, integrating theme of this chapter.

Mechanization and automation have been increasingly important technological forces. Machine skills have increasingly been substituted for human skills and capital for labor. At first, only the simplest manual and perceptual-motor skills were mechanized in industry and agriculture. These were skills like moving, lifting, pulling apart, shaking, and mixing. During the past three decades, with rapid advances in computer hardware and software, increasingly sophisticated perceptual, motor, and decisional skills have been automated. Examples of these skills are moving, rotating, and inserting a subassembly and deciding to turn a system on or off or change the rate of reaction when some value exceeds a threshold or enters an out-of-tolerance zone.

So-called fixed automation has had a major impact on work-systems design and worker behavior and on patterns of employment. It has also contributed to unemployment levels, including chronic and structural unemployment, but so far to a lesser degree. With the development and widespread implementation of the "factory of the future" and "office of the future," impacts on both work-systems design and unemployment are likely to be quantitatively and qualitatively different from those up to now. Computer-aided design (CAD), advanced information systems, sophisticated techniques of systems integration, robotics, and computer-aid manufacturing (CAM) are the dominant technological features of these emerging organizations.

Many of the features of the industrial mass production revolution have been criticized on a number of grounds. Industrialization itself has been held responsible for the breakup of long established patterns of community and family life, usually for the worse. The fragmentation of jobs, specialization of tasks, and emphasis on efficiency have been held to be both dehumanizing and counterproductive. Thus, developments like Frederick W. Taylor's scientific management, the Gilbreths' time and motion study, and Henry Ford's automobile assembly line can eventually lead to diminishing productivity returns and even negative results.

In the 1920s, following the famous Hawthorne studies, it became widely recognized that attention to worker traits could affect productivity. The Hawthorne studies led to the human relations school of thinking. However, there has been no unanimous agreement as to just what worker traits are of greatest importance and just what are the human relations. The Hawthorne studies suggested that management awareness and attention improved worker productivity. Other researchers believed that friendliness among workers on the job was a major determining factor. Sociotechnical systems theorists argue that their field is not human relations or group dynamics, and that systems productivity involves much more than friendliness on the job, if indeed this factor is involved at all.

Over the past five decades many psychological, psychosocial, sociological, and economic factors have been investigated in terms of their purported effects on systems productivity. Representative examples are motivation, learning, group dynamics, role structure, and reward structure. Studies have focused on the individual, the group, and the whole organization. I believe that the key factors in all productive human achievement are the need for control over one's self, one's immediate environment, and one's destiny and the perception that this control exists. These factors may variously explain, amplify, and integrate sociotechnical systems theory, the Maslow hierarchy of motives theory, and Hertzberg two-factor theory, the McClelland-Atkinson theory of power, achievement, and affiliation, the White theory of competence, the Seligman theory of learned helplessness, and several theories of intrinsic and extrinsic motivation. References to original sources are made in De Greene (1982). Personal control can be greatly restricted both by machines and processes and by organizational designs, especially of the hierarchical, bureaucratic kind. The results can be depression, lack of confidence, defensive and evasive behaviors, low morale, job dissatisfaction, hostile-aggressive behavior, and reduced health—all leading to lowered productivity.

Productivity and the factors contributing to it have been extensively studied. Total factor productivity can be defined as output per unit of input. A more common measure of productivity is output per person-hour. A Cobb-Douglas production function can be defined as

$$P = a L^{\alpha} C^{\beta}; \ \alpha, \beta < 1.0, \ \alpha + \beta = 1.0$$

where production or output P represents a multiplicative relationship between labor L and capital C, and a is a constant. The units are physical, not monetary.

Productivity as a concept and as a measurable entity is more complex than these preliminary definitions would suggest. The units of input and output are not independent, and feedback loops both link inputs to one another and inputs with outputs. Outputs must be viewed in terms of both intended and unintended outputs and of both quality and quantity. Thus, effective productivity P_e might be expressed in terms of four categories of inputs—capital C, labor L, technology T, and natural resources R—and of unintended environmental consequences or externalities E and poor quality products P_q as

$$P_e = C + L + T + R - E - P_q$$

For example, effective productivity could be greatly reduced by huge costs associated with cleaning up environmental pollution, settling lawsuits stemming from the use of toxic substances on the job, and recalling faulty products.

Figure 3.1 shows the overall nature of sociotechnical evolution. Locally, the curve represents the growth to saturation of a capability, followed by a mutation or breakthrough that initiates the next stage of growth. The evolutions of transportation systems and of computers are representative examples.

FIGURE 3.1. Evolution of Sociotechnical Systems.

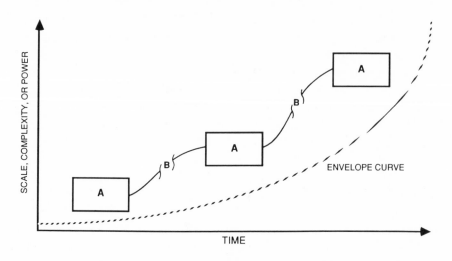

Sequences of logistic curves, bounded by an exponential or hyperbolic envelope curve, have characterized human evolution since the earliest Paleolithic. Stages of very rapid change, B may discontinuously break longer periods of slower continuous change, A. The most unstable periods occur around the inflection point of the logistic curve and following long periods of stable equilibrium.

TABLE 3.1. Percent Rate of Annual Growth of Gross Domestic Product per Employed Workers, 1965-79

Country	1965-73	1973-79
United States	1.6	0.3
Belgium	4.3	2.7
Canada	2.4	0.4
France	4.5	2.9
West Germany	4.3	3.1
Italy	5.8	1.7
Japan	9.1	3.4
Netherlands	4.6	2.6
United Kingdom	3.4	1.1

Source: Adapted from *The Productivity Problem* (Washington, DC: Congressional Budget Office, 1981).

Many observers, including me, believe that the evolution of world civilization has entered a stage of major transformation. One trend of particular concern here is the decline in the growth of labor productivity, which is shown in Table 3.1.

HISTORICAL AND EVOLUTIONARY PERSPECTIVES

The body of knowledge about sociotechnical systems involves both theory and applications work that evolved over the past 35 years. There is no single correct sociotechnical systems approach that excludes alternative approaches. Research and applications will depend on a great many factors, including life-cycle phenomena of products, technologies, and organizations, kinds and degrees of automation, kinds of work and skills, constraints imposed on and by equipment and software design, support by management and often by labor unions, cost constraints, and so forth.

Early Work at the Tavistock Institute on Industrial Production Systems

The first formal studies of sociotechnical work systems were performed at the Tavistock Institute of Human Relations, London. The early Tavistock research was influenced by the open-systems theory of Ludwig von Bertalanffy and by work in experimental social psychology, clinical psychology, and sociology. It also was a reaction against both the industrial engineering espoused in Frederick W. Taylor's scientific management, on the one hand, and human relations, on the other.

The term sociotechnical system was first used by Trist and Bamforth (1951), who were studying the impacts of technological change in a British deep-seam coal mine. Mining had traditionally involved groups of two or three men working closely together but almost autonomously. Each miner performed a variety of tasks, jobs were essentially interchangeable, control was internal, and worker satisfaction derived from performing the total job. The psychosocial and task needs fit one another; sociotechnically, they were congruent.

The new technology was designed to replace the costly manual method. Mechanical coal cutters and conveyers represented a mass production technology capable of extracting a long wall of coal but necessitating a different individual and group work organization. Work was shredded into narrowly defined, unvarying tasks allotted to three shifts of 10 to 20 miners each. The main task interrelationships were now among the shifts, not within a work group. The complex, rigid system was sensitive to both social and technical perturbations, and problems arising at one stage aggravated performance at successive stages. Production declined, absenteeism mounted, and intragroup rivalry became common.

Later research compared the sociotechnical design with a design combining the new technology with elements of the traditional social-psychological work structure: greater independence of the strict technological cycle, self-selection of team members, and a greater variety of worker skills. The latter led to an increase in productivity from 78 to 95 as defined by percentage of the coal face potential, a reduction in absenteeism from 20 percent of possible shifts to 8.2 percent, and a large increase in the percentage of production cycles that were normal and in advance rather than behind.

Research in other industrial-production settings in several countries demonstrated the same principles that continue today to be the basic underpinnings of the sociotechnical systems approach to work-systems design. Mechanization or automation is introduced in an attempt to reduce the costs of manual systems and to increase productivity. Equipment layouts, work flow, and workloads are studied by industrial engineers. But counter to expectations, productivity is low, and behaviors, like absenteeism and damage to equipment and materials, increase. Following sociotechnical redesigns, which attack the system as a whole, not just its constituent parts, productivity improves and undesirable behaviors decrease.

Tavistock researchers determined early that for a given technology and a given environment, a variety of social subsystems and work structures could be applicable. One design could usually be found superior to others. The technological subsystem imposes requirements on the social subsystem, and productivity is a function of how effectively the social subsystem meets those requirements.

The organization as an open system interchanges both matter and energy with its environment. The organization is also informationally a closed-loop system, that is, positive and negative feedback determine growth and regulatory processes. The organization is thus cybernetic, but the term "cybernetic(s)" is rarely if ever used in the older sociotechnical systems literature. Nevertheless, early research stressed the importance of the technological subsystem in organizational self-regulation, that is, in maintaining equilibrium or steady state in the face of fluctuations in the external environment. The technological subsystem was viewed in the early Tavistock studies as one of the major boundary conditions of the social subsystem by mediating between the organization and the external environment. Thus, the term "sociotechnical system" was coined because "social system" was considered to be insufficient. (Most of the terminology in this chapter represents the evolution of my own thinking. In some cases, the original terminology was different. For example, what I have called the "technological subsystem" might have been referred to by the original authors as the "technical system" or the "technological component.")

F. E. Emery, E. J. Miller, A. K. Rice, and E. Trist were among the chief "founding fathers" of sociotechnical systems theory and applications at the Tavistock Institute. Pioneering work was also carried on by P. Herbst at Tavistock and in Norway. Good sources for understanding the early history and continued evolution of the sociotechnical systems paradigm are Emery (1959, 1977, 1982), Emery and Trist (1965, 1973), and Trist (1981, 1983). See also De Greene (1973), especially for extensions to macrosystems.

Tavistock researchers identified dimensions of the technological subsystem and of the social subsystem, which was often called the work-relationship structure. Analysis of the two subsystems, their interrelationships, and the joint contribution to organizational performance continue to be basic to sociotechnical systems studies. The technological subsystem has usually been viewed as a given that adapts to perturbations from the external environment, imposes demands not only on the work structure but also on the internal design, differentiation, and mission of the organization, and sets limits to what can be done.

The technological subsystem consists of equipment, plant layout, manufacturing processes, and raw materials. The dimensions of the technological subsystem include characteristics of raw materials; environmental characteristics of the work setting; space required for the production process, speed of throughput, and requirements for two or more shifts; the level of mechanization or automation (usually the most important dimension); the operations and processes required by production and their grouping into phases; the relative criticality

of the different operations; and the boundary conditions of maintenance and supply. The nature of these dimensions has, of course,
been modified over the evolution of sociotechnical systems. For
example, the kind and quality of information, rather than the characteristics of raw materials, are of greater significance to information
systems. Supervision and quality control are often viewed as boundary
conditions, and modern technologies offer potential as much as constraint.

Analysis of the technological subsystem provides insights about
the structure and function of the social subsystem, especially regarding the jobs and tasks required. Although there is no one-to-one relationship between the two subsystems, most sociotechnical systems
have reflected a great deal of technological determinism. Ideally, this
would not be the case, and the technological and social subsystems
would be co-planned and co-developed and would co-evolve with the
factory, facility, office, and organization. In reality, heavy capital
investment in plant and equipment precludes much change to the
technological subsystem. Evolution toward more flexible production
and office technology may alter this picture.

The social subsystem consists of individuals and their characteristics and interrelationships. Analysis of the social subsystem involves
determining tasks and task interdependencies that define the work
system. The work system relates people to both technology and to
each other. The term "occupational role," with its sociological level
of emphasis, bridges the gap between the work structure and the individual worker. The role helps define the group social structure. The
social subsystem possesses both social and psychological properties.
Dissatisfaction with either the role, including interpersonal relations,
or the work can lead to lower productivity.

The work system and the production organization are not social
systems as psychologists, social psychologists, and sociologists might
argue, nor are they technological systems as often seen by engineers
and computer scientists. Rather, they are holistic sociotechnical systems, characterized by complex mutual cause and effects and interdependencies among social and technological factors. They can be
analyzed at many hierarchical levels. One approach, developed by
Herbst (discussed in De Greene, 1973, pp. 50–52), involves the analysis of operations by individuals (assembling a piece of equipment),
operations by machines (trimming and cutting metal sheets), and
operations on materials (welding, inspecting, storing). Sequences of

such analyses lead to allocations of people to machines, people to processes, and processes to machines. The resulting systems structures are, respectively, the social subsystem, the plant layout, and the manufacturing system, which interact to yield the sociotechnical system.

Many authors refer to the "optimization" of the sociotechnical system design. The term is often used informally, but maximization of productivity and minimization of undesired behaviors like absenteeism or intentional damage to equipment or materials are possible in the rigorous mathematical sense. Usually, however, systems measures, including outputs, are varied and even contradictory. For example, productivity may be increased at the expense of morale. Optimizations of complex systems are therefore unlikely.

The Spread of the Paradigm

By the early 1970s sociotechnical kinds of designs had been applied to organizations and operations in a number of countries. The relationship of these applications to the original Tavistock studies is not always clear. Often the designs are called "job enlargement," referring to a work system focused at the group, not the individual, level, in which workers share and rotate among most or all the tasks.

The most familiar of these efforts involved the design of a new Volvo automobile assembly plant that opened in 1974 at Kalmar, Sweden. This plant lacks the traditional assembly line. Construction costs were 10 percent more than those of other Volvo plants, but morale and factors like job turnover, down from 35 to 10 percent, were improved over those at other plants. The design philosophy was to restore much of the atmosphere and many of the practices of a small pre-Industrial Revolution craftsman's shop in the context of a large production industry. The work group as a whole became responsible for assembling a car, sharing the various tasks involved. Some of the design innovations developed at the Kalmar plant, for example, task rotation within work group and self-selection of teammates, were implemented at traditional Volvo assembly plants. Volvo as a whole has evolved into a progressive, organic firm and has implemented other improvements in working life such as flexible hours. In the years 1976 through 1978, its automobile productivity rose 20 percent.

The Organization as a Sociotechnical System

In the dynamic world of open systems, any hierarchical level of organization of matter, energy, and information has complete meaning only with reference to the levels above and below, that is, the subsystem(s) and suprasystem or environment. A sociotechnical work system must therefore be viewed not only as the outcome of interaction between the social and technological subsystems but also in terms of the organization in which it is embedded. A sociotechnical design, optimized at the work-systems level, may be an emphemeral thing in the absence of total organization design incorporating an adaptivity and resilience to environmental buffeting and continual commitment by management.

The need to view the entire organization as a sociotechnical system was recognized by the original Tavistock researchers (see, for example, Emery [1959]). Researchers were concerned with the impact of the technological subsystem on the internal differentiation and integration of the organization as the subsystem played its major role of self-regulation in the face of environmental disturbance. Here the studies of the Tavistock school interface with other research on organization design as a function of environmental structure and change and of top management behavior. The research of Burns and Stalker, Woodward, Lawrence, and Lorsch, Chandler, and Child (referenced in De Greene, 1982) also led to a better understanding of congruence or fit between an organization and its environment and of the characteristics of mechanistic versus organic designs. Collectively, this kind of research led to the contingency theory of organizations. In most instances an organic design is more compatible with a sociotechnical systems design in terms of a holistic approach to work system, worker autonomy and participation, and organizational adaptivity to rapid environmental change.

Tavistock researchers contributed to the development of two of the most important social themes of contemporary work organization: quality of work life and industrial democracy.

Quality of Work Life

Attitudes toward specific work and entitlement and behavior on the job have changed greatly in the past 20 years. Commitment has decreased, and alienation has become widespread. This has been especially evident among American and British assembly workers whose high pay, compared with that of other hourly workers, and relatively generous fringe benefits have been seen to contrast sharply with declining productivity and quality of output.

The contrast is especially stark when comparisons are made with the pay, work behavior, and output of foreign assembly line workers, especially the Japanese. This devolution of work behavior is due to many factors, including increased education, the spread of democratization and the concept of rights, and the buffering effects of social welfare. Although such social change is worldwide, it is considerably damped in countries, especially in West Germany and East Asia, where strong cultural obligations to work itself, as opposed to working for pay and fringe benefits, still continue. To many observers, the dehumanization of work that accompanied the Industrial Revolution in Britain and America has finally come home to roost.

There is a widespread belief today that the quality of work life should be improved for its own sake, as a major responsibility of an enlightened society, as well as a spur to increases in productivity. Better technology-work-systems matches offer one main opportunity for improvements. Another is the search for alternative design ideas in foreign production methods. For example, high Japanese productivity is associated with high participation by workers in decision making and with methods of arriving at group consensus.

A study of Guest (1979) illustrates the implementation of a quality of work life program at the General Motors automobile assembly plant at Tarrytown, New York. In the early 1970s the plant had very high levels of absenteeism, job turnover, operating costs, and grievances under consideration. Relations among labor, the union, and management were hostile, and productivity was low. Nevertheless, there was insight that something had to be done to prevent further deterioration. A quality of work life program was initiated, and the cessation of truck assembly provided the opportunity to redesign the plant. At first, traditional methods of design were employed. Engineers and technical specialists laid out the plant and equipment, planned the work flow, and developed charts and blueprints. These results were presented to supervisors. However, one supervisor suggested involving the workers, as experts in their own right. Workers made hundreds of suggestions, many of which were adopted. Workers, management, and the union began to cooperate on a large scale in solving future problems.

By December 1978, more than 3,300 workers had gone through a quality of work life training program. The plant became one of the best among 18 in its division. In the Tarrytown case, as in many others, improvements stemmed largely from redesign of the social subsystem. That is, worker participation in decision making and mutual cooperation of all stakeholders in problem solving led to increased motivation, morale, and job satisfaction. Changes in the technological subsystem were slight. Unlike the design at the Volvo plant in Kalmar, Sweden, the Tarrytown plant retained its assembly line. The repetitive conveyer-paced tasks, 60 cars per hour, remained fundamentally unchanged. The bureaucratic hierarchy remained intact.

Industrial Democracy

Industrial democracy extends the process of democratization to most aspects of organization life. Even more than quality of work life, industrial democracy can represent an end in itself, beyond any improvements in productivity and profits. Industrial democracy in this ideal form is a goal most often seen in Scandinavia. However, industrial democracy programs have been implemented in several other European countries, in Yugoslavia, and in Israel, but so far to a lesser extent in the United States.

Industrial democracy varies among applications and may include one or more of the following features: greater worker decision making and control at the work-systems level, for example, through design of semiautonomous work groups; design of offices, living quarters, dining facilities, parking lots, and the like on an egalitarian basis in which status differences are eliminated; elimination of features that pace workers, such as assembly lines, and provision of flexible working hours and reduced working hours once production quotas are met; participation through elected representatives at all levels of corporate management; and ownership of companies by workers, typically following mass stock purchases. Some of these features are easier to implement than are others, which represent longer range goals. Some features, worker councils as in West Germany, for example, are legislated by government.

Industrial democracy is sometimes viewed as a successful blend of capitalism and socialism in which most companies would remain privately owned, with top management making the final decisions, but workers or their representatives would participate at all levels in decisions about plant design, moves, and shutdowns; equipment procurement; work schedules and rules; employee hiring, firing, transfers, and training; worker housing; fringe benefits; and overall planning. Quality of work life, morale, productivity, and profits would increase and be sustained because power and decision making and the rewards of work would be nearly equally shared. Thus, although the immediate work task might remain distasteful, further erosion of total job satisfaction could be arrested.

Alternatives to Hierarchy

The legacy of the Industrial Revolution is seen not only in the production work system but also throughout the organization. The hierarchical bureaucratic design, with its attendant specialization of jobs and top-down flow of control, has been widely criticized as a generator of alienation and job dissatisfaction. Bureaucracy has been criticized as being obsolete at a time of increasing democratization of all aspects of life. Perhaps worst of all, bureaucracies are seen to be obsolescent because of rigidity, slowness of response, and lack of adaptivity at times of rapid environmental change. Dating from ancient times and intensified to fit the needs of the Industrial Revolution, hierarchical bureaucratic designs stimulate the search for alternatives or at least fine tuning.

Herbst (1974, 1976) has studied design alternatives to hierarchy. Two forms warrant particular attention: semiautonomous work groups and matrix organizations. In both cases the development of lateral communications is emphasized. Deciding is reunited with doing.

In semiautonomous work groups, the fragmentation of jobs and tasks in space and time is minimized by reuniting in one job such factors as operations, maintenance, supply, inspection, quality control, and supervision. The need for outside specialists is greatly reduced. Ideally, members share the same values, and status differences are minimized. Rewards accrue from knowledge and capability. The remaining functions of supervision and of management become those of providing resources to the working groups and providing information on organizational goals and plans.

Semiautonomous work groups may be of matrix design, as may be the total organization. Ad hoc problem-solving teams, which can react quickly to emergencies, are one form of matrix design. These are considered to be self-adaptive, learning systems. Leadership roles change according to the situation.

Evaluation of the Sociotechnical Systems Approach

Holistic in concept, the classical sociotechnical systems approach is limited by the context in which it is applied and by interfaces with other approaches. Poor management support, the hostility of unions, economic limitations and setbacks, poor human factors design, and systems evolution are examples of variables that can affect the meaningfulness and permanency of sociotechnical design. Experimental autonomous work groups can be resented by other groups who perceive favoritism. Supervisors and managers may resent loss of control. Unions may see the development of autonomous work groups as a step toward union-busting. Representative discussions and evaluations have been made by Cherns (1976), De Greene (1973, 1982), Van Der Zwaan (1975), and Trist (1981).

One of the major early experimental sociotechnical studies was made in 1953–54 by A. K. Rice in automatic and nonautomatic textile mills at Ahmedabad, India. Miller (1975) made a follow-up study after 16 years. Rice had introduced semiautonomous group systems, that is, small internally led groups of workers responsible for the entire system of weaving on a group of looms. By 1970, only one out of four, the nonautomatic experimental group, maintained the same work structure and level of performance. Two loom sheds retained some features of the sociotechnical design. In the fourth, the group structure had largely disappeared. Regression in the two automatic looms was interpreted in terms of loss of the necessary boundary-sustaining conditions as changes occurred in the external environment of suppliers, markets, and competitors. Miller believes that the problem was one of maintaining equilibrium within a constantly changing system trajectory, not just within a static range of tolerable steady states. Management's drive to maximize production in the short term led to a longer term increase in maintenance problems.

Rice's original design was consistent with modern ecological concepts of design for maximization of resilience and minimization of disaster (see Holling, cited in De Greene, 1982) as opposed to maximization of production efficiency. The latter typically leads to loss of variability and contraction of the boundaries of systems stability with a concomitant loss of self-regulation. Miller's study is both a valuable follow-up of sociotechnical systems-external environment co-evolution and an indication of the evolution of sociotechnical systems theory itself.

MACROSYSTEMS FORCES

Since the early 1970s the concept of sociotechnical systems has been applied to contexts far beyond those of work system and organization design (De Greene, 1973, 1978, 1981, 1982). Sociotechnical systems studies now encompass the macrosystems of national and international society, systems such as nuclear and conventional power generation, health services, education, transportation, trade and finance, the city, the region, and the arms race/international-security system. Each macrosystem reflects the emergent properties of organizations and work systems at lower hierarchical levels. Indeed, the most challenging unsolved problems are those at the macrosystemic level, and in the absence of better understanding of macrosystem forces, work system and organization designs may be fragile and ephemeral things. In addition, productivity is more a function of global than of local forces.

There is, accordingly, a great interest, especially among systems engineering groups, in topics like technology and society, technological assessment and impact, and the social responsibility of engineers. For a number of years, the National Academy of Sciences/National Research Council had an active Council on Sociotechnical Systems. This section discusses features of the life cycle of technology, of products, and of organizations, with particular reference to the design of the "factory of the future." It concludes with a consideration of evolutionary trends in the social macrosystem.

Life Cycles of Technologies, Products, and Organizations

Trends in the development of computer-based rationalization, artificial intelligence, planning, design, manufacturing, systems integration, and robotics seem likely to increase greatly productivity as measured by total output quantity, quality, and variety and by output her person-hour. However, the nature of work will also change in the direction of greater demands on abilities and skills and probably in the direction of lessened importance of production teams.

Many observers agree that the organizational profile will be less triangular in the future. With the elimination of less skilled blue-collar and white-collar jobs, the organizational profile may become diamond-shaped. Many observers foresee the elimination of numbers of middle management jobs, a structural change that occurred in the 1981–82 recession, and the bulge in the middle might reflect the increased participation of technical experts. Eventually, the profile could resemble a rectangle or even an inverted triangle as the routine tasks of production, information processing, and management are automated, but an increased staff becomes necessary for environmental assessment, long-range planning, and the handling of emergencies and contingencies.

The Factory of the Future

The factory of the future will not be totally revolutionary because considerable automation has already been accomplished. One example is the machine tool, such as a lathe, numerically controlled (NC) by its own computer. Automated transports, materials storage and retrieval systems, and simple robots provide other examples of equipment under local computer control. Different equipment can be grouped into a single manufacturing cell with a corresponding savings in movement, labor, and costs. In turn, the separate equipment can be brought under integrated computer control, producing an automated manufacturing cell. This cell can be reprogrammed to make a variety of kinds of products, hence the term "flexible automation" as opposed to the older, special-purpose "hard automation." At the next hierarchical level of integration, one can speak of flexible manufacturing systems and flexible automatic factories. The number of workers in the last may be as low as one per shift, and it is significant that they are usually referred to as managers.

The factory of the future is likely to combine the efficiency and relatively low cost per unit of mass production with the person-based greater flexibility of batch production. New generations of equipment will operate 24 hours a day, producing many kinds of high-quality units at relatively low costs. Sensing, monitoring, surveillance, regulation, and control will utilize layers of computer hardware and software. The work force will consist largely of a small and professional number of systems managers.

As used here, the functions of the factory of the future include not only computer-aided manufacturing (CAM) but also the engineering tasks that can be subsumed under computer-aided design (CAD). A number of routine activities are already being eliminated. New data bases reduce the need for lengthy searches for design criteria, tolerance limits, specifications, and so on. Three-dimensional, full color, interactive computer graphics permit the consideration, comparison, and evaluation of a wide variety of alternative designs. Computer simulations enable the designer to test parts and products, outside the laboratory, under conditions of various environmental stressors. Advances in artificial intelligence, for example, in making possible better figure-ground distinctions, may further automated design. CAD and CAM themselves are being further integrated through direct control of machinery on the factory floor via computer graphics. The highly integrated, automated CAD/CAM-based factory will be managed at a top level in which planning of and quick-response control over processes, products, amounts, and mixtures will be incorporated into design. Holistic displays of total factory operation can be provided via computer animation. Total factory simulation will aid test and evaluation and help specify where preventive maintenance is needed.

The coordination, communication, and integration of so many components, modules, and subsystems, involving complex interactions among both hardware and software, seems guaranteed to yield some mammoth failures. Software design continues to be a major impediment to the development of advanced automated systems. Design, interfacing, debugging, and integration of components in a hierarchical scheduling and control system are especially difficult.

As has been the case with the life cycles of technologies, products, and organizations up to now, the factory of the future will learn by doing and through experience. In the early stage, most knowledge will be in the heads of planners, designers, managers, consultants, and others. Over time, expert systems will be developed. The evolution to holistic automated-knowledge systems can be thought of as a reversal of the trend to even greater fragmentation and specialization of tasks that characterized the Industrial Revolution. As discussed earlier, sociotechnical work-systems designs attempted the same kind of reversal, and there may be little need for this kind of retrofit effort in emerging organizations if design is done correctly the first time.

So far, the artificial intelligence systems are not really so intelligent, but many of the tasks and skills in factory and office do not require high levels of human abilities anyway. As long as certain rules and protocols can be specified, expert systems can be designed as is the case now in some areas of chemistry, medicine, and mineralogical prospecting. These systems are usually tailor-made to a particular cognitive style, and some must be calibrated to a single individual. A better organization of known features of knowledge is still necessary.

Productivity will be a function of the capital-intensive factory and work-systems design just discussed. It is well to bear in mind that similar developments are taking place in Western Europe and elsewhere, especially in Japan. Considerable redundancy of production capacity and variety, and the capability to change production in quantity and quality without hiring and firing large numbers of workers, suggest further that future employment may be much less than is often projected.

Parallels are often made with the decline of U.S. agricultural workers from some 50 percent of the work force after the Civil War to the current 3 percent. Some observers estimate that as few as 5 percent of the U.S. work force will, by the turn of the century, be employed in production industry. In the past ex-farmers, displaced factory workers, and new immigrants found jobs in an expanding economy. But today many industries, for example, steel, suffer from world overcapacity. The automobile industry is reaching a saturation level. Jobs have migrated to the developing countries under the auspices of both American and foreign firms. Observers note large reductions in the work force, which are due to automation and technological change, in industries ranging from coal mining and meat packing to automobile manufacture and textile manufacture to printing and telecommunications. Environmental constraints may limit further growth. However, demographic changes will lead to fewer new job entrants over the next decade, which could mitigate the unemployment problem or even create a local labor shortage in jobs in which the young are needed or perceived to be needed, while exacerbating the problem among older workers.

Historically, automation and technological change have created jobs, eliminated jobs, and modified jobs. The computer field, manual and semiautomatic printing, and clerical work in banks provide familiar examples. Changing from electromechanical to electronic switching in the communications industry both eliminated jobs and upgraded the level of remaining jobs.

Sociotechnically, the problems of job loss, on the one hand, and the design and improvement of remaining and future jobs, on the other hand, are interrelated. In many areas a buyer's market from the corporate point of view is likely to continue. Many workers may be motivated mainly to retain their jobs, even though these jobs are inherently as repulsive as ever. Worker behavior that contributed to lower productivity in the past may change. Management attitudes may harden. As discussed earlier, some sociotechnical designs may be considered relics of the past and luxuries that are no longer needed. Training programs, as ameliorative solutions to unemployment, may be greatly reduced in industry unless government exerts great pressure.

Consider now the nature of jobs in the factory of the future. Such a factory may be run, that is, managed, by as few as several tens of people. Jobs will probably resemble those in electrical power control, air traffic control, and military systems, such as submarines, underground missile control centers, and computerized command, control, communications, information, and intelligence (C^4I^2) systems more than those on assembly lines.

This does not necessarily represent a militarization of civilian industry, although there are already some minor trends in that direction. Rather, computerized automation, the importance of dynamically updated real-time information, the importance of regulation and control of sequences, interactions, and patterns, and the necessity to detect abnormal, out-of-tolerance or threatening conditions will require well-educated, highly skilled, alert, and motivated personnel. These jobs will largely be professional.

The physical environment of the factory may little resemble the hot, noisy, dirty, often dangerous factory of old. Parts of the factory may be dark. Sensitive equipment will require careful control of environmental factors like temperature, humidity, and atomospheric composition. Robots have already taken over many of the dirty, unpleasant, and dangerous jobs like welding and spray painting. This trend should be accelerated in the future.

Nevertheless, by Murphy's law, it is possible to design the total factory work system improperly. Jobs could continue to be fragmented, requiring operators, not systems managers, to spend long hours monitoring display consoles under conditions of isolation, boredom, and sensory deprivation and without authority to take important corrective actions. Layers of supervisors could be added, impoverishing the lower level jobs, and introducing unneeded delays into operations.

The integrating capability of the new automation could be greatly reduced by imposing the specialization-based, variety-reducing work system of yesterday. In a work system that should be largely nonhierarchical, introduction of the old chain of command, with status and privileges associated with ranks, could introduce conflict among members. Denial of ownership privileges could further increase alienation and decrease motivation and job satisfaction. The work force in such a factory might be resentful and unhappy, but effects on productivity in a capital-intensive, automated setting are difficult to predict. Both government and corporate management might take a hard line on worker grievances and strikes. It is likely that worker hostility would be expressed as passively overlooking out-of-tolerance conditions and by active vandalism and occasional sabotage.

Another factor is human engineering. Unfortunately, human engineering design and sociotechnical systems design have been poorly if at all integrated in the past. Lessons should be learned from poor designs for air traffic control, electrical power generation (for example, Three Mile Island and Consolidated Edison in New York City), and some military systems. Poorly designed display consoles and control centers could greatly degrade the integration and coordination provided by the automated system and therefore the integrity of the sociotechnical system. Great pains should be taken to avoid ad hoc collections of existing meters, dials, switches, and knobs.

In brief, most of the coordination, control, and integration will be performed automatically in the cybernetic factory. Sensors, computers, and servomechanism-type controls will be embedded in individual equipment, robots, and manufacturing cells. Data base management and computer networking will be extensively used. C^4I^2 systems design can provide a holistic view of total factory function and operation. Congruence between the technological and social subsystems will not require a corresponding hierarchy in the social subsystem, even given that top management will retain final authority, decision making, and control. The major challenge will be the management of complexity, and complexity is best managed by seeing the system as a whole. Boundaries between the factory and the office of the future will become blurred.

Because of the instability and chaos in the present stage of world transformation, it is possible that widespread realization of the factory of the future will be delayed for decades, if, indeed, it ever takes place. If so, there would be islands of fully rationalized automation. Most surviving factories would be semiautomatic, and many tasks requiring fine discriminations, decisions, checking, adjustments, and manipulations would still require considerable numbers of less skilled workers. Classical sociotechnical designs would still be appropriate.

Getting from Here to There

Technologies, products, and organizations change over their life cycles in a number of ways, but notably from novelty to confirmation, innovation to growth, more dynamic to more static, more problem-solving oriented to more routine, and loosely coupled to rigid and inflexible. Discontinuities and structural change, loss of environmental fit, and an ever mounting complexity are the overarching problems of modern organizations.

Ayres and Steger (1982) use a life-cycle approach to explain a number of contemporary economic and sociotechnical changes. Briefly, a product goes through six phases, each with its own attributes:

1. *Conception*, when new ideas dominate.
2. *Birth*, when the prototype of a new product is developed.
3. *Childhood*, characterized by a diversity of models and designs, general-purpose machines, and machine-specific skilled labor.
4. *Adolescence*, characterized by improved designs, fewer models, and reduced rates of change. Labor skills are product-specific. Phase 4 marks the transition to large-scale production. Ayers and Steger perceive it to be a rewarding stage, to be prolonged.
5. *Maturity*, characterized by slow evolutionary change and standardized products. Automation is on a large scale, and the labor force is semiskilled. Many large factories today are in this phase. Much of production has been or is being transferred outside the country.

6. *Senescence*, when hard automation has been standardized and packaged by capital goods specialists. Products are commodity-like.

The kinds and numbers of jobs, and hence sociotechnical design, are heavily dependent on these dynamics. Standardization of machines and methods of production eliminates the need for highly educated and skilled labor. Knowledge, accrued through learning by doing and experience, can be built into machines and processes. Factories can be designed almost on a turnkey basis. Generous loans to the developing countries, coupled with much lower labor costs there, almost guarantee the emigration of industries and jobs.

Just as products, technologies, and industries evolve, so also must work systems co-evolve. Typically, evolution has progressed from manual technology using general-purpose machines through semi-automated technology to the present specialized hard automation. Capital is continually substituted for labor, especially skilled labor. Large capital investments prevent much modification of either products or production equipment. The system increasingly delimits what is possible. Incentive to innovate, both technologically and socially, is reduced. Sociotechnical systems learning is gradually internalized in machine and process design. The level of skills required decreases. Eventually, major innovation and design may become vested in the capital-equipment maker, and no change may be possible for as long as 20 years, severely constraining local options. This represents a major structural change. With the internalization of knowledge, experience is no longer necessary, and a manufacturing capability with its attendant jobs can readily be transferred outside the originating industrialized country. Foreign competition may then further weaken the mature and stagnant industry. At home, socio-technical redesigns are those discussed earlier, for example, job enlargement, better team building, and profit sharing. At a higher level, clamor for protective tariffs and voluntary restrictions on exports may further destabilize the international system.

Further, the markets for many products in the industrialized countries are rapidly becoming saturated. Marchetti (1983) fitted three parameters to the logistic equation in a study of car populations in nine highly industrialized countries. Saturation levels are predicted to occur at about the same time in all the countries regardless of when widespread diffusion began. The final number of cars differs by country, of course, but in all cases, saturation will occur by approximately the turn of the century or earlier. Simply, later starters like the Japanese moved faster to catch up. Marchetti believes that this worldwide behavior represents a "quasi-biological, internally generated determinism," in which during the active growth phase economics, engineering, marketing, and the media play minor roles as stimuli. This interpretation fits well into my own field-theoretic framework (De Greene, 1978, 1981, 1982). Saturation of product markets in the industrialized countries worldwide, coupled with the emigration of manufacturing capabilities, can mean that whole industries are entering the final phase of their life cycles. Because a large industry like the automobile industry helps support the makers of glass, rubber, paints, lubricants, fuels, and so forth, major retrenchment or collapse of the former can be expected to aggravate the unemployment problem. Theoretically, these huge industrial complexes are metastable, just waiting for one more perturbation or increment in a continuous force to trigger catastrophic collapse.

One step toward the factory of the future is the embedding of computers in individual products and pieces of equipment. The use of microprocessors is now widespread and increasing at a rapid pace (Shaiken & Lund, 1981). The long-term employment effects of microprocessor applications are systemic and not easy to decipher. However, job content is affected in many blue- and white-collar categories. Light electronic assembly tends to expand in factories accompanied by reductions in the production of mechanical parts. Final inspection shifts in favor of in-process electronic testing. The assembly jobs are less skilled, but designer and supervisory jobs require higher skills. Training and retraining requirements increase.

Changes in job contents within a single company may lead both to layoffs and to new hirings. Productivity using fewer workers may increase, but expansion of market share can at least temporarily boost employment by the firm. However, increased competitiveness can reduce the market share and hence employment of other firms. In the longer run, the life-cycle phenomena discussed earlier, for example, standardization and a proliferation of similar products, could have the net effect of reducing employment. In a number of firms studied, productivity increased while employment either remained the same or decreased.

Large reductions in employment are likely in firms that retain the old methods, sell conventional products, or make components whose functions can be performed much better electronically, thereby losing market share. Demand for software is expected to create a large number of programming jobs. As mentioned earlier, jobs created may not equal jobs lost.

In the longer range, the threat of microprocessors to numbers of present and future jobs is great. This is causing major changes in the strategies of the labor unions and in the behavior of organized labor, as already discussed. Unions are demanding much greater participation in decisions about technology. Innovative proposals for preserving jobs are being made. For example, productivity gains employing fewer workers could be translated into creating socially useful products, thus retaining jobs (Shaiken & Lund, 1981). Fears of workers and unions seem justified. Shaiken and Lund cite evidence that in France, by 1990, 30 percent fewer workers may be needed to produce a given amount of work in the banking and insurance industries; a study by Olivetti Corporation of eight international firms in electronics found an average 20 percent employment decrease between 1969 and 1978.

Another step toward the factory of the future is to utilize the best experience now available with the design and manufacture of the total manufacturing system. Here, the Japanese experience is invaluable. The *kanban* ("just-in-time") system ensures that materials and components are available just before they are needed, thus reducing in-process inventory and improving the quality of operations. Tight coupling in time and space means that the system will break down unless maintenance is consistent and defects are eliminated beforehand. Thorough maintenance is performed during the third shift. Suppliers must provide high-quality materials and parts. *Jidoka* allows any worker to stop operations if he perceives a defect or potential malfunction. These practices mean that considerable effort is directed beforehand to anticipating and planning around difficulties. Active involvement by the work force and with the authority to shut down operations appear to be strongly motivating factors.

Finally, there is further reason for concern about actual applications of new computerized manufacturing technology. Theoretically, applications may violate Ashby's law of requisite variety, namely, that there must be at least as much variety in regulation and control as there is in the system being regulated. Human beings generate variety that management often finds objectionable and tries to stifle. Humans also generate variety necessary to cope with the unexpected in production operations. In addition, some applications represent continuations of Taylorism, the superimposition of nineteenth-century scientific management onto the latest computer-based designs.

Shaiken (1984) has reviewed some of these misapplications, which appear to be purposeful. The final report of the Machine Tool Task Force, a large effort funded and guided by the U.S. Air Force, argues that increased productivity and profitability will stem from a reduction of human variability. Reduction can be accomplished by complete automation or by reducing the skill levels needed in operations, maintenance, and manufacturing. Other studies indicate that, paradoxically, flexible manufacturing systems can be used to take away the control over production rates and quality that workers and unions now have.

Shaiken cites three cases. In the first, CAD resulted in breaking down the traditional interactions between the designer in the shop office and the machinist on the shop floor. As is often the case when computer models are used, the designer began to misinterpret the model as being the real world (see De Greene, 1982). In a British aircraft factory, a decimal point was accidently moved one place to the right. A worker, following specifications, built a component ten times the correct size, but the designer did not immediately recognize the error! Much smaller errors might never be detected.

The second case involved the introduction of computerized numerically controlled machine tools into seven small metalworking shops. Centralized control increased, overall skill requirements decreased, and many skilled workers complained of routine and boredom. Although computers provide the potential to enrich jobs, the option selected in all seven shops was centralized control of production in order to reduce reliance on highly skilled workers. Under these conditions, a variety-rich job involving detailed planning and control of work is reduced to simple monitoring with concomitant atrophy of skills that might be needed in emergencies and increased job dissatisfaction. Many workers found most satisfying those situations in which the machines and processes did not operate according to plan!

The third case involved a computerized management information system for monitoring and scheduling, installed in two plants of a large manufacturing company. When a worker starts or stops any phase of a job, the information is keyed into a terminal. A supervisor can then call up the details of departmental activities, resulting in both direct monitoring of and control over the worker. The system can be used to increase the pace of work consistently and to reduce local control of production rates on the shop floor.

Just as there is no single future, so there are alternative future factories and offices. System evolution involves passing myriad bifurcation points beyond which lie structures with differing stability characteristics and permanence. Computer-based technology will probably increase productivity. Probably the technological subsystem will be optimized at the expense of the social subsystem, which may be greatly reduced in size in the long run through automation. Workers as a whole will probably have poorer bargaining powers and may be motivated principally by the need to survive. A work force with lessened expectations, coupled with a labor surplus and a reduction in alternatives and increased management control, could be capable of little further enhancement of productivity. The fewer, higher level jobs are likely to receive management endorsement in enrichment and to be intrinsically motivating and, unless extreme blunders are made, are likely to be highly productive. Productivity enhancement will, I propose, jump to the higher sociotechnical level of design and management for complexity. In the longer run, classical sociotechnical interventions and redesigns at the level of mass production and routine information processing may have less significance than they do today. The necessity to avoid the social instability accompanying mass unemployment is likely to shift the emphasis to creating a maximum number of jobs under the circumstances, and productivity would have to be weighed against job elimination.

SUMMARY

The field of sociotechnical systems embodies theory and applications devoted to understanding and improving the fit between social or societal and technological factors and forces. The sociotechnical systems approach was first applied to the analysis and design of industrial-production systems. Mismatches between the social and technological subsystems can lead to low motivation and morale, job dissatisfaction, and lower levels of productivity. Analysis and design of the two subsystems within the framework of a holistic sociotechnical system can often ameliorate these problems.

Over the past 35 years theory has expanded, and applications have increased in kind and systems level. There is more rapprochement if not better integration with other approaches to work-systems design, motivation, morale, and job satisfaction, and productivity enhancement. The sociotechnical systems paradigm now applies to organizations and to the macrosystems of society. However, there is no one way to analyze or design sociotechnical systems, and practitioners caution against rigidly following any set of steps and procedures.

The sociotechnical systems approach is not a panacea for the myriad problems of work-systems, organizational, and societal productivity. As with other effective approaches to analysis, design, and management, it serves its users best by providing heuristics and the opportunity for intelligent choices among different systems configurations.

Since inception, sociotechnical systems theory and methodology have evolved; systems of work, organizations, and societies have also evolved. This chapter was written within the overarching theoretical frameworks of the turbulent-field environment and of the evolution of systems and environments past critical thresholds beyond which structural change takes place. It has been argued that the present time represents a major stage of historical transformation. Past sociotechnical systems designs have not always persisted. It is likely that the acceleration of computerized automation and its application to "factories and offices of the future" will provide new challenges and opportunities for sociotechnical systems theory and methodology.

REFERENCES

Ayres, R. U., & Steger, W. A. (1982). *New strategic options created by flexible automation* (Working Paper No. 82-20b). Pittsburgh: CONSAD Reserach Corp.

Cherns, A. (1976). The principles of sociotechnical design. *Human Relations, 29* (8), 783-792.

Congressional Budget Office. (1981). *The productivity problem.* Washington, D.C.

De Greene, K. B. (1973). *Sociotechnical systems: Factors in analysis, design, and management.* Englewood Cliffs, NJ: Prentice-Hall.

De Greene, K. B. (1978). Force fields and emergent phenomena in sociotechnical macrosystems. *Behavioral Science, 23*(1), 1-14.

De Greene, K. B. (1981). Limits to societal systems adaptability. *Behavioral Science, 26*(2), 103-113.

De Greene, K. B. (1982). *The adaptive organization: Anticipation and management of crisis.* New York: Wiley.

Emery, F. E. (1959). *Characteristics of socio-technical systems* (Rep. No. HRC 527). London: Tavistock Institute of Human Relations.

Emery, F. E. (1977). *The emergence of a new paradigm of work.* Canberra: Australia National University, Centre for Continuing Education.

Emery, F. E. (1982). New perspectives on the world of work: Sociotechnical foundations for a new social order? *Human Relations, 35*(12), 1095-1122.

Emery, F. E., & Trist, E. L. (1960). Socio-technical systems. In C. W. Churchman & M. Verhulst (Eds.), *Management sciences, models and techniques* (Vol. 1, pp. 83-97). London: Pergamon Press.

Emery, F. E., & Trist, E. L. (1965). The causal texture of organizational environments. *Human Relations, 18*(1), 21-32.

Emery, F. E., & Trist, E. L. (1973). *Towards a social ecology: Contextual appreciation of the future in the present.* New York: Plenum Press.

Guest, R. H. (1979, July-August). Quality of work life—Learning from Tarrytown. *Harvard Business Review,* 76-87.

Herbst, P. G. (1974). *Socio-technical design: Strategies in multidisciplinary research.* London: Tavistock Institute of Human Relations.

Herbst, P. G. (1976). *Alternatives to hierarchies.* Leiden, The Netherlands: Martinus Nijhoff.

Marchetti, C. (1983). The automobile in a system context: The past 80 years and the next 20 years. *Technological Forecasting and Social Change, 23,* 3-23.

Miller, E. J. (1975). Socio-technical systems in weaving, 1953-1970: A follow-up study. *Human Relations, 28*(4), 349-386.

Shaiken, H. (1984). Automation in industry: Bleaching the blue collar. *IEEE Spectrum, 21* (6), 77-79.

Shaiken, H., & Lund, R. T. (1981, January). Microprocessors and labor: Whose bargaining chips? *Technology Review*, 37-39, 44.

Trist, E. L. (1981). The evolution of sociotechnical systems as a conceptual framework and as an action research program. In A. H. Van de Ven & W. E. Joyce (Eds.), *Perspectives on organization design and behavior* (pp. 19-87). New York: Wiley.

Trist, E. L. (1983). QWL and the 1980s. In H. Kolodny & H. van Beinum (Eds.), *The quality of working life and the 1980s* (pp. 43-54). New York: Praeger.

Trist, E. L., & Bamforth, K. W. (1951). Some social and psychological consequences of the longwall method of coal-getting. *Human Relations, 4*, 3-38.

Van Der Zwaan, A. H. (1975). The sociotechnical systems approach: A critical evaluation. *International Journal of Production Research, 13* (2), 149-163.

II KNOWLEDGE REPRESENTATION AND DECISION MAKING

This section is concerned with the interrelated areas of knowledge representation in artificial intelligence (AI) and behavioral decision making. Knowledge representation, using some inference scheme, provides advice or agreements, but in most real-world situations the human remains responsible for making decisions in the context of broader considerations. Artificial intelligence is concerned with symbol-manipulation processes that produce intelligent action. It involves some important interactions between humans and machines, normally incorporating human experience and expertise in a particular knowledge domain.

Knowledge-based expert systems are AI problem-solving programs designed to operate in narrow domains of knowledge, performing tasks normally performed by human experts. Such expert systems are usually built around two components, collectively called the "problem-solving engine." The knowledge-based component contains all of the relevant domain-specific information, allowing the computing system to perform as a specialized, intelligent problem solver. The inference engine component controls the deductive process and implements the best strategy for a particular problem.

Much of the research in AI has focused on effective methods for representing and organizing knowledge. Some representations are declarative-based logical formalisms, stylized rules, and semantic nets and frames. The heart and power of an expert system is the knowledge base, composed of a large collection of facts, definitions, procedures, and heuristics acquired directly from a human expert. Human experts have comprehensive knowledge of a particular, specialized domain, deep understanding of problems in that area, and capability to solve some of these problems. Experts use rules of thumb or heurestics for making guesses when information is incomplete or inaccurate, and recognize appropriate techniques for solving certain classes of problems (for example, how to make a medical diagnosis). "Knowledge engineers" are the link between the human expert and the computing system. They extract knowledge and rules of thumb from experts and then formalize, represent, and test the knowledge within the computing system. Thus the current view taken is that the expert's knowledge is the reason for expert performance in a restricted domain. Knowledge representation and inference engines or schemes provide the mechanisms for the problem-solving engine to use the expert's knowledge.

The inference engine or control system is the reasoning process or body of procedures that acts in the knowledge base. After the knowledge-based structure or organization is defined, the control system can be built. Generally, the process involves the structuring of nested "if-then-else" or "if-and if-then" statements, permitting the evaluation of alternatives. Today's expert systems separate the control strategy from the knowledge base. This allows the same inference engine to be used with an expanded or changed knowledge base. The development of a highly general inference engine would be of great value in expert systems.

Turning to behavioral decision making, it has been shown that a major difficulty of decision makers is their inability to process the large amount of information needed in complex decision problems. Traditional decision analytic techniques assume that decision makers have detailed information about all aspects of the problem, including a complete set of alternatives or actions, specifications of outcome for each alternative, and good criteria to evaluate choices. In complex practical decision making, these conditions rarely exist. Indeed, individuals are unable to process a large volume of information, and decision alternatives are multidimensional as are the decision maker's goals. Thus, a principal aim of behavioral decision-making research is to develop strategies and aids for dealing with complex decision making.

Behavioral decision making attempts to understand the decision process and to make it more effective; it attempts to integrate descriptive and normative approaches and to combine cognitive and quantitative aspects of decision making. Decision-making models envision a varying number of interrelated steps or phases in the decision-making process. These steps generally include problem recognition, information gathering, developing and evaluating alternatives, and choice. Rarely are the activities associated with these phases carried out sequentially in actual practice, nor are the activities that are thought to characterize each phase confined only to that phase.

In developing decision aids, decisions are often classified as programmed (repetitive, routine) or nonprogrammed (complex, unique). Important decisions that are unique can benefit from the use of decision analytic techniques, providing time and resources are available. These techniques assume that problems can be logically structured into alternatives, outcomes, values, and uncertainties. In practice, however, informed intuition is generally the primary tool used. Here it may be helpful to make the decision maker aware of the host of informational and perceptual biases that are known to influence the process negatively. Aids that may be used for repeated decisions are rules (linear regression models, multiattribute utility), computer-based decision support systems, and simulations.

Much research is needed to improve the young technology of decision aiding. In the area of decision structuring, some promising research areas are dynamic structuring (using insights gained from iterations), goal formulation and acceptance, and option generation. In the area of measuring values, techniques are needed to elicit judgment of probabilities and utilities. One promising research area is to explore interactive value measurements obtained through a dialogue with the decision analyst. Another research approach is to provide more realism in the decision problem used for study. Research is also needed in validation methodologies so that the quality of a decision could be better evaluated.

In this section three chapters deal with a variety of AI research issues. First, the philosophy and practice in knowledge representation are reviewed. Then an account is given of conversational systems, a contrasting and novel approach taken in knowledge representation. The last chapter on AI provides a detailed explanation of how knowledge-based expert systems function. One general conclusion the reader may reach is that the use of expert systems in more complex situations such as the automated office is not "just around the corner." Even if practical and theoretical limitations are solved, future acceptance depends on their potential for increasing productivity and the ease of use.

The final chapter in this section is concerned with a description of behavioral decision-making research and the presentation of a case study. One conclusion here is that our new insights into cognitive decision making can now be incorporated into the design of decision support systems to make better use of the information provided.

An important achievement of artificial intelligence research is the development of a technology for aiding problem solving. In one type of system, "expert systems," the heart of the system is a knowledge base, a large collection of facts, definitions, and rules of thumb acquired directly from a human expert. In another type, "conversational systems," the system functions as an intelligent intermediary that computes agreements. In the introductory chapter of this section, Dik Gregory argues that each approach is based on quite different perspectives of knowledge representation. The problem here is how to formalize and capture the meaning and use of human knowledge in some applications so that a computing system might be used to solve problems for that application. Any attempt to represent knowledge must contain a set of assumptions about the nature of knowledge, at least implicitly.

There has been a continuing debate about the structure and acquisition of knowledge since the time of the early Greeks. The debate involves an interaction between the two broad philosophical positions of realism and idealism. The philosophical position taken today leads to different views on what type of an AI system to build and how it might be constructed. After characterizing the two philosophies, Gregory provides a detailed examination of recent approaches of knowledge representation in AI. Realists conveniently divide the AI problem into the representation of the memory structure, attaching facts to it (acquisition) and using the facts (inferencing). The goal is to construct an artificial, thinking entity that takes the place of a human expert. A user then could talk to this entity, ask questions, and get answers. Idealists develop a formalism for representing the process in which two entities (people, machines, or a combination of both) come to share the same meaning for a particular concept. The goal is the construction of a communication medium that can bring a current user into coherence with other users who may exist only as representational agreement structures and are open to incorporating new perspectives. For Gregory, it matters which perspective is used, not because one of them is necessarily correct but because each yields rather different theories of what AI might be made to do and how it might be constructed.

In Chapter 5, Gordon Pask and Dik Gregory first describe conversation theory and a computer-implementable protolanguage before turning to three computer applications based on the theory. Conversation theory is the outcome of 25 years of research largely carried out by Pask and his associates. It belongs to the philosophical perspective of idealism that naturally produces an emphasis on conversation and knowledge as a process by which agreements are reached and thereby enriches the understanding of the conversational participants. The very process of conversation, according to the theory, forces us into consciousness. It is the role of conversational systems to "show up" the implications of that process in action. Of primary concern in conversation theory are conversations in a language, L, that lead to concept sharing. Here, a concept is regarded as a dynamic entity that can be applied in an L-processor, such as a human brain, as a process to yield mental images or overt behavior. Concept sharing takes place by means of transactions that give rise to hard, observable data known as agreements. Lp is a representational language that models both the process by which knowledge becomes meaningfully articulated and the public concept structures that emerge as outcomes to that process. Conversational systems, then, focus on how an understanding of events may become shared between user and system and how the incorporation of new events changes the structure of understanding.

Intelligent, computer-based conversational systems are different from expert systems. They do not provide answers; rather they are facilitators that connect us to the world in a particular way. They are intended to show us the way information changes by refocusing our awareness. The authors describe an application, THOUGHT-STICKER, the name given to Lp implemented as a computer program for eliciting and representing knowledge. It is currently being used in research on advanced tutorial systems for embedded training and in an intelligent support system sensitive to learning styles of its users. Another system, CASTE (course assembly system and tutorial environment), is a tutorial system that matches information to be learned to individual learning styles and learning progress. Various research projects are in progress using CASTE. Finally, the team decision system (TDS) is discussed, which is a simulation system designed to improve decision-making behavior of tactical commanders. All three systems concern the process of interpersonal and intrapersonal communication as essentially the same process. The outcome of conversations are agreements about understanding, made observable by modeling them as executable processes in a modeling facility.

Dana S. Nau, in Chapter 6, provides a detailed review of theory and practice of knowledge-based computing systems or expert computer systems. He begins by rejecting two common myths about AI: that highly intelligent computers and computer programs already exist, and that computers cannot be very intelligent because they "can only do what we tell them to do." With the dramatic increase in computing power and equally dramatic decrease in computing costs, researchers are very actively engaged in designing computer systems to accomplish tasks that normally require human experts. Knowledge-based expert systems are AI problem-solving systems designed to operate in very narrow, problem-specific domains, performing tasks with the competence of a skilled expert. What makes them unique is that the problem-solving information appears explicitly in a knowledge base that is manipulated by a separate control structure, using domain-independent techniques to search for solutions. Expert systems development requires the use of human experts to solve problems, even though the experts sometimes are not able to explain how they solve a problem. Recently, expert systems techniques have been used in operational systems in determining unknown chemical compounds, medical diagnosis, installing and monitoring computer systems, and discovering ore deposits. It is the aim of many researchers to use expert systems to enhance office productivity, but such applications, according to Nau, await progress in a number of technical areas.

In an expert computer system, there are three levels of operation: data, knowledge base, and control structure. Data are representations of the specific problem to be solved. The knowledge base encodes problem-solving knowledge relevant to the domain of expertise of the expert computing system. The control structure is a computer program that decides which rules to apply. The author describes techniques for capturing expert knowledge and representing facts. He also describes some simple and more elaborate control strategies for rule-based systems and non-rule-based approaches. Nau raises a number of problems associated with expert systems. One problem is the large amount of effort and money involved, generally due to software limitations. Another problem is that the amount of time necessary to encode knowledge is very lengthy, and may be partly due to our limitations in understanding human problem solving. Additionally, most systems are not user-friendly, nor are they designed for long-term maintenance. Finally, potential users are overly optimistic in their expectations about what applications are appropriate for expert systems and the level of performance that can be achieved.

Assuming that an AI knowledge representational or expert system can assist in obtaining desired information, the user generally will need to incorporate that information into a larger organization-based decision problem. For Ruth H. Phelps, Rebecca M. Pliske, and Sharon A. Mutter, in Chapter 7, "decisions" must be defined broadly enough to encompass the variety of behaviors decision makers perform. They must include subjective judgments, choices, solutions to problems, and the absence of these activities. Thus, the authors define a decision as a general problem to be solved, either ill-defined or well-defined at the outset, structured or unstructured, subjective or objective. Their focus is on the thinking processes involved in decision making rather than on the decision or choice itself. Contemporary study of decision making also includes decision theory, based on the axioms of expected utility theory, and decision support systems, based on interactive computer systems and theoretical organizational decision making. The psychological or cognitive decision-making approach emphasized here is composed of a number of distinct models of decision making, all concerned with subjective factors in decision making, such as values, perceived worth, and conflict resolution. Many of these models attempt to capture mental events that may influence the process.

The authors detail research organized according to a cognitive processing model of decision making, which they developed. The model includes five discrete stages: problem recognition, problem definition, generation of alternative solutions, implementation of solutions, and evaluations. This five-stage cognitive model was adapted for use in aiding strategic intelligence decision making. A case study detailing that application is presented. The authors conclude that there is a clear trend toward research aimed at understanding cognitive processes in decision making. Hopefully, this new emphasis on cognitive variables may lead to the design of decision support systems concerned with how to use information cognitively.

They also suggest that the research data available on human strengths and weaknesses in decision making should serve as a basis for providing prompts in decision support systems. A great deal of attention has been given to developing an information base for decision making; now more attention should be given to developing procedures, based on research findings, to help the decision maker know what to do with this information.

4

PHILOSOPHY AND PRACTICE IN KNOWLEDGE REPRESENTATION

Dik Gregory

One of the very difficult problems in artificial intelligence (AI) that continues today is that of knowledge representation. The issue has been how to formalize and capture the meaning and use of human knowledge in some subject matter area so that it might be used to solve problems in that area by a computer. One of the reasons why this is such a difficult problem is that it includes the earlier but just as hard problems of what knowledge is and how it is obtained from the world. Any attempt to represent knowledge must contain, at least implicitly, a set of assumptions about what knowledge is, and yet this is a puzzle that people have been thinking about and debating for several thousands of years.

What should be clear at the outset is that all those who make any sort of contribution to the problem of knowledge representation *do*, in fact, make *some* assumptions whether or not implicitly. There are some in the AI community (Buchanan, 1981; Nilsson, 1983, for example) who feel that the issues of knowledge representation are solved or nearly solved, and that the big question is that of knowledge acquisition. The view taken in this chapter is that claims like this are neither right nor wrong, but instead the consequences of incorporating a particular set of assumptions about what knowledge is

The views and opinions contained herein are those of the author and do not necessarily reflect the position of the U.S. Army Research Institute for the Behavioral and Social Sciences, or the Admiralty Research Establishment, U.K.

and how human beings come to know the world in which they live. There are other assumptions, less familiar to AI, whose adoption leads to the view that the issues of knowledge acquisition, representation, and utilization are so intimately related that it makes little sense to do other than address them simultaneously.

The main purpose of this chapter is to organize discussion of several recent approaches to the problem of knowledge representation by reference to the ancient but still continuing debate on the problem of knowledge. After a short characterization of the two broad positions taken in this debate—realism and idealism—a detailed view will be presented regarding the approaches to knowledge representation made by Quillian, Anderson & Bower, Woods, and Brachman on

TABLE 4.1. Realism versus Idealism in Relation to Knowledge and Its Representation

	Realism	Idealism
Focus	● Reality is matter	● Reality is what matters
Assumptions	● Form of the world is independent of observational process ● Knowledge is correspondence to a world state	● Form of the world depends on observational process ● Knowledge is process of knower-connection with world
Goals	● Discovery of it-referenced truth ● Prediction and control	● Self- and other-referenced elucidation of meaning ● Understanding of process
Methods	● Reductionism ● True/false logics ● Tools (which expose knowledge)	● Constructivism ● Coherence logics ● Tools (which create forms of knowledge)
Manifestations	● Newtonian physics ● Comate's sociology ● Behaviorism	● New physics ● New cybernetics ● Hermeneutic psychology
Approaches to knowledge representation in AI	● Semantic net theories (Quillian, Anderson & Bower, Woods, Brachman) ● Conceptual dependency, scripts (Schank)	● MOP theory? (Schank) ● KRL? (Bobrow & Winograd) ● THOUGHTSTICKER (Pask) ● Recent Winograd
Types of AI systems	● Expert systems —Automatized consultants —Detection of error —Correction by reference to canonical model	● Intelligent support systems —Real-time cognitive modeling —Detection of inconsistency —Innovation by communication with other perspectives

semantic nets; Schank on conceptual dependency, scripts, and memory organization packets (MOPs); Bobrow and Winograd on knowledge representation language (KRL); and Pask on conversation theory, the protolanguage, Lp, and THOUGHTSTICKER. The aim is to show how these theorists have been influenced by one or the other of the two philosophical positions on knowledge, and indeed just how influential a particular philosophical starting point is for how the problem of knowledge representation is conceptualized, and hence how approaches to solving it are designed.

In the end, it matters from which philosophical perspective one operates, not because one of them is necessarily correct but because each yields rather different views and theories of what an artificial intelligence might be made to do to enhance human productivity and how it might be constructed. The chapter ends with a discussion on the qualitatively different sorts of AI systems that follow logically from different views of what knowledge is and from different conceptualizations of what the knowledge representation problem is.

Though this chapter has been written as an introduction first to the philosophical orientations and then to the approaches to AI that they organize, the chapter sections may be read in any order. Table 4.1 provides an overview and summary of the entire chapter for reference purposes.

KNOWLEDGE

The Questions of Ontology and Epistemology: What Is Real? How Can You Find Out? And What Does It Mean to Know the Answer?

The two biggest questions that have caught the attention of the great philosophers since the early Greeks have concerned the nature of the universe, on the one hand, and the process of coming to know it, on the other. The first question is that of ontology. What is the structure of being? What is the true base substance of the universe? What is real: mind or matter? The second question is that of epistemology. How can we find out about the true nature of the universe, or indeed can we? Could it be that although there is a true nature, we cannot know it because of the distorting effect of the activity that we invoke to look? Even further than this, could it be that the answer to one depends on the other? Could it be that there is a true reality for every epistemological process?

The story of how these questions have been approached over the millennia is of course a complex one, but for the purposes of this chapter can be cast essentially as a tension between two major focuses of attention: One focus has been on the notion of reality as consisting of matter. This focus may be referred to generically as the realist[1] perspective; and it embraces the philosophies and enterprises of nominalism, reductionism, mechanism, empiricism, positivism, materialism, formal (two-valued) logic, magic, alchemy, correspondence theories of truth, modern science, and the scientific method. The other main focus emphasizes reality as consisting of what matters, that is, what objects mean to us, the assigners of meaning. We will refer to this focus as the idealist perspective. This second perspective embraces the philosophies and enterprises of sophism, skepticism, apologism, scholasticism, holism, all religions, multivalued logics, coherentist theories of truth, symbolic interactionism, ethnomethodology, hermeneutics, second-order cybernetics (that is, the cybernetics of cybernetics), and the new (post-Einsteinian) physics.

The World According to Realism

The central focus in the world according to realism is that of a subject/object dualism. What this means is that the world of objects is assumed to exist entirely independently of a perceiving organism. If I walk into my family room and notice with one or more of my senses the television, the sofa, the carpet, telephone, walls, windows, and blinds, then I do not imagine that all these objects cease to exist the moment I walk out again. These objects exist whether or not I do, or choose to, perceive them. The consequence of a subject/object dualism is that ontological "what is?" questions are rendered logically distinct from epistemological "how do we know what is?" questions. In the realist perspective, we are free to investigate the reality of the objects around us using whatever methods of inquiry we can conjure. Whatever methods we do use will not affect the objects we investigate, for after all the objects exist independently of our methods for asking questions about them.

Ontological realism goes back to the early Greeks with Democritus (460–370 B.C.), who postulated that objects were composed of different combinations of various numbers of the same material—tiny, identical atoms. Much later Galileo (1564–1642) went much farther than this, claiming that not only was matter atomic in nature but that the atoms co-acted in blind but lawful motion. Even later, Newton (1642–1727) replaced the idea of direct contact with that of attracting and repelling forces, thereby extending the theory sufficiently to embrace the entire material universe. The task of realist science became that of discovering the true structure of objects and their relationships to one another and the representation of these discoveries as laws. The discovery of such knowledge depended for its value on the fact that it could be used for prediction and control and on the fact that such knowledge transcends the particular moment and circumstances of its elucidation. The new injunction invoked in the sixteenth century by philosophers like Vives (1492–1540), to go out and observe the universe in order to obtain an understanding of its nature, led to the emergence of empiricism as the dominant means of inquiry. Knowledge and truth became questions of correspondence: What is true corresponds to reality, and correspondence is ascertained by observation and empirical verification.

Epistemological realism is the notion that objects are not transmuted in the act of answering the questions we ask of them. What this also means is that experimentation necessarily takes place against an external referent, making our results "it-referenced." This means that for experimental results to count as valid, they must have a truth value that is not affected by the observer or the materials/ participants used in the experiment. The truth value must find existence in an absolute sense. We seek knowledge and results that are publicly observable, and we insist that any facts that emerge from our inquiries pass the test of repeatability before they are admitted as such. The instruments used in our inquiries are a way to get an accurate reflection of what exists; hygrometers measure that bit of reality called relative humidity, and IQ tests measure that bit of reality called intelligence.

It should be obvious that the assumptions of realism are the very underpinning of science and scientific method, and of course such science has been extraordinarily successful. The technological achievements of nuclear physics, the space program, computing, and medical science have been spectacular, and yet all this time, since the views of Democritus, there has been another side to the story.

The World According to Idealism

The central assumption of idealism is that observers are fundamentally connected to the world by their acts of observation. Observers help to create and shape what is observed so that observations are always "self-" or "other-referenced," but never it-referenced. This means that it is not possible to determine the meaning of something via an external referent existing "out there," but only by apprehending the context in which the "something" is or can be viewed. In this view of things, knowledge and truth are not objective realities, but rather matters for agreement within some universe of discourse.

As a philosophy, idealism is as ancient as realism. For Plato (427?–347? B.C.), a contemporary of Democritus, the only true reality was the world of Mind, and the only true objects in the world therefore, were Ideas. Plato's reality was an exclusively intensional one that was independent of, and irrelevant to, the extensional world of material objects; for Plato the existence of material was immaterial. Since Plato, several attempts to incorporate the commonsense notion of the existence of matter were made, including those by Aristotle (384–322 B.C.), Zeno (336?–264? B.C.), St. Augustine (354–430), Aquinas (1225?–1274), and notably Abelard (1079–1142). A strong form of idealism emerged again, however, with the teachings of Bishop Berkeley (1685–1753). Berkeley concluded that the objects in a room literally depended for their existence on their perception by someone. The fact that objects are often to be found in the same position as we last perceived them to be was not dependent on the notion that they really existed, but on the fact that when no human was around to perceive them, God was doing so. In more recent times, Immanuel Kant (1724–1804) and others of the German school have agreed with Berkeley's contention that knowledge is confined to ideas that are constructed from sensations. But, in addition, Kant argued that man was at liberty to form ideas about the outer world, God, freedom, and morality through acts of Reason, and that he could function *as if* this outer world existed. Because of his view that we are free to construct an Idea of the world in which we may live and know our moral lives, Kant is regarded as the founding father of modern idealism.

At this point it must be emphasized that idealism is not so much a contrast to realism, as a different perspective producing different emphases. As has been shown, the focus changes from "objects *are* matter" to "objects are *what matters*." It is not that idealism denies the existence of a material world (except in the Berkeleyan extreme), but rather than it concentrates on meaning-assignment in that material world. An object may be in the material world, but unless it has meaning for an observer, it remains opaque and impenetrable: it really is "out there" and its relation to the rest of that observer's knowledge is unknown; in fact, it might as well not exist. However, once meaning has been assigned to the object, including its conceptualization as an object of mystery, it becomes part of the world of meaning for that observer, who is not an observer in the classical, realist sense, but a subjective interpreter of that object. Other interpreters may or may not relate the object into their "scheme of things" in the same way. The point is that the idealist perspective requires to account for the notion that the same material object can be incorporated into different interpreters' cognitive systems in different ways, with different relations, and hence have (perhaps greatly, perhaps slightly) different meanings. To this extent, that "same material object" *is* a different object for each interpreter.

The idealist position with regard to the measuring instruments of science is that they are extensions of the knower—they operate as elements in the construction of (scientific) reality. The IQ test and the notion of IQ scores are themselves part of the definition of intelligence. The hygrometer is an integral part of the meaning of the concept of relative humidity. The meaning of the notions of intelligence and relative humidity *allows* the notion of measuring them to make sense, and vice versa.

A true/false logic is inappropriate to the idealist position. Instead, what is required is a coherentist theory of truth underwritten by logics of coherence, distinction, and analogy with which we can model our construction, not of the truth, but of our coherent schemes about reality. What is true is what we can agree on at any particular time and place. Contradictions, conflicts, and ambiguity are resolved by a process of agreement that is inescapably bound up with the values and interests of the participants. Objectivity in idealist terms is a social agreement: What is objectively so is what we agree is objectively so. If researchers see the world in the same way, it is because they have similar interests, values, purposes, motives, methods, dispositions, politics. Agreement rests not on the duplication of results, but on a commonality of perspective, which in turn produces similar results (Smith, 1983).

Realism, Idealism, and Science

The early successes of realist science, with its emphases on observation, measurement, prediction, and control, were spectacular. It was understandable when the same thinking and methodologies came to be applied to the study of ourselves and the societies we formed. Descartes (1596–1650), a major architect of the age of mechanism, had been responsible for the conceptualization of the body as a sub-mechanism within the great mechanism of nature that had lasted for nearly 200 years when the positivism of Augustus Comte (1798–1857) arrived. Comte's notion was of an evolution of a hierarchy of sciences from mathematics through physics to the most recently evolved science of sociology. The time seemed right to him for an inquiry in which knowledge about society could be acquired through the application of controlled scientific measures. This would produce, he anticipated, a collection of social facts that were indisputably true, as distinct from knowledge that was intuitive, subjective, and unscientific. Comte's positivism, taken up and recast as the logical positivism of the Vienna Circle in the 1920s, served as profound and powerful directives to the essentially realist conception of ourselves and our relationship to the world that dominates today. This conception was transported into psychology by the advent of behaviorism in which independently observable behavior rather than subjective experience was emphasized. More generally, psychology and the social sciences found themselves having to adopt the perspective of realist science in order to be taken seriously (Levine, 1974), and the validity of the investigations of psychologists came to depend on the correct use of experimental paradigms insisted upon by realist science.

Unfortunately, as Shotter (1975) points out, the application of realist science to ourselves has produced a difficult and extraordinary paradox. The problem is that the laws of human behavior that the experimental psychologist hopes to discover by holding himself in logical distinction from his subjects, as he "manipulates" his subjects' behavior, must also explain his own behavior as an experimenter performing activities designed to discover the laws of human behavior.

In more recent times psychologists and philosophers such as Rogers (1951), Taylor (1971), Shotter (1975), Gauld and Shotter (1977), Fransella (1975), and Campbell (1984), among others, have argued for the adoption of an alternative, hermeneutic[2] framework for psychological investigations. This new framework represents a turning away from the goals and assumptions of realist science, to adopt what is essentially an idealist position. In the role afforded by this latter position, the goal of the psychologist changes from one of prediction and control to the elucidation of experience through entering the contexts that he or she creates with experimental participants.

What is intriguing is that this same philosophical shift is also taking place in other areas of human inquiry. Of particular note here is the area of the new cybernetics, otherwise known as the cybernetics of cybernetics (von Foerster, 1974) or second-order Cybernetics (Glanville, 1979, 1982). Whereas the original cybernetics of Wiener's (1948) day was concerned with the study of observed systems, the new cybernetics deals with the study of observing systems. The important point that the new cybernetics makes is that any description or observation of a system must incorporate the perspective of the particular observer doing the observing, who is therefore engaged in an act that is as creative as it is descriptive.

Perhaps the most surprising shift to an idealist-like perspective is in the area of particle physics. Here, investigators have been forced from the view that matter is composed of discrete "building-block" particles that are independent of them, the observers, to the apparently extraordinary position that the process *itself* of investigating the sub-molecular world contributes to the properties and structure of that world (Capra, 1977; Zukav, 1979).

In the macro world of objects, as well as in the micro world of particles, the adoption of an idealist perspective allows us to choose to perceive and construe the objects around us in any of many different ways. In doing so, however, we prohibit, or at least limit for the duration of our construction, other ways of construing. Furthermore, the constructions we do place upon the objects of our attention are subject to the tacit "agreement" of those objects if we are to trade any meaning with/through them that is of practical value. I may, for example, interpret an object as a desk. Having done so, my thoughts are constrained by the notion I have applied to the object so that I may now think of it as a surface for my papers or as a set of containers for writing accessories; but I am unlikely to think of it any more, as the host of other meanings for which I was previously free to assign to it. But my success in continuing to treat the object as a desk, and indeed (assuming I have had previous experience with the form of such objects), the reason why I assigned the desk-meaning to the object in the first place is because I expect the object itself to be capable of supporting the notion of "desk." It is not that the object *is* a desk in absolute terms, but rather that the way it defines itself supports the notion of "desk" in a way that it does not support my notions of "flying machine" or "chicken soup." I do not create the existence of objects in the world, rather I am free to create meaning for them that their existence may or may not be able to support. If they do support my meaning that I establish by practical interaction and test with them, then they contribute to the coherency of the world that we construct and share with each other. If they do not, then I am free to continue to insist on the meaning I want to give to them, but only at the risk of attracting the attentions of those in our society who make it their profession to check the coherency of its members (that is, psychiatrists).

The view of the structure of matter forced upon us by quantum mechanics turns out to be analogous to Aristotle's view. Just as Aristotle tried to unify the independence of matter with the importance of acknowledging what matters to us, the observers of matter, so, more than 2,000 years later, quantum physics is showing us that we may define what objects are, as long as our definition is congruent with the object's definition of itself. Quantum physics removes a kind of arrogance that has allowed us to claim that we seek and declare the true reality of objects-in-the-world, by demonstrating to us that these very same objects answer our questions in ways that prevent answers to other questions that we nevertheless might have asked of them,[3] but additionally, that there are some questions for which the only answer is silence. The conclusion that a particular form of matter supports (or does not support) the notion of "desk," as distinct from "actually being" a desk provides some insight into the process of analogy, claimed by some cognitive theorists (including Pask, 1980; Winston, 1977; Schank, 1982) to be of fundamental importance to the processes of learning, thinking, and innovation. It is easier to see how an object that merely *carries* our notion of desk may be reconstrued to carry the analogous notions of "platform to stand on," "surface to sit on," and "lunch table" than if that object was in absolute terms a desk. It is here that it becomes clear that Aristotle's philosophy is analogous rather than isomorphic with quantum mechanics, because while they both share the fusion of idea with matter, they differ over the question of the initial residence of the idea. For Aristotle, the idea was in the matter striving to emerge. For quantum mechanics the idea is infused into the matter by the act of observation. Aristotle's conversation is with the world. The conversation of particle physicists is with *themselves* by *consent* of the world.

The next sections attempt to demonstrate that it is the difference between these two types of conversation—*with* an external world and *through* (that is, with ourselves, by consent of) an external world—that separates the two main forms of approach to knowledge representation afforded by the perspectives of realism and idealism, respectively.

KNOWLEDGE REPRESENTATION

From the foregoing descriptions of the assumptions of realism and idealism, it may be anticipated how researchers operating from each position conceptualize the problem of knowledge representation.

It follows from the realist position that knowledge is a kind of commodity that is logically distinct from its knower. This means that its articulation may be expressed in any convenient language, and having been expressed, may be purveyed, transported, learned, taught, and manipulated to some end. Knowledge consists in collections of facts that are true of the world that they represent. Their truth or falsehood may be objectively determined and their place in a representation depends on whether or not they correspond with some object, state, or relationship that exists in the world being represented. Since the world is by nature a complex entity that is reducible into ever more simple units, and finally into fundamental elements, so knowledge of the world is equally representable as (non-overlapping, "partition") hierarchies of concepts where the place of each concept is fixed in relation to the others.

The problem of knowledge representation for the realist, then, is to find a representational scheme in which he or she can capture the way the world *is* in terms of the facts that are true of it, and the relationships between its facts, and to specify a knowledge utilization engine that can interpret those facts in order to arrive at conclusions that are consistent with, and true in, the world being represented. One of the obvious problems to be solved in this formulation occurs in the knowledge acquisition phase, where there are innumerable opportunities for the misrepresentation of the way the expert really understands facts, their relationships, and how they are used to draw conclusions and solve problems. The realist view that has been generally taken in AI is that this may be because the expert does not have articulable access to her or his own processes because the representational language is a clumsy medium for expressing expertise, or even because the knowledge engineer has difficulty understanding the subject matter. Whether or not there is a representational problem of this type, what is *not* in dispute is the question of whether or not knowledge of the world is being represented.

From the position of idealism, knowledge consists not of independent bodies of facts but rather as connections that are created by knowers to attach themselves to the world in which they live. Knowledge is not merely articulated in some convenient language, but is *allowed* by the language of its expression. Idealists require logics and representations that do not seek to capture the relationships that are presumed to exist in the world, but instead that capture the relationships that the idealists construct between themselves and the world. The representations that are sought focus on consistency rather than on objective truth. In the event that consistency is compromised, there must be some representational process that detects the inconsistency and presents it for resolution; resolution proceeds by a process of agreement that depends on the perspectives of the knowers. Since knowledge is not a reflection of the way the world "really" is, its representation is not presumed to be capturable as a fixed hierarchy of nodes and relations. Rather, knowledge must be minimally representable as a heterarchy in which nodes may play more or less primitive roles with respect to other nodes, dependent on the particular perspectives, circumstances, and purposes pertaining when they are attended to.

The problem of knowledge representation for an idealist is to find a means of representing the process of understanding and its outcome, *what is understood.* Representation can only proceed by a process in which the participants in the process share the meaning that each participant has for the situation. This sharing through, for example, a process of strict conversation (Pask, 1980) results in a representation that is true for both, that is, coherent, but different to the situation that both were in at the start—any conversation that takes place results in the exchange of concepts that are forever changed in the process of exchange. So, in addition to the representation of shared meanings, any knowledge representation system created from the perspective of idealism must be able to represent how the data structure changes by the entry of another perspective, that is, investigator/questioner/student/expert. That is to say, it must also represent the process by which meanings *become* shared.

The next few sections identify and characterize several different approaches to knowledge representation. The aim is to show how the philosophical roots of each have influenced their formalisms and approaches to significant degrees. While the semantic net approaches of Quillian, Woods, Brachman, and Anderson and Bower are essentially realist in origin, Schank's story is one of a gradual movement from the perspective of realism to one more congruent with idealism. Winograd, it seems, has always been essentially idealist, although his recent work acknowledges this perspective more explicitly than before. Finally, it will be seen that Pask's approach has, from the beginning, embraced the assumptions of idealism.

Quillian, Woods, Brachman, and Anderson and Bower: Semantic Nets

In 1968 Quillian wrote a seminal paper in which he introduced a semantic net formalism for the representation of memory. This formalism has been subsequently developed and widely drawn on by AI researchers seeking a means to represent knowledge. Quillian's original notion was for a hierarchy of concepts represented at the nodes of a network and connected by links such that a concept was, for example, either a superset of a collection of others "below" it or a property of one "above" it. According to Brachman (1977, p. 127), Quillian's general aim was to

> develop a formal encoding scheme rich enough to reflect the structure of human "semantic memory," yet uniform enough to be manageable by general procedures. . . . This simple representational format would presumably allow the encoding of large bodies of factual information, and would facilitate the interpretation of new material in terms of large quantities of previously stored information ("assimilation"). In this way it might be used to help simulate the reading and understanding of text.

But Brachman goes on to note the failure of this early hope, observing that no uniform notation evolved, no algorithmic procedures for encoding information became established, and no general assimilation mechanisms currently exist.

In his analysis of what went wrong, Brachman notes how nodes and links have been used, often it seemed without their authors' awareness, to stand for quite different sorts of entity—facts, sets, instances. In an earlier paper, Woods (1975) had sought to take stock of the status of semantic network theories and came to much the same conclusions. In particular, Woods had emphasized the importance of representing the intensions of concepts. As Rumelhart and Norman (1983) note, while the extension of a concept is the set of things that it denotes, the intension of a concept is its internal structure, by virtue of which it denotes what it denotes. (Cf. Aristotle's contention that the intension of a thing was inside each of its extensions.) Brachman (1979) recalled many of Woods's criticisms, arguing in particular that it was not enough to assume that the class of all extensions of a concept would constitute that concept's intension.

Brachman's KL-ONE (1979a, b) was an attempt to implement his ideas for a semantic network that was based on a fundamental rethinking of what concepts and links were. Central to Brachman's proposals was a set of primitive (axiomatic) links that amounted to an epistemological foundation for semantic nets. All concepts in his structured inheritance nets (SI-Nets) were represented and related by different types of links, such that they were related both in a between-concepts inheritance hierarchy and also internally, as a within-concepts structure. The meaning of a concept was represented by both its superconcept and by its own internal structure. Brachman's emphasis on KL-ONE as based on a set of epistemological primitives is both significant and insightful. He argues (1978) that one of the most difficult tasks facing the knowledge engineer has been to decide at what level of abstraction to break knowledge down. The problem here is how to decide what the most fundamental units are for a particular domain. If the level chosen is too fine grained, then the representation may become overencumbered by large amounts of irrelevant detail. If, on the other hand, the detail is too coarse grained, then the representation system may not be able to support distinctions that are both relevant and important. In addressing this question, Brachman looked back over the previous (ten) years of semantic net theory to identify several different theoretical types of representational primitive, that is, means of net construction, noting that most schemes in the past had used mixes of these, often unknowingly. These types included

1. *Implementational primitives.* Here the primitives are pointers and atoms. What can be constructed with them is limited to an associational data structure, having no representational facility. Brachman cites the early work of Shapiro (1971) as being the best example, but comments that many semantic net systems have implementational primitives as part of their constructional methodologies. An example is Hendrix's (1975a, b) partitions that serve as node-grouping devices. The point is that the partitions play no part in the theory and have no representational significance. Brachman also notes that the concept of frames (Minsky, 1975) is an implementational one, being no more than "fancy data structures, and not representational structures."

2. *Logical primitives.* These do have representational import, and while Brachman agrees that predicate calculus is logically adequate to do the job, nevertheless, knowledge representation can be done with more communicative power by resorting to epistemological primitives, as KL-ONE.

3. *Epistemological primitives.* Here "the focus . . . shifts away from predication, and onto objecthood." This new focus enables an emphasis on the intensionality of concepts—their internal structure—as opposed to their extensions in terms of properties and attributes.

4. *Conceptual primitives.* This even higher level type of primitive is characterized by Brachman as being among the oldest of the types. For example, Schank's (1972) conceptual dependency theory depended on the notion that any concept could be broken down into a mix of up to 11 primitive concepts or (human) ACTS, such as GRASP, MOVE, and ATTEND. Brachman notes that the central question here is what particular concepts and cases are to be taken as primitive. This question does not arise at the epistemological level because although the notion of the *role* of a concept is primitive, no *particular* role is primitive.

5. Finally, *language primitives* reflect the (idealist-like) Whorfian thesis that any representation of the world, like cognition, is constrained by the particular language through which the world is observed. The example given here is Martin's (1977) OWL. Such a system as this is at variance with Schank's (realist) rationale for a con-

ceptual level primitive set that "representations should reflect the important properties of relationships inherent in the world rather than those in the constructor of the Knowledge Representation language," but allows the authors to claim an "almost trivial" provision for the expressive power of English in a computer language.

As an implementation of an epistemological primitive set, with its concomitant emphasis on the structural representation of a concept's intensionality, KL-ONE is probably the most sophisticated and principled semantic net theory so far. In speaking of the intention behind the KL-ONE network to represent "the beliefs about the world (and other possible worlds) as conceived by a single, thinking being" and "not intending to attempt to capture the world "as it really is," only the conception of it by an individual perceiver," Brachman (1979b) begins to approach an idealist perspective to knowledge representation. While it is certainly an important idealist notion to want to represent the particular conception of the world by a particular perceiver, Brachman's system is not, however, an idealist system.

That Brachman's work is quite different from an idealist approach is evident from the fact that although an SI-Net (like other semantic nets) contains the *outcome* of the interaction of the knowledge engineer with the representee(s), an idealist-driven enterprise is also concerned with a representational system that includes a logic for the *process* of this interaction. It is in this sense that Pangaro and Nicoll (1983) want to "delete the knowledge engineer" and replace her or him with a logic that allows the "knowledge" that is represented to continue to "live" in the representation, sensitive to ambiguities as they are introduced. The idealist does not construe knowledge as a static inscription of objects (intensional or not) in a data base, but as a *process of knowing.* Indeed, the former confusion between a concept's intension and extension that Brachman and others have sought to clear up seems to be a direct result of the realist predisposition to see objects as physical entities rather than as stabilizations of meaning between two communicants. When one focuses on a world of objects "out there," it is natural, given the task of representing knowledge, to represent "them" and the "relations" between "them." This is contrasted with the alternative approach that seeks to represent the relationship between ourselves as knowers and what it is we know. The acknowledgment of intensionality was an important step in the move to represent meaning, but it is still very much a realist solution. It is as if Brachman has taken the essentially idealist notion of intensionality and tried to apply to it a true/false correspondence logic that is essentially realist.

Anderson and Bower's (1980) work on human associative memory (HAM) is based on a revision of the early associationists and of semantic net formalisms and constitutes a more recent psychological theory of human memory pertinent to AI's requirement for knowledge representation. The program they have written functions in a question and answer domain and consists in a fact-retrieval system linked to a simple but elegant parser for the input/output of facts. The program that Anderson and Bower would like to write, they say, would have an extremely large data base and, most importantly, a comprehensive solution to the "interface problem." This solution would enable the program to comprehend (for example) the *Encyclopaedia Britannica* as an adult can do, by virtue of the facts that the adult is "a very competent speaker or reader of the language, has an enormous store of world knowledge and is very adept at inference and problem solving."

The interface problem is indeed a problem of enormous dimensions, and Anderson and Bower dismiss it as a Utopian goal, arguing instead for a "subset of the adult's sophistication." It is perhaps the conceptualization of the interface problem and what its resolution would bring that most separate realist- and idealist-driven AI systems. Explication of this separation is presented later. For now it should be understood that the two different sorts of systems that result from the two philosophies should not be thought of as rival solutions for the same problem but as two different solutions to two different problems.

The HAM theory is firmly rooted in realist assumptions that emerge particularly clearly when its authors list five systematic considerations they believe will assist in the construction of a plausible knowledge representation:

1. The representation should be capable of expressing any conception that a human can formulate or understand.
2. The representation should allow for relatively efficient search for and retrieval of known information; specific information should remain relatively accessible even when the data files grow to encyclopedic proportions.

3. The representation should saliently exhibit the substantive information extracted from a given input. It should not be influenced by the peculiarities of the particular natural language in which that information was communicated.
4. For reasons of parsimony, the representation should involve a minimum of formal categories; it should make a minimum of *formal* (structural or syntactic) distinctions at the outset; more complex distinctions would be built up by the construction rules for concatenating primitive ideas.
5. The representation must allow for easy expression of concatenation operations, by which "duplex ideas" can be constructed out of "simple ideas." This means, for example, that the representation should allow easy expression of conceptual hierarchies, or multiply embedded predications, or allow one to predicate new information on any old information-structure.

Each of these criteria for a knowledge representation may be qualified or disputed from the perspective of idealism.

On the first criterion there is no dispute so long as the representation has the capacity to incorporate not just the understanding but the context or perspective from which the understanding is constructed.

The second criterion clearly assumes an image of memory as "containing" a large number of facts through which a search must be made to retrieve a particular fact. This view of knowledge as a commodity is at variance with the idealist view of knowledge as inseparable from epistemology—knowledge as a constructive and reconstructive process of knowing.

The idealist would dispute the possibility for the third criterion ever to be achieved. The essential argument here is that natural languages are not codes, but rather the basis from which codes (such as representational systems) are possible. Information is not independent of natural language, although it may be independent of any code to which natural language gives rise. As with the first criterion, the minimal point is that the influence of the context and perspective of the knower of the represented knowledge must be accounted for; for without these, the meaning evaporates or, at the very least, is seriously compromised.

In the fourth criterion, the influence of the early associationists and the concomitant assumption of the reducibility of concepts to some set of primitives are shown. While realist theories look for distinctions of meaning in terms of the genealogy of primitives, idealist theories of knowledge representation focus on logics that can detect the loss of distinction between the meanings of concepts, that is, a means of ambiguity detection in terms of a breaking down of consistency. Furthermore, because a concept's status may change from being primitive-like to one requiring explanation itself, an idealist system must be able to represent knowledge and understanding in a dynamic, relativistic way that allows one child's primitive to be another adult's concatenation.

Again, in the fifth criterion, the notion of reducibility and hierarchy is expressed. In contrast, idealism demands structures that are heterarchical whose entities may take on both primitivity *and* "topichood," as circumstances demand.

Schank: Conceptual Dependency, Scripts, and MOPs

In discussing Brachman's work, Schank's theory of conceptual dependency was mentioned in which Schank (1975) hypothesized 11 primitive concepts that he believed underlay the representation of all concepts. This notion of reducibility is, as has been noted on several occasions now, one of the hallmarks of realism. So, of course, is Schank and Abelson's (1977) claim that what is represented should "reflect the important properties of relationships *inherent in the world*" (emphasis added).

Schank's conceptual primitives, called acts, were divided into four main groups:

- Physical actions of people:
  PROPEL
  MOVE
  INGEST
  EXPEL
  GRASP
- Change of state acts:
  PTRANS—physical transition of an object
  ATRANS—abstract transition of an object, as change of ownership
- Instrumental acts:
  SPEAK
  ATTEND

- Mental acts:
  MTRANS—mental transition of information
  MBUILD—mental building of thoughts, ideas, and the like

The kind of representational structures that emerged from this analysis was quite different from semantic net structures. Schank was not interested in representing whole sentences, but rather in representing the meanings encoded in those sentences—the "point" of what was being communicated. As he reflects in Schank (1980), his interests at that time were guided by the problem of machine translation, and his special concern was over the question of how a representation of meaning could be used in the generation and parsing of natural-language sentences. He notes that the recent emphasis over his conceptual acts as primitives was not the main point of his work then. In fact, Schank was attempting to construct a natural-language-independent meaning structure that he hoped could be used to guide a parsing program. But the enterprise ran into a serious problem that had not been encountered before: Schank saw that the disambiguation of sentences relied to a large extent on background knowledge of the world. Schank solved this with a set of modifying conceptual semantics that eventually led to a position where the parsed sentence had more in it than its pre-parsed state. Schank focused more and more on the importance of tacit knowledge: His comment that "clearly we needed a memory full of facts about the world in order to do any sensible understanding" (1980) is a realist's way of acknowledging the importance of the hermeneutic circle—an apparent paradox that says that in order to understand something, you already have to be very near understanding it.

Schank saw that his enterprise was not so much that of natural-language processing, but that of the problem of belief systems in general, with the added problem of the representation of meaning, knowledge, and memory. The mechanisms of inference became central as Schank realized that his primitive acts were important because they helped him think about what inferencing mechanisms might exist. He and his co-workers identified four types of causal links that together were believed to constitute the inference process. RESULT and ENABLE were held to be the forward and backward causal rules for the physical acts, and REASON and INITIATE were the forward and backward links for mental acts. The obvious influence of realist assumptions here should be clear in the reference to causal rules (laws) operating on conceptual primitives (the atomic "building blocks" of thought). In applying these ideas once again to the problem of the understanding of text, Schank's group realized something was missing. Causal connections seemed adequate for tying together local regions of text, but some sort of framework was needed for weaving together sequences of causal chains. This is where the idea for *scripts* came from. Scripts became a convenient conceptual entity for saying what sort of things to expect given the occurrence of some event. The question then arises as to where these scripts come from. Schank answered that they are generated or invoked by the formulation of *plans*. Now the question arises about why a particular plan is in progress, and the answer is that it is hatched following the specification of *goals*. Finally, consciousness of *themes* would allow inferences about what sorts of goal an actor might pursue.

The attention to scripts, plans, goals, and themes marked the beginnings of an idealist-like concern with perspective, context, and taking into account the way in which speakers are connected with the worlds in which they live. But Schank's arrival at the notion of scripts, plans, goals, and themes only generated more questions. In particular, Schank notes that a key insight was to notice that scripts ought to be more than just data structures; they ought to say something about memory too. The question of the moment, then, was to ask how far the notion of scripts compared with the way people's memories worked. Schank set about investigating this question by looking at the way people both remembered and confused things.

Schank offers a number of types of memory experience that were claimed to be hierarchically organized. These included:

- *Event memory*—not dissimilar to what psychologists know otherwise as episodic memory. It is responsible for our being able to describe in detail what happened when we went to the dentist yesterday.
- *Generalized event memory*—a collocation of events whose common features have been abstracted. Here we find information that pertains in general to "going to the dentist."
- *Situational memory*—containing information about specific situations in general. Thus, for example, here we find the similarities shared by going to the doctor, the dentist, the optometrist— "waiting rooms."

- *Intentional memory*—where we find the similarities shared by all societal services.

Next Schank asks the crucial question of where scripts fit into this partitioning of memory. His answer marks another turning point, for it is that there are no scripts in memory at all. Schank reaches the conclusion that his postulated levels of memory are sufficient to allow the construction of scripts as they are required. This is now becoming very near to the idealist notion of knowledge as knowing—the process of constructing and reconstructing observer relationships with the world.

Having established that script application is a reconstructive process rather than the retrieval of some complete data structure, Schank proceeds to inquire after the organization of memory. He asks two questions that seem relevant: How does any given experience get stored so that it will provide a capability for understanding new experiences in terms of it? Second, why do recognition confusions occur?

As it turns out, the fundamental process of memory that lies at the heart of the answers to both these questions for Schank is the process of *reminding.* Schank argues that reminding is vital for the bringing to mind of relevant memories to help process new experiences. He claims, furthermore, that reminding is not restricted to those occasions when we experience it as a conscious process, but that it happens all the time even if we are not aware of it. Walking through my back door into my kitchen reminds me of previous times when I did this, and this helps me to understand my surrounding. Walking through your back door into your kitchen for the first time reminds me of when I do this at my house, and again helps me to understand what I see. In this second case, however, what I am reminded of is more likely to be a conscious activity due to more differences between the two situations.

Instead of scripts as the units of memory, Schank supposes that they are constructed "on demand" from bundles of concepts called memory organization packets, or MOPs. MOPs are said to be the subject of the continuing creation and organization of abstractions of similarities of different experiences. Schank sees memory as a "morass of MOP strands." At one end of each strand is the most abstract generalization of the part of the particular experience that is marked by the other end. The storage of abstractions of our experiences lends a certain efficiency to memory, for it means that more is available whenever we have to understand new experiences. But, importantly, a by-product of experience-abstraction is memory confusion. Memory and the processing of new situations work, argues Schank, through the mechanism of meaning abstraction, but it is precisely this organization of experiences that allows an imperfect memory. We are reminded of previous experiences through the activation of MOPs, but at the expense of those details of the original experiences that were not organized by the reminding MOPs.

Schank's recent theory is consistent to some extent with the perspective of idealism. This is evidenced, for example, by the emphasis on memory as the process of reminding in which new events are interpreted in terms of a current structure of understanding (that is, self-reference), the result of which serves to change that structure. This view is certainly incongruent with the state theories of memory assumed by the semantic network theorists.

Schank's notion of being able to take and represent different perspectives on a situation or concept emphasizes a heterarchical, rather than hierarchical, fixed view of knowledge and is, again, not compatible with the realist concern for what particular concepts "really" mean. It may be observed, however, that there are still some important points of difference between Schank's current position and the one that he is approximating. In particular, although they are less emphasized these days, Schank still has a commitment to the notion of a set of absolute primitives. This leads Schank to the goal of constructing a theory of cognition and into a discussion of the structure of human memory. As we shall see, the distinction is between, in Schank's case, focusing on and modeling observed regularities in persons' cognitive structures, as against, in Winograd's and Pask's cases, focusing on and modeling the regularities that emerge as public concepts (see Pask and Gregory in this volume) between people when they communicate.

Bobrow and Winograd: SHRDLU, KRL, and Beyond

Even a cursory analysis of the spectacular and enormously influential arrival of the SHRDLU program demonstrates that Winograd (1971, 1972, 1973) began very near to the idealist view. SHRDLU was the subject of his doctoral thesis and is a program for natural-language conversation between a human user and a simulated table-top world of differently shaped and differently colored blocks. SHRDLU differed in significant ways from previous (and concurrent) attempts at computerized natural-language conversation, and perhaps the main such difference was the explicit attempt made to model the speaker as well as knowledge about the world—in this case, toy blocks. As Winograd (1980) points out, the previous, simpler model of natural-language understanding had rested on the following basic (as seen here, realist) assumptions:

1. Sentences in a natural language correspond to facts about the world.
2. It is possible to create a formal representation system such that
   - For any relevant fact about the world there is a corresponding structure in the representation system;
   - There is a systematic way of correlating sentences in natural language with the structure in the representation system that correspond to the same facts about the world; and
   - Systematic formal operations can be specified that operate on the representation structures to do "reasoning." Given structures corresponding to facts about the world, these operations will generate structures corresponding to other facts, without introducing falsehoods.

With SHRDLU, Winograd attempted to provide an explicit representation of the cognitive context of the human user. This enabled the program to reason not just about the domain of blocks but also about the focus and structure of the current conversation it was having with a user about the domain. The explicit acknowledgment of the interpretative activities of the understander is, of course, much more of an idealist concern, although Winograd became concerned over the ad hoc nature of the speaker-representations created by the system. The nature of his concern at this time was realist-oriented, however, for the speaker-representations he was after were "structures that exist in the mind."

The second main distinguishing feature of SHRDLU concerned the way in which word meanings were defined as *programs*. In this way, as Winograd points out, it was at least theoretically possible to take any arbitrary number of contextual factors into account. This was rather different from semantic net systems, for example, in which a concept was defined in terms of its parts, often in hierarchical relation. The problem remained for Winograd, however, that no hint was provided as to what particular contextual factors to include for any word definition. In addition, Winograd came to see that the problem extended to the meaning of most words (not just adjectives). It is the case that the meaning of a word (or phrase) changes dependent on the context and purposes of the conversation. Winograd gives the example of the word "bachelor" against its dictionary definition of "unmarried, adult, human male," and asks us to consider its aptness when applied to the pope, a member of a monogamous homosexual couple, and an independent career woman. The key point is that to utter a word as part of some expression is to take a perspective on the meaning of that word and, further, to communicate that particular meaning to a hearer.

A third main distinguishing feature was an emphasis on the use of language as triggering action. The idea being modeled was that an utterance registered in a hearer as an activity. This was achieved in Winograd's program by a formalism in which the meaning of a sentence was represented as a command to carry out some action—for example, a user's question was interpreted by the program as a command to generate an answer. Winograd reports that although this was an important idea, nevertheless, natural language is much more than the conveyance of a fact from A to B, but an interpretive activity that depends on the whole of our cognitive capabilities. Focusing again on the importance of accounting for the *perspective* of conversational participants, Winograd notes that in conversation every statement is the answer to a question that may or may not be explicit but is at least implicit in the context of the exchange. Similarly, every answer to a question is preceded at least implicitly by another question of the form "why do you want to know?"

The fourth and final point of departure of SHRDLU from previous approaches to representation concerns the way in which facts about the domain were encoded in the program. Contrary to tradition, Winograd represented facts as programs that could execute rather than as declarative statements about the world. The procedural/declarative controversy is one of the recurrent themes in AI and knowledge representation and one that has been characterized by several (for example, Rumelhart and Norman, 1983). The controversy turns on whether knowledge should be represented as descriptive ("knowledge about") statements that are then subjected to inferencing mechanisms or as prescriptive ("knowledge how") procedures that execute—or, indeed, some combination of both. The point here, though, is not that Winograd used one or the other, but rather that the "reasoning" of the program that used these fact-programs was underwritten by a deductive knowledge that Winograd subsequently argued only corresponds to a small amount of human reasoning.

The reflective criticisms that Winograd made of SHRDLU led directly, with the partnership of Bobrow, to the specification for a new knowledge representation language, or KRL (Bobrow and Winograd, 1977). In fact, KRL is both a high-level AI programming language and a theory of knowledge representation (Lenhert & Wilks, 1979).

The feature of KRL that has generated the most controversy is its disavowal of primitives. This feature follows from Winograd's earlier concern to find a way to treat inputs to the system other than as items to be stored or commands to be executed. In particular, Bobrow and Winograd claim, like Schank, that objects and events are not generally reducible and can only be represented through "multiple views." Bobrow and Winograd's concern in KRL is to open up the possibility for a word to have different meaning profiles, rather than have its meaning rooted, "once and for all," in some arrangement of primitives. But, for example, Lenhert and Wilks cannot accept this and conclude that KRL's formalisms are inadequate to deal with what they feel is a fundamental problem of memory representation. This is the paraphrase problem; if you input something like "Tom gave a peanut to Tim," you require your representation system to be able to respond to the question "Did Tim get a peanut from Tom?" The controversy, they claim, is over whether decomposition into primitives or, on the other hand, pattern matching is likely to result in a solution to this problem. In their view, it is only by collapsing sentences into an internal primitive representation that underlies the meaning of *both* the Tim/Tom sentences that there is any chance of resolution.

In a reply to this challenge, Bobrow and Winograd (1979) once again express their disbelief in a system of primitives, since for them, as for idealism, "the process of understanding is always one of drawing inferences, not one of simple storage . . . primitivity is with respect to the current knowledge state of the system, and with respect to the language or the world which it reflects." Bobrow and Winograd react to Lenhert and Wilks' invocation of the "paraphrase problem" by showing that the latter's formulation of the problem is faulty. It is, they say, based on the misguided notion that the problem is "In order to answer this question, what is the chunk of memory that is equivalent in meaning?" Bobrow and Winograd claim that a more difficult question, and one that is more appropriate to everyday situations is "What is the purpose of this question, so that I might decide which things are relevant, and draw the appropriate inferences from them?" They do not claim that KRL has an answer to this sort of question, but suggest that resorting to the notion of primitives does not provide the solution either.

KRL is probably the closest implementation of an idealist-type knowledge representation system. In the time since the conception and specification of KRL, it is interesting to note Winograd's (1980) attention being drawn explicitly to the principles of hermeneutics, and in the same breath, to Maturana's notions in the field of biology, of systems as "plastic," yet closed. Here the conception of the living, self-organized system as plastic follows from the notion that its structure can be changed by its activity; yet the system is also closed in the sense that its activity at any moment is fully determined by its current structure. Maturana (1970a, b) and his student Varela (Varela, Maturana, & Uribe, 1974) have been responsible for elaborating this concept, now known as autopoiesis, meaning literally "self-production," in the context of living systems.

With KRL in a sense behind him, Winograd is intrigued by the idealist notion that the activity of an organism—or analogously, a concept—may be better understood as something that is determined by its own structure, which in turn determines its own activity, as opposed to the more familiar realist formulation that activity is a reflection of the externally perceived world. He sees in this view that

> The focus is shifted away from the structure of the phenomena that led to the perturbations (of the system) toward the structure of changes in the ongoing activity of the system as it is perturbed. This view meshed well with the "triggering" view of language understanding. . . . The central questions to be asked of an utterance are those dealing with the changes in activity that it triggers, not with its correspondence to a world it describes (1980, p. 223)

Winograd has explicitly turned away from the realist's preoccupation with truth correspondence and with modeling the "structure of memory" to the idealist focus on modeling the processes of sharing meaning and the structure of agreement within perspectives and between people.

Beyond KRL, Winograd sees the need for a "calculus of language acts." This will include

- *A logic of illocution*—needed to express the responsibility that the speaker has for the kind of effect he expects his utterance to have in the hearer, for example, promises or demands, irrespective of the content of the utterance.
- *A logic of argument*—needed to make potentially defensible (that is, coherent) statements in the event of ambiguity becoming manifest.
- *A logic of breaking down*—needed to enable the "de-axiomatization" (my term) of the conversation, in the event that the statements that are uttered do have to be defended (that is, ambiguity resolution is required).

In considering the implications for what we have characterized here as the adoption of an idealist perspective, Winograd foresees systems already adumbrated by Pask's conversation theory, as we shall see below. Winograd notes that while the prevalent view in AI is to design expert systems stand-ins for people, nevertheless, the adoption of a different philosophical perspective produces an entirely different view of the computer's role in an intelligent system. "It is not a surrogate expert, but an intermediary—a sophisticated medium of communication." This change in focus changes the nature of the problem—from how to ensure it computes the correct answer to how to arrange for the system to cope with a mismatch between it and its user.

Pask: Conversation Theory

Winograd's idealist concern is for a calculus of language acts that leads him to the notion of the computer as an intelligent communications facilitator. Operating from very much the same philosophical perspective, Pask has been concerned with representing the processes by which meaning is exchanged between individuals, and how the incorporation of another's perspective on the world into one's own perspective changes one's own knowledge in possibly fundamental ways. The outcomes of Pask's concern are conversation theory and its computer-implementable formalization, the protolanguage Lp (Pask, Scott, & Kallikourdis, 1973; Pask, Kallikourdis, & Scott, 1975; Pask, 1976, 1980). The technical details of conversation theory, Lp, and a knowledge representation system known as THOUGHT-STICKER are elaborated elsewhere in this volume by Pask and Gregory. What follows is a descriptive overview of the approach.

Conversation theory arose some 15 years ago in a training context when Pask sought to apply a cybernetic perspective to the construction of adaptive training devices. Pask construed the interaction of the student with such a device as like a conversation in that each side of the interaction was required to transfer information to the other side. The student had to give the machine information about what she or he knew so that the machine could be adaptive, and the machine had to transfer information about its subject matter based on this information. Pask's perspective was that for such transfers of information to take place, the conversational participants had to become entrained with each other, synchronized by means of some common focus of attention. This led later to the notion of consciousness as the process of at least two conversational participants simultaneously sharing the meaning of a concept.

Following von Foerster's (1960) notion of self-organization, Pask held that conversations were prime examples of self-organizing systems in that information transfer continued until stability was achieved. At this point, stability could turn into ossification unless the system was perturbed, perhaps by new information that caused ambiguity to arise. The idea of a conversation as a self-organizing process to stability was further extended to the content of conversations, namely, concepts. Concepts were also conceived of as collections of self-organized processes, which were organizationally closed insofar that they were stable and autonomous, and yet informationally open to each other in that they helped to give meaning to one another. Furthermore, while concepts seemed to collect in clusters so that all the members of a cluster made sense together—that is, were coherent with each other—nevertheless, there was clearly a requirement for each concept to maintain its distinction from its neighbors. A logic of coherence and distinction had begun to emerge—a logic that underpinned the processes of coming to a stable conversational agreement. What had begun as a cybernetic approach to teaching machines was turning into a major psychological theory of memory, thought, and the processing of meaning.

In conversation theory, the minimal unit for psychological observation—indeed, the minimal meaningful psychological unit—is held to be a conversation between two individuals in some mutually comprehended language over some domain. Formally speaking, the purpose of the participants in the conversation is to exchange the meaning that each concept has for them in the domain until they get to the point where each has an understanding of the domain not only in their own terms and from the original perspectives that they had on the subject matter but also in the other's terms and from the other's perspective. The referents for knowledge about the world are the conversational participants themselves. Each participant allows the process of conversation, under certain conditions, to synchronize each with the other, to transfer information across the relation built between them and to construct a model of the other's understanding. In so doing, the information that originated with each becomes forever changed. The participants do not just adapt to each other; they change each other into different individuals who nevertheless retain their original identities. The process of conversation is both productive and reproductive.

The truth value of a conversational agreement is a coherence truth that does not preclude the possibility, however, for conversational partners to introduce (a convenient simulation of) factual truth to the extent that they also agree about the validity of some appropriate criterion test. Lp, standing for protolanguage or protologic, is the formalization of the conversational processes that underpin conversation theory and is, hence, a model of them. What is represented in Lp is shared knowledge over an agreed meaning of concepts made by two or more participants who are conversing in some universe of discourse. The process by which agreement is reached, and by which ambiguity is discovered, resolved and re-represented as an explicated analogy relation, *is* the process of knowledge acquisition. Furthermore, because Lp models this process, there is a very real sense in which the knowledge that is represented through Lp is "alive"—perturbable and beholdable—by new perspectives on the domain. Indeed, the meaning of a concept is represented in Lp by its repertoire, that is, the total number of ways it may be derived from other concepts with which it is coherent. This idea is much the same as the "multiple views" of Bobrow & Winograd and the MOP strands of Schank.

The utilization of knowledge represented through Lp is enabled by the procedural embedding of the meaning of each concept in (at least one) manipulatable model that is accessible to both conversational participants. These models and modeling facilities can take many forms—formulas, diagrams, text, command sequences—but are insisted upon, since it is only by their manipulation that agreements about understandings can be demonstrated by the participants to each other. We should emphasize that the participants can be taken to mean two different, but simultaneous, perspectives in the same person, or two different perspectives in the same person on different occasions, or two different people at simultaneous or different times, or in general, any two distinguishable L-processors. We are talking about cognitive individuals, or what Pask calls psychological or P-individuals.

The utilization of knowledge via model manipulation in Lp may take place either in a training context or in an operational one. In the former, the manipulations are made by a machine-tutor as part of an exposition of the subject matter to a student, but also by the student, to "teach back" his understanding to the tutor. In the case of an operational context, the manipulations are done by a machine-adviser to check understanding with the operator or to achieve some task in the domain, and by the operator for similar reasons. Systems requiring these capabilities have been described elsewhere as intelligent support systems (Gregory & Sheppard, 1981; Sheppard, 1981, 1982; Gregory 1982).

It should be clear that an intelligent support system is quite different from the surrogate nature of the expert system discussed by Winograd. The rather different image of an AI system as an intelligent communications channel that is possible when one takes an idealist perspective provides the opportunity to address some important classes of tasks where the expert system surrogate is not appropriate at all. In fields requiring complex, tactical decision making, the decision maker cannot look for an answer from the machine because none yet exists. In these cases the requirement is for a system that can help the decision maker to (re-)formulate the problem coherently and that can help him or her to innovate solutions by forging analogies between the user's present situation and previously represented situations and performances, both of the current, and other, users. In the process of making these intelligent connections, inconsistencies would be detected and resolved that would produce in turn a changed but coherent and therefore enriched representation.

This kind of communication in which users are "put in touch" with themselves and others is clearly beyond even Nilsson's 1983 AAAI presidential appeal for "Expert Systems that can model their users," for they require the embodiment of "living" expertise as opposed to the mapping of human users onto static representations of experts who "died" (Pangaro & Nicoll, 1983) the moment the knowledge engineer finished coding. It is not obvious how communicative, "living" systems can come about without also the appropriate philosophical shift from realism with its concomitant assumptions of observer independence of facts and their logical connectivity to a convenient form of idealism and the development of logics that allow the expression and resolution of conflict and agreement between interacting individuals. What is fundamental to the enterprise of constructing an intelligent support system is precisely the unification of the acquisition, representation, and utilization of knowledge that is offered by the adoption of a rather different position on what should be represented and of the logics, like Lp and Winograd's image, that flow from that position.

SUMMARY

The debate on the structure and acquisition of knowledge of the world has continued since the time of the early Greeks and has involved an interaction between the two main philosophical positions of realism and idealism. The different philosophies of realism and idealism are important to the enterprise of AI in that AI draws on its own scientific and philosophical traditions, as well as those of experimental psychology, for answers to what it takes to be problems of knowledge acquisition, representation, and utilization. Depending on which philosophical position one uses, one is led to ask quite different questions and/or look for quite different answers with respect to, for example, the nature of knowledge and what should be represented. In turn, this leads to different images of what sort of AI system one should build.

Through a detailed look at selected but representative pursuits in AI (with respect to knowledge representation), this chapter has shown how the assumptions of realism have affected the decisions and questions of those working in the field. The general comments can be summarized by the rather different conceptualizations of what Anderson and Bower (1980) call the "interface problem."

For (realist) investigators like Anderson and Bower, who attempt to capture knowledge in a semantic net, the interface problem is how to arrange for an inferencing ("thinking") process to operate over a collection of facts to determine the answer to a question, or perhaps to incorporate some new fact into the fact structure (memory). Prerequisites of the problem, therefore, are a formalism for representing the structure of the facts in memory, where memory is imagined to be a kind of container with an internal structure to which facts are attached, and the specification of the inferencing process. The metaphorical nature of the computer for brains has evaporated. Knowing and knowledge, like software, are imaged as consisting of programs and data bases. The represented facts are taken to mean something by virtue of their correspondence with objects out in the real world, as well as, perhaps, by the structure of themselves as (intensional) objects in their own right (Brachman's KL-ONE). The problem conveniently divides into those of the representation of the memory structure, the elucidation and attachment of the facts (acquisition), and the use of them (inferencing). The most obvious goal of the enterprise is to construct an artificial, thinking being that can take someone's, or several people's, place, that one can "talk" to and obtain answers from.

The interface problem for the idealist is how to arrange for two entities (machines, people, or a combination) to come to share the same meaning for a particular concept. A concept is not an object that is stored in some pigeonhole, but the process of consciousness of one entity with another over an agreement about what a token stands for. Memory is imaged as the process of remembering (or to use Schank's term, reminding); to remember is to take a perspective on the world, that is, to unfold and thereby create the current structure of agreements "underneath" some particular understanding. What is required is a formalism for representing the process by which two entities that live in different worlds can come to inhabit the same world, the process by which the nature of the analogies between the two entities becomes articulated. The goal of this approach is the construction of a communication medium that can bring a current user into coherence with other users who may exist only as represented agreement-structures, but who are informationally open to the incorporation of, or use by, new perspectives. Such a system as this is intelligent not because it has been made to "think" about what it "knows," but because it can create active partnerships between users who are separated in space and time. One does not talk to it, but through it; one does not get answers from it, but with it; one is not the object of intelligent (partial) replacement, but the subject of intelligent support.

While Pask's conversation theory and the THOUGHTSTICKER representational system, originating from second-order cybernetics, has always belonged to an idealist perspective on human interactions, some of those working in knowledge representation are now reaching out in this direction. It has been argued that with his MOP system, Schank is trying to grasp idealist notions about the importance of analogy as a model of agreement, while keeping his feet on a realist ground paved with sets of conceptual primitives to which our higher order concepts are said to be ultimately reducible. From the days of SHRDLU, however, Winograd appears to have made the transition completely, and with it, the image of a different kind of AI system has arisen for him—a system that functions as an intelligent intermediary that computes agreement rather than an oracle that computes answers that may or may not have any meaning or import for a client that it will never know or understand.

ACKNOWLEDGMENTS AND NOTES

I am indebted to many for their perceptive and valuable comments on earlier drafts of this paper. Most notably these include Sharon Mutter, George Lawton, and Jonathan Kaplan of ARI; Gordon Pask of Concordia University; Paul Pangaro, Heather Harney, and Jeffrey Nicoll of Pangaro Incorporated; and Abraham Birnbaum. I am especially grateful to Jeffrey Nicoll for the insightful time we spent discussing and investigating the physics of conversation.

1. It is important to remember that throughout this chapter the terms "realism" and "idealism" are used in these very broad senses to indicate general perspectives rather than particular philosophical schools.

2. The term "hermeneutical" comes from the Greek *hermeneuo*, meaning "I interpret, explain, make clear," and was originally concerned with the elucidation of meaning of ancient texts.

3. Electrons can be asked about their speed or location, but not both simultaneously. If speed is chosen, then the electron can be made to answer precisely, but at the expense of rendering the notion of location meaningless.

REFERENCES

Anderson, J. R., & Bower, G. H. (1980). *Human associative memory: A brief edition.* Hillsdale, NJ: Erlbaum Associates.

Bobrow, D. G., & Winograd, T. (1977). An overview of KRL, a knowledge representation language. *Cognitive Science, 1*, 3–46.

Bobrow, D. G., & Winograd, T. (1979). KRL: Another perspective. *Cognitive Science, 3*, 29–42.

Brachman, R. J. (1977, October). *What's in a concept? Structural foundations for semantic networks* (BBN Rep. 3433). Also *International Journal Man-Machine Studies, 9*, 127–152.

Brachman, R. J. (1978). *Theoretical studies in natural language understanding: Annual report* (BBN Rep. No. 3888).

Brachman, R. J. (1979a). On the epistemological status of semantic networks. In N. V. Findler (Ed.), *Associative networks: Representation and use of knowledge by computers.* New York: Academic Press.

Brachman, R. J. (1979). *An introduction to KL-ONE* (BBN Rep. No. 4274).

Buchanan, B. (1981). *Knowledge acquisition for expert systems.* Paper presented at the NATO Symposium on Human and Artificial Intelligence, Chateau de Chapeau Cornu, Lyon, France.

Campbell, D. T. (1984). *Science's social system of validity-enhancing collective belief change and the problems of the social sciences.* Draft for book based on September 1983 conference at University of Chicago: Potentialities for knowledge in social science, Eds. D. W. Fiske & R. A. Shweder.

Capra, F. (1977). *The Tao of physics* New York: Bantam.

Foerster, H. von. (1960). On self-organising systems and their environments. In *Self Organising Systems*. Eds. M. C. Yovitz & S. Cameron. Pergamon: New York.

Foerster, H. von. (1974). *The cybernetics of cybernetics.* Urbana: University of Illinois.

Fransella, F. (1975). *Need to change?* London: Methuen.

Gauld, A., & Shotter, J. (1977). *Human action and its psychological investigation.* London: Routledge & Kegan Paul.

Glanville, R. (1979). The form of cybernetics—Whitening the black box. In *Proceedings of the Twenty-fourth Society for General Systems Research Annual Meeting*, Houston. Louisville: KY: Society for General Systems Research.

Glanville, R. (1982). Inside every white box there are two black boxes trying to get out. *Behavioral Science*, 27.

Gregory, D. (1982). What's a conversation between friends? In *Proceedings of MOD Seminar on the Application of Machine Intelligence to Defence Systems.*

Gregory, D., & Sheppard, C. (1981). Work programme and rationale: Applied Psychology Unit Man Computer Studies Section. In *The Technical Cooperation Program: Technical Panel UTP-2* (Training Technology), paper on artificial intelligence.

Hendrix, G. G. (1975a). *Partitioned networks for the mathematical modelling of natural language semantics* (Tech. Rep. NL-28). Austin: Department of Computer Science, University of Texas.

Hendrix, G. G. (1975b). Expanding the utility of semantic networks through partitioning. In *Proceedings of the Fourth International Conference on Artificial Intelligence* (pp. 115-121). Tbilisi, Georgia, USSR.

Lenhert, W., & Wilks, Y. (1979). A critical perspective on KRL. *Cognitive Science, 3*, 1-28.

Levine, M. (1974). Scientific method and the adversary model: Some preliminary thoughts. *American Psychologist*, 661-677.

Martin, W. A. (1977). OWL. In *Proceedings of the Fifth International Joint Conference on Artificial Intelligence* (pp. 985-987). Cambridge, MA.

Maturana, H. R. (1970a). *The biology of cognition* (Biological Computer Laboratory Res. Rep. 9.0). Urbana: University of Illinois.

Maturana, H. R. (1970b). *Biology of language* (Biological Computer Laboratory BCL Rep. 9.0). Urbana: University of Illinois. Also in R. W. Rieber (Ed.), (1977). *The neuropsychology of language.* New York: Plenum Press.

Minsky, M. (1975). A framework for representing knowledge. In P. H. Winston (Ed.), *The psychology of computer vision.* New York: McGraw-Hill.

Nilsson, N. J. (1983). Presidential address. AAAI (American Association for Artificial Intelligence). Washington, DC.

Pangaro, P., & Nicoll, J. F. (1983). Deleting the knowledge engineer. In *Proceedings of MOD Seminar on the Applications of Machine Intelligence to Defence Systems.*

Pask, G. (1976). *Conversation theory: Applications in education and epistemology.* Amsterdam: Elsevier.

Pask, G. (1980). Developments in conversation theory. Part I. *International Journal Man-Machine Studies, 13*, 357-411.

Pask, G., Kallikourdis, D., & Scott, B. C. E. (1975). The representation of knowables. *International Journal of Man-Machine Studies, 7*, 15-134.

Pask, G., Scott, B. C. E., & Kallikourdis, D. (1973). A theory of conversations and individuals. *International Journal of Man-Machine Studies, 5*, 443.

Quillian, M. R. (1968). Semantic memory. In M. Minsky (Ed.), *Semantic information processing.* Cambridge, MA: MIT Press.

Rogers, C. R. (1951). *Client centered therapy.* London: Constable.

Rumelhart, D. E., & Norman, D. A. (1983). *Representation in memory* (ONR Rep. 8302. CHIP 116). San Diego: University of California.

Schank, R. C. (1972). Conceptual dependency: A theory of natural language understanding. *Cognitive Psychology, 3*, 552-631.

Schank, R. C. (1975). *Conceptual information processing.* New York: North-Holland.

Schank, R. C. (1980). Language and memory. *Cognitive Science, 4*, 243–284.

Schank, R. C. (1982). Looking at learning. In *Proceedings of 1982 European Conference on Artificial Intelligence*, Orsay, France.

Schank, R. C., & Abelson, R. (1977). *Scripts, plans, goals and understanding.* Hillsdale, NJ: Erlbaum Associates.

Shapiro, S. C. (1971). *The MIND system: A data structure for semantic information processing* (Tech. Rep. R-837-PR). Rand Corp.

Sheppard, C. (1981). *Applied Psychology Unit Man Computer Studies Section: Rationale and work programme 1981/1983* (Rep. E1/P4.1/198/81). Teddington, Middlesex, England: Admiralty Marine Technology Establishment.

Sheppard, C. (1982). Beyond expert systems. In *Proceedings of MOD Seminar on the Application of Machine Intelligence to Defence Systems.*

Shotter, J. (1975). *Images of man in psychological research.* London: Methuen.

Smith, J. K. (1983, March). Quantitative versus qualitative research: An attempt to clarify the issue. *Educational Researcher*, 6–13.

Taylor, C. (1971). Interpretation and the sciences of man. *Review Metaphysics, 25*, 3–51.

Varela, F., Maturana, H. R., & Uribe, R. (1974). Autopoiesis: The organization of living systems, its characterization and a model. *Biosystems, 5*, 187–196.

Wiener, N. (1948). *Cybernetics.* Boston: MIT Press.

Winograd, T. (1971). Procedures as a representation for data in a computer program for understanding natural language (MAC-TR-84). *MIT Project MAC.*

Winograd, T. (1972). *Understanding natural language.* New York: Academic Press.

Winograd, T. (1973). A process model of natural language understanding. In R. C. Schank & K. M. Colby (Eds.), *Computer models of thought and language.* San Francisco: Freeman.

Winograd, T. (1980). What does it mean to understand language? *Cognitive Science, 4*, 209–241.

Winston, P. H. (1977). *Artificial intelligence.* Reading, MA: Addison-Wesley.

Woods, W. A. (1975). What's in a link? In D. G. Bobrow & A. Collins (Eds.), *Representation and understanding.* New York: Academic Press.

Zukav, G. (1979). *The dancing Wu Li masters: An overview of the new physics.* New York: Bantam.

5

CONVERSATIONAL SYSTEMS

Gordon Pask and Dik Gregory

Conversation is something that we carry on with each other as a matter of course. We rarely stop to think very much about it, let alone study it; and yet if one does pause to consider it, one very quickly sees that conversation is a process of the most fundamental importance to the task that we all have in connecting ourselves with each other and with the world in which we live. Conversation is not just natural language; it is natural language in action—the process by which we make deliberate use of language to render ourselves and the world understandable to each other.

Conversation theory is the outcome of some 25 years (the name "conversation theory" is rather newer than this) of investigation and experimentation into the processes by which we come to understand (and misunderstand) each other's views, and the dynamics of incorporating the perspectives of others into the structure of our own understanding. One of the practical findings of conversation theory is that it has a formal dual that manifests as a logic, or more precisely, a protologic, called Lp.[1] Lp is a protologic (equivalently, a protolanguage) rather than a logic (or language) in two senses. First, it is *fundamental* because it is believed to underlie (that is, enables) what-

The views and opinions contained herein are those of the authors and do not necessarily reflect the position of the U.S. Army Research Institute for the Behavioral and Social Sciences, the Admiralty Research Establishment, U.K., or the Social Research Council (London).

ever natural language is used for communicating with each other. In this sense, it is a model of the processes by which natural language works to make us understandable to each other. Second, Lp is *proto* because it is *primitive* by comparison with the logic naturally available to us as processors of language. That is to say, the processes that Lp specifies are not claimed to be perfect, isomorphic, or complete copies of the processes modeled. What is important about Lp is that it is an extensible, refinable environment in which to explore the exchange of meaning between two or more conversational participants.

The development of conversation theory and Lp has led to systems that provide new insights into the enterprises of knowledge representation and intelligent computer-aided training, as well as into the issues of complex decision making. In this chapter observations are made about conversation theory and Lp. Following these observations is a discussion of three systems whose development has been motivated by the import of these observations. These systems are THOUGHTSTICKER, a knowledge acquisition and representation system; CASTE, an intelligent tutorial system; and the team decision system, a simulation designed to exteriorize the otherwise internal conversations of thought required for complex decision making. Although this chapter has been organized to cover the theory before its practical implementations, it is left to the reader's own priorities as to which to read first.

It is worth noting at the outset that conversation theory belongs to a philosophical perspective that is rather unfamiliar to the broad mainstream of science. This perspective is that of *idealism*, which naturally produces an emphasis on conversation, meaning, and knowledge as processes by which agreements are reached and by which these agreements then change and enrich the understanding of the conversational participants. This philosophy may be contrasted with the approach of philosophical *realism*, which is more concerned with discussing meaning and knowledge in terms of truth correspondence with a world that is held to be logically distinct from its observers. Gregory argues (this volume) that it is only possible to appreciate fully the contribution of approaches like conversation theory to the problem of knowledge representation by being aware of this rather different, idealist philosophy. Although this chapter was designed to stand on its own, a deeper perspective may be reached if it is read in conjunction with Gregory's Chapter 4 on the philosophy and practice in knowledge representation.

CONVERSATION THEORY

Conversation theory is fully described in Pask (1976, 1980). It is a theory of interpersonal and intrapersonal cognition that derives from a wealth of experimental findings (Pask & Scott, 1973; Pask, Kallikourdis, & Scott, 1975) to account for the way in which intelligent entities communicate with each other. In terms of both concept and philosophy, the theory is congruent with recent activities in a wide range of human thinking and endeavor, including the hermeneutics movement in psychology (Taylor, 1971; Gauld & Shotter, 1977), second-order cybernetics (von Foerster, 1974; Glanville, 1979, 1982), Maturana's (1970, 1977) research on living systems, and the fundamentals of quantum mechanics (see Zukav, 1979). This congruency derives from the insistence of all of these disciplines that observers of the world are not independent of the events and objects that they observe, but that they help to give form and meaning to the world by the very process of observation. Observing something is as creative an act as it is descriptive.

As its name suggests, conversation theory is concerned with conversations between individuals that take place in a language, "L." A conversational language has many characteristics of a natural language in contrast to a logical or programming language. For example, L must be able to express commands and responses to them, to generate questions and a multitude of answers, to create metaphors that designate analogies, to express stories and allegories, and to establish a sense of self and other reference. All of this is needed over and above the descriptive and expressive power of a standard logic. It should be noted, however, that L need not be verbal: Music, ballet, mime, gesture, and art are all legitimate conversational languages.

Of primary concern in conversation theory are conversations in some L that lead to *concept sharing.* Here, a concept is regarded as a dynamic entity that can be applied in an L-processor (such as a human brain) as a process to yield an intellectual or tangible product, such as a mental image or an overt behavior. This dynamic and productive idea of a concept has a great deal in common with Bartlett's (1932) interpretation of a skill and Kelly's notion of a personal construct (1955), recently revitalized and extended by Shaw (1980).

Concept sharing takes place by means of transactions that give rise to the hard, observable data of conversation theory. These data are known as agreements. The term "agreements" is intended to connote not just agreement but also agreement to disagree and how and why disagreements prevail, since utter accord is seldom (if ever) encountered. There is likely to be, for example, a great deal of accord between different people about geometrical concepts like "sphere," or everyday concepts like "cup and saucer," "walking," or "flying in an aircraft"; by contrast, there may be little or no shared concepts of "beauty" or the act of falling in love. Whatever personal concepts are stated, the shared and common part of these personal constituents is referred to as a *public concept.*

Clearly, public concepts must be common to at least two individual conversational participants. Quite often, however, they are very much wider in scope. Concepts may be public for a team, an institution, a culture, a nation, or indeed any arbitrary group whose members converse. A public concept may be smaller (more restricted) or larger (more encompassing) than a personal concept. Whichever it is, it is always the case that the process that produces the public concept, concept sharing, enriches the personal concepts of the participants. This is because conversational concept sharing converts what is known into a form such that it becomes known that it is known: The process of conversation produces consciousness of two conversational participants with each other about an agreement to understand something in a particular way.

It is important to understand that the conversation theoretic notion of a conversational participant is somewhat broader than usual. For example, an individual may be a person such as each of the two authors of this paper, being biologically distinct and having different brains. Alternatively, an individual may be a *perspective* shared by more than one biological brain such as the two authors of this chapter considered *together* as the joint authors of this chapter. In this latter case, the whole content of the chapter may be viewed as a public concept. More widely, an individual may be a societal entity such as a persistent system of beliefs, hypotheses, or allegiances. Individuals may also exist as dynamic, cohesive organizations contained in any one brain, namely, the different beliefs and hypotheses (all of which are concepts), that we debate in thought.

This definition of an individual is very much related to what conversation theory images a concept to be. In conversation theory, a concept is a stable process capable of two kinds of activity: It is both reproductive and productive. This means that its execution in a brain produces both a reproduction or redefinition of itself as well as a production of either a mental image or an overt behavior. Minimally, an individual is a single such concept, both autonomous and yet ready to combine with other individuals. This autonomy of a concept (alias, individual) is much the same kind of thing as von Foerster's (1960) notion of "organizational closure"; the "readiness to combine with others" is an important qualification, however, and refers to the capacity of an organization that is stable to be, nevertheless, informationally open. The two notions taken together—organizational closure and informational openness—are equivalent to Varela et al.'s (1974) notion of autopoeisis in which living systems are imaged as stable organizations whose current structure completely determines the range of activities that may be performed, but where the performance of any one may subsequently change the system's structure.

In conversation theory, the combination and juxtaposition of concepts that are personal to individuals may lead to conflict. It is the resolution of this conflict (the emergence of new structure) that leads, in turn, to novelty of the kind known as creative and to innovation or tangible invention if its product is socially agreed to have value.

Lp: A PROTOLANGUAGE

Duality

As the formal dual of conversation theory, and implemented as a suite of computer programs known as THOUGHTSTICKER (discussed below), Lp expresses fundamental aspects of agreement, including agreements to disagree, and how the resolution of ambiguity perturbs the conversational structures being modeled. Lp is important as a class of knowledge representation systems that is quite different from semantic networks and most other current representational formalisms of artificial intelligence (AI). This difference stems from two essential premises of Lp, both consistent with the philosophy idealism and both implementing the central claims of conversation theory.

First, what may be represented is neither objective knowledge about an objective world nor personal knowledge shared in the process of conversation. The concept of "table" does not mean anything simply because it is an object that exists independently of us; nor does it mean anything to me simply because I can experience a table. In order that we may both understand the notion of "table," either you and I must become conscious with each other over it (that is, agree what it means) or I have to *know* that I experience the meaning of "table" (that is, agree with its meaning with myself). In either case, we must express our agreement through some mutually agreed modeling facility (for example, the world of physical objects) in order to make our agreement demonstrable. Lp represents not the meanings of things but agreements about what things mean. These agreements are public concepts.

The second premise of Lp is that since we are representing our agreements about what things mean, and since these agreements may change or require modification as the conversation proceeds, then it is important to include in the representational system the process by which public concepts arise, therefore, how conflict is detected and agreements are made. In the more traditional approach to knowledge representation found in AI, this process occurs outside the representation system when the knowledge engineer converses with a domain expert. Lp is a representational (proto)language, then, that models both the process by which knowledge becomes meaningfully articulated and the public concept structures that emerge as outcomes of that process.

The approach to representation that Lp affords is important precisely because of its emphasis on modeling the process of agreement. In this way, it leads to novel applications in intelligent computer support systems for training and complex decision making, as is discussed below.

History

Lp emerged from the requirement to perform empirical work with conversation theory, and it is in this sense that Lp is the formalization of the theory; but it did not emerge initially as a protologic. Since about 1970 it was quite evident that empirical work in conversation theory required a maplike representation of public concepts and their relation to each other. This map organized groups of public concepts into coherences designating agreements (and agreements to disagree) and, in so doing, also indicated what might be accessed and learned by a participating newcomer. In the context of education or training, it became more appropriate to refer to public concepts as topics and to think of the entire structure as a representation of what may be known or believed. Such a maplike and momentarily static structure had to be able to evolve, however, to accommodate further topics as they made their appearance through learning, discovery, and innovation.

Several evolvable, heterarchical[2] structures were tried and proved successful in allowing systematic classification of learning strategies by learning participants. This was achieved by charting what participants aimed to learn, what their immediate subgoals were, and what (with learning) came to be demonstrably understood. It was noted at this time that exclusively hierarchical representation of the topics was something to be avoided since it produced only one view on the subject matter obtained by focusing on one topic and its possible derivation from the others.

Besides the notion of heterarchy, the reproductive capability of stable topics (noted earlier) was also respected from the outset. This reproductive capability refers to the conversation theoretic image of concepts as processes (as opposed to states) that upon execution are able to reproduce each other's meaning. This reproducibility was imaged in the representations by a local cyclicity of entailment relations among the members of concept clusters. In other words, the meaning of each concept in a coherent cluster was imaged as being derivable from its cluster members.

By 1973, these evolvable, maplike structures for representing knowledge had come to be known as entailment meshes, and the process of specifying operations to manipulate the knowledge structures was begun. Most of the important mesh manipulations that were to be completely specified were at least glimpsed during this time, and some were made manifest as prototype programs by 1974. It was well appreciated, for example, that several entailment meshes must be able to coexist; that due to evolutionary enhancements they might be merged into one mesh; and, conversely, that one mesh might bifurcate (split) into several in order to maintain the degree of distinction between topics needed to support the asserted coherencies. The topics of distinct meshes might also be related by analogies, preserving a difference and a similarity, distinct meshes might be analogously related in toto. About 1975–76, it became increasingly obvious that entailment meshes, together with their analogical relations, were graphical expressions in a language of coherency, distinction, process, and analogy. This language became known as Lp. Its embodiment in a computer program was called THOUGHTSTICKER.

THOUGHTSTICKER

Overview

THOUGHTSTICKER is capable of eliciting and representing knowledge as entailment meshes of public concepts. Early implementations date back to 1974 and have included versions written in LISPN, BASIC, and Hewlett Packard Pascal. Most recently, versions have been written in TLC LISP and extended Microsoft BASIC for the Apple IIe[3], and in ZetaLisp for the Symbolics 3600 LISP Machine.[4]

Essentially, THOUGHTSTICKER is a system that encourages a subject matter author to converse with him- or herself and to represent the results of that conversation as clusters of concepts that are related coherently and possibly analogously. During the course of representation, THOUGHTSTICKER checks newly proposed clusters for consistency with assertions already made, and in the event of a conflict, proposes resolution possibilities. Each public concept that is related in the mesh must be attached to a model, for example, a computer program, that is capable of yielding an instance of the concept.

Representing Public Concepts

A formal representation of the term "public concept," is presented in the following equation:

$$Execution \text{ (all models of } T) \longrightarrow T = <\text{Models } T; \text{``}T\text{''}>$$

This expression means that if all the models of a public concept called T are executed, then an indefinitely large class of descriptions or behaviors are yielded, designated by "T." The right-hand side of the representation says that this is logically equivalent to saying that the public concept T is constituted by all of its models and the results of their execution. If T is a table, then the concept of table is given by all of the procedures taht could be executed that would produce an instance of table (drawings, physical constructions, pointing at one, imagining one) plus the result of doing all of these. A user of THOUGHTSTICKER may make any desired assertion with the requirements that he or she can indicate which words or phrases designate the key parts of the assertion and can provide definitions or models of them.

Figure 5.1 depicts three words standing for concepts, chosen by a user as key and represented by THOUGHTSTICKER as a coherence. (In the interests of brevity a description of the vital process of specifying models is not presented here.) This grouping is an assertion that is interpreted by THOUGHTSTICKER as follows: The meaning of each of the three concepts is derived not just from its interpretability as a collection of models but also by its ability to bind together, and derive from, the other concepts with which it is coherent. Public concepts are characterized by their producibility (model executions) and their reproducibility (from the combination of other public concepts). The premise of THOUGHTSTICKER is that we can take the notions of typing and chair and reproduce from them the notion of a surface at which to sit while typing—a table. In the act of doing this we (re-)specify a procedural model whose execution results in an image of a table, and if we require, the physical creation of one.

FIGURE 5.1. Simple Coherence

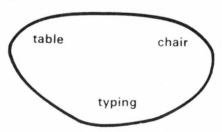

Any public concept must bind (relate together) at least two other distinct public concepts to form a coherence. This restriction is necessary because in a grouping of just two concepts, there is not enough specified to distinguish between them. If the execution of one reproduces the other, then a fundamental ambiguity occurs: They must be considered identical. Another way of seeing this is to recall that coherences such as in Figure 5.1 are, in fact, relations of coherence—a logical adhesion of processes. Not only do public concepts cohere but whatever sticks them together is also a public concept. In the case where a coherence boundary is placed around two distinct concepts—and only two—the ambiguity may be resolved by naming the *boundary* as the concept that distinguishes between the already named pair.

Coherences can overlap each other. If they do, they are called distributive. An example of the distributivity of the public concept, "table," is shown in Figure 5.2. Each of the two coherences in the figure may be taken as a different perspective on the public concept of table. Neither the number of public concept names inside one boundary nor the number of boundaries enclosing any one public concept are limited as long as the distinction of each public concept is preserved.

FIGURE 5.2.

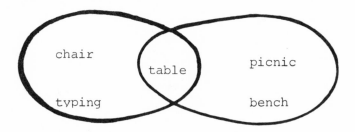

Any complex of coherences is an entailment mesh. Figure 5.3 illustrates a simple mesh.

Now it must be understood that a mesh of public concepts that are related together coherently and in which each designates at least one executable model is inherently nondirectional and nonactionable. To convert a mesh into a directed, active form, it must be unfolded from the perspective of one (or perhaps several) arbitrary public concepts. Only Lp expressions that are capable of unambiguous unfoldment are legal Lp expressions.

The operation in THOUGHTSTICKER that produces mesh unfoldments is called Prune. Figure 5.4 is the result of pruning Figure 5.2 to give the perspective on the mesh from the point of view of the

FIGURE 5.3. A Simple but Illustrative Mesh.

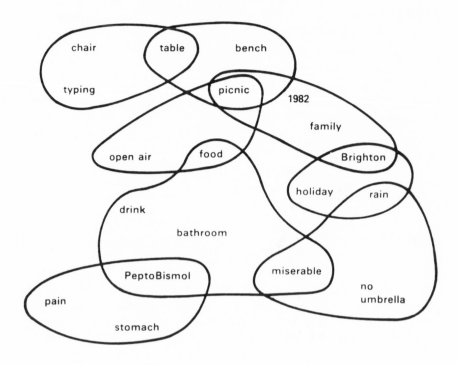

FIGURE 5.4. The Pruning of Figure 5.2 Under "bench"

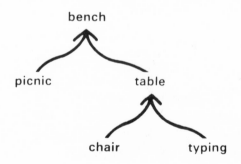

public concept "bench." The meaning of the pruning in Figure 5.4 is that it forms a kind of directed map depicting the way that the author understands "bench." The different "levels" that the concepts seem to occupy are not hierarchical levels at all, but rather measures of conceptual distance. Generally speaking, this map is a plan of action to "achieve" in some appropriate sense the notion of "bench." If the mesh is being authored for the purposes of subsequent tutorial delivery, this "achievement" would correspond with learning what a bench is. In this context, the pruning may be construed as a learning strategy. For a mesh of relations in a tactical domain, pruning structures might be better considered as decision-making strategies leading to the achievement of some specified goal state. At the very least, Figure 5.4 is a graphical representation of how its author can re-create the meaning of "bench" for her- or himself.

Pruning structures can become quite elaborate of course. Figure 5.5 shows a pruning of the relatively simple mesh of Figure 5.3, again under "bench." A pruning includes all of the public concepts in a mesh, and the superimposition of all the prunes of a mesh is the mesh itself. Selective prune, or Selprune, operates on a pruning to dissect it into structures that represent *single* action or learning strategies. The superimposition of all the Selprunes of a prune is that prune.

FIGURE 5.5. A Pruning of Figure 5.3 from the Perspective of "bench."

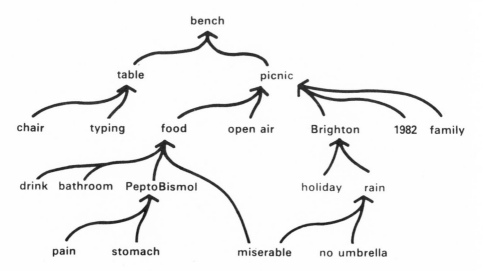

In addition to functioning as the unfolding operators for entailment meshes, Prune and Selprune are important discoverers of any structural ambiguities that may exist. Consider Figure 5.6. On the face of it, the two assertions represented in Figure 5.6 are entirely

FIGURE 5.6. Two Coherences?

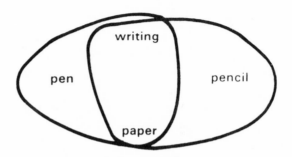

reasonable. To THOUGHTSTICKER, however, they represent a fundamental conflict, and this is because of the necessarily strict way in which THOUGHTSTICKER applies the notions of coherence and distinction. If the structure in Figure 5.6 under "pen" and "pencil" is pruned simultaneously, then it becomes clear that both of these public concepts have exactly the same derivation, as depicted in Figure 5.7.

FIGURE 5.7. A Structural Ambiguity.

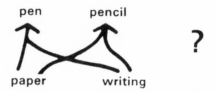

The question that the Prune/Selprune operations cannot resolve without further information is "What is derived from paper and writing—pen or pencil?" At this point, THOUGHTSTICKER can offer several resolution possibilities:

1. Perhaps "pen" and "pencil" are two different tokens standing for the same public concept? If this is the case, the two clusters fit exactly over each other and a note is made that the tokens are equivalent. We might agree here by considering that the only point we wished to make was for the notion of an inscriptive device. On the other hand, we will reject this possibility if it is important to us to preserve the distinction between pen and pencil.

2. Well, in that case, suggests THOUGHTSTICKER, perhaps one or both of the clusters is incomplete. If this is so, then we must add at least one more public concept to at least one of the clusters. This is equivalent to saying that although the public concepts are asserted to be distinct, not enough distinction has yet been represented. In our example the ambiguity could be resolved by Figure 5.8.

FIGURE 5.8. Resolution by the Addition of Distinction.

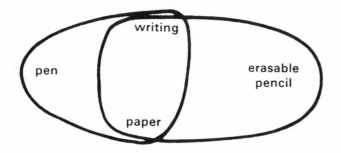

3. The third possibility forces us to confront the idea that more than one public concept is being glossed by one (or both) of the tokens, "writing" and "paper." It might be the case, for example, that what we had meant to represent was not simply "writing" but the two notions of "writing formal letters" and "writing notes to ourselves." Now we could simply respecify "writing" in each case with our newly evolved terms, but to do so would involve losing valuable information. After all, we are talking about writing in both cases. Meaning can be refined in THOUGHT-STICKER by bifurcating (splitting) "writing" and linking the two new public concept representations with an analogy relation,

characterized by similarity and difference terms. Figure 5.9 graphically illustrates the analogical resolution of the ambiguity.

FIGURE 5.9. Resolution by Bifurcation.

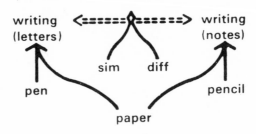

The essential point about an analogy relation is that it designates a different sort of entity compared with a public concept. It represents a vantage point from which to consider the similarities of, and differences between, the expressions being connected. It designates not a public concept but a place where different perspectives on the mesh (prunings) can be synthesized and considered together. Analogy relations can be imaged as kinds of gateways to higher order representations, for the result of combining perspectives is not unlike what Kelly (1955) called a personal construct. We would call it a public construct, however, and a construct it *is* when considered from within the mesh that gave rise to it. The fact is, though, that this construct also resides in a mesh of higher order, and from within its own mesh, it is a public *concept* coherently related with other public concepts.

The THOUGHTSTICKER operation that acts on an analogy to transform a construct into a concept is the process of Condense. The obverse operation is Expand, and it clearly follows that any public concept represented in a mesh is at least potentially expandable into analogously related pruning structures of a whole new mesh containing (relatively speaking, lower order) public concepts. What is important to note here is that concepts represented through THOUGHTSTICKER do not have any a priori "grain" at which they belong, but adopt a "level" that is appropriate, relative to each other. It is certainly the case that the condensed analogy of Figure 5.9 is of a higher order with respect to its expanded prunings; but it is also quite conceivable that it may be part of other coherences that are at the same order as its expansion. The "size" of public concepts varies locally with their use.

One special kind of analogy relation is better known as a generalization. This occurs when a public concept is made to stand for a coherence of other public concepts existing at a lower relative order. It is possible to author some structures in THOUGHTSTICKER that produce a mandatory requirement to condense to a generalization. This form of conflict resolution is called for when particular kinds of embedded structures are created, as in the lower half of Figure 5.10.

FIGURE 5.10. A Mandatory Condense to a Genrealization.

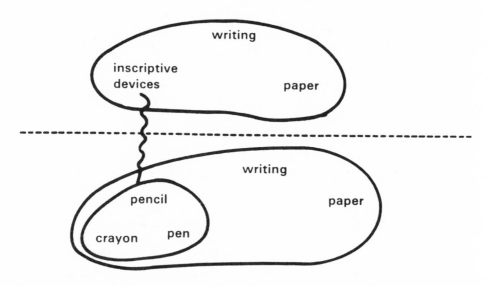

In Figure 5.10 a problem arises because a subset coherence was authored. The problem is that logically different orders of statements are being mixed at the same order. In resolving the problem by generalizing <pencil pen crayon> to <inscriptive devices>, one is, in a sense, leveling out the "size" of the concepts. The resolution emphasizes that it is not appropriate to distinguish between different forms of inscriptive devices to make the point designated by the larger coherence. Another way of saying this is that the "point" of <pencil pen crayon> *in the context of the larger coherence* is that they are all similar in terms of their capacity as inscriptive devices. Generalizations are public concepts that organize other (relatively) lower order public concepts in terms of their similarities. The analogy represented in Figure 5.9 designates a public construct that organizes (relatively) lower order prunings of public concepts in terms of their similarities *and* differences.

There are other THOUGHTSTICKER operations that are important to the system but that require no more than a mention in the context of this chapter. Of these, perhaps the principal operation is that of Saturate. This process takes as its arguments the concepts that have so far been represented and produces new, canddate clusters for consideration by the author. The process is a kind of inference, and suggests only those clusters that, if added to the mesh, would not cause structural ambiguity to arise.

This summary of THOUGHTSTICKER has been necessarily brief, aiming only to give an idea of the kind of representational system it is. More complete and detailed information may be found in Pask (1979). From this summary, however, it is possible to isolate five important points of departure from other approaches to knowledge representation.

1. First, THOUGHTSTICKER represents the meaning of knowledge as what is agreed between conversational participants (who may be two distinct perspectives in the same person). These agreements are observable, public knowables insofar that their understanding can be demonstrated by participants to each other by observing each other as they manipulate models of the agreements in some suitable modeling environment. This approach is quite different from the conventional one in AI and psychology (with the particularly notable exception of Gestaltism) in which knowledge is viewed as a reflection of the objects and their relationships that are presumed to exist in an external world. In this latter view, the validity of knowledge depends on the ability of the world to remain unchanged by our attempts to describe it,

and unconnected to us in the face of our attempts to connect with it.

2. This leads to the second point, which is that the emphasis in THOUGHTSTICKER is on a logic of coherence and distinction rather than on a more familiar logic of truth and falsehood. In a world of agreement it is appropriate to determine inconsistency rather than falsehood, and when it is found, to offer ways to resolve it. Furthermore, it is precisely the detection and resolution of conflict that lead to the creation of new perspectives. By contrast, in a world of facts and assertions about the way the world "actually" is, irrespective of one's observations of it, it is natural to determine the truth or falsehood of one's knowledge. In this latter view the goal is never to genuinely resolve conflict, but to avoid it by sweeping away the inaccuracies and artifacts produced by "unscientific methods" or "bad experimental design" until what is left is the "true picture."

3. The insistence in THOUGHTSTICKER that what is represented is a public concept is also an important point of departure from other sorts of representational systems. Here the key notion is that what is represented is *shared* meaning. This gives rise to the notion that the meaning of concepts cannot be represented by their location with respect to their subsets and supersets. To an important extent, they receive their meaning from the sum total of all the perspectives that contribute to it. A concept is not an object but a repertoire of the ways it is understood. A concept is best represented, then, not as a node in a hierarchy, for example, as in semantic net representations, but as an entity with multiple profiles that are derivable from many different directions.

4. Related to the last point is the somewhat radical notion embodied in THOUGHTSTICKER that there is no place for specifying which concepts are more primitive than others in any absolute sense. The primitivity of a concept is always in relation to the circumstances of its use and its generation.

5. Finally, THOUGHTSTICKER incorporates, by philosophical design, the notion that whatever is represented is perturbable and beholdable by new authors. One of the bugbears of knowledge engineering in AI is the difficulty encountered in attempting to make the accounts of two different experts agree. This has even led to expert systems sources being deliberately restricted to one

to avoid (not resolve) the difficulty. THOUGHTSTICKER's logic is designed precisely to compute the extent to which two or more people do agree, and in the event of disagreement, to provide an environment in which the conflicts can be explored and resolved, and the representation changed and enriched by the result.

Current Uses of THOUGHTSTICKER

The microcomputer implementation of THOUGHTSTICKER is currently being used and developed at Concordia University by Gordon Pask. This use is primarily aimed at representing subject matters for the CASTE tutorial system discussed next. In addition, however, THOUGHTSTICKER is being investigated as an interface to ABL/W4, a software design environment invented by W. Jaworski. This work is proceeding in partnership among Pask, Jaworski, Morton, and Small. The same microcomputer version of THOUGHTSTICKER is also available to the U.S. Army Research Institute, where its relevance is being investigated, with CASTE, for learning strategy research and as an authoring system as part of an advanced tutorial technology for embedded training systems.

The Symbolics 3600 Lisp Machine version of THOUGHT-STICKER is currently one of the experimental conversational modeling systems under investigation at the Admiralty Research Establishment in Teddington, England. As such, it forms part of a work program designed to construct an intelligent support system (Gregory & Sheppard, 1981; Gregory, 1982; Sheppard, 1982) whose essential feature is that of sensitivity to the operational and learning styles of its users. This sensitivity (manifest as a user modeling capacity) is used by the system to select (and possibly design) either job aiding or learning support that is specifically tailored to the user and the situation he or she is in. The image of an intelligent support system requires a rather different kind of artificial intelligence than is being worked on for the most part elsewhere. In particular, such a system functions as a communications medium between current and previous users, bringing them into coherence and detecting conflict, rather than as a closed, imperturbable, answer-giving expert system of the MYCIN (Shortliffe, 1974) kind.

CASTE

Overview

CASTE is an acronym for *c*ource *a*ssembly *s*ystem and *t*utorial *e*nvironment. It is a facility for promoting learning in which students are modeled in terms of their learning style, are presented new information in a way that is consistent with their style and with what is currently understood, and which insists on the demonstration of student understanding via the appropriate manipulation of a model in a modeling facility. The earliest and most complete implementation of CASTE was constructed in England in 1972 and used in a number of schools for a variety of subject matters, including probability theory, mathematics, genetics, chemistry, physics, and history. The implementation was a mixture of electronic and mechanical subsystems that in 1974 was converted into a portable CASTE-type system called INTUITION (Pask, 1974). More recently, fully computer-based prototype CASTE systems have been produced on a multiple Apple microcomputer system, running compiled, extended Microsoft BASIC, and on the Symbolics 3600 Lisp Machine running ZetaLisp.

Tutorial Learning

History

CASTE is a set of techniques implemented as software, designed to exteriorize, and hence observe, the process of learning as a conversation between the student and her- or himself, moderated by a tutor. In some ways it parallels the Piagetian method[5] in that it does not rigidly structure or determine the way in which any individual learns about a subject matter, academic or otherwise. However, unlike the Piagetian school of thought, the research has always been aimed at obtaining more rigorously interpretable data than is possible to extract from the dialogue with even the most expert interviewer.

Work on learning strategies was begun by Gordon Pask in the 1950s with respect to the teaching of keyboard skills and the measurement of the levels of uncertainty (confusion) tolerable to the student. These early research projects led to the development of

SAKI, the Self Adaptive Keyboard Instructor (Pask, 1958, 1982) for the teaching of touch typing. In the course of this research, certain interesting and consistent observations were made. Not only was there a distinct polarity in the amount of uncertainty tolerable to students, but the students appeared to be learning the skill in two quite dissimilar ways. In one case, the students appeared to be learning the keyboard layout letter by letter and then group sets of keys together until a total picture emerged. In the other case, students were clumping certain keys together from the start. The students with low tolerance of uncertainty tended to fall into the first (step-by-step) category of learning, whereas those with high tolerance tended to fall into the second (clumping) category.

These findings were subsequently confirmed by a series of experiments that used an entirely different subject matter involving the learning of a complex taxonomy. From these studies emerged a clear indication of two main learning strategies:

1. Serialists were characterized by their tendency to follow a step-by-step learning procedure, concentrating on simple, closely defined hypotheses relating to one topic at a time. At the extreme, this could lead to the pathology of "improvidence"—failing to see or (mis-)using analogies that would lead to shortcuts in the learning.
2. Holists tended to form more complex hypotheses involving several topics at once. Further analysis made it clear that holists subdivided into:
   • Irredundant holists, who made effective use of analogies in their explanations
   • Redundant holists, who made much wider use of analogy to the point of highly personalized invention
   In the extreme, exclusive use of a holist strategy could lead to the pathology of "globe-trotting" in which analogies are invented and used to a point where they interfere with the recall of the subject matter.

It was argued (Pask, 1977) that these strategies were manifestations of psychologically more fundamental learning styles: operation learning (manifesting in a serialist strategy) and comprehension learning (holist strategy). As extreme styles, they each represented an incomplete approach, and hence a pathology. Between these, however, was the versatile learner who was able to operate on the subject matter in either way as appropriate to produce effective learning.

It followed that students who favored one learning style were much more dependent on the nature of the subject matter representation than those who were versatile. Specifically, it was found that when students' learning styles were deliberately mismatched with subject matter representation, their learning performances were significantly impaired. While "matched" students had retained an average of 80 percent of the material six weeks after the experiment, the "mismatched" students' average was only 10 percent. The method of testing used in all these studies was called "Teachback," and it evolved out of the difficulties of establishing an "understanding" in the strict sense of conversation theory. While multiple choice and "fill in the blanks" type testing had been ruled out from the start as measures of understanding, it had still been noted that particularly articulate students who did not fully understand a topic could nevertheless convincingly talk around the early versions of the test technique. In the fully evolved form of Teachback, no topic can be said to be understood until the student can explain an example of the topic to the experimenter, and then explain how this model was derived from the original material. A carbon copy of the experimenter's examples was automatically disallowed. Students were required to demonstrate understanding of a topic by being able to "do" that topic—modeling or demonstrating in some sense that was sufficient to allow the experimenter (tutor) to agree that it was understood.

In the computer-based version of CASTE, the student demonstrates understanding most conveniently by manipulating a software model. Understanding may also be demonstrated by asking the student to play a particular role, for example. Any manipulation of the model via paddles, light pen, or typed action that gives the desired result as required to demonstrate understanding would be acceptable by CASTE. Thus, a relatively liberal dialogue is maintained between tutor and student in which individual variations are incorporated into a framework that ensures learning has taken place. One of the ways that CASTE is unique is that, unlike other computer-aided learning systems, a strict definition of understanding is maintained as the basis for tutoring.

Operations

At the core of the system is a data structure represented as an entailment mesh of topics (alias, public concepts) produced by THOUGHTSTICKER. Each topic in this mesh is associated with a description and its relations to other topic descriptions and a model, for example, a software program.

The learner is at liberty to select any topic as a focus of interest and attention. This becomes the aim topic. Once an aim topic has been established, there are several things that might be done next, depending on the needs and preferences of the student. For example, if the student is a serialist, the entailment mesh could be pruned and selpruned (see above) under the aim topic. The Selprune that included most topics already understood would be chosen, and learning subgoals would be set up and tutored by the system until the aim topic could be meaningfully presented. On the other hand, if the student had been diagnosed by CASTE as a holist, the student might receive tutorial material on the aim topic at once. In either case, whichever topic is actually selected, the student receives a description in text and, where appropriate, in pictorial form, and is asked to demonstrate understanding by explaining it in terms of related topics. If the explanation, based on an example of the topic is successful, then the topic is marked as understood by CASTE. In other words, the topic is marked understood if the student can produce an example of the topic as well as its reproduction from topics with which it is related. If the topic cannot be demonstrated to have been understood, then a different learning route (Selprune) may be selected by CASTE, or a different demonstration of the topic given, or a different aim topic selected altogether by the student or system.

There are numerous refinements of this procedure and different emphases have been selected for investigation with more recent versions of CASTE. Some of these emphases have included creating the facility for the system to make informed selections of new aim topics based on what the student currently understands and experimenting with the pruning of topic relations through analogies. Learning through an analogy in CASTE is a little like encountering a discontinuity in the mesh. It may seem but a short "distance" between one topic and another to which it is analogously related; however, it may be a very long "conceptual distance" between the same two topics when only coherent relations of entailment are considered. It is also conceivable, of course, for two topics to be entirely unrelated except by analogy.

By way of summary of our description of CASTE, drawn below are some comparisons and contrasts between this computer-based learning system and other, more traditional approaches to computer-aided instruction (CAI).

1. *Origins and focus.* CAI has tended to be technology-driven, concerned with an approach to learning that fits in with what is easy for computers to (be made to) do. This is where multiple choice/fill-in-the-blanks testing and one-thing-at-a-time presentation come from. By contrast, the development of CASTE has been motivated by such questions of the form

- How do people learn?
- How do people transfer and incorporate meaning?
- What is it to understand?
- How can computers help?

2. *Course design.* CAI has concentrated on a linearization of its subject matter, preordering it from what is deemed simple to what is deemed complex. CASTE has concentrated on ensuring the consistency of the subject matter. Sequencing the material and determining what is difficult is left for the student to decide.

3. *Student progress.* In CAI, the paths through the subject matter are predefined and the student's location on a path is defined by a test-branch-test procedure. In CASTE, the student has complete freedom to explore and many different ways to learn about any one topic. Furthermore, partial learning is emphasized in CASTE, so that understanding a topic just one way out of many represented is sufficient to be judged as understanding, even though that understanding is yet to become enriched.

4. *Student model.* In CAI, the model of the student is an implicit one, embodied in the way the author structures the subject matter. The model is expressed in terms of the errors the student is anticipated to make and in the branching that is authored to remedy them. This also means that the model is diagnostic; the author presumes to be able to know what misconceptions the student will have and how best to correct them. In CASTE, the system's model is expressed in terms of the extent of current student understanding as demonstrated by the student's successful manipulation of topic-models. The

extent of the student's understanding is equivalent to the extent that the system and the student share agreement over the meaning of the topics in the mesh. CASTE uses its model of the student to select the currently best understood topics to explain the least understood. There is no diagnosis of error in CASTE. Instead, a growing, shared vocabulary is used to explain student-determined difficulties, interpreted in CASTE as agreements yet to be established.

5. *Modeling facilities.* These are largely left out of CAI systems. Notable exceptions are certain of the intelligent tutorial systems that often use an explicit simulation as a modeling facility (Burton & Brown, 1979; Goldstein, 1979; Brown, Burton, & de Kleer, 1981; Sleeman, 1982). Conversation theory, which underlies CASTE, demands a manipulatable environment in which to question, discover, and demonstrate the meaning of topics.

6. *Measuring understanding.* This is confined in CAI to relatively shallow measures, such as multiple choice tests. CASTE requires a Teachback facility in which understanding must be demonstrated via the novel manipulation of a topic model by the student. In this way, agreements about what topics mean can be exteriorized as the observables of tutorial conversations.

Current Uses of CASTE

The multiple Apple microcomputer configuration of CASTE is being extended and developed at Concordia University by Gordon Pask. One particular issue of immediate concern relates to the enrichment of CASTE's modeling facilities via videodisc technology. Another relates to the system's tolerance of, and enrichment by, students who become effective model manipulators, but whose representations may be qualitatively different from the expert representation(s) used by CASTE to teach the same students.

A previous incarnation of CASTE, again running in compiled Microsoft BASIC but utilizing only one Apple microcomputer, is being used at the U.S. Army Research Institute to investigate its potential when applied to the training of a visual recognition task. In addition, an experiment is in progress to test certain features of the same system with respect to learning retention of a complex, academic subject matter.

The Symbolics Lisp Machine version of CASTE is currently being evaluated for its contribution to the Admiralty Research Establishment's intelligent (tutorial) support system program.

TEAM DECISION SYSTEM

Overview

The team decision system (TDS) is a simulation of some of the significant features of command, control, and communication, including the assignment of responsibility, planning, and the often adverse consequences of overkill actions that disrupt the environment. The importance of these features and issues is that they are all germane to the task of decision making in a complex environment.

There have been two implementations of the TDS, both the U.S. Army Research Institute. The first was implemented on a mix of computing machinery, in a mix of LISP, BASIC, and Assembly languages, and was completed in 1979. The second is written in Apple Pascal and implemented on a network of Apple microcomputers, communicating through a Corvus hard disk.

A Simulation Environment

The central ideas of the TDS are these: Each TDS commander has charge of at least two spaceships. Each ship is controlled by a separate computer and acts in a shared environment of star bases connected by trade routes. The economies of the star bases are measured in terms of energy units and are maintained by the exchange of trading barges along the routes. The base economies would flourish by trade but, at the start of a simulation, the universe is invaded by marauders—mobile objects that move to trade routes and destroy barges. As a result, commanders must act in a mercenary way to eliminate the marauders or at least to minimize the damage done by them.

The movement and countermarauder activity of ships are controlled by commander-specified tactics (programs, but expressed in tactical terms) that, unless the commander intervenes, will act autonomously, reexecuting whatever they did last. A commander is required to assign tactical responsibility and to divide attention between the ships and the star bases. Action designed by the commander to eliminate marauders that turns out to be excessive for the situation casues a "hole" in the space of the simulation that will block the navigation of ships, or if the space is punctured on a trading route, will impede the passage of trading barges. Either occurrence is a nuisance, but the blockage of a trade route has an adverse effect on one or more base economies so serious that the hole must be repaired. Repairs call for cooperative action between the ships and require the expenditure of an amount of energy.

The point of the simulation is that it exteriorizes the decision making of the commanders by ensuring that everything a commander does, or plans to do, is done through one or more of the spaceships he or she commands. Tactics may be sequences of if-then-else statements of any length and may call for the execution of a further tactic. Unconditional tactics are also possible by issuing direct orders to spaceships. It is important to emphasize that tactics govern information retrieval as well as operations, such as maneuvering, destroying marauders, docking with star bases, repairing, and so on. Furthermore, a tactic in one ship may call for another tactic in the same ship or in a different one.

Current Uses of TDS

TDS has realistic features that are seldom present in a simulation. An object or action or complex of actions in TDS may be usefully considered as a public concept; if so, TDS functions as a modeling facility. As a modeling facility, TDS may be used with CASTE.[6] In this case, CASTE may demonstrate tactics to the student via TDS, and the student may demonstrate understanding via tactic construction from differently initialized states of the environment.

As well as a modeling facility, TDS may also be used in place of an Lp author by connecting it with THOUGHTSTICKER. Here THOUGHTSTICKER would adopt input from TDS that is necessarily restricted to actions and objects that are part of the TDS environment; they could not include commanders' beliefs and forecasts, for example. The advantage of such a connection is that it allows operational models to be developed that are essentially models of the tacticians generating the tactics in TDS. The importance of this is that representations of tactical behavior (that is, sequences of commands) expressed as public concepts designating executable models could be produced automatically through THOUGHTSTICKER. The executable entailment mesh that results could be set to take over from the commander in the event of prespecified emergency conditions to restore the status quo. Not only would the sequence of activities be determined by pruning and selpruning under the desired goal state but the Selprune would be highly pertinent to the commander's preferred command style since the structure was derived from the commander in the first place.

Alternatively, a mesh automatically produced in this way could be used by the commander that generated it to become better aware, and hence to evaluate his or her own tactical performance, or to become aware of process conflicts in decision making. These ideas are important to the notion of intelligent decision-making support. The second version of the TDS, a prototype, is running at Concordia University and at the U.S. Army Research Institute.

SUMMARY

This chapter has presented the fundamentals of conversation theory, together with descriptions and discussion of three computer systems whose roles and interfaces have been constructed from it. The construction of these systems has been possible because conversation theory has a computer-implementable dual called Lp, a protolanguage, with the capacity to express and manipulate agreements and the process of their emergence between conversational participants.

THOUGHTSTICKER is a suite of computer programs that operationalizes Lp and functions as a knowledge acquisition and representation system. CASTE is a tutorial system that delivers entailment meshes produced through THOUGHTSTICKER to students to match the presentation of material with individual learning styles and with the extent to which the material is already understood. Finally, the team decision system (TDS) is a simulation environment specifically designed to exteriorize the decision-making behavior of tactical commanders. If the TDS is connected to THOUGHTSTICKER, the represented behavior is imaged as Lp expressions and the commanders as authors. The result is an executable mesh that may be used by its author to study or aid his or her own decision making. Alternatively, meshes produced by commanders may be loaded into CASTE and then connected to the TDS that now will be able to function as a modeling facility for demonstrations of topics by both systems and student.

All three systems were brought into existence by conceiving of the process of interpersonal communication (between people) and intrapersonal communication (between different perspectives in the same person, that is, thought) as essentially the same conversational process. In this view, the outcomes of conversation are agreements over understandings, rendered observable by modeling them as executable processes in a modeling facility.

Conversational systems focus on how an understanding of events and situations may become shared between user and system, on how the incorporation of a new event or perspective permanently changes the structure of understanding so that even "identical" events may be perceived differently on successive occasions, and on how the process of sharing understanding may give rise to innovation. As such, conversational systems have special import for the enterprise of knowledge representation for intelligent tutorial and intelligent operational support. The role of the computer is not that of the instructor or the expert but the understander and facilitator; it is not the loudspeaker of the way things are but the amplifier that shows us the possibilities that arise when we connect ourselves with the world in particular ways. Conversational systems do not confront us with information but with the way information changes us, focusing and refocusing our awareness. According to conversation theory, it is the very process of conversation that forces us into consciousness, and for any domain of inquiry, it is the role of conversational systems to amplify, elucidate, and show us the implications of that process in action.

ACKNOWLEDGMENTS AND NOTES

The authors gratefully acknowledge the incorporation in this chapter of some original material on the history of CASTE written by Paul Pangaro.

1. Work on conversation theory and Lp has been supported over the last 15 years by the Social Science Research Council (London), the U.S. Army Research

Institute for the Behavioral and Social Sciences (Washington, D.C.), and the Applied Psychology Unit of the Admiralty Research Establishment (Teddington, England).

2. Here topic-maps should be understood to contain no inherent hierarchical or directional structure.

3. For the Admiralty Research Establishment, Teddington, England, and the U.S. Army Research Institute, Washington, D.C., respectively.

4. For the Admiralty Research Establishment, Teddington, England.

5. Piaget and his associates perfected the technique of highly structured interviews between a trained experimenter/interviewer and child to establish the ages at which some forms of thought occur. The Piagetian interviews are usually, but not always, based on some concrete object around which the conversation is structured. For example, two vessels of different shapes, both containing the same volume of water, might be used to see if a child is capable of abstracting the concept of conservation of volume of fluid.

6. The uses of TDS described in this chapter are all set in the future. The interconnections between TDS and CASTE and THOUGHTSTICKER do not exist at the time of writing and therefore are presented as ideas rather than as implementations for which detailed specifications exist.

REFERENCES

Bartlett, F. C. (1932). *Remembering.* Cambridge: Cambridge University Press.

Brown, J. S., Burton, R. R., & de Kleer, J. (1981). Knowledge engineering and pedagogical techniques in the SOPHIE I, II, & III (Cognitive and Instructional Sciences Tech. Rep.). In D. Sleeman & J. S. Brown (Eds.), *Intelligent tutoring systems.* New York: Academic Press.

Burton, R. R., & Brown, J. S. (1979). An investigation of computer coaching for informal learning activities. *International Journal of Man-Machine Studies, 11,* 5–24.

Foerster, H. von. (1960). On self-organizing systems and their environments. In M. C. Yovitz & S. Cameron (Eds.), *Self organizing systems.* New York: Pergamon Press.

Foerster, H. von. (1974). *The cybernetics of cybernetics.* Urbana: University of Illinois.

Gauld, A., & Shotter, J. (1977). *Human action and its psychological investigation.* London: Routledge & Kegan Paul.

Glanville, R. (1979). The form of cybernetics—Whitening the black box. In *Proceedings of the Twenty-fourth Society for General Systems Research Annual Meeting*. Houston 1979. Louisville, KY: Society for General Systems Research.

Glanville, R. (1982). Inside every white box there are two black boxes trying to get out. *Behavioral Science, 27*, p. 1-11.

Goldstein, I. P. (1979). The genetic graph: A representation for the evolution of procedural knowledge. *International Journal of Man-Machine Studies, 11*, 51-77.

Gregory, D. (1982). What's a conversation between friends? In *Proceedings of MOD Seminar on the Application of Machine Intelligence to Defence Systems*.

Gregory, D., & Sheppard, C. (1981). Work programme and rationale: Applied Psychology Unit Man Computer Studies Section. In *The Technical Cooperation Program: Technical Panel UTP-2* (Training Technology), paper on artificial intelligence.

Kelly, G. (1955). *The psychology of personal constructs* (Vols. 1, 2). New York: Norton.

Maturana, H. R. (1970). *The Biology of cognition* (Biol. Computer Lab. Res. Rep. 9.0). Urbana: University of Illinois.

Maturana, H. R. (1977). Biology of language. In R. W. Rieber (Ed.), *The neuropsychology of language*. New York: Plenum Press.

Pask, G. (July, 1958). Electronic keyboard teaching machines. *Journal of the National Association for Education and Commerce*. Reprinted in R. Glaser & A. Lumsdaine (Eds.) (1960). *Teaching machines and programmed learning* (Vol. 1, pp. 336-349). Washington, DC: National Education Association.

Pask, G. (1974). *Final report on SSRC research programme HR 2371/1* (Vols. I & II). Richmond, Surrey, England: System Research.

Pask, G. (1976). *Conversation theory: Applications in education and epistemology*. Amsterdam: Elsevier.

Pask, G. (1977). *Third progress report on SSRC research programme HR 2708*. Richmond, Surrey, England: System Research.

Pask, G. (1979). *A protolanguage (Lp: The THOUGHTSTICKER language).* Woodville Ho., Richmond, Surrey, England: System Research.

Pask, G. (1980). Developments in conversation theory, Part I. *International Journal of Man-Machine Studies, 13*, 357-411.

Pask, G. (1982). SAKI: Twenty-five years of adaptive training into the microprocessor era. *International Journal of Man-Machine Studies, 17*, 69-74.

Pask, G., Kallikourdis, D., & Scott, B. C. E. (1975). The representation of knowables. *International Journal of Man-Machine Studies, 7*, 15-134.

Pask, G., & Scott, B. C. E. (1973). CASTE: A system for exhibiting learning strategies and regulating uncertainty. *International Journal of Man-Machine Studies, 5*, 17-52.

Shaw, M. J. (1980). *On becoming a personal scientist.* London: Academic Press.

Sheppard, C. (1982). Beyond expert systems. In *Proceedings of MOD Seminar on the Application of Machine Intelligence to Defence Systems.*

Shortliffe, E. H. (1974). MYCIN: A rule-based computer program for advising physicians regarding antimicrobial therapy selection (Memo AIM-251). Stanford, CA: AI Laboratory, Stanford University.

Sleeman, D. H. (1982). Inferring (mal) rules from pupils' protocols. In *Proceedings ECAI-82: 1982 European conference on artificial intelligence*, Orsay, France.

Taylor, C. (1971). Interpretation and the sciences of man. *Review of Metraphysics, 25*, 3-51.

Zukav, G. (1979). *The dancing Wu Li masters: An overview of the new physics.* New York: Bantam.

6

KNOWLEDGE-BASED EXPERT SYSTEMS

Dana S. Nau

ARTIFICIAL INTELLIGENCE

Artificial intelligence (AI) is that area of computer science whose goal is to develop computer systems that exhibit behavior we would call intelligent. AI is receiving a great deal of publicity lately, and there are a number of misconceptions about its capabilities and limitations expressed in comments similar to the following:

- "I think computers are getting too intelligent, and I'm afraid they might get out of control."
- "Great! Where can I find an expert computer program to do X for me?"
- "I don't think that computers can ever be intelligent, because they can only do exactly what we call them to do."

This chapter is intended to clear up such misconceptions by providing a tutorial on a subfield of AI known as knowledge-based computing or expert computer systems.

AI includes several areas of research, some of which are listed below:

Research is being done on computer programs that can understand "natural" languages (that is, human languages, as opposed to computer languages).

Work is being done on computer programs for such perceptual tasks as speech understanding and computer visions.

Robotics, which overlaps research in the field of mechanical engineering, finds application in automated manufacturing and assembly. Work is also being done on integrating vision and robotics.

A number of problem-solving methods, some general, some specific, find application in many of the other areas of SI listed here. Work has been done on problem-solving techniques for game playing, automated program construction, theorem proving, trial and error search, and commonsense problem solving.

Computer learning is one of the most difficult tasks being explored. Various techniques are being examined for getting computers to learn how to recognize something, how to play a game, or how to synthesize concepts or techniques for use in problem solving.

Although much AI research is directed toward developing artificial intelligence using whatever techniques seem feasible, some researchers are doing research specifically on emulating the thought processes carried out by humans in solving various problems. This is called cognitive modeling.

An expert computer system is a computer system that uses a combination of domain-independent and domain-specific problem-solving knowledge to achieve a high level of performance in an area that would normally require a human expert. Because of their potential applicability to a wide variety of problems, expert computer systems are currently of interest to researchers in many different areas of academia, industry, and government.

Two Myths About AI

Expert computer systems will be discussed in more detail in the following pages, but let us first discuss the three reactions mentioned at the beginning of the chapter. These reactions arise from two common myths about AI.

The first myth is that highly intelligent computers and computer programs already exist. This is simply not true. Although artificial intelligence has made some significant advances lately, it will be a long time before machines approach the thinking capabilities of human beings. The current state of affairs is illustrated in Figure 6.1.

FIGURE 6.1. Current Intelligence in Humans and Machines.

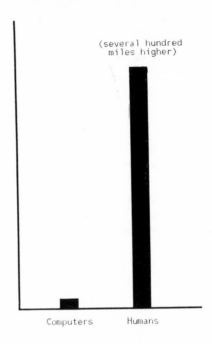

The second myth is that computers can never be very intelligent because they can "only do what we tell them to do." This is not true either. There are ways to program computers to do things that are not explicitly told to them, and expert computer systems techniques are one such way.

Expert Computer Systems

Table 6.1 contains a very brief list of expert computer systems for various problem domains that illustrates the range of applicability of expert computer systems. In addition, several computer systems and languages have been developed to provide tools for creating expert systems for various problem domains. These systems include Age (Newell & Simon, 1963; Aiello & Nii, 1979), Ars (Stallman & Sussman, 1977), Emycin (Melle, 1979), Expert (Weiss, Kulikowski, Amarel, & Safir, 1979), Hearsay-III (Erman, London, & Fickas, 1981), KAS (Hayes-Roth, Waterman, & Lenat, 1983), KMS (Reggia, 1981),

TABLE 6.1. Some Existing Expert Systems

System Name	Application	Comments	References
Ace	Prediction of problems in telephone lines	In use by AT&T	Stolfo & Vesondo (1983)
AQ11	Diagnosis of plant diseases	Can synthesize its own rules; has sometimes produced rules better than those proposed by experts	Chilausky, Jacobsen, & Michalski (1976)
Casnet	Diagnosis and treatment of glaucoma		Weiss et al. (1978)
Centaur	Interpretation of pulmonary (lung) function tests	Successor to Puff	Aikins (1980)
Dendral	Hypothesizing molecular structure from mass spectrograms	Has discovered new molecules	Buchanan & Feigenbaum (1978)
Dipmeter Advisor	Oil exploration	In use by Schlumberger	Davis et al. (1981)
EL	Analyzing electrical circuits		Stallman & Sussman (1977)
No name	Diagnosis of abdominal pain	Outperforms physicians	de Dombal (1975)
E	Diagnosis of strokes	Implemented using KMS; outperforms physicians	Zagoria & Reggia (1983)
Internist	Diagnosis in internal medicine	One of the largest knowledge bases of any expert computer system	Pople (1977)
Macsyma	Mathematical formula manipulation		Moses (1971)
MDX	Diagnosis of liver disorders		Chandrasekaran et al. (1979)
Molgen	Planning experiments in molecular genetics		Martin et al. (1977)
Mycin	Diagnosis and treatment of infectious diseases		Davis, Buchanan, & Shortliffe (1977)
Prospector	Mineral exploration	Has discovered new ore deposits	Hart, Duda, & Einaudi (1978)
Puff	Interpretation of pulmonary (lung) function tests	Implemented using Emycin	Osborn et al. (1979)
TIA	Treatment of transient ischemic attacks	Implemented using KMS	Reggia et al. (1984)
VM	Monitoring a patient's breathing after surgery		Fagan (1980)
XCON	Configuring computers	Outperforms technicians; in use by Digital Equipment Corporation	McDermott & Steele (1981)

OPS5 (Forgy, 1980), RLL (Greiner & Lenat, 1980), and Rosie (Fain, Hayes-Roth, Sowizral, & Waterman, 1982). Such systems typically provide formats or languages for representing both procedural knowledge and declarative knowledge, control structures for manipulating this knowledge, and interfaces for interaction with human users.

Earlier we characterized an expert computer system as one that achieves a high level of performance in an area that normally requires a human expert. From this characterization it may not be obvious why a computer system for medical diagnosis qualifies as an expert computer system and why a computer system for a task such as payroll accounting does not. After all, both tasks, if done manually, require a highly trained human being. To understand the difference, one must examine the nature of human problem solving.

The problems that human beings can solve can be roughly divided into two classes. The first class consists of the problems that we can solve that we can also explain how to solve. Examples include adding columns of numbers, sorting arrays of numbers, and payroll accounting. If we can explain exactly how to solve a problem, an ordinary computer program can be written to solve the problem.

There are also problems that humans can solve but cannot explain how to solve. For example, each of us can recognize the faces of our various colleagues and friends, but yet we cannot describe them to others in such a way that others are able to recognize them. As another example, physicians go to medical school for many years to learn how to make medical diagnoses, but yet at no time are they taught explicitly how to diagnose medical cases. Instead, they learn it through experience. In fact, internships after completing medical school are designed to generate additional experience.

Problems that humans can solve but cannot explain how to solve are possible candidates for solution using AI techniques. One set of AI techniques that is sometimes useful includes the techniques used in expert computer systems. These incorporate ways to capture expert knowledge to put it into a knowledge base and make use of it in problem solving.

Capturing Expert Knowledge

An expert who is given a specific problem in his or her domain of expertise will reach a specific conclusion. In some problem domains the expert may be able to explain how that specific conclusion was reached. For example, a given expert may produce an argument such as the following: "If *a* were true, then this would provide very strong evidence that *b* were true. Thus I checked to see whether *a* were true and concluded that it probably was, since *c* and *d* were present." From this argument one may extract the following two rules of inference: If *a* THEN conclude *b* (certainty = 0.9) and If *c* and *d* THEN conclude *a* (certainty = 0.7), where "very strong evidence" has been translated into "certainty = 0.9" and "probably" has been translated into "certainty = 0.7."

The following is a similar kind of rule taken from an existing medical expert system (Reggia, Pula, Price, & Perricone, 1980):

```
IF      serum K + = low
        and myotonia = absent
        and serum T4 = high
THEN  paralysis type = thyrotoxic (0.8)
        and paralysis type = hypokalemic (0.2)
```

However, useful knowledge cannot always be extracted from experts in this way. For example, talented computer programmers and chess players have worked for many years designing computer programs to play chess, but yet the most successful chess-playing computer programs operate in ways very different from the way human chess players play chess (Biermann, 1978; Robinson, 1979; Truscott, 1979). Even when useful knowledge can be gotten from experts and encoded as rules, it still does not tell exactly what to do in a given situation, for many of the rules may be applicable at once. Thus, some mechanism is necessary to decide which rules to apply and which paths of inference to follow in certain situations. This mechanism usually involves a trial and error search.

In conventional computer programs, there are two levels of operation: data and program. The program is an encoding of the knowledge necessary to solve problems in some domain, and the data are a representation of the specific problem to be solved. Expert computer systems, because of the rules and the necessity of searching around for a solution, are organized in a rather different way. In an expert computer system, there are three levels of operation: data, knowledge base, and control structure. The data are a representation of the specific problem to be solved. The knowledge base, which usually consists of rules similar to the examples above, encodes problem-solving knowledge relevant to the domain of expertise of the expert computer system. The control structure is a computer program that encodes some fairly general problem-solving knowledge. It decides which rules to apply if more than one rule is applicable at a given time, when (or whether) to backtrack if the path being explored seems unproductive, and so forth.

A Simple Example

The following example was developed by James Reggia at the University of Maryland. Suppose a personal robot is instructed to do our household chores. In looking through our house one morning, we find that it is infested with bugs. The task is to program the robot to get rid of the bugs. The problem is that there are many different kinds of bugs, and the robot should take different actions, depending on what bugs it finds. Ticks and Japanese beetles, for example, are harmful and should be killed. Spiders, ladybugs, and crickets are benign and should simply be moved outside. Praying mantises are beneficial bugs to have in the garden because they will eat other bugs that might hurt the plants. Thus, they should be moved to the solarium and encouraged to stay there. Table 6.2 contains a simple taxonomy of the bugs.

The following rules can be used to tell which class a bug is in (arachnid or insect):

TABLE 6.2. A Simple Taxonomy

Class	Type	Name	Characteristics
Arachnid		Spider	Benign
		Tick	Harmful
Insect	Beetle	Ladybug	Benign
		Japanese beetle	Harmful
	Orthoptera	Cricket	Benign
		Praying mantis	Beneficial

C1: IF antennae = 0 and legs = 8 THEN class = arachnid
C2: IF wings = 0 THEN class = arachnid
C3: IF antennae = 2 and legs = 6 THEN class = insect
C4: IF wings ≠ 0 THEN class = insect

If a bug turns out to be an insect, the following rules can be used to tell which type of insect it is (beetle or orthoptera):

T1: IF class = insect and size = small and shape = round THEN
type = beetle
T2: IF class = insect and size ≠ small and shape = elongated THEN
type = orthoptera

The following rules can be used to determine the name of the bug:

N1: IF class = arachnid and leg length = long THEN name = spider
N2: IF class = arachnid and leg length = short THEN name = tick
N3: IF type = beetle and color = orange and black THEN name =
ladybug
N4: IF type = beetle and color = green and black THEN name =
Japanese beetle
N5: IF type = orthoptera and color = black THEN name = cricket
N6: IF type = orthoptera and color = green and size = large THEN
name = praying mantis

Once the identity of the bug has been established the following rules tell what actions to take:

A1: IF (name = spider | name = cricket | name = ladybug) and loca-
tion ≠ outside
THEN first action = grasp bug
and second action = move to outside
and third action = release bug
A2: IF name = Japanese beetle | name = tick
THEN first action = swat bug
and second action = grasp bug
and third action = put in jar
A3: IF name = praying mantis and location ≠ solarium
THEN first action = grasp bug
and second action = move to solarium
and third action = release bug

A4: IF name = praying mantis and location = solarium
   THEN first action = get bug from jar
      and second action = release bug
      and third action = none

The control strategy, which we call Handle-Bugs, is described below. Handle-Bugs uses what is called a goal-driven (or top-down), depth-first (or backtracking) problem-reduction approach.

Step 1. Let G be the goal Handle-Bugs is trying to achieve, and let S be the set of all rules that might be capable of satisfying G. Let R be the first rule in S: (Each clause in the antecedent (the IF part) of R determines a new problem to be solved. For example, in order to determine whether "class = arachnid" is satisfied in rule N1, one must solve the problem of finding out the bug's class. Such a problem is called a subproblem or subgoal.)

Step 2. Let A be the antecedent of R. For each clause C of A, invoke Handle-Bugs recursively with the corresponding problem P as its goal; and if it is found that A cannot be satisfied, then go to step 3. Otherwise, once A has been satisfied, return from Handle-Bugs with the returned value being the consequent (the THEN part) of R.

Step 3. If there are any rules left in G, then let R be the next one. Otherwise, return from Handle-Bugs with the returned value being "failure."

Suppose the robot finds a bug. Then the following actions occur:

1. Handle-Bugs is invoked with the goal of deciding what action to take. There are four rules that might tell what action to take: A1, A2, A3, and A4.
2. First A1 is tried. To satisfy its antecedent, it is necessary to solve two subproblems: finding out the bug's name and the robot's location. The first subgoal is to find out the bug's name. There are six rules that might tell the name: N1 through N6.
3. First N1 is tried. Its antecedent requires finding out the bug's class and its leg length. First the bug's class is checked. There are four rules that might tell the class: C1 through C4.
4. C1 is tried. Its antecedent requires finding out the number of antennae and the number of legs. First subgoal, the number of antennae, is checked. Suppose it is 2. Then the antecedent of C1 cannot be satisfied, since it requires that the number of antennae be 0. Thus C1 is inapplicable.

5. C2 is tried. Its antecedent requires finding out the number of wings the bug has. Suppose the bug has 2 wings. Then the antecedent of C2 is not satisfied, since it requires that the number of wings be 0. Thus C2 is inapplicable.

6. C3 is tried. Its antecedent requires finding out the number of antennae and the number of legs. The number of antennae is already known to be 2. This antecedent is thus satisfied, so the number of legs is checked. Suppose the number is 6. Then the antecedent for C3 is completely satisfied.

7. C3 concludes that the bug is an insect. This solves the subgoal of finding out the bug's class (see number 3 above).

8. The antecedent of N1 cannot be satisfied since it requires that the bug be an arachnid. Thus N1 is not applicable.

9. Rule N2 is tried. Its antecedent requires finding out the bug's class and its leg length. The bug's class is already known to be "insect." This means that N2 is not applicable since it requires that the bug be an arachnid.

10. Rule N3 is tried. Its antecedent requires knowing the bug's type and its color. First the bug's type is checked. Two rules are applicable: T1 and T2.

11. T1 is tried. Its antecedent requires knowing the bug's class, size, and shape. The bug's class is already known to be "insect." Suppose the size is small and the shape is round. Then the antecedent to T1 is satisfied.

12. T1 concludes that the bug is a beetle. This satisfies the subgoal of finding out the bug's type (see number 10 above).

13. The antecedent of N3 is satisfied so far, and no work is begun on the second subgoal relevant to N3: finding out the bug's color. Suppose that the color is orange and black. Then the antecedent of N3 is completely satisfied.

14. N3 concludes that the bug is a ladybug. This satisfies the subgoal of finding out the bug's name (see number 2 above).

15. So far, the antecedent of AI is satisfied, so the second subgoal relevant to AI is investigated: finding out the robot's location. If we suppose that the robot is inside, then the antecedent of AI is completely satisfied.

16. AI concludes that the actions to be performed are to pick up the bug, go outside, and release the bug. The ultimate goal is solved, so Handle-Bug terminates.

This example illustrates the interplay among the three levels of an expert system. In this example, the data consisted of facts such as "color = orange and black" or "type = beetle." The knowledge base consisted of various rules. Often several of them were applicable at once, and the control structure used a goal-directed backtracking search to choose which rules to apply.

There are other types of knowledge bases and control strategies (a control strategy is the particular problem-solving strategy used by the control structure). This example does illustrate the basic method of how some expert computer systems work.

REPRESENTING FACTS

In the last section, the data being manipulated were simple facts of the form "attribute = value." Such simple data structures are adequate for many problem domains, but in some cases more powerful structures are required for representing knowledge. Several approaches are introduced in this section; for more detail, see Mylopoulos (1980), Nilsson (1980), and Winston (1977).

First-Order Logic, Frames, and Semantic Networks

One way to represent declarative knowledge is in statements of first-order logic (FOL). Simple declarative facts can often be represented in FOL as instantiated predicates. A predicate is a function whose possible values are TRUE and FALSE. For example, we might define NEGATIVE(x) to be TRUE if the numeric argument x is negative and FALSE if x is nonnegative. An instantiated predicate is a predicate whose arguments have been given specific values, for example, NEGATIVE(-3). More complicated statements may require more complicated representations, as in the use of

$$(\forall x)(\forall y)\ (R(x, y) \rightarrow R(y, x))$$

for the statement that the relation R is symmetric.

Two other ways of representing declarative knowledge are frames and semantic networks (Minsky, 1975; Nilsson, 1980; Winston, 1977; Schubert, 1976; Findler, 1979). Although frames and semantic networks were developed independently by researchers working on different kinds of problems, they share a number of common elements and both may be thought of as stylized representations of FOL statements. As such, they do not give any more representational power than a simple list of FOL statements, but they have a number of computational and intuitive advantages. Given an object, all the information about the object may be found in the same place, and it is easy to find out information about related objects. In addition, frame systems and semantic networks often allow ways to specify default values for pieces of information about an object when that information is not explicitly given.

Many different variants have been proposed for frame-based knowledge representation, but most of them include the idea of having different types of frames for different types of objects, with fields or slots in each frame to contain the information relevant to that type of frame. For example, a frame for a published paper might be a data structure including slots for the author, the title, the name, volume, and date of the journal in which the paper appeared, as well as the beginning and ending page numbers. To describe a particular paper, a copy of this frame would be created, and the slots would be filled in with the pertinent information about the particular paper being described.

Semantic networks (or semantic nets) are like frames in the sense that the knowledge is organized around the objects being described, but here the objects are represented by nodes in a graph and the relationships among them are represented by labeled arcs. This difference has more to do with the way in which the information is presented to the user than anything else. In practice, the internal computer representation of a semantic network system may be the same as for a frame system.

Example: Representing a Set of Related Facts

Consider the following set of facts:

Al is an electrician.
Al lives in Manassas, Virginia.

These facts can be directly represented in FOL by creating predicates called OCCUPATION and ADDRESS, and writing

OCCUPATION(Al, electrician) & ADDRESS(Al, Manassas, Virginia).

For convenience, we will often omit the occurrences of & and put the predicates on separate lines. Now consider the facts

Al is an electrician.
Al lives in Manassas, Virginia.
Al took a pen from Judy.

"Al" and "Judy" are presumed unambiguously to identify the people they refer to. However, "a pen" could conceivably refer to any of a number of different pens, and we do not know which one. To talk about the pen in FOL, we need an appropriate way to refer to it. One approach is to use an existential quantifier. (Briefly, an existential quantifier is a mathematical way of saying "there exists." For more details, the reader is referred to Nilsson [1980 or 1971]. For specific information on how quantifiers and other logical constructs can be handled using frames and semantic networks, see Nilsson [1980] or Schubert [1976].) This approach would yield the FOL statements

($\exists$x) (ELEMENT-OF(x, pens) & TAKE(Al, x, Judy)
OCCUPATION(Al, electrician)
ADDRESS(Al, Manassas, Virginia)

Interpreted literally, these statements mean

There is an x such that x is a pen and Al took x from Judy.
Al is an electrician.
Al lives in Manassas, Virginia.

Another way is to give the pen a name:

ELEMENT-OF(D, pens)
TAKE(Al, D, Judy)
OCCUPATION(Al, electrician)
ADDRESS(Al, Manassas, Virginia).

The meaning of this is roughly

Al took a pen (call it D) from Judy.
Al is an electrician.
Al lives in Manassas, Virginia.

The name D, which is called a Skolem constant, is slightly different from an ordinary name. If the text later refers to a pen called E, it might well be the same pen as D, because all we know about D is that it was taken by Al from Judy.

To put this information into frames, it is first necessary to decide what kinds of frames to use. Schank (1972, 1975) and Winston (1977) have developed a "theory of conceptual dependency" that, among other things, attempts to represent most events in terms of a small number of primitive actions. Each such primitive action may be represented by a single kind of frame.

For example, Schank's theory would treat certain meanings of "take" and "give" as two examples of the same phenomenon: a change of location. The frame for a change of location is

frame name: _____
frame type: change of location
source: _____
destination: _____
agent: _____
object: _____

where the source is the person or thing from which the object is taken, the destination is the person or thing to which the object is given, and the agent is the one who performs the transfer. Thus, for "give" the agent is the same as the source, and for "take" the agent is the same as the destination.

If we use this approach for the sentences

Al took a pen (call it D) from Judy.
Al is an electrician.
Al lives in Manassas, Virginia.

the result is as follows:

frame name: change1
frame type: change-of-location

source: Judy
destination: Al
agent: Al
object: D
frame name: D
frame type: pen
. . . (various slots pertaining to pens)

frame name: occupation1
frame type: occupation
worker: Al
job: electrician

frame name: address1
frame type: address
addressee: Al
location: Manassas-Virginia

All of the above information can be translated directly back into first-order predicate logic, but the formulas will look somewhat different than before. This time, every predicate is binary, and the first argument to each predicate is the frame name.

ELEMENT-OF (Change1, change-of-location-events)
SOURCE (change1, Judy)
DESTINATION (change1, Al)
AGENT (change1, Al)
OBJECT (change1, D)
ELEMENT-OF (D, pens)
ELEMENT-OF (occupation1, occupation-events)
WORKER (occupation1, Al)
JOB (occupation1 electrician)
ELEMENT-OF (address1, address-events)
ADDRESSEE (address1, Al)
LOCATION (address1, Manassas-Virginia)

Putting this information into a semantic net would create a structure similar to that shown in Figure 6.2.

Several computer languages have been developed to provide ways to manipulate frames and semantic nets. Examples are KRL (Bobrow

FIGURE 6.2. A Simple Semantic Net.

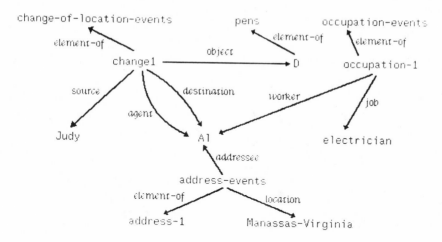

& Winograd, 1977), FRL (Goldstein & Papert, 1977), NETL (Fahl-man, 1979), and KLONE (Brachman, 1979).

CONTROL STRATEGIES FOR RULE-BASED SYSTEMS

As stated earlier, expert computer systems are composed of three different levels: control structure, knowledge base, and data. In most, but not all, expert computer systems, the knowledge base is composed of rules or operators, in which case the expert computer system is called a rule-based system. These rules normally consist of two parts: a "condition" part and an "action" part (the IF and THEN parts, respectively, of the rules in the bug example).

Most control strategies for rule-based systems involve search, but there are different ways this search can be done. Several different approaches are described in this section.

State-Space Search

To describe various search strategies, it will be useful to consider a simple puzzle called the 15-puzzle. The 15-puzzle consists of a square frame containing 15 square tiles and a square hole. The tiles are numbered from 1 to 15, and may be moved around by moving a tile into the hole if the tile and hole are adjacent. The goal is to get the squares in order, as depicted in Figure 6.3.

FIGURE 6.3. The 15-puzzle.

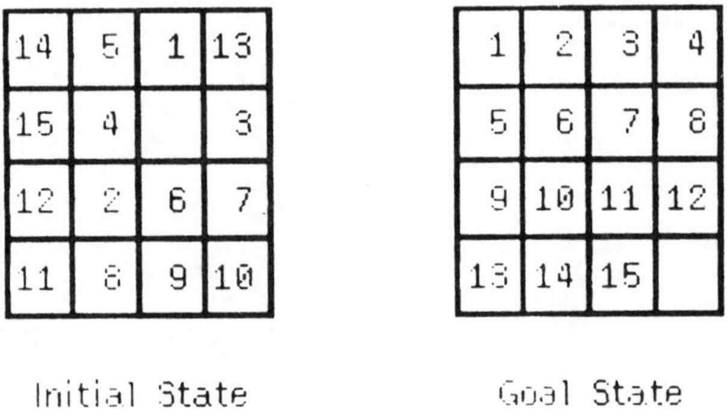

14	5	1	13
15	4		3
12	2	6	7
11	8	9	10

1	2	3	4
5	6	7	8
9	10	11	12
13	14	15	

Initial State   Goal State

The various possible moves can be represented by the following set of operators:

D1: IF tile 1 is above the hole THEN move tile 1 down
L1: IF tile 1 is to the left of the hole THEN move tile 1 to the right
R1: IF tile 1 is to the right of the hole THEN move tile 1 to the left
U1: IF tile 1 is below the hole THEN move tile 1 up
D2: IF tile 2 is above the hole THEN move tile 1 down
. . . (59 other rules) . . .

Though there are 64 operators, only four of them, at most, are applicable at any one time. When an operator is applied to a configuration of the puzzle, the operator will transform the configuration into another configuration of the puzzle. The set of all configurations of the puzzle may be represented as a directed graph in which every node is a puzzle configuration. There will be an arc from a node x to a node y only if there is an operator that transforms x into y. Each node of such a graph is called a state, and the entire graph is called the state space for the problem. Figures 6.4 shows a portion of the state space for the 15-puzzle.

The simplest kind of search technique to use for this problem is called a state-space search. The basic idea is to start at the initial

FIGURE 6.4. A Portion of the State Space for the 15-puzzle.

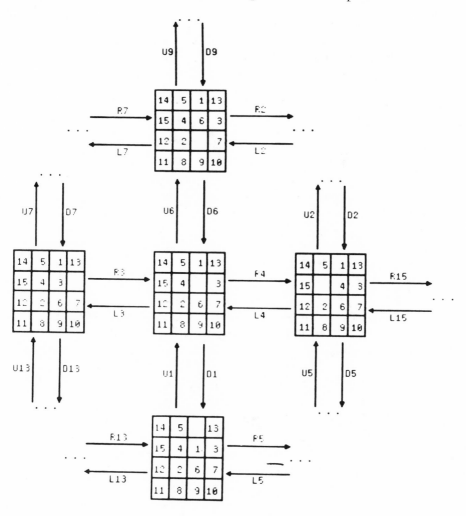

problem state and keep applying operators until a solution is found. Many different paths may lead to a solution, though certain paths cost less than others or may be preferable for other reasons. State-space search programs are based on the following procedure:

PROCEDURE state-space:
1. s := initial state
2. path := NIL /*list of operators used so far*/
3. WHILE s is not a goal DO
4.   ops := [operators applicable to s]
5.   nondeterministically select an operator r from ops
6.   path := concatenate(path, r)
7.   s := r(s) /*apply r to s*/
8. END
9. RETURN path
END state-space

The nondeterministic selection in line 5 is similar to the operation of a nondeterministic Turing machine: It is assumed that the procedure somehow guesses exactly the right operator to apply to keep it on an appropriate path to the goal. Since real computer procedures usually cannot be guaranteed such omniscience, practical space-search procedures must include ways to recover if the procedure goes down an inappropriate path.

One way to recover in case of error is called backtracking. The basic idea is to explore a path as far as possible; if the path turns out to be a dead end, then back up to the last previous state and try another operator. Backtracking procedures are based on the procedure given below.

PROCEDURE backtrack (s, p):
        /*s is the current state*/
        /*p is the sequence of states which was followed to get to s*/
1. IF s is a goal THEN RETURN NIL /*the null sequence*/
2. IF decide-to-backtrack(s, p) THEN RETURN 'fail'
3. ops := [operators applicable to s]
4. FOR EVERY r∈ops DO /*iterate through the list of operators*/
5.   path = backtrack (r(s), concat(p, r(s)))
        /*r(s) is the state resulting from applying r to the state s */

6.   IF path ≠ 'fail' THEN RETURN concat(r, path)
            /*return the sequence of operators found to get from s to
               a goal*/
7. END
8. RETURN 'fail'
END backtrack

Backtracking has a significant drawback: In some cases, the procedure can go off on an infinitely long path and never reach a solution. However, such cases do not normally arise in expert computer systems applications, and most expert computer systems use backtracking control strategies.

Another type of state-space strategy is a breadth-first search, which expands all paths simultaneously at the same rate. Since a breadth-first search examines all possible paths, it is guaranteed to find a solution if one exists—but at the expense of large amounts of time and memory. There are also various heuristic search strategies that keep track of several paths but explore some of them faster than others. For more detail, see Nilsson (1980).

State-space searches can often be done either in the forward direction, by starting at the initial state and applying operators to try to produce a goal state, or in the backward direction, by starting at the goal state and applying inverses of the operators to try to reach the initial state. When the operators are in the form of IF-THEN rules, a forward search is often called a data-driven or antecedent-driven search, and a backward search is often called a goal-driven search. Exactly which search direction will be more efficient depends on two factors: (1) whether the operators are more easily computable than their inverses or vice versa and (2) the structure of the search space. For example, in the search space shown in Figure 6.5a, a forward search will involve fewer operator applications than a backward search, but in the search space shown in Figure 6.5b, the reverse will be true.

Propagation of Constraints

Propagation of constraints is a special kind of state-space search in which special characteristics of the problem being solved are used

FIGURE 6.5. Two State Spaces. In Each Case, S is the Start State and G is Goal State.

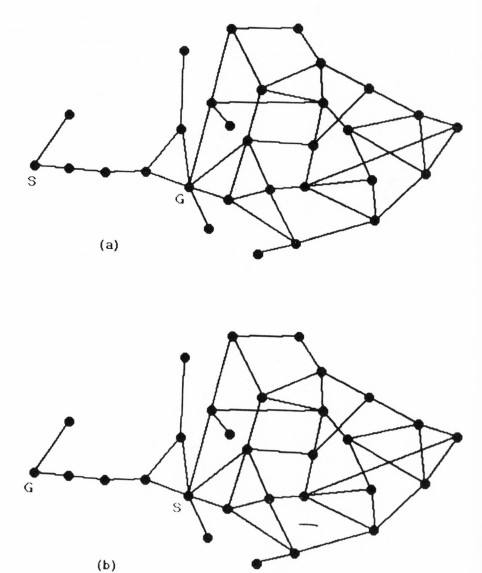

(a)

(b)

in deciding which operator or rule to choose next. When this can be done, it often avoids the necessity of backtracking. One should consider using propagation of constraints whenever each problem state can be represented as a graph (thus the state space will consist of a graph whose nodes are also graphs) having the following properties:

1. Each arc may be assigned various values, and initially, some of the values will be known but not others.
2. Associated with each node is a set of constraints on the values associated with the arcs incident to the node.
3. The goal is to assign values to the arcs in such a way that all constraints are satisfied simultaneously.

As an example of propagation of constraints, consider the electrical circuit shown in Figure 6.6a. Suppose (as is shown in the figure) the voltage of the battery and the resistance of each resistor are known but the voltage at each resistor terminal and the current through each resistor are unknown. This circuit may be represented as a graph in which each node represents a circuit element or a junction of three or more wires, and each arc represents a wire. Associated with each arc are two values: the voltage present at that wire and the current flowing through that wire. At each node are constraints that are derived from Ohm's law and Kirchhoff's current law. The resulting graph is illustrated in Figure 6.6b.

Given the values of certain circuit parameters, the constraints may be sufficient to determine the values of other circuit parameters. For example, if V_1 is known to be 100 and I_1 is known to be 1, then the constraint

$$C_S : V_1 - V_2 = 70 I_1$$

associated with resistor R_1 requires that $V_2 = 30$. In this case, we say that V_1 is completely determined by the existing constraints.

The control structure for propagation of constraints is as follows:

PROCEDURE propagate:
1.   record any values of any variables whose values are already known
2.   WHILE there are variables which have not been assigned values DO
3.   IF there is a variable V such that
                 V has not been assigned a value
                 and V is completely determined

FIGURE 6.6. An Electrical Circuit and Its Associated Constraint
Graph.

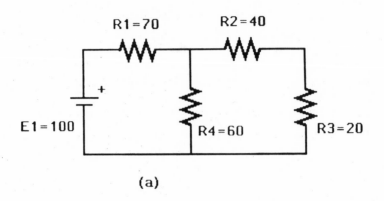

(a)

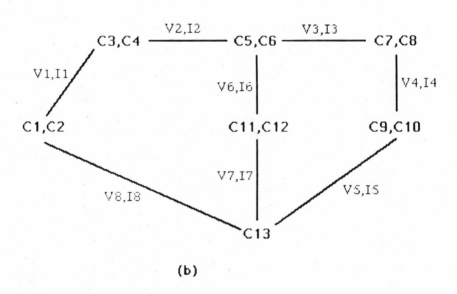

(b)

The constraints are as follows:

$C_1 : V_1 = V_8 + 100 \qquad C_6 : I_2 + I_3 + I_6 = 0 \qquad C_{11} : V_6 - V_7 = 60 I_6$
$C_2 : I_1 = I_8 \qquad\qquad C_7 : V_3 - V_4 = 40 I_3 \qquad C_{12} : I_6 = I_7$
$C_3 : V_1 - V_2 = 70 I \qquad C_8 : I_3 = I_4 \qquad\qquad C_{13} : V_5 = V_7 = V_8$
$C_4 : I_1 = I_2 \qquad\qquad C_9 : V_4 - V_5 = 20 I_4 \qquad C_{14} : I_5 + I_7 + I_8 = 0$
$C_5 : V_2 = V_3 = V_6 \qquad C_{10} : I_4 = I_5$

258

4. THEN
5. record the value determined for V
6. ELSE
7. nondeterministically choose a plausible value for
some variable
8. ENDIF
9. ENDWHILE
END propagate

For many problems, the nondeterministic choice in line 7 of the procedure may be handled in any of the ways discussed earlier for statespace search. For the electrical circuit of Figure 6.6, the appropriate way to handle the choice is somewhat different: to assign some variable a constant as its value without specifying the value of the constant. Later on, if the value of the constant becomes completely determined, then the constant is replaced by its value wherever it appears.

The reason that propagation of constraints is a kind of statespace search is that every constraint corresponds to several statespace operators—one operator for each argument to the constraint. The "state" on which these operators operate is the current state of knowledge about the values of the variables on the graph. For example, the predicate P_s discussed above corresponds to the operators

IF V_1 and V_2 are known THEN assign $I_1 = (V_1 - V_2)/70$
IF V_1 and I_1 are known THEN assign $V_2 = V_1 - 70 I_1$
IF V_2 and I_1 are known THEN assign $V_1 = V_2 + 70 I_1$

When operators such as these are used, then the propagation of constraints procedure may be rewritten as

PROCEDURE propagate2:
1. record any values of any variables whose values are already known
2. WHILE there are variables whose values are not known DO
3. IF there is an operator whose preconditions are satisfied
4. THEN
5. apply the operator
6. ELSE
7. nondeterministically choose a plausible value for
some variable

8.　　　ENDIF
9.　ENDWHILE
END propagate2

Propagation of constraints can be used to solve the problem illustrated in Figure 6.6. As an initial condition, suppose that $V_8 = 0$. Then V_1, V_5, and V_7 are completely determined by constraints C_1 and C_{11}, which require that $V_1 = 100$ and $V_5 = V_7 = 0$. At this point, no other variables are completely determined, so some variable must be set equal to a constant. Suppose V_4 is set equal to e. Then from C_9, $I_4 = e/20$, so from C_8 and C_{10}, $I_3 = I_5 = e/20$. Thus from C_7, $V_3 = 3e$. Thus from C_5, $V_2 = V_6 = 3e$, and so from C_{11} and C_{12}, $I_6 = I_7 = e/20$. Thus from C_6 and C_4, $I_1 = I_2 = e/10$. Thus from C_3, $e = 10$. Thus $I_1 = 1$, $I_2 = I_3 = I_4 = I_5 = I_6 = I_7 = 0.5$, $V_2 = V_3 = V_6 = 30$, and $V_4 = 10$. And, finally, from C_7, $I_8 = 1$.

The kind of reasoning done on the circuit is what is done by Stallman and Sussman's EL program (Stallman & Sussman, 1977). EL also incorporates techniques for analyzing active devices such as transistors and diodes in DC circuits. This is done using the "method of assumed states," in which the operating characteristics of the device are modeled as a number of piecewise-linear regions, and an assumption is made about which region the device is operating in. If

FIGURE 6.7. Search Tree for a BACKTRACK Search.

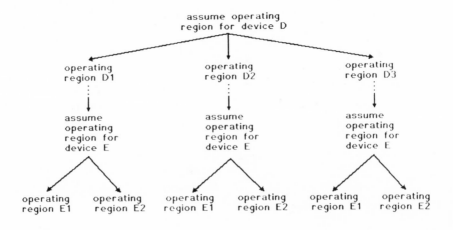

the assumption is wrong, it will eventually lead to a contradiction, and backtracking will be necessary.

One trouble with backtracking is the "combinatorial explosion" that may arise in large search spaces. For example, suppose device D has operating regions D_1, D_2, and D_3, and device E has operating regions E_1, and E_2. If the two devices are in the same circuit, then six combinations of operating regions are possible. Suppose that independent of the operating region for D, the circuit is such that E cannot be operating in region E_1. If a backtrack search assumes operating regions first for D and then for E (see Figure 6.7), then during the course of its search it may eventually try each of the three combinations (D_1, E_1), (D_2, E_1), and (D_3, E_1), even though it may have been possible to tell that no combination involving E_1 would work. To avoid such problems, EL notes which assumptions were responsible for an error whenever one occurs and never makes that combination of assumptions again.

Problem Reduction

One alternative to state-space search is a technique known as problem reduction. This is the strategy used in some of the early problem-solving systems, such as GPS (Newell & Simon, 1963) and STRIPS (Fikes & Nilsson, 1971). Here the problem is partitioned, or decomposed, into subproblems (each of which can be solved separately) in such a way that combining the solutions to the subproblems will yield a solution to the original problem. The subproblems may each be further decomposed into sub-subproblems, which may be even further decomposed until "primitive" problems are generated that can be solved directly.

Example

Consider the 15-puzzle again. As illustrated in Figure 6.8, the problem of getting from the initial state to the goal state may be decomposed into the following four subproblems:

1. The problem of getting the first row in order
2. The problem of getting the first two rows in order, given that the first row is in order

FIGURE 6.8. An AND/OR Graph for Solving the 15-puzzle by Problem Reduction.

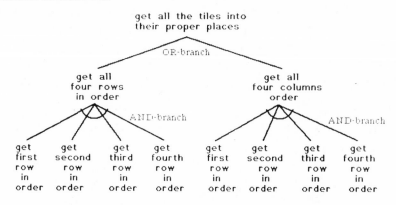

3. The problem of getting the first three rows in order, given that the first two rows are in order
4. The problem of getting all four rows in order, given that the first three rows are in order

Each subproblem may in turn be solved by dividing it into even smaller subproblems. For example subproblem 1 could be decomposed into the sub-subproblems of getting each of the four tiles in the first row into its proper place. The solution to the original problem is produced by concentrating the solutions to the various subproblems.

AND/OR Graphs

Obviously, there may be more than one way to decompose a problem. For example, the 15-puzzle could have been decomposed into the subproblems of getting the four columns correct, rather than the four rows. All possible decompositions of a problem can be graphically represented in a problem-reduction graph or AND/OR graph (see Figure 6.9), in which each OR branch represents a choice of several alternate decompositions, and each AND branch represents a particular way of decomposing a problem. Indeed, Figure 6.8 is an AND/OR graph.

Some decompositions of a problem may lead to solvable subproblems; others may not. To solve a problem using problem reduc-

FIGURE 6.9. An AND/OR Graph Produced by Dendral.

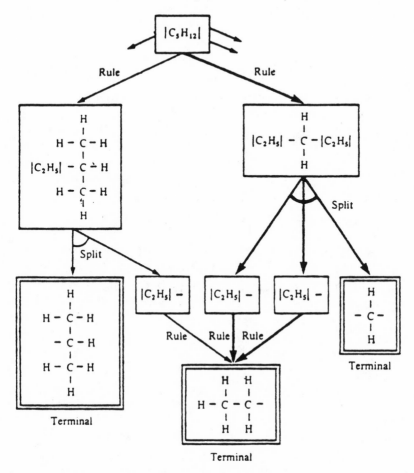

Source: Taken from Nilsson (1980, p. 44). Copyright ©Morgan Kaufmann Publishers. Reprinted by permission.

tion, a decomposition must be chosen that yields solvable subproblems. In turn to solve each of these subproblems, decompositions must be chosen that yield solvable sub-subproblems, and so forth. Thus, a problem solution is represented by a solution graph, which may be defined recursively as follows:

Let n be a node in an AND/OR graph G, and let N be a set of terminal nodes in G. One may think of the nodes in N as the set of solvable primitive problems. A solution graph in G from n to N is then defined as follows:

1. If $n \in N$, then the graph containing the single node n is a solution graph in G from n to N.
2. If G' is a solution graph from m to N and if G contains an OR branch B in which m is a child of n, then the graph containing n, B, and G' is a solution graph in G from n to N.
3. If G_1, G_2, ..., G_k are solution graphs from n_1 to N, n_2 to N, ..., n_k to N, respectively, and if there is an AND branch B in which n_1, n_2, ..., n_k are the children of n, then the graph containing n, B, and each of the graphs G_1, ..., G_k is a solution graph in G from n to N.
4. There are no other solution graphs in G from n to N.

Just as there may be many different paths to a solution when state-space search is used, there may be many different solution graphs when problem reduction is used. Depending on the problem, the preferred solution may be any solution graph, the solution graph of least (or highest) cost according to some cost criterion, or solution graphs satisfying other criteria.

Directionality

Just as with state-space searches, problem-reduction searches can use either a goal-driven approach (sometimes called backward chaining) or a data-driven or antecedent-driven approach (sometimes called forward chaining). Handle-Bugs, presented earlier in this chapter, used backward chaining, and an example of forward chaining appears in Dendral (Feigenbaum, Buchanan, & Lederberg, 1971; Buchanan & Feigenbaum, 1978), a computer system that proposed plausible chemical structures for molecules given their mass spectrograms.

Dendral uses a "plan, generate, and test" technique. First, in the planning phase, constraints on the problem solution are inferred from mass spectrometry data. Second, in the generation phase, the program generates all molecular structures satisfying both these constraints and some general chemical constraints. Third, in the testing phase, the proposed structures are tested in a more sophisticated manner for compatibility with the mass spectrometry data.

The generation phase of Dendral's operation is an antecedent-driven problem-reduction search. Dendral contains a number of operators, each of which takes some of the atoms in a chemical formula and replaces them with one or more pieces of molecular structure. The problem decomposition is done by considering each of these pieces of structure independently and applying other operators to it to fill in more details. Examples of this are illustrated in Figures 6.9 and 6.10.

One difficulty with problem reduction is that the subproblems may not be independent of each other, and thus it may not be possible to combine their solutions into a solution for the original problem. This is one reason for Dendral's testing phase: to eliminate those "solutions" proposed in the generation phase that do not actually work.

FIGURE 6.10. Chemical Structures Produced by Dendral from the Problem Shown in Figure 6.9.

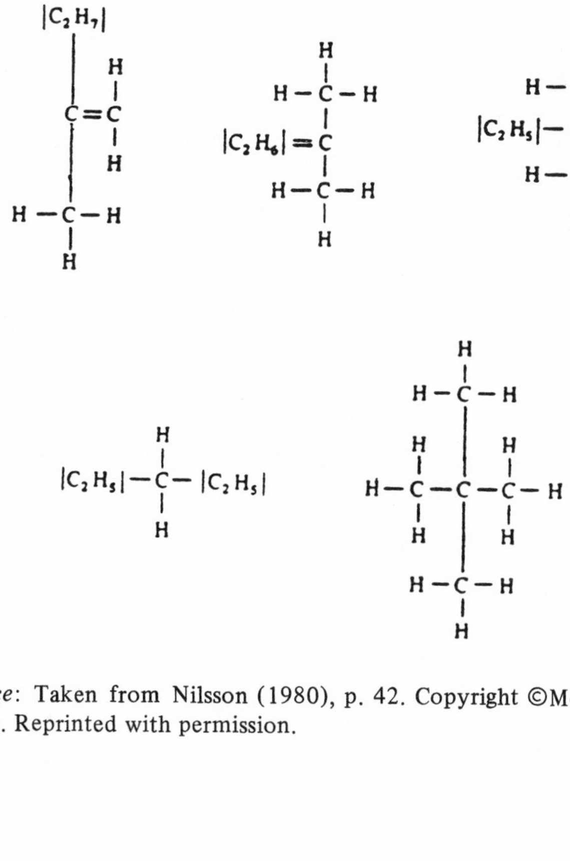

Source: Taken from Nilsson (1980), p. 42. Copyright ©Morgam Kaufman Publishers. Reprinted with permission.

MORE ELABORATE FORMS OF RULES

In the bug example, the clauses in the rules were all of the form "attribute = value." Often it is desirable to be able to represent more general kinds of information in the rules or operators in a knowledge base. This section discusses several ways to do this.

Prolog

Often operators are required that are applicable to every problem state matching a certain pattern. For example, rather than

IF V_1 and V_2 are known THEN assign $I_1 = (V_1 - V_2)/70$

the following is more general:

IF V_k and V_{k+1} are known THEN assign $I_k = (V_k - V_{k+1})/70$

where k is any positive integer. Prolog (Clocksin & Mellish, 1981; Kowalski, 1979) is a computer language that incorporates an easy way to do such things.

Prolog is an outgrowth of AI research on theorem proving. In resolution theorem proving, both the statement to be proved and the relevant facts to be used in the proof are represented as statements in FOL (see "Representing Facts" above), and a control strategy called resolution is used to attempt to prove the desired statement (Loveland, 1978; Nilsson, 1971). Prolog operates in the same way, but with a restriction: Only certain kinds of FOL statements are allowed, as shown in Table 6.3.

Prolog may be considered either a resolution-based theorem prover or a problem-reduction problem solver. This is because a formula such as

GREATER(x, z) :- GREATER(x, y) & GREATER(y, z)

can be thought of either as the logical statement that $x > z$ whenever $x > y$ and $y > z$, or as a rule or operator of the form

IF GREATER(x, y) & GREATER(y, z) THEN assert GREATER(x, z)

TABLE 6.3. Types of Statements Allowed in Prolog

Statement	Meaning
$:-A.$	A is a goal
$A.$	A is an assertion
$A :-B_1, \ldots, B\eta.$	$B_1 \ \& \ldots \& B\eta \rightarrow A$

Note: A and all of the B's must be predicates, and all variables appearing in these predicates are considered to be universally quantified (that is, the statement is taken to be true for all possible values of the variables).

A Prolog program may contain several different ways to establish a predicate. For example, in addition to the Prolog statement above, one might also have the statement

GREATER$(x, z) :-$ LESS (z, x)

The solution of a problem presented as a set of Prolog statements is found by doing a depth-first search of the corresponding AND/OR graph until an instantiation of a set of assertions is found that provides a solution graph. For example, if a Prolog program is written to compute the factorial function the program will make use of built-in Prolog functions for addition and multiplication. Although some Prolog implementation allow equations such as "$a + b = c$" to be written directly, we assume that addition and multiplication are handled by two predicates called PLUS and MULT, as described below.

PLUS(a, b, c) is a predicate that is true if $a + b = c$. Although values must be given for at least two of the arguments, the third one may be a variable. If one of the arguments is a variable, then Prolog will set that variable to a value that makes the equation "$a + b = c$" true. MULT(a, b, c) is a predicate that is true if $ab = c$. Although values must be given for at least two of the arguments, the third one may be a variable. If one of the arguments is a variable, then Prolog will set that variable to a value that makes the equation "$ab = c$" true.

To write the Prolog program, a predicate FAC should be defined so that FAC(w, x) will be true only if $w! = x$. If this is done correctly then a statement such as "$:-$FAC(3, x)" will cause x to be set to $3!$:

FAC(1, 1)
FAC(n, r) :-PLUS(m, 1, n), FAC(m, s), MULT(n, s, r)
:-FAC(3, x)

The first statement of this program asserts that $1! = 1$. The second statement asserts that

if $m = n - 1$, $m! = s$, and $r = ns$, then $n! = r$

or, in other words

$n! = n(n - 1)!$

The third statement means "find an x such that $x = 3!$"

To execute this program, Prolog invokes a resolution theorem prover that may be thought of as doing a depth-first search on the AND/OR graph shown in Figure 6.11. The events, in the order that they occur, are as follows:

1. To try to find an x such that FAC(3, x) is true, Prolog first tries to match FAC(3, x) against the fact FAC(1, 1). Since the first arguments don't match, this fails.
2. Prolog then tries to match FAC(3, x) against the conclusion of the rule

   FAC(n, r) :-PLUS(m, 1, n), FAC(m, s), MULT(n, s, r)

   To do this, it is first necessary to create a copy of the rule having slightly different variable names:

   FAC(n1, r1) :-PLUS(m1, 1, n1), FAC(m1, s1), MULT(n1, s1, r1)

   This is to avoid later confusion about which variables are which. The conclusion of this rule does match FAC(3, x) if 3 is substituted for $n1$ and $r1$ is substituted for x. Three subgoals are thus produced: PLUS(m1, 1, 3), FAC(m1, s1), and MULT(3, s1, r1).
3. The first subgoal, PLUS(m1, 1, n1), is satisfied if 2 is substituted for $m1$ and 3 is substituted for $n1$. This must be done everywhere $m1$ and $n1$ occur, so the second subgoal becomes FAC(2, s1).
4. Prolog tries to solve FAC(2, s1) by matching it against FAC(1, 1). This fails since $1 \neq 2$.
5. Prolog tries to match FAC(2, s1) to the conclusion of the rule

FIGURE 6.11. A Search Tree for Prolog.

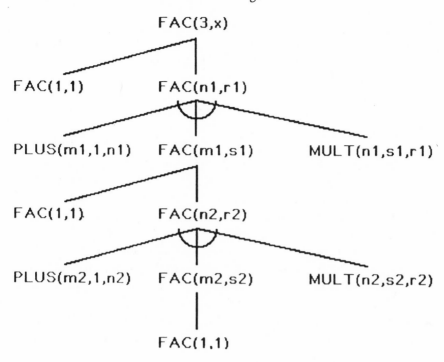

FAC(n, r) :-PLUS(m, 1, n), FAC(m, s), MULT(n, s, r)

As before, Prolog must first create new variable names:

FAC(n2, r2) :-PLUS(m2, 1, n2), FAC(m2, s2), MULT(n2, s2, r2)

FAC(3, x) does match FAC(n2, r2), provided that 2 is substituted for n2 and r2 for s1. Since these substitutions must be done everywhere, the third subgoal mentioned above becomes MULT (3, r2, r1). Three new subgoals are created: PLUS(m2, 1, 2), FAC (m2, s2), and MULT(2, s2, r2).

6. The subgoal PLUS(m2, 1, 2) is satisfied if 1 is substituted for m2. Since this must be done everywhere, the subgoal FAC(m2, s2) becomes FAC(1, s2).

7. FAC(1, s2) is satisfied because it matches FAC(1, 1) if 1 is substituted for s2. Since this substitution must be made everywhere, the subgoal MULT(2, s2, r2) becomes MULT(2, 1, r2).

8. MULT (2, 1, r2) is satisfied if 2 is substituted for $r2$. Since this substitution must be made everywhere, the only remaining un-examined subgoal becomes MULT (3, 2, r1).

9. MULT(3, 2, r1) is satisfied if 6 is substituted for $r1$. Since this substitution must be made everywhere, FAC(3, r1) becomes FAC (3, 6), and the problem is solved.

Certainty Factors

In knowledge-based problem solving, often it may not be com-pletely clear whether certain facts are true or whether certain causal relationships hold. Thus, it is often useful to be able to assert these facts or relationships with less than absolute certainty. The following approach is often used for these assertions.

If there is some evidence in favor of a statement, then a certain amount of belief in the statement is warranted based on this evidence. This amount of belief can be represented by a number between 0 and 1, called a measure of belief (or MB). Similarly, if there is some evi-dence against the statement, then a certain amount of disbelief is warranted which can be represented by a number between 0 and 1, called a measure of disbelief (MD). The certainty factor (or CF) of the statement is then defined as

$$CF = MB - MD$$

Thus the CF is a number between −1 and 1. If the CF is positive, then the statement is thought to be true (with absolute certainty if the CF is 1). If the CF is negative, then the statement is thought to be false (with absolute certainty if the CF is −1).

When this approach is used, rules will also have certainty factors associated with them. For example, the Mycin rule

```
PREMISE    ($and (same cntxt infect primary-bacteremia)
           (membf cntxt site sterilesites)
           (same cntxt portal gi)
ACTION     (conclude cntxt ident bacteroides tally 0.7)
```

has the following meaning (Davis, Buchanan, & Shortliffe, 1977):

IF   (1) the infection is primary-bacteremia

          (2) the site is one of the sterilesites

          (3) suspected portal entry is the gastrointestinal tract

THEN conclude (with a certainty factor of 0.7) that the organism
is bacteroides

If a rule does not allow a fact to be concluded with absolute certainty, then many different alternatives may be possible. For example, the following rule, taken from a KMS knowledge base (Reggia, et
al., 1980), asserts that under certain conditions a medical patient
may have either of two different types of paralysis—one with a certainty of 0.8 and the other with a certainty of 0.2:

IF   serum K+ = low and myotonia = absent and serum T4 = high

THEN paralysis type = thyrotoxic (0.8)

         and paralysis type = hypokalemic (0.2)

When rules such as these are used, MBs, MDs, and CFs are computed as follows:

1. First, the CF for the antecedent (the IF part of the rule) is computed. The antecedent is normally an expression containing *and*
and *or* operations. The CF for a conjunct such as "A and B" is
taken to be the minimum of the certainties for A and B. The CF
for a disjunct such as "A or B" is taken to be the maximum of the
certainties for A and B. The rule will not fire at all unless the CF
of its antecedent is above some positive cutoff value (for example, Mycin uses 0.2 as its cutoff).
2. If the rule has a positive CF, it will affect only the MB of the
statement mentioned in its consequent (its THEN part). First, an
MB for the statement is computed by multiplying the CF of the
antecedent with the CF of the rule. Then this MB and the old MB
for the statement are combined as if they were independent
probabilities:

New MB = 1 – (1 – old MB) (1 – MB produced by the rule)

If the rule has a negative CF, the computation is similar but affects the MD of its consequent rather than the MB.

3. Once the new **MB** or **MD** has been computed for the statement, its CF is computed in the usual way:

CF = MD – MB

For example, suppose we have the following facts:

A known with CF = 0.7
B known with CF = 0.3
C known with CF = 0.5
D known with **MB** = 0.7 and **MD** = 0.5 (whence CF = 0.3)
H known with CF = 0.8
I known with CF = 0.7
J known with CF = 0.5

and suppose that the following rule is invoked:

IF (A & B) / C, THEN CONCLUDE D (0.8)

Then, as shown in Figure 6.12, the MB for D produced by the rule is 0.4. This is combined with the old MB for D as

MB = 1 – (1 – 0.7) (1 – 0.4) = 0.82

and then the CF is computed as

CF = MB – MD = 0.84 – 0.5 = 0.32

There are several systems (for example, Emcyn [Melle, 1979], Mycin [Davis, et al., 1977], Puff [Osborn, Fagan, Fallat, McClung, & Mitchell, 1979], and KMS.PS[1] [Reggia, 1981; Reggia, et al., 1980]) that use this kind of computation on data having a form similar to

attribute = value (with some CF)

and use a backward chaining problem-reduction control strategy. However, this control strategy must be modified somewhat because of the certainty factors. The procedure usually looks something like this:

FIGURE 6.12. A Search Graph for Find-Value.

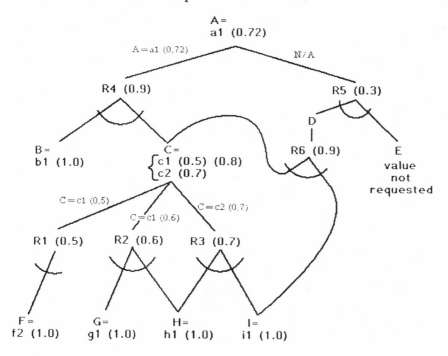

Computing the MB produced by a rule.

$$\left.\begin{array}{l} CF(A) = 0.7 \\ CF(B) = 0.3 \end{array}\right\} CF(A \& B) = 0.3 \left.\begin{array}{l} \\ \end{array}\right\}$$

$$\left.\begin{array}{l} CF(C) = 0.5 \end{array}\right\} (CF\,(A \& B)\,/C) = 0.5 \left.\begin{array}{l} \\ \end{array}\right\} MB \text{ produced by rule}$$
$$CF(\text{rule}) = 0.8 \left.\begin{array}{l} \\ \end{array}\right\} \begin{array}{l} = CF \text{ (premises)} \times CF \text{ (rule)} \\ = 0.4 \end{array}$$

PROCEDURE Find-Value (GOAL):
    IF GOAL is user input data THEN
            ask user the value of GOAL
            IF user gives a definite answer THEN
                assert the answer (with CF)
                RETURN
            ENDIF
    ENDIF
    LOOP1: FOR each rule R relevant to GOAL DO

```
            LOOP 2: FOR each premise P of R DO
                IF P has not been traced THEN
                    call Find-Value(P)
                ENDIF
                IF CF(premises) ≤ 0 THEN
                    continue(LOOP1)
                ELSE IF CF(premises) = 1 THEN
                    break(LOOP2)
                ENDIF
            END LOOP2
            assert GOAL = concl(R) (change CF)
            IF the CF is 1 THEN
                mark GOAL as traced
                RETURN
            ENDIF
        END LOOP1
        mark GOAL as traced
        IF GOAL still unknown AND haven't asked the user
        THEN ask the user the value of GOAL
        RETURN
END Find-Value
```

The operation of Find-Value is illustrated in the following example. Suppose a system is given the following rules:

1. IF $F = f2$ THEN $C = c1$ (0.5)
2. IF $G = g1$ & $H = h1$ THEN $C = c1$ (0.6)
3. IF $H = h1$ & $I = i1$ THEN $C = c2$ (0.7)
4. IF $B = b1$ & $C = c1$ THEN $A = a1$ (0.9)
5. IF $D = d1$ & $E = e1$ THEN $A \neq a1$ (0.3)
6. IF $C = c2$ & $I = i2$ THEN $D = d1$ (0.9)

and suppose the following are data known to the user:

$B = b1, E = e1, F = f2, G = g1, H = h1, I = i1$

If the goal is to find the value of A, then Find-Value will generate the AND/OR graph as shown in Figure 6.13. Find-Value does its search in the same manner as Handle-Bugs and Prolog. The only significant differences are the following:

1. Certainty factors are computed as discussed above.
2. Unlike Prolog, predicates with variables are not allowed. There is no theoretical reason why they could not be allowed, but such an extension has not been documented in the literature.
3. Unless a fact is established with a CF of 1 or −1, Find-Value will continue to invoke additional rules bearing on that fact.

NON-RULE-BASED APPROACHES

In the computer systems discussed so far, the knowledge bases were all in the form of simple IF-THEN rules, and the control strategies were all forward-chaining or backward-chaining search strategies of some sort. These systems are summarized in Table 6.4. Although most expert computer systems operate in this way, there are a number that use other approaches. A few such approaches are described in this section.

TABLE 6.4. Examples Grouped by Search Strategy

	State Space	Problem Reduction
Forward chaining	15-Puzzle EL	Dendral
Backward chaining	15-Puzzle	Handle-Bugs Prolog Find-Value

Pattern-Invoked Programs

All the knowledge bases discussed so far consist of simple operators or production rules. Such entities are special cases of a more general concept called a pattern-invoked program. A pattern-invoked program is a computer program that consists of two parts: an IF part and a THEN part. As with production rules, the pattern-invoked programs never explicitly call each other, but are instead invoked by some control structure if their IF parts are satisfied. However, rather than being simple entities, such as conjuncts or disjuncts of predicates, the IF and THEN parts of pattern-invoked programs may be large and complex programs. AI languages such as Planner (Hewitt, 1972) and Conniver (Sussman & McDermott, 1972) were developed in the early 1970s to provide control structures to manipulate pattern-invoked programs.

One system developed more recently is Hearsay-II, a system for understanding spoken commands. Hearsay-II is in no way an expert system; its performance does not compare with that of a human being. However, the techniques used in its construction are of interest to designers of expert systems. As with most systems for natural-language understanding, Hearsay-II is restricted to a small subset of the English language, in this case, document retrieval commands. This domain restriction, along with various restrictions on what sentence constructions the speaker may use, allows the use of a context-free semantic grammar to describe the language.

As with most systems for speech recognition, Hearsay-II can be used only by one user at a time and must first be turned (in this case, by means of 20 to 30 training utterances) to understand that user's speech pattern. Once the system has been tuned, however, no speaker adaptation is required (in contrast to commercially available systems that require the speaker to say one word at a time, with pauses in between). Table 6.5 summarizes the reported performance of Hearsay-II (Erman, Hayes-Roth, Lesser, and Reddy, 1980).

TABLE 6.5. Performance of Hearsay-II

Test data	23 utterances, brand new to the system, run blind. 7 words/utterance (average); 2.6 seconds/utterance (average)
Accuracy	9% sentences misunderstood; 10% sentences not word-for-word correct but meaning understood anyway
Computing resources	60 million instructions per second of speech on a PDP-10
Time required to comprehend speech	On the order of 10 times the length of the utterance

Source: Adapted from Erman, et al., 1980, p. 239.

The pattern-invoked computer programs used in Hearsay-II are called knowledge sources (KS's). The system contains approximately 40 KS's, each responsible for a different kinds of task. Each KS consists of a condition program, which evaluates whether the KS is applicable, and an action program, to accomplish whatever results the KS is to produce. The KS's range in size from 5 to 100 pages of source code each (30 pages is typical), and each KS has up to 50,000 bytes of its own local data storage.

The KS's communicate with each other by posting messages on a global data structure called the blackboard. The blackboard is divided into several levels, which can be thought of as the various levels at which subproblems are located in a problem-reduction tree. In order from highest to lowest, the levels are (1) database interface, (2) phrase, (3) word sequence, (4) word, (5) syllable, (6) segment, and (7) parameter. The condition program of each KS tests events occurring at a particular level or levels of the blackboard, and the action program of the KS puts hypotheses at a particular level or levels of the blackboard.

For example, there is a KS called SEG, whose responsibility is to digitize the input signal, measure various signal parameters, divide the signal into phonelike segments, and assign to each segment several alternate possibilities for what phoneme it might be. SEG's action program tests events occurring at the parameter level of the blackboard and posts messages on the segment level. Another KS, called POM, looks at the messages posted on the segment level and posts (on the syllable level) hyptheses for what syllables are present in the input. Another KS, called VERIFY, checks information on both the phrase and segment levels and posts messages (on the word level) regarding the consistency between various segment hypotheses and contiguous word-phrase pairs. A KS called PARSE takes sequences of words on the word-sequence level, and parses them into phrases that are posted on the phrase level. PARSE consists of an encoding of the grammar for the task language as a network and procedures for searching the network to parse a sequence of words.

The control structure that controls the KS's consists of a blackboard monitor and a scheduler. The blackboard monitor notes all messages that are posted on the blackboard and creates entries on scheduling queues for any KS whose applicability conditions might be satisfied. For each KS condition program or action program on the queues, the scheduler creates a priority. The highest priority activity is removed from the queues and executed. Although most of the KS's operate in a data-driven manner (that is, examining messages at lower levels of the blackboard and posting messages at higher levels), there are some (VERIFY) that also operate in a goal-driven way.

For a large, complex problem such as speech understanding, the ability to use pattern-invoked programs more complicated than simple rules offers several advantages. Since the KS's can be arbitrarily complex—and arbitrarily different in their internal operation—this provides a way to implement whatever problem-solving approach is most appropriate at each level of processing. Each KS may itself be a small knowledge-based problem solver whose internal processes have only local effects rather than causing potential interactions with the entire system. This alleviates the problem associated with "combinatorial explosions" that often occur when search techniques are used on very large problems. For example, when portions of Hearsay-II were experimentally rewritten as a production system, the production system version was found to run approximately 100 times as slow (McCracken, 1979).

The structure of Hearsay-II has been separated from the Hearsay-II knowledge base for use as a tool for designing expert computer systems. This tool is called Hearsay-III (Erman, London, & Fickas, 1981). The relationship between Hearsay-II and Hearsay-III is analogous to the relationship between Mycin and Emycin: Hearsay-III consists of the Hearsay-II control structure and environment with all of the facilities for creating a knowledge base but without any of the domain knowledge specific to speech recognition.

Bayesian Classification

Although all the systems discussed so far have been based on the use of pattern-invoked programs, many of the more successful expert computer systems for diagnostic problem solving are based instead on statistical pattern classification techniques such as Bayesian pattern classification (Duda & Hart, 1973; Rogers, Ryack, & Moeller, 1979; deDombal, 1975; Matthys, Fischer, Ulrichs, & Ruhle, 1979). In the Bayesian approach, knowledge is represented by a set of probabilities. For example, suppose there are n possible diagnoses or outcomes associated with some features. If D_i is the ith outcome, then $P(D_i)$ is the prior probability of D_i, that is, how commonly D_i occurs in the general population. If S is the set of features present in a particular case, then $P(S \mid D_i)$ is the conditional probability of S given the presence of D_i. If we know $P(D_i)$ and $P(S \mid D_i)$ for every D_i, application of Bayes' theorem will give us

$$P(D_i \mid S) = \frac{P(D_i)\,P(S \mid D_i)}{\Sigma_j\, P(D_j)\,P(S \mid D_j)}$$

where $P(D_i \mid S)$ is the posterior probability of each D_i for a given set of features. Knowing $P(D_i \mid S)$ for each D_i indicates which D_i is most likely to be present in a given situation.

For example, according to Synder, Ramirez-Lassepas, and Lippert (1977), for heart attack patients, the a priori probabilities of brain damage are

$P(\text{no impairment}) = 0.62$
$P(\text{impairment}) = 0.38$

The conditional probabilities for various signs and symptoms are given in Table 6.6. Now suppose that a heart attack patient is found to have s_2, s_4, s_5, and s_7 (no spontaneous breathing, no purposeful response to pain, pupillary light reflex, and oculocephalic reflex). If

TABLE 6.6. Conditional Probabilities of Various Signs and Symptoms

Symptom or Sign s_i	$P(s_i \mid \text{no impairment})$	$P(s_i \mid \text{impairment})$
s_1: Spontaneous breathing	0.67	0.15
s_2: No spontaneous breathing	0.33	0.85
s_3: Purposeful response to pain	0.57	0.15
s_4: No purposeful response to pain	0.43	0.85
s_5: Pupillary light reflex	0.89	0.42
s_6: No pupillary light reflex	0.11	0.58
s_7: Oculocephalic reflex	0.69	0.33
s_8 No oculocephalic reflex	0.31	0.67

each of these signs and symptoms is assumed to be independent of each other, then according to Bayes' theorem

$$P(\text{impairment} \mid S) = \frac{P(\text{impairment})\, P(s \mid \text{impairment})}{P(\text{impairment})P(S \mid \text{impairment}) + P(S \mid \text{no impairment})P(\text{no impairment})}$$

$$= \frac{P(\text{impairment}) \prod_{i=2,4,5,7} P(s_i \mid \text{impairment})}{P(\text{impairment}) \prod_{i=2,4,5,7} P(s_i \mid \text{impairment}) + P(\text{no impairment}) \prod_{i=2,4,5,7} P(s_i \mid \text{no impairment})}$$

$$= \frac{0.62 \times (0.85 \times 0.85 \times 0.42 \times 0.33)}{0.62 \times (0.85 \times 0.85 \times 0.42 \times 0.33) + 0.38 \times (0.33 \times 0.43 \times 0.89 \times 0.69)}$$

$$= 0.652$$

There are a number of restrictions that must be satisfied to use the Bayesian approach, and various ways have been tried to overcome them (Reggia, Nau, & Wang, 1983a). However, when these restrictions can be met, the Bayesian approach can produce outstanding performance. For example, in a recent test on a set of 100 patients, the E system, which was implemented in KMS.BAYES (Reggia et al., 1980), produced diagnoses that were significantly more accurate than those produced by experienced physicians (Zagoria & Reggia, 1983).

Abductive Problem Solving

The production rules in rule-based systems such as Handle-Bugs, Prolog, and Find-Value use production rules of the form

IF condition THEN assert conclusion

to construct chains of deductive reasoning showing that the existence of some initial set of conditions leads to some set of ultimate conclusions. Such reasoning derives from the rule of modus ponens: if "*A* implies *B*" is true and if "*A*" is true, then "*B*" is true. However, diagnostic problem solving is basically an abductive process rather than a deductive one. Abductive inference derives from a rule that goes in the reverse direction from modus ponens: If "A implies B" is true, and "B" is true, then *possibly* "A" is true.

In diagnostic problems where more than one disorder occurs simultaneously, the usual deductive approach used in production rule systems can lead to problems. To describe these problems, a formal definition of a diagnostic problem is required.

Solutions to Diagnostic Problems

A diagnostic problem can be anything from diagnosing a medical patient to troubleshooting a piece of electronic hardware to figuring out why a car won't start. However, every diagnostic problem domain has the following characteristics:

1. There are various disorders that can occur in that domain that may or may not be present in specific diagnostic problems. The set of all possible such disorders shall be called D. For now, it is assumed (perhaps erroneously) that all members of D are independent of each other.
2. If a disorder d is present, then it may cause one or more symptoms, signs, or manifestations of its presence. The set of all possible manifestations in a given problem domain may be called M. Let $C \subseteq D \times M$ be the relation between disorders and the manifestations they cause; that is, $(d, m) \epsilon C$ if and only if d is capable of causing m. Assume that when a disorder occurs, it does not necessarily always cause all of the manifestations it is capable of causing (this is often the case in real-world diagnostic problems).

Thus, a problem domain may be specified as a three-truple $<D, M, C>$.

Within a problem domain, a diagnostic problem occurs when one or more manifestations are present. Thus, a diagnostic problem P may be specified as a four-tuple $P = <D, M, C, M^+>$, where $M^+ \subseteq M$ is the set of all manifestations that are actually present. Given P, the task is to find the set of disorders $D^+ \subseteq D$ that is responsible for the presence of the manifestations in M^+.

It may not be possible unambiguously to determine D^+ since there may be more than one set of disorders capable of causing $M+$. Several possible criteria have been proposed to determine D^+, a few of which are listed below:

Criterion 1. D^+ is the set of all disorders capable of causing any of the manifestations in $M+$.

Criterion 2. Every set of disorders capable of causing M^+ is a possibility for the identity of $D+$, and all alternate possibilities should be found. Thus, finding the diagnosis is equivalent to finding the set of all implicants of a Boolean expression.[2]

Criterion 3. Not all of the alternate hypotheses produced by criterion 2 need be considered. If all disorders are independent of each other, then the simplest possible explanation for a set of manifestations M^+ is a set of disorders having the smallest cardinality of any of the sets of disorders capable of causing M^+. From Ockham's razor, such a smallest set of disorders is most likely to be the correct diagnosis. Each of the possibly several smallest sets of disorders capable of causing M^+ is an alternate hypothesis for the identity of D^+. Thus, finding the diagnosis is equivalent to solving a generalization of the set covering problem (Reggia, Nau, & Wang, 1983a; Reggia, Nau, & Wang, 1983b).

Criterion 4. More than just the smallest sets should be considered. For example, suppose that M^+ can be caused either by one very rare disorder d_1 or by two very common disorders d_2 and d_3. Then even though d_1 is a simpler explanation, $[d_2, d_3]$ should also be considered as a hypothesis. In general, the possible alternate hypotheses for the identity of D^+ are all sets E of disorders such that E can cause M^+ and no subset of E can cause M^+. Therefore, finding the diagnosis is equivalent to finding the prime implicants of a Boolean expression.[3]

Example

Consider a problem domain in which there are four independent disorders, d_1, d_2, d_3, and d_4. Suppose that disorder d_1 can cause manifestation m_1; disorder d_2 can cause manifestations m_1 and m_2; disorder d_3 can cause manifestations m_2, m_3, and m_4; and disorder d_4 can cause manifestation m_4; and that a disorder does not always cause all of the disorders it is capable of causing. Suppose that both m_1 and m_2 are present. In this case, criterion 1 gives the answer

$$d_1 \ \& \ d_2 \ \& \ d_3$$

Criterion 2 gives the answer

$$(d_1 \& d_3) \mid d_2 \mid (d_1 \& d_2) \mid (d_2 \& d_3) \mid (d_1 \& d_2 \& d_3)$$

Criterion 3 gives the answer

$$d_2$$

and criterion 4 gives the answer

$$(d_1 \& d_3) \mid d_2$$

Consider how a production rule system might perform. The problem domain knowledge may be written naively in the form of production rules:

R1: IF m_1 THEN d_1 (c_1)
R2: IF m_1 & m_2 THEN d_2 (c_2)
R3: IF m_2 & m_3 & m_4 THEN d_3 (c_3)
R4: IF m_4 THEN d_4 (c_4)

where c_1, c_2, c_3, and c_4 are certainly factors. In the diagnostic problem described above, these rules produce

$$d_1 \& d_2$$

which does not fit any of the four criteria. Part of the problem is that not enough rules fire because each rule requires the presence of all of its preconditions. This problem can be handled by adding additional rules referring to all combinations that can be caused by each disorder:

R 5: IF m_1 THEN d_2 (c_5)
R 6: IF m_2 THEN d_2 (c_6)
R 7: IF m_2 THEN d_3 (c_7)
R 8: IF m_3 THEN d_3 (c_8)
R 9: IF m_4 THEN d_3 (c_9)
R10: IF m_2 & m_3 THEN d_3 (c_{10})
R11: IF m_2 & m_4 THEN d_3 (c_{11})
R12: IF m_3 & m_4 THEN d_3 (c_{12})

If these rules are added, then the system will produce, with varying certainties

d_1 & d_2 & d_3

These results all fit criterion 1. Indeed, it can be shown in general that the results produced by these rules on other problems in this problem domain always fit criterion 1.

It seems fairly clear that criterion 1 is not really an adequate characterization of the solution to a diagnostic problem. However, if restricted to using rules of the form

IF manifestations THEN disorder

then the production rule approach cannot be made to satisfy criterion 2, 3, or 4 because the only conclusions it will be able to produce are conjuncts of disorders.

An Abductive Approach

Part of the reason why the usual rule-based approach cannot produce diagnoses satisfying criterion 2, 3, or 4 is that the information contained in the production rules is simply incorrect. The underlying causal knowledge is not of the form

IF manifestations THEN disorder

typically found in rule-based expert systems, but is instead of the form

IF disorder THEN manifestations

Suppose, for example, that a manifestation m can be caused by any of the disorders d, e, and f. If m is present, then the presence of d, or of e, or of f cannot be deduced. The correct action would instead be to postulate d, e, and f as alternate possible hypotheses for what is causing m.

In the above example, suppose it is also known that d, e, and f were the *only* disorders capable of causing m. Then it could be correctly deduced that at least one of d, e, and f must be present. This idea, which can be generalized and stated as a theorem relating abductive inference to deductive inference to deductive inference (Nau

& Reggia, 1984), is at the basis of an approach to diagnostic problem solving developed by Reggia, Nau, & Wang (1983a). An algorithm capable of producing answers satisfying criterion 3 has been implemented for one of the subsystems of KMS (Reggia, et al., 1980) and has successfully been used in implementing knowledge-based diagnostic problem solvers in several different domains (Reggia, et al., 1983a). This algorithm is summarized below (for a more detailed treatment, see Reggia, et al., 1983a, 1983b). The algorithm is currently being extended to criterion 4 and is producing satisfying solutions (Reggia, et al., 1984).

The algorithm, which is called HT, makes use of three main data structures:

1. MANIFS $\subseteq M^+$ is the set of manifestations known to be present so far, that is, our current hypothesis for the identity of M^+.
2. SCOPE $\subseteq D$ contains every disorder capable of causing at least one of the manifestations in MANIFS (note that this is the answer criterion 1 would produce).
3. FOCUS is the family of all smallest sets of disorders capable of causing MANIFS. This is the set of alternate hypotheses for D^+ according to criterion 3. In order to represent the alternate hypotheses compactly, FOCUS is represented as a disjunct of conjuncts of disjuncts and is manipulated directly in that form.

At the top level, HT is a hypothesize-and-test loop that looks roughly as follows:

PROCEDURE HT
1. MANIFS := SCOPE := FOCUS := $\emptyset$
2. while not all of M^+ is known do
3.   perform a test to discover a new manifestation $m \in M^+$
4.   MANIFS := MANIFS $\cup$ {m}
5.   SCOPE := SCOPE $\cup$ {$d \in D$ | $(d,m) \in C$]}
6.   adjust FOCUS to accommodate m
7. endwhile
8. return FOCUS
end HT

The knowledge base for HT is a set of frames, one for each disorder $d \in D$. The frame for a particular disorder d contains all the information available about d—what manifestations it is capable of causing, what conditions govern whether it may occur, and so on. These frames thus define the causal relation C. In addition, the frames contain information (analogous to certainty factors) about how likely it is to cause each of its manifestations, and this information is used to determine the relative likelihoods of the various alternate hypotheses.

In adjusting FOCUS to accommodate a new manifestation m, there are two possible cases that may occur:

1. Some of the sets of disorders in FOCUS may be capable of causing MANIFS $\cup \{ m \}$. In this case, it can be proved that the smallest family of disorders capable of causing MANIFS $\cup \{ m \}$ is a subfamily of FOCUS. Thus, FOCUS must be adjusted to remove the sets of disorders that no longer work.
2. MANIFS $\cup \{ m \}$ cannot be caused by any set of disorders in FOCUS. In this case, it can be proved that each smallest set of disorders capable of causing MANIFS $\cup \{ m \}$ has cardinality exactly one more than the cardinality of each smallest set of disorders capable of causing MANIFS. In this case, FOCUS must be completely recomputed, but the problem is not as difficult as it might be in general since we know exactly how many disorders will appear in each set.

The operation of HT used in the Example section above is illustrated below. Just how tests are generated in line 3 is described in Reggia et al. (1983). The final result produced is independent of the order in which the manifestations are discovered. Assuming that m_1, m_2, and m_3 are present and that they are discovered in that order, then the following events occur:

1. Initially, MANIFS = SCOPE = FOCUS = $\emptyset$.
2. m_1 is found to be present. Then MANIFS is set to $\{ m_1 \}$. SCOPE is set to $\{ d_1, d_2 \}$, the set of all disorders that can cause m_1. MANIFS can be caused by d_1 alone or d_2 alone, so FOCUS is the expression

    $$d_1 \mid d_2$$

3. m_2 is found to be present. The disorders capable of causing m_2

are d_2 and d_3. These are added into SCOPE, yielding SCOPE = $\{d_1, d_2, d_3\}$. MANIFS can still be caused by d_2, but not by d_1. Thus FOCUS is the expression

$$d_2$$

4. m_3 is found to be present. The only disorder capable of causing m_3 is d_3; thus, SCOPE does not change. No single disorder can now explain MANIFS. Thus FOCUS is recomputed, looking for sets of two disorders each. Both $\{d_1, d_3\}$ and $\{d_2, d_3\}$ work, and thus FOCUS is represented as the expression

$$(d_1 \mid d_2) \ \& \ d_3$$

5. No more manifestations are found. Thus, HT terminates and returns FOCUS, which is the correct answer according to criterion 3.

SUMMARY

Expert systems are commonly defined as computed systems that use problem-specific problem-solving knowledge to achieve high levels of performance in fields that normally require human experts. It may not be clear from this definition what distinguishes such a system from an ordinary applications program. Certainly, applications programs make use of specialized problem-solving knowledge, and many of them reach high levels of performance. Probably the main differences are the following:

1. In expert systems, the domain-dependent problem-solving information appears explicitly in a knowledge base rather than appearing only implicitly as part of the coding of the program. This knowledge base is manipulated by a separate control structure, which uses domain-independent techniques to search for and elaborate upon various possible solutions to the problem.
2. Just as with applications programs, expert systems cannot be developed for a problem without the availability of human experts who know how to solve the problem. But expert systems can sometimes be developed in problem domains where the human experts cannot explain how they solve the problems they solve.

During the last several years, expert systems techniques have begun to find a number of applications outside artificial intelligence research laboratories. Dendral has been used by university and industrial chemists on a number of problems. R1 saves Digital Equipment Corporation several million dollars each year as an aid in installing computer systems. AT&T's Ace is routinely used as an aid in telephone line maintenance. And Prospector has discovered new ore deposits (Campbell, Hollister, Duda, & Hart, 1982). For the success of expert computer systems in other applications, progress will be required in several areas.

One problem is the amount of effort it takes to build an expert system. Some expert systems have taken as many as 10 to 25 worker-years to build and have cost as much as $1 million to $2 million. One reason for this is the lack of software tools for implementing expert computer systems. Progress is currently being made in this direction with tools for building expert systems (such as Age, Art, Emycin, Expert, Hearsay-III, KEE, KMS, Loops, and OPS-5).

A second problem is the amount of time necessary to take the knowledge from an expert in some problem domain and encode it in a knowledge base. This is partly because of a lack of adequate tools for this task, and partly because of the large gaps that still remain in our understanding of human problem solving. Some of the knowledge that an expert uses to solve a problem often cannot be made consciously accessible to the expert or to others without a great deal of effort. This has been one of the motivations for some of the recent research on machine learning (Michalski, Carbonell, and Mitchell, 1983).

A third issue is that because expert systems have until recently been largely experimental, it has not been necessary to design such systems for long-term maintenance or to construct them to be "friendly" to a community of users who may not have a sophisticated knowledge of computers. For example, users are less likely to believe the conclusions reached by an expert system unless it can justify or explain its conclusions in an understandable and convincing way (Teach & Shortliffe, 1981). Although a number of researchers are doing work on justification and explanation facilities in expert computer systems (Davis, et al., 1977; Swartout, 1981; Hasling, Clancey, and Rennels, 1984; Reggia and Perricone, 1983; Reggia, Perricone, Nau, and Peng, 1985a, b), more attention will have to be paid to such real-world details in order to develop useful expert systems for real-world problems.

Fourth, expert systems are currently something of a fad, and expert computer systems technology is being oversold. Recent publicity and hyperbole about expert systems have led many potential users to have overly optimistic expectations about the potential applicability, ease of use, and level of performance of expert systems. Simply because it sounds sophisticated, some people are using the term "expert system" indiscriminately to describe relatively conventional computer programs, and others are attempting to build expert systems for tasks that could perhaps better be solved using conventional techniques. Expert systems are potentially useful for a number of problems, but unless potential users take a more cautious view of the potential of expert systems, they run the risk of disappointment with the performance of the systems they buy or build.

NOTES

1. KMS has three subsystems: KMS.PS, which is based on production rules; KMS.BAYES, which is based on Beyesian classification; and KMS.HT, which is based on a generalization of the set-covering problem. The user can select which approach appears best for the problem domain under consideration and build an expert computer system using that approach.

2. If B is a Boolean expression and C is a conjunct of variables appearing in B, then C is an implicant of B if the statement "$C \rightarrow B$" is true for all possible values of the variables in B and C. For example, the implicants of $(a \ \& \ b) \mid c$ are $a \ \& \ b$, c, and $a \ \& \ b \ \& \ c$.

3. If B is a Boolean expression, then C is a prime implicant of B if C is an implicant of B and there is no other implicant C' of B, which is also an implicant of C. For example, the prime implicants of $(a \ \& \ b) \mid c$ are $a \ \& \ b$ and c. For a more detailed discussion, see Kohavi (1970).

REFERENCES

Aiello, N., & Nii, H. (1979). *Building a knowledge-based system with AGE* (Tech. Memo HPP-79-3). Stanford, CA: Stanford University, Computer Science Department.

Aikins, J. S. (1980, August). Prototypes and Production Rules: A Knowledge Representation for Computer Consultations, Ph.D. Dissertation, Tech. Report STAN-CS-80-814, Dept. of Computer Sciences, Stanford University.

Biermann, A. W. (1978, September). Theoretical issues related to computer game playing programs. *Personal Computing*, 86–88.

Bobrow, D. G., & Winograd, T. (1977). An overview of KRL, a knowledge representation language. *Cognitive Science, 1* (1), 3–46.

Brachman, R. (1979). On the epistemological status of semantic networks. In N. V. Findler (Ed.), *Associative networks: Representation and use of knowledge by Computer* (pp. 3–50). New York: Academic Press.

Buchanan, B. G., & Feigenbaum, E. A. (1978). Dendral and Meta-Dentral: Their applications dimension. *Artificial Intelligence, 11*, 5–24.

Campbell, A. N., Hollister, V. F., Duda, R. O., & Hart, P. E. (1982, September). Recognition of a hidden mineral deposit by an artificial intelligence program. *Science, 217*, 3, 927–929.

Chandrasekaran, B., Gomez, F., Mittal, S., & Smith, J. (1979, August). An Approach to Medical Diagnosis Based on Conceptual Structures. *Proceedings of the Sixth International Joint Conference on Artificial Intelligence.* Tokyo, pp. 134–142.

Chilausky, R., Jacobsen, B., and Michalski, R. S. (1979, August). An Application of Variable-Valued Logic in Inductive Learning of Plant Disease Diagnostic Rules. *Proceedings of the Sixth Annual International Symposium on Multi-Valued Logic*, Utah.

Clocksin, W., & Mellish, C. (1981). *Programming in PROLOG.* New York: Springer-Verlag.

Davis, R., Buchanan, B. G., & Shortliffe, E. (1977). Production rules as a representation for a knowledge-based consultation program. *Artificial Intelligence, 8*, 1, 15–45.

Davis, R., Austin, H., Carlbom, I., Frawley, B., Pruchnik, P., Sneiderman, R., & Gilreath, J. A. (1981, August). The Dipmeter Advisor: Interpretation of Geological Signals. *Proceedings of the Seventh International Joint Conference on Artificial Intelligence.*

deDombal, F. (1975). Computer assisted diagnosis of abdominal pain. In J. Mitchell (Ed.), *Advances in medical computing* (pp. 10–19). New York: Churchill-Livingston.

Duda, R., & Hart, P. (1973). *Pattern classification and scene analysis.* New York: Wiley.

Erman, L. D., Hayes-Roth, F., Lesser, V. R., & Reddy, D. R. (1980, June). The Hearsay-II speech-understanding system: Integrating knowledge to resolve uncertainty. *Computing Surveys, 12*(2), 213-253.

Erman, L. D., London, P., & Fickas, S. F. (1981). The design and an example use of HEARSAY-III. *Proceeding of the Seventh International Joint Conference on Artificial Intelligence* (pp. 409-415).

Fagan, J. M. (1980, June). VM: Representing Time-Dependent Relations in a Medical Setting, Ph.D. Dissertation, Computer Science Dept., Stanford University, Stanford, CA.

Fahlman, S. E. (1979). *NETL: A system for representing and using real-world knowledge.* Cambridge, MA: MIT Press.

Fain, J., Hayes-Roth, F., Sowizral, H., & Waterman, D. (1982). *Programming in ROSIE: An introduction by means of examples* (Tech. Rep. N-1646-ARPA). Santa Monica, CA: Rand Corp.

Feigenbaum, E., Buchanan, B. G., & Lederberg, J. (1971). Generality and problem solving: A case study using the DENDRAL program. In B. Meltzer & D. Michie (Eds.), *Machine Intelligence 6.* Edinburgh: Edinburgh University Press.

Fikes, R. E., & Nilsson, N. J. (1971). STRIPS: A new approach to the application of theorem proving to problem solving. *Artificial Intelligence, 2* (3/4), 189-208.

Findler, N. (Ed.). (1979). *Associative networks: Representation and use of knowledge by computers.* New York: Academic Press.

Forgy, C. L. (1980). *The OPS5 User's Manual* (Tech. Rep. CMU-CS-8-135). Pittsburgh: Carnegie-Mellon University, Computer Science Department.

Goldstein, I., & Papert, S. (1977). Artificial intelligence, language and the study of knowledge. *Cognitive Science, 1* (1), 84-123.

Greiner, R., & Lenat, D. (1980). A representation language language. *Proceedings of the First Annual National Conference on Artificial Intelligence.*

Hart, P. E., Duda, R. O., & Einaudi, M. T. (1978). A Computer-Based Consultation System for Mineral Exploration, SRI International, Menlo Park, CA.

Hasling, D. W., Clancey, W. J., & Rennels, G. (1984). Strategic explanations for a diagnostic consultation system. *International Journal of Man-Machine Studies, 20*, 3–19.

Hayes-Roth, F., Waterman, D. A., & Lenat, D. B. (1983). *Building expert systems.* Reading, MA: Addison-Wesley.

Hewitt, C. (1972). Description and theoretical analysis (using schemata) of PLANNER: A language for proving theorems and manipulating models in a robot (Tech. Rep. 258). Cambridge, MA: Massachusetts Institute of Technology, Artificial Intelligence Laboratory.

Kohavi, Z. (1970). *Switching and finite automata theory.* New York: McGraw-Hill.

Kowalski, R. A. (1979). *Logic for problem solving.* New York: North-Holland.

Loveland, D. W. (1978). *Automated theorem proving: A logical basis.* New York: North-Holland.

Martin, N., Friedland, P., King, J., & Stefik, M. J. (1977). Knowledge-Based Management for Experiment Planning in Molecular Genetics. *Proceedings of the Fifth International Joint Conference on Artificial Intelligence*, pp. 882–887.

Matthys, H., Fischer, J., Ulrichs, H., & Ruhle, K. (1979). Functional patterns of different lung diseases for computer-assisted diagnostic procedures. *Progress in Respiration Research, 11*, 188–201.

McCracken, D. L. (1979). Representation and efficiency in a production system for speech understanding. *Proceedings of the Sixth International Joint Conference on Artificial Intelligence* (pp. 556–561).

McDermott, J. & Steele, B. (1981, August). Extending a Knowledge-Based System to Deal with Ad Hoc Constraints. *Proceedings of the Seventh International Joint Conference on Artificial Intelligence*, pp. 824–828.

Melle, W. van (1979). A domain-independent production rule system for consultation programs. *Proceedings of the Sixth International Joint Conference on Artificial Intelligence.*

Michalski, R. S., Carbonell, J. G., & Mitchell, T. M. (1983). *Machine learning: An artificial intelligence approach*. Palo Alto, CA: Tioga.

Minsky, M. (1975). A framework for representing knowledge. In P. H. Winston (Ed.), *The psychology of computer vision* (pp. 211-277). New York: Mc-Graw-Hill.

Moses, J. (1971). Symbolic Integration: The Stormy Decade, *Communications of the ACM, 14*, pp. 548-560.

Mylopoulos, J. (1980, June). An overview of knowledge representation. *Proc. Workshop on Data Abstraction, Databases, and Conceptual Modeling* (pp. 5-12).

Nau, D. S., & Reggia, J. A. (1984). Relationships between abductive and deductive inference in knowledge-based diagnostic problem solving. Reprinted in Kerschberg, M. ed. (1985), *Expert-Database Systems*.

Newell, A., & Simon, H. A. (1963). GPS, a program that simulates human thought. In E. A. Feigenbaum & J. A. Feldman (Eds.), *Computers and thought*. New York: McGraw-Hill.

Nii, H. P., & Aiello, N. (1979). AGE (attempt to generalize): A knowledge-based program for building knowledge-based programs. *Proceedings of the Sixth International Joint Conference on Artificial Intelligence* (pp. 645-655).

Nilsson, N. J. (1971). *Problem-solving methods in artificial intelligence*. New York: McGraw-Hill.

Nilsson, N. J. (1980). *Principles of artificial intelligence*. Palo Alto, CA: Tioga.

Osborn, J., Fagan, L., Fallat, R., McClung, D., & Mitchell, R. (1979, November). Managing the data from respiratory measurements. *Medical Instrumentation, 13*, 6.

Pople, H. E. (1977). The Formation of Composite Hypotheses in Diagnostic Problem Solving: an Exercise in Synthetic Reasoning. *Proceedings of the Fifth International Joint Conference on Artificial Intelligence*, pp. 1030-1037.

Reggia, J. A. (1981, October). *Knowledge-based decision support systems: Development through KMS*. Ph.D. Dissertation (Tech. Rep. TR-1121). College Park: University of Maryland, Computer Science Department.

Reggia, J. A., Nau, D. S., & Wang, P. Y. (1985). Diagnostic expert systems based on a set covering model. Reprinted in Reggia, J. A., & Tuhrim, S. (1984, November), *Computer-Assisted Medical Decision Making.*

Reggia, J. A., Nau, D. S., & Wang, P. Y. (1983a, November). Diagnostic expert systems based on a set covering model. *International Journal of Man-Machine Studies*, 437-460.

Reggia, J. A., Nau, D. S., & Wang, P. Y. (1983b, December). *A theory of abductive inference in diagnostic expert systems* (Tech. Rep. TR-1338). College Park: University of Maryland, Computer Science Department.

Reggia, J. A., A., Peng, Y., & Nau, D. S. (in preparation). A formal model of diagnostic inference. Part Three. Exploring the nature of parsimony.

Reggia, J. A., & Perricone, B. T. (1983). *Answer justification in medical decision support systems based on Bayesian classification.* College Park: University of Maryland.

Reggia, J. A., Perricone, B., Nau, D. S., & Peng, Y. (1985a, April). Answer justification in abductive expert systems for diagnostic problem solving, Part I: Abductive inference and its justification. *IEEE Transactions on Biomedical Engineering.* Volume No. BME-32, No. 4, p. 263-267.

Reggia, J. A., Perricone, B., Nau, D. S., & Peng Y. (1985b, April). Answer justification in abductive expert systems for diagnostic problem solving, Part II: Supporting plausible justifications, *IEEE Transactions on Biomedical Engineering.* Volume No. BME-32, No. 4, p. 268-272.

Reggia, J. A., Pula, T. P., Price, T. R., & Perricone, B. T. (1980, November). Towards an intelligent textbook of neurology. *Proceedings of the Fourth Annual Symposium on Computer Applications in Medical Care* (pp. 190-199).

Reggia, J. A., Tabb, D. R., Price, T. R., Banko, M., & Hebel, R. (1984). Computer-Aided Assessment of Transient Ischemic Attacks: A Clinical Evaluation. *Archives of Neurology.*

Robinson, A. L. (1979). Tournament competition fuels computer chess. *Science, 204* 1396-1398.

Rogers, W., Ryack, B., & Moeller, G. (1979). Computer-aided medical diagnosis—Literature review. *International Journal of Biomedical Computing, 10,* 267-289.

Schank, R. (1972). Conceptual dependency: A theory of natural language understanding. *Cognitive Psychology, 3, 4.*

Schank, R. C. (1975). *Conceptual information processing.* New York: North-Holland.

Schubert, L. K. (1976). Extending the expressive power of semantic nets. *Artificial Intelligence 7,* 2, 163-198.

Snyder, B., Ramirez-Lassepas, M., & Lippert. D. (1977). Neurologic status and prognosis after cardiopulmonary arrest. *Neurology, 27,* 807.

Stallman, R. M., & Sussman, G. J. (1977). Forward reasoning and dependency-directed backtracking in a system for computer-aided circuit analysis. *Artificial Intelligence, 9,* 135-196.

Stolfo, S. J., & Vesonder, G. T. (1983). ACE: An Expert System Supporting Analysis and Management Decision Making, Tech. Report, Dept. of Computer Science, Columbia University.

Sussman, G. J., & McDermott, D. (1972). From PLANNER to Conniver, a genetic approach. *Proceedings of the Fall Joint Computer Conference, 41* (p. 1171).

Swartout, W. R. (1981, August). Explaining and justifying expert consulting programs. *Proceedings of the Seventh International Joint Conference on Artificial Intelligence* (pp. 815-822).

Teach, R., & Shortliffe, E. (1981). An analysis of physical attitudes regarding computer-based clinical consultation systems. *Computers and Biomedical Research, 14,* 542-558.

Truscott, T. R. (1979, June). Minimum variance tree searching. *Proceedings of the First International Symposium on Policy Analysis and Information Systems* (pp. 203-209). Durham, NC.

Weiss, S. M., Kulikowski, C. A., Amarel, S., and Safir, A. (1978). A Model-Based Method for Computer Aided Medical Decision-Making. *Artificial Intelligence II,* 2, p. 145-172.

Weiss, S. M., Kulikowski, C. A., Amarel, S., & Safir, A. (1979). EXPERT: A system for developing consultation models. *Proceedings of the Sixth International Joint Conference on Artificial Intelligence* (pp. 942-947).

Winston, P. H. (1977). *Artificial intelligence.* Reading, MA: Addison-Wesley.

Zagoria, R. J., & Reggia, J. A. (1983). Transferability of medical decision support systems based on Bayesian classification. *Medical Decision Making, 3.*

7

IMPROVING DECISION MAKING: A COGNITIVE APPROACH

Ruth H. Phelps, Rebecca M. Pliske, and Sharon A. Mutter

What is a decision? The answer seems quite obvious. Decisions are choices among alternatives: which car to buy, which applicant to hire, where to locate the new plant. A decision may be between doing and not doing: to build now or wait, to be or not to be. However, a little reflection will reveal that real-world decision makers make many other types of decisions that are not so easily categorized: how much to invest, how to improve employee morale, how to reduce attrition, how to achieve a balanced budget, and the list goes on. These decision makers are also solving problems, and only some of the decisions they make are choices among alternatives. Thus, "decision" must be defined broadly enough to encompass the variety of behaviors decision makers perform. To the practitioner of decision making, the definition of decision making must include subjective judgments, choices, solutions to problems, and the absence of these activities. For the systems designer, the definition must convey the idea that the decision maker needs support for problems much greater than the selection among alternatives. A decision is therefore a general problem to be solved that may be well or ill-defined at the outset, structured or unstructured, subjective or objective.

This chapter differs from most other discussions of decision making in that it focuses on the cognitive processes involved in decision making rather than on the decision or choice itself. Specifically, emphasis is placed on the mental or thinking processes that are basic to decision making, the deficiencies or errors that are associated with these processes, and methods of compensating for these deficiencies in processing. This emphasis on cognitive processing has considerable practical value for practitioners and systems designers seeking to improve the quality of decision making. Indeed, this chapter will show how a cognitive model for decision making can be of greater benefit in aiding decision making and designing decision support systems than the more traditional approaches to this process.

To support this goal, the chapter has been divided into three sections. The first section briefly summarizes the major approaches to decision making and highlights the ways in which these approaches are limited in their description of human decision-making behavior. The second section presents a detailed look at both the cognitive "steps" of decision making and the natural limitations in decision making that arise from processing deficiencies in these steps. The third section describes a case study in which the cognitive model presented in the second section has been adapted to the specific class of decisions involved in military intelligence analysis. This case study shows how the model can be of great value in delineating and improving the cognitive processes involved in real-world decision making.

APPROACHES TO STUDYING DECISION MAKING

There are three major categories of approaches to the contemporary study of decision making.[1] Although all do not share a concern for understanding the cognitive processes, features from each approach have been incorporated into the stage model presented in the next section. The first category is decision theory, which includes those approaches philosophically derived from economics and mathematics. Decision theory analysts and, to a lesser extent, operations researchers typically apply this approach. The second category is loosely called decision support systems and includes approaches from the disciplines of systems engineering, business, organizational information systems, and management science. The third category is psychological decision making, including basic and applied research from the fields of cognition, social judgment, and measurement. For each category the origins and methods will be briefly described.

Decision Theory

Decision theory is based on the axioms of expected utility theory as constructed by the mathematician T. Von Neuman and the economist O. Morgenstern (1947). Expected utility theory itself is derived from the value theory of nineteenth-century economists as well as from the famous Bernoulli expression: The worth of a decision is determined by the probability of events and their associated utilities. Decision theory has been applied to choices between risky options (for instance, two gambles), riskless options (two cars), as well as multiattributed options (two jobs that vary in salary, location, and interest). It is by far the most widely used method for aiding decision makers in the real world.

For the decision theorist, the "decision" is defined as the logical selection of one alternative from a set of many alternatives, the associated probabilities of occurrence, and the relative utility (value) of each alternative. More importantly, however, it is assumed that the decision maker is completely rational and should behave in accordance with the theory. There is no room for personal deviations once the probabilities and utilities have been assigned.

The decision theory method involves obtaining the decision maker's utilities (values) and probabilities for each alternative, multiplying them together, and designating the alternative with the highest score as the most "preferred." Extensive research (for example, the classic work by Mostellar & Nogee, 1951) has been conducted to test the axioms underlying the theory and the best method for extracting utilities and probabilities from decision makers (Davidson, Suppes, & Siegel, 1957; Tversky, 1967). Despite this early research, two problems plague decision theoretic techniques: (1) obtaining valid utilities and probabilities and (2) assuming the decision maker is completely rational. To counter these problems, decision makers are often coached by a trained decision analyst who acts not unlike a psychotherapist in counseling a client to arrive reasonably at a solution.

Decision Support Systems

The notion of decision support systems, a relatively recent approach to decision making, evolved from two main research fields: interactive computer systems and theoretical organizational decision making. Simon's (1960) seminal book, *The New Science of Management Decision*, provided a description of decision making that differed from decision theory in that it emphasized the "bounded rationality" of human decision-making abilities. That is, people are limited in the amount of information they can process and the methods they use to integrate information. Furthermore, Simon argued that if these limitations could be transcended, then decision-making effectiveness would be enhanced. The marriage of the human with the interactive computer was deemed to be the best method for achieving these new heights for decision makers.

Computers are extremely effective for organizing, storing, and retrieving information in either raw or summarized form. Consequently, the major contribution of the decision support approach has been the design of automated support for decision makers who must deal with large volumes of information. However, decision support system research is guided by little theoretical work beyond Simon's ideas and loose behavioral models. Moreover, the attempts to automate information processing and decision making have emphasized that our understanding of decision making is fuzzy—a computer cannot be told to do what we ourselves cannot define. The net effect is the development of decision support systems that do not support decision making.

Psychological Decision Making

The last approach that will be discussed in this chapter is composed of a number of distinct psychological models of decision making. However, all of these models are similar in that they are concerned with subjective factors in decision making, such as values, attitudes, perceptions of others, perceived worth, and resolution of conflict. Moreover, many of these models emphasize the mental events that influence these factors and that are presumed to lead to overt decision-making behavior. Historically, these models trace their origins to the methods and concerns of nineteenth-century psychologists. Much of the recent work in this area is derived from the theories of Brunswick (1955), Heider (1958), and Thurstone (1927). A very excellent and thoughtful review of the major psychological approaches can be found in Hammond, McClelland, and Mumpower (1980). The focus of psychological approaches to decision making is on describing both quantitatively and qualitatively how people actually make decisions, especially noting deviations from theoretically optimal models of behavior such as Bayes' theorem. Psychological approaches use mathematical models only as reference points for measuring human behavior—they are not typically used as prescriptive algorithms for optimal behavior.

Psychologists use scientific methods for evaluating the influence of variables on decision-making behavior in laboratory settings. The most common paradigm is to present hypothetical decisions to experimental participants and then analyze the decision process by measuring and manipulating such variables as decision consistency, accuracy, use of various types and amounts of information, methods of integrating information, effects of feedback, small group interactions, the use of individual decision strategies, and the effects of memory and perception, to name but a few.

The major contribution of the psychological decision-making approach has been the massive number of experiments that collectively have begun to expose both the environmental variables (how information is presented and formatted, information overload, context effects) and the cognitive variables (mental strategies, cognitive limitations, memory processes) that influence decision-making behavior. Although the use of laboratory studies may somewhat restrict the generalizability of results, many of the findings appear so consistent and robust that they can be applied to real-world settings with a good deal of confidence.

Unfortunately, there seem to be few psychologists who are interested in making the transition between basic research in cognitive processes and practical applications in decision making. In the next two sections of the chapter an attempt is made to bridge this gap by outlining a model of cognitive processes in decision making, by summarizing pertinent research on cognitive processes in decision making, and finally, by applying this model to a real-world decision-making situation.

A COGNITIVE PROCESSING MODEL
OF DECISION MAKING

The model that follows is called a stage model because several discrete stages or phases of decision making are identified. Many different stage descriptions of the decision-making process have been proposed (see, for example, Janis & Mann, 1977; Sage, 1981); however, the five stages shown in Figure 7.1 and discussed below seem to

FIGURE 7.1. A Cognitive Processing Model of Decision Making.

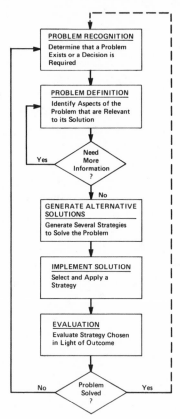

be the most useful conceptualization of the decision-making process in a problem-solving context. Although the stages are presented as discrete, sequential steps, the decision maker may execute an operation in two or more stages simultaneously. Furthermore, in some decision-making situations, the decision maker may not explicitly perform the operations specified in each stage; however, similar cognitive processes are involved implicitly in all decision behavior.

Problem Recognition

In stage 1, the decision maker must recognize that a problem exists or that a decision needs to be made. This is one of many important "predecision" processes that occur prior to the actual choice of a course of action. As Corbin (1980) points out, this is an often neglected aspect of decision making. Clearly, before any decision can be made, a decision maker must recognize when and if a decision *needs* to be made. It is important to realize that, for a variety of motivational reasons, decision makers may "recognize" that a problem exists but choose either to ignore or delay the decision (that is, choose *not* to decide). Alternatively, decision makers may be unaware that an occasion for choice exists. This is often the case in ambiguous situations when the information presented to the decision maker is insufficient or inappropriately summarized. For example, an entrepreneur may fail to recognize that a decision about the addition of a new product line needs to be made due to lack of appropriate information, such as an up-to-date market analysis.

The cognitive processes of perception, attention, and memory are particularly relevant at this initial stage in the decision-making process. Decision makers acquire information about potential problems through their sense modalities (their eyes, ears, and so on) that respond to external stimuli (lights, sounds, and the like) in the environment. In any particular decision-making environment, there is more information than a single decision maker can process at a given time. There are essentially two types of capacity limits on our information processing. First, there is a peripheral limitation because each of our sensory modalities is limited in that we can only receive (see, hear, smell) so much sensory information at one time. Second, many theorists (see Kahneman, 1973; Norman & Bobrow, 1975) have proposed that there is a central pool of capacity that is shared by all the sense modalities. Thus, when a piece of incoming information (an input) is compared to information stored in memory, it must compete with inputs from all other sense modalities. Because decision makers have information processing systems with limited capacities, they must be selective in what they attend to, that is, they can only attend to a subset of the available information in their environment.

This stage of the decision-making process is likely to be affected by the amount of experience the decision maker has in a particular context. Inexperienced decision makers may fail to detect problem situations because they fail to attend to critical changes that have taken place in the environment. On the other hand, experienced decision makers may be very skilled at detecting patterns of early warning signals that indicate a potential problem exists.

Problem Definition

After the decision maker recognizes that a decision problem exists, the problem must be clearly defined. The decision maker forms an internal representation or "mental model" (Gentner & Stevens, 1983) of the decision problem that relates the problem to other knowledge stored in memory. Research indicates that this is a crucial stage in the decision process, because unless decision makers have identified the important aspects of the problem in question, they may fail to consider the optimal solution (Gettys, Kelley, Pliske, & Beckstead, 1983).

Structured versus Unstructured Problems

Decision problems vary a great deal in terms of how structured or defined they are. Most psychological research on problem solving has focused on well-defined or highly structured problems in which people are given a clearly specified problem statement that explains the "goal state," the "present state," and the "permissible operations" they may use to get to the goal state from the present state (Newell & Simon, 1972). For example, in the well-known "Tower of Hanoi" puzzle, shown in Figure 7.2, the goal state and present state might be specified as "To solve the problem you must move all three disks from peg A (present state) to peg C (goal state)." Problem solvers would also be given a set of permissible operations by which they may move toward the goal state: "You may move one disk at a time from one peg to another"; and they would be explicitly told about the existing constraints: "You can never place a larger disk on top of a disk smaller than itself."

In contrast to the Tower of Hanoi puzzle, decision makers in the real world are often faced with a totally unstructured or ill-defined problem in which they may have only a fuzzy idea about the goal state and their present state. The permissible operations usually must be generated by the decision maker, who may be uncertain about the

FIGURE 7.2. Initial and Goal States for the Tower of Hanoi Puzzle.

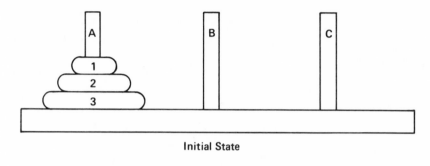

Initial State

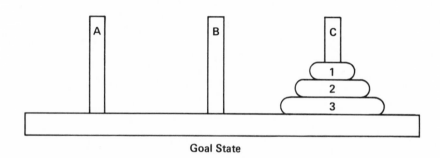

Goal State

existing constraints. Consider an example from Gettys (1983) of a military field commander who experiences a surprise attack. The commander's present state will not be clearly specified until additional information, such as damage and casualty reports, is received. The commander's goal state may also be unclear because the original goal may no longer be attainable. The permissible operations may be undefined due to lack of information about present resources and existing constraints. When faced with an unstructured problem, decision makers must provide their own structure as they construct their mental model of the problem. That is, they must fill in the details of the goal state, present state, permissible operations, and existing constraints by gathering additional information and recalling information from memory.

In sum, decision makers must often make inferences based on limited data in order to provide a complete mental representation from which they can proceed to generate alternative solutions.

Research indicates that the nature of this mental representation is very critical because changing people's mental representation or perspective of the problem often alters (even reverses) their preferences of alternative solutions to the problem (Tversky & Kahneman, 1981).

Analogies Help Define the Problem

One way to define and clarify a problem is to recall similar or analogous problems solved previously. Research indicates that people have difficulty detecting these problem "isomorphs" even with highly structured problems (Reed, Ernst, & Baneji, 1974; Simon & Hayes, 1976). That is, after solving a problem, people, given a second problem with the same basic structure as the first problem, tend not to recognize that the second problem can also be solved with the same strategy. However, other research (Gettys, et al., 1983) indicates that when people are explicitly told that two semistructured problems can be solved using similar strategies, they are able to apply solutions generated for solving the first problem to the solution of the second problem. Recently, cognitive psychologists have begun to examine how people process analogies and metaphors (Gentner, 1982; Ortony, 1979). We anticipate that this research will improve our future understanding of how people recognize similar problems.

Gathering Additional Information Helps Clarify the Problem

A critical activity during the problem definition and clarification stage is the gathering of additional information about the decision problem in question. A great deal of research by cognitive psychologists indicates that people demonstrate systematic biases in their information gathering behavior.[2] Most of these studies compare people's behavior in tasks involving information acquisition and analysis to the normative results that would have occurred if the people had followed an "optimal" information gathering procedure. The literature describing this research is very extensive and only a brief summary of selected studies will be discussed in this chapter. Recent texts by Nisbett and Ross (1980), Hogarth (1980), and Kahneman, Slovic, and Tversky (1982) offer excellent reviews. Generally, this research has indicated that most people have difficulty sorting relevant from irrelevant information that is available to them from both external sources and from their own memories. First, discussed are the biases in the recall of information from memory, then the biases in selecting information from external sources.

Biases Influence Recall of Information from Memory

When we recall information from memory, we do not recall all information equally well. For example, the order in which you receive information will affect your ability to recall that information; items that are first in a series are better remembered. Vivid information is likely to attract and hold our attention, so it is more likely to be recorded in our memory in a retrievable format. Concrete information (which also tends to be more vivid) is easily "imaginable" because it usually includes sensory details. Research indicates that concreteness and imaginability can improve our ability to recall information from memory (Bower, 1972). Personal information, or information that is obtained firsthand through one's own senses, is also more likely to be remembered than information received second-hand.

Because both our attention and our memory processes are selective, vivid or concrete information may have greater impact on our judgment than abstract information of objectively greater value. "Objective" information is often presented to the decision maker in aggregated, statistical, or summary form (such as a table of percentages) that lacks concreteness and emotional interest. "Subjective" data are often in the form of vivid anecdotes that subsequently have a more powerful effect on the decision maker's judgment than the objective data. In fact, a substantial amount of research indicates decision makers tend to neglect summary statistics, such as base rate of occurrence, in favor of concrete, anecdotal information (Borgida & Brekke, 1981; Tversky & Kahneman, 1982).

When we recall information from memory, we must also be careful to separate actual facts from previous inferences we have made. Cognitive psychologists have repeatedly demonstrated that when we recall information from memory we often reconstruct this information rather than retrieve verbatim memory records of previous events. People tend to record general descriptions of events and then fill in the details when they are asked to recall the event. These details are usually consistent with what we would logically infer or assume given the general description, but because recall is reconstructive it is not always veridical. For example, research indicates that the testimony of eyewitnesses to events such as traffic accidents can be influenced by subtle changes in the way in which they are questioned (Loftus & Palmer, 1974). This research suggests that decision makers can be led to recall inaccurate information that may subsequently affect their judgment.

Biases Influence Selection of Information from External Sources

In addition to relying on information stored in memory, decision makers often seek information from external sources, such as written reports, data bases, or other colleagues, as they attempt to clarify the decision problem in question. This additional information should help to reduce the decision maker's uncertainty about the situation. Normative decision theorists have labeled such information "diagnostic" information and contrast it with "nondiagnostic" or irrelevant information, which refers to information that does not differentiate between alternative options or reduce uncertainty. Cognitive psychologists have repeatedly demonstrated that people tend to modify their judgments based on nondiagnostic information (Lichtenstein, Earle, & Slovic, 1975; Troutman & Shanteau, 1977). Other research indicates that when people are given an inference task in which they can request additional information (or data) to aid them in making their judgment and they are presented with both diagnostic and nondiagnostic information, they tend to select the nondiagnostic data that should "normatively" have absolutely no impact on their judgment; they then use this information to revise their judgment (Kern & Doherty, 1983).

When decision makers seek additional information about a particular problem, they are also subject to a bias known as confirmation bias. According to Doherty, Mynatt, Tweney, and Schiavo (1979), confirmation bias can be inferred from two different forms of behavior: (1) when a person fails to change his or her opinion in the face of nonsupporting or contradictory evidence, and (2) when a person selects information favoring his or her hypothesis (or initial point of view) while ignoring information that contradicts that hypothesis. These behaviors have been observed in laboratory tasks with both novices (Wason, 1960; Mynatt, Doherty, & Tweney, 1978) and scientists as subjects (Tolbert & Phelps, 1984) and with scientists in their natural working environment (Mitroff, 1974).

Knowing When to Stop

Decision makers must determine at what point they should stop seeking additional information about the problem and begin considering alternative solutions. Numerous studies describe people's search strategies over various cost and risk conditions (for example, Edwards, 1965; Irwin & Smith, 1957). It appears that people feel they must collect information, even when the information is useless (Lanzetta & Driscoll, 1966). There is no set rule that decision makers can use to determine when they have sufficient information. Corbin (1980) suggests that people continue to collect additional information until they reduce their "subjective uncertainty" below some acceptable point, at which time they proceed in the decision-making process.

In sum, the problem definition and clarification stage is a very critical stage in the decision-making process because it affects behavior in all the subsequent stages. If decision makers fail to construct complete and veridical mental models of the decision problem in question, then it is unlikely that they will subsequently generate and/ or ultimately choose the optimal solution to the problem. As stated previously, research indicates that changing decision makers' mental models of the problem can change their preferences for alternative solutions to the problem (Tversky & Kahneman, 1981). It is not always easy for decision makers to construct complete and veridical mental models because many real-world decision makers are forced to supply their own structure by retrieving information from memory and by seeking additional information from other sources.

Generate Alternative Solutions

Decision makers must assess the decision situation and determine what type of method of solution they want to use.[3] Can you simply use a "seat-of-the-pants" approach to solve the problem, or should you consider more elaborate, formal approaches to solving the problem? There is no simple answer to this question, because the appropriateness of the chosen method of solution will be determined by the specific decision situation in question.[4] However, it is generally considered preferable to use a systematic, rational method of solving the problem rather than a haphazard or irrational approach.

The interactive nature of the different stages in the decision-making process becomes readily apparent when we begin to consider the generation of alternative methods of solution. Often, the very process of clarifying and defining the decision problem in question results in the spontaneous generation of solutions to the problem. Alternatively, decision makers may start to generate solutions to the problem and realize that their problem definition was incomplete; this may necessitate the acquisition of additional information to clarify the problem representation, but at some point decision makers must stop acquiring additional information and start to consider alternative methods to solve the problem.

Problem Constraints

When considering alternative methods of problem solution, decision makers must identify existing constraints (that is, factors that will dictate which solutions are feasible) and select a method of solution that is most appropriate given these constraints. Most decision behavior occurs in situations where time, money, and the sophistication of the decision maker (that is, the ability to carry out different methods of solution) are all salient constraints. Although some constraints are relevant to the consideration of alternative methods, decision makers should eliminate any unnecessary constraints. A somewhat simplistic example from the psychological research on problem solving may help illustrate this point. Consider the well-known nine-dot problem shown in Figure 7.3a. The problem solver is

FIGURE 7.3. The Nine-Dot Problem (a) and Its Solution (b).

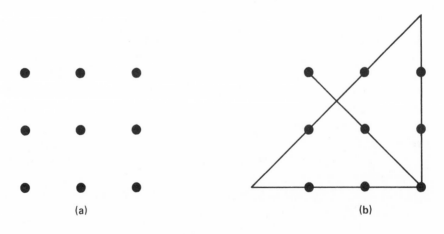

(a)　　　　　　　　　　　　　(b)

told to draw four straight lines through all nine dots without lifting the pencil from the paper. Research indicates that people usually "see" a square boundary around the nine dots; they assume this boundary is a constraint on potential solutions to the problem and never consider the solution shown in Figure 7.3b (Gick & Holyoak, 1979). Similarly, decision makers may "see" time pressure as an unavoidable constraint when in fact that particular constraint could be removed (they could get an extension on their deadline).

Decision Strategies

Various decision strategies can be used by decision makers to choose which solution they wish to implement. Decision makers may choose an optimizing strategy in which they determine the expected cost (not necessarily just the financial cost) and benefit of the outcome associated with all solutions and then, based on this "cost/benefit" analysis, select the optimal solution. Although this strategy increases decision makers' chances of selecting the optimal solution, it can often be very time consuming and expensive. Optimizing techniques include such methods as linear programming, decision analysis, and various forecasting techniques.

Alternatively, decision makers may use a satisficing strategy in which they generate alternative solutions until they come up with a solution that satisfies a minimal set of criteria. They make no attempt to compare all alternative courses of action; they essentially implement the first reasonable solution that comes to mind. This strategy is definitely less time consuming than optimizing, but it will often lead to a less than optimal solution.

There are a variety of heuristic strategies used by decision makers when selecting among alternative courses of action. Heuristics are rules of thumb for simplifying complex problems in a way that increases the probability that a solution will be found within a reasonable amount of time. Decision makers may choose a compensatory decision rule that permits a high value on one dimension of an alternative to make up for (or compensate for) a low value on another dimension. For example, when choosing an apartment, an excellent location (a high value on the location dimension) may make up for the small size (a low value on the size dimension). Similarly, when choosing between alternative methods of solution, the high cost of bringing in a decision analyst might be compensated for by the expected improvement in the quality of the final decision. Various forms of the general linear model have been used to describe compensatory decision rules (Dawes & Corrigan, 1974).

Instead of using a compensatory heuristic, decision makers may choose to use a noncompensatory rule that does not permit a high value on one dimension to compensate for a low value on another dimension. Many different types of noncompensatory decision rules have been studied. For example, lexicographic rules are noncompensatory rules in which the dimensions are ordered according to their importance to the decision maker, and then the alternatives are ordered with respect to their values on the most important dimension; the next most important dimension is only taken into account when there are ties on the more important dimension (Keeney & Raiffa, 1976). Elimination by aspects is a specific variation of a lexicographic rule in which the probability that a particular dimension will be considered in the decision is proportional to the importance of dimension (Tversky, 1972).

In their efforts to determine which rule best describes decision makers' choice behavior when they are given a set of alternative solutions, cognitive psychologists (Billings & Marcus, 1983; Dawes & Corrigan, 1974; Einhorn, 1970, 1971) have generally found that decision rules will vary as a function of the decision task (Einhorn & Hogarth, 1981). Generalizing this research to the selection of a method of problem solution, it is recommended that this selection of a decision strategy should only be made after there is an adequate understanding of the problem at hand.

Generation of Alternative Solutions

In contrast to the large research literature exploring the alternative decision rules used by decision makers to select among an existing set of alternative solutions, there has been very little cognitive research investigating people's ability to generate a set of alternative solutions. The research that has been done is not very encouraging, for it indicates that people have difficulty generating a wide variety of solutions to problems (see Gettys, 1983, for a review). People tend to generate a few acceptable solutions to the problem and then report they have "run out of ideas." This finding has been demonstrated with both expert (Mehle, 1982) and nonexpert subjects (Gettys, Manning, & Casey, 1981; Pitz, Sachs, & Heerboth, 1980).

Similar behavior has been described in both organizational decision making (Simon, 1976) and decision making in a military setting (Phelps, Englert, & Mutter, 1984).

When generating alternative methods for solving the problem, decision makers must determine whether the decision problem should be solved by a single individual or by a group of individuals. Groups usually take more time to make decisions than do individuals; however, group decision methods allow for the pooling of information from many difference sources, which can be particularly beneficial when dealing with ill-structured problems requiring the synthesis of novel solutions (Casey, et al., 1984). However, when decision makers work together in groups they must avoid a variety of problems that Janis (1972) has labeled "groupthink." For example, members of a group tend to develop an illusion of invulnerability that may encourage excessive optimism and risk taking. Another result of groupthink is that members of a group who express opposing views may be pressured by other group members and ostracized if they resist. The negative aspects of group problem solving may be avoided by use of brainstorming (Van Gundy, 1981) and other related methods, such as synectics (Mitchell, et al., 1975).

Implement Solution

After decision makers have generated alternative methods for solving the decision problem, they implement one or more of these methods. Rational methods are usually systematic sets of procedures that may require the decision maker to complete the following subtasks either implicitly or explicitly: evaluate information (is the information valid, which information is most important), assess probabilities of events (events that may happen in the future, the frequency of past events, the probability that one event may cause another), and integrate the information and the probability assessments in a logical manner.

Research by cognitive psychologists has repeatedly demonstrated that people are subject to a number of cognitive limitations that may affect their ability to implement successfully their chosen method. In general, we know that people have definite limitations on their ability to combine information and make mental calculations. Often decision makers will reduce the cognitive demands of the decision situation by oversimplifying the decision problem. To compensate for these limitations, many of the structured, analytic methods used to solve decision problems (such as decision analysis) decompose the problem into a series of judgments that should make it easier for the decision maker to perform successfully. However, decision makers still display systematic biases when using decomposition methods, especially with respect to the estimation of probabilities.

People do not behave like intuitive statisticians (Nisbett & Ross, 1980); that is, they do not follow the principles of probability theory in judging the likelihood of uncertain events. Instead, people use judgmental heuristics (mental shortcuts) to compute subjective probabilities, and these heuristics can lead to inaccurate judgments; thus, they are often referred to as judgmental biases. Decision makers continue to use heuristics because they are effective in reducing their cognitive load, they take less time than unbiased algorithmic approaches, and they usually provide at least a "ball park" estimate of the probability in question. We will briefly summarize several of the commonly used judgmental heuristics.

Representativeness

People evaluate the probability of an event according to how similar that event is to its "parent population" and/or according to the degree to which the event reflects the salient features of the process by which it was generated (Kahneman & Tversky, 1972). In other words, we think events are more "likely" when they are similar to our expectations. For example, the sequence of heads and tails in a series of coin tosses, HHTHTH, is judged to be more probable than the series HHHTTT (which is actually equally probable) because the former series is perceived to be more random and thus more reflective of the process by which it was generated. Similarly, the personality description "intelligent, meticulous, and self-centered" is judged to be a more probable description of a graduate student in computer science than a graduate student in psychology because the personality description is more similar to people's stereotype of computer scientists than of psychologists (Kahneman & Tversky, 1973).

Availability

People tend to estimate the likelihood of an event occurring by the ease with which instances or occurrences can be brought to mind

(Tversky & Kahneman, 1973). For example, when asked to judge the probability of suicide among college students, decision makers may recall no such occurrences among their acquaintances and assign this event an inaccurately low probability. The availability heuristic helps explain people's misperceptions and faulty decisions with regard to national hazards (Slovic, Fischoff, & Lichtenstein, 1982) because media coverage and vivid films of low probability events (such as in *Jaws* or *The China Syndrome*) increase the *perceived* riskiness of low probability hazards.

Anchoring

In many situations, people have initial estimations of probability values (an anchor) and must revise these values as new information becomes available. For example, you and your friend are trying to estimate the probability that you will win the lottery this week. She estimates the odds are 1/1,000. According to the anchoring heuristic, you would use this value as a starting point and "adjust" it to be more in line with your expectations—perhaps you would estimate the odds as 5/1,000. Research indicates that adjustments are typically insufficient; different starting values yield different estimates that are biased toward the initial values (Tversky & Kahneman, 1974). Continuing with our example, if your friend had originally estimated the odds to be 100/1,000 (instead of 1/1,000), according to the anchoring heuristic you would have also estimated the odds to be more in favor of your winning (for example, 50/1,000).

In addition to the heuristics that can produce biased judgments, decision makers should be wary of another bias called "belief perseverance" (Lord, Lepper, & Ross, 1979). It is common knowledge that first impressions are very critical; psychological research has confirmed this intuition and demonstrated that people have great difficulty revising their initial opinion even when the evidence that created the original opinion is totally discredited. It seems that once we have postulated a set of casual connections to explain an event (for example, Bill doesn't deserve the promotion, and he only got it because he's the boss's nephew), we have great difficulty revising our explanation even when we find our assumptions are false (Bill is not the boss's nephew? Well, he sure doesn't work hard enough to deserve the promotion). A recent study (Pliske & Gettys, 1983) has replicated and extended the work on belief perseverance in a decision-making context. This work indicates that once decision makers have explained why one particular outcome may result from taking a particular course of action, they have difficulty generating alternative outcomes that may occur in the future.

Evaluation

In the final stage of the decision-making process, decision makers evaluate their choice behavior. In this stage, the decision makers should evaluate the entire decision process that they have completed, not simply evaluate whether their final choice was the "right" one. Outcome feedback is the main source of information for evaluating the quality of our decisions. We choose to implement a particular solution to the problem, and if it works (the outcome is favorable) then we have reason to believe we have chosen the correct solution. Accurate outcome feedback is the only way we have to evaluate our decision behavior validly. Unfortunately, in most decision situations, complete and accurate outcome feedback is unavailable. This is the case when choices must be made and actions taken to solve long-term problems for which the outcome will remain unknown for years to come.

In many decision situations, we have incomplete outcome feedback because we do not know what would have resulted from courses of action we chose not to take (Einhorn, 1980). For example, when an employer chooses to hire a particular person and not another, the employer will never know what would have happened if the rejected person had been hired.

Incomplete outcome feedback can often be misleading; it is possible for decision makers to implement a nonoptimal solution to a problem that for reasons outside their control solves the problem (not unlike the adage "He has more luck than brains"). In this case the decision maker would be "rewarded" for choosing a nonoptimal solution. For example, a marketing executive chooses not to introduce a new product line because he does not like the name of the product, even though all the marketing research data indicate that the product will be a huge success. Subsequently, the product, which was marketed by another firm, is found to contain a cancer-causing substance. This outcome could reinforce the marketing executive's reliance on his own intuitive judgment and may cause him to ignore totally the more objective market data in the future. Similarly, it is also possible for a decision maker to implement a normatively optimal solution that proves to be suboptimal due to the occurrence of extremely rare environmental factors. For example, a patient decides not to take a vaccine because the risk of contracting the disease (1 chance in 10 million) was smaller than the risk of complications from taking the vaccine (5 in 1,000), but then contracts the disease. In this case, the decision maker is "punished" for choosing to implement a rational course of action.

Decision makers' ability to learn from experience is limited by the "hindsight" bias (Fischoff, 1975) or the "knew-it-all-along" bias (Wood, 1978) that refers to people's tendency to exaggerate what they could have anticipated in foresight. People tend to view what has happened in the past as having been inevitable and also claim that it was "inevitable" before it happened. People tend to think that others should have been able to anticipate events better than they actually can and they even misremember their own predictions in that they exaggerate in hindsight what they knew in foresight. A well-known historical example of the hindsight bias is the bombing of Pearl Harbor. After the Japanese *surprised* the United States at Pearl Harbor, everyone seemed to agree this event was "inevitable."

The hindsight bias can be particularly devastating to decision makers because it can prevent them from learning from existing outcome feedback. If we misremember our own predictions and the predictions of others, so that we always think the predictions made in the past were more accurate than they were, we are unlikely to make any changes in our forecasting behavior. In other words, you cannot learn from mistakes you deny you ever made!

This concludes the discussion of the cognitive processes underlying decision making. Throughout the description of these processes, a number of cognitive biases were identified that can affect a decision maker's ability to make optimal decisions. The intention in presenting this research was to make clear that cognitive processes are an important aspect of decision making and that the biases they produce must be considered by those who wish to improve decision making. The next section, illustrates how knowledge of the cognitive process underlying decision making can be used in an applied setting to improve decision making.

USING THE COGNITIVE MODEL TO IMPROVE
DECISION MAKING: A CASE STUDY

Decision making occurs on both a small and a large scale in day-to-day living as well as on the job. The cognitive model for decision making that was presented in the previous section can be applied to most if not all situations in which a decision must be made; it is a general problem-solving model that can be flexibly adapted to many types of decisions. In what follows, it is shown how this general cognitive model has been adapted to improve decision making in a real-world context. To illustrate, a case study is presented in which the general cognitive model was tailored to create a problem-solving model for military intelligence analysis. A brief description of the intelligence field and a review of the study's history provide an introduction to the application of the general model.

Military Intelligence Analysis

The ultimate goal of military intelligence analysis is to predict enemy behavior. In military intelligence, the enemy is any country or force that aggressively imposes policies counter to U.S. policies on the United States or on any allied nation. Intelligence is created to anticipate better enemy capabilities, intentions, actions, and reactions. As such, it is of critical importance to our national security and must be as accurate and reliable as possible. However, due to the constraints under which intelligence is created, accuracy and reliability are often difficult to achieve and can be further compromised by poor decision-making procedures (remember Pearl Harbor).

There are a number of constraints on decision making in the intelligence arena. Some of these apply to both strategic (long-range global projections) and tactical (short-range situational projections) intelligence, and some are unique to each type. For example, in both types of intelligence the information upon which decisions are based can be of questionable reliability and validity. Moreover, in both types of intelligence the information is typically not obtained directly by the analyst making the decision; it passes through a chain of analyses and arrives in summarized form. Important information can be missing from this summary altogether. Tactical intelligence analysts have the added disadvantage of time pressure; their decisions must be made "yesterday." On the other hand, the short turnaround time for tactical intelligence allows these analysts the benefit of feedback on the success of their decisions.

Strategic analysts have little time pressure, but may never know the outcome of their decisions because they are projecting far into the future. In addition, these analysts may be creating intelligence for which no current information is available (for example, the penetrability of Soviet armored vehicles in the year 2010). Clearly, strategic intelligence analysts are faced with difficult conditions for decision making. In combination with poor decision-making skills, this can lead to inaccurate and unreliable intelligence. For this reason, strategic intelligence analysis was targeted as an area in which the cognitive model for decision making could aid the analyst and lead to a better intelligence product.

Based on the assumption that a systematic cognitive approach could enhance the decision-making processes required for strategic intelligence analysis, a project was undertaken to develop a model specifically for these processes. The initial phase of the project involved a three-year investigation into the job environment of intelligence analysts and the range of cognitive processes these individuals use in conducting analysis (Montgomery, Thompson, and Katter, 1979). This extensive investigation was necessary to determine demands and constraints imposed by the environment and limitations in analysts' cognitive processes that would be important considerations in tailoring the general cognitive model (see Figure 7.1) to a specific model for strategic analysis. The final phase of the project involved the actual development of the model for strategic intelligence analysis and the creation of a "tool kit" of methods and techniques that allowed the analyst to avoid, or at least ease, the consequences of cognitive limitations associated with each step in the model (Thompson, Hopf-Weichel, & Geiselman, 1984; Phelps, Englert, & Mutter, 1984).

A Cognitive Model of Strategic Intelligence Analysis

The cognitive model of intelligence analysis is diagrammed on the right in Figure 7.4; on the left is the general cognitive model presented in Figure 7.1. A comparison of the two models shows that the steps are quite similar in both content and sequence. However, the

FIGURE 7.4. A Cognitive Model of Strategic Intelligence Analysis (right) and the General Cognitive Processing Model of Decision Making (left).

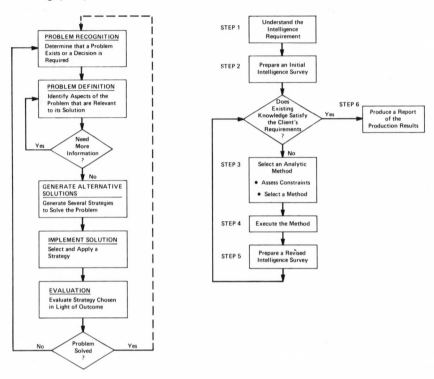

Source: Phelps, Englert, and Mutter, 1984, p. 5-3.

description of the steps for the intelligence model has been tailored to be more consistent with the vocabulary of the intelligence analyst. For example, in step 1, the analyst must "understand the intelligence requirement." Functionally, this translates to deciphering what action, if any, needs to be taken as a result of a question or request from a client–Do I have a problem to solve? In step 2, the analyst must "prepare an initial intelligence survey." In this step the request or problem is further defined by gathering and analyzing readily available information from either internal (memory) or external (data files) sources. The analyst then decides whether additional information gathering is required. If the data at hand are sufficient to answer the question, then a report is produced.

Note that the wording of the decision diamonds in the general model and the intelligence model are substantially different. This intentional difference reflects the real-world demands of the intelligence environment. The analyst is encouraged to use information that is immediately available to answer the intelligence requirement as soon as possible, with as few resources as possible. Therefore, the original question of whether additional information is needed becomes the new question of whether the client's requirement can be answered without gathering more information. As discussed earlier, people generally have difficulty determining when to terminate information gathering, and in the area of intelligence analysis it is advantageous to encourage analysts to think in terms of having adequate information rather than maximal information.

If additional analysis is required, then the analyst progresses to step 3 and selects a method for conducting the analysis. Note that the intelligence model explicitly focuses on assessing decision making and environmental constraints. As we pointed out in the discussion of problem recognition, people implicitly assume some unnecessary constraints and fail to recognize others. Therefore, the intelligence model explicitly directs the analyst to examine constraints using specially designed worksheets.

In both the general model and the intelligence model, the fourth step is to execute the method or decision-making strategy. However, in the fifth step, the analyst is again directed toward a job-relevant behavior, that is, creating a decision solution that will satisfy a client rather than engaging in a subjective evaluation process. It should be noted, however, that the analyst is indeed required to conduct an evaluation as part of the process of revising the intelligence survey. If the revised survey is evaluated as satisfactory, then the analyst converts the knowledge and solutions to the problem to a format understandable by the client.

This model for strategic intelligence serves as a basic guide to the process of creating intelligence. It provides the analyst with a set of clear-cut procedures that, when used, enhance the quality of decision making and problem solving and, ultimately, lead to a better intelligence product. However, as discussed throughout this chapter, there are many cognitive limitations that can hinder the processes of decision making and problem solving. To aid the intelligence analyst further, the matrix in Table 7.1 was provided. In the first column the steps in the intelligence model with supporting tasks are listed. In the

TABLE 7.1. Matrix of Intelligence Steps, Tools, and Methods

Steps and Tasks	Basic Tools and Concepts	Suggested Methods and Techniques*

Step 1. Understand the Intelligence Requirement
  Know client needs
  Translate requirements into specific objectives and tasks
	Communication skills
	Identifying assumptions
	Recognizing biases
		Techniques
		  Goal analysis
		  Mission flow diagrams
		  Client profile checklist
		  Expert opinion

Step 2. Prepare an Initial Intelligence Survey
  Identify what is known
  Identify what is unknown
  Identify areas of uncertainty
  Identify memory/data shortfalls
  Recognize threat
  Develop a threat model
  Define/formulate the problem
	Problem representation (see general problem solving)
	Identifying assumptions
	Pattern recognition and matching
	Probability assessment
	Memory skills
		Methods
		  Cut and paste
		  LRPE
		  Scientific method (steps 1 and 2)
		  Change signals monitoring (step 1)
		  War gaming—modeling
		Techniques
		  Intelligence survey checklist
		  Expert opinion
		  Exponential smoothing
		  Historical analogy
		  Leading indicators
		  Precursor events
		  Scenarios
		  Time lines

Step 3. Select an Analytic Method
  Assess constraints
  Formulate hypotheses
  Formulate plans
	General problem solving
	Identifying assumptions
	Pattern recognition and matching (recognizing similarities in different requirements)
	Decision-making strategies
		Methods
		  Scientific method (step 2)
		Techniques
		  Worksheet to establish constraints and resources
		  Brainstorming
		  Cost-benefit analysis
		  Decision matrices
		  Decision theory
		  Goal analysis
		  Mission flow diagrams
		  Multiattribute utility (MAU)
		  Relevance trees
		  Synectics
		  System analysis

Step 4. Execute the Method
  Collect data
  Evaluate data
  Interpret data
  Develop estimates
  Evaluate hypotheses
  Identify possibilities
	Pattern recognition and matching
	Identifying assumptions
	Recognizing biases
	Probability assessment and decision theory
		Methods
		  Change signals monitoring (step 3)
		  Cut and paste
		  LRPE
		  Scientific method (steps 3 and 4)
		  War gaming—simulation
		Techniques
		  Anomalous event matrix
		  Bayesian analysis
		  Breakthroughs
		  Canonical trend variation
		  Critical event filters
		  Delphi
		  Decision matrices
		  Decision theory
		  Intuitive analysis
		  KSIM
		  MAU
		  Panels
		  Relevance trees
		  Worksheet for identifying informational value of data (Appendix H)

Step 5. Prepare a Revised Intelligence Survey
  Predict future threat
  Impact assessment
  Evaluation
	Probability assessment
	Identifying assumptions
	Recognizing biases
		Methods
		  Change signals
		  Monitoring (step 4)
		  Cut and paste
		  LRPE
		  Scientific method (steps 4 and 5)
		Techniques
		  Bayesian analysis
		  Cross-impact analysis
		  PAMNACS and DENS
		  Dynamic models
		  KSIM
		  Probabilistic forecasting
		  Scenarios
		  Time lines
		  Trend extrapolation

Step 6. Produce a Report of the Production Results	Communication skills
	Identifying assumptions
	Probability assessment
		Techniques
		  ITAC Writer's Guide
		  Ideal product checklist
		  Expert opinion

Note: A method is a broad general approach that has components which can be applied to many of the steps in conducting strategic intelligence analysis. A technique is a more specific tool for doing a particular task. Several different techniques may be useful within a general method.
Source: Phelps, Englert, & Mutter (1984), p. G-5.

second column, labeled "Basic Tools and Concepts," the cognitive skills required to execute successfully each step and its supporting tasks are listed. In the third column, methods and techniques specifically selected to aid in the execution of the cognitive skills are listed.

Because intelligence analysts are not experts in decision making and analytical methodology, additional aids were provided to help them know when to use the methods and techniques listed in Table 7.1. A matrix of the characteristics of each technique or method (type of data required, time required, type of output) was provided to help them determine the feasibility of executing the technique under their individual constraints and resources. Again, the critical aspect for improving decision making was to relate directly the techniques to their specific situation and context.

The preceding discussion has shown how the cognitive model of decision making was tailored to produce a specific model for intelligence analysis. The intelligence model then served as a procedure to guide analysts in a systematic approach to solving a specific problem. The model also served as a framework for sensitizing them to the need to support their cognitive skills with aids and techniques designed to counteract biases and cognitive limitations. This detailed level of support for the intelligence analyst was only possible following an in-depth analysis of environmental demands and an interpretation and adaptation of the general cognitive model for that environment.

CONCLUSIONS

As evidenced by the large literature cited in this chapter, there is clearly a trend toward delving deeper into the decision processes to understand the underlying cognitive processes. This unmistakable increase in the concern for the role of human cognitive processes and decision-making variables in the quality of decisions, as well as in the design of decision support systems, should ultimately be beneficial for the applied researcher and practitioner. While the introduction of cognitive issues to management decision making was made more than 20 years ago (Simon, 1960), it is only very recently that the general decision-making field has expended any intensive efforts to study underlying cognitive variables. This trend is evidenced by the appearance of a special issue of the *SMC Transactions* (July/August 1982) on human information processing factors that included articles specifically addressing human decision-making strengths and weaknesses. In addition, the journal of the American Institute for Decision Sciences, *Decision Sciences*, published a special state-of-the-art issue for decision making under uncertainty that included major discussions of cognitive variables underlying decisions (Winkler, 1982, pp. 522, 525).

It is hoped that an increased research and development emphasis on the cognitive variables can help redirect the current trend in improving decision making—decision support systems that provide more quantity and sophistication in the information available to a decision maker without concern for how to use the information cognitively. In general, decision support systems are automated data base systems with, perhaps, a layer of automated data analysis and fusion (synthesis) provided, along with statistical analyses and summaries. Only occasionally, however, do such systems contain support for the actual decision-making and cognitive processes, even though there are many techniques currently available.[5] In addition, as demonstrated in this chapter, there is a great deal of research available on the human strengths and weaknesses that could serve as a basis for providing prompts ("remember to look at the base-rate information that could disconfirm your options, consider the following information"). In short, a great deal of attention has been given to the development of the information base for decision making but not enough to incorporating the research findings to develop procedures to help the decision maker know what to *do* with the information. The demonstration of how the decision-making process can be improved by an understanding of the underlying cognitive processes should aid the practitioners and systems designers in increasing the quality of individual decision making and, in turn, the effectiveness of their organizations.

SUMMARY

To encompass the full range of decisions that must be addressed by both systems designers and practitioners who want to improve the quality of decision making, it is necessary to define decision making in a broad context. Therefore, in this chapter a decision is defined as a general problem to be solved. It may be well or ill-defined at the outset, structured or unstructured, subjective or objective. As background, the origins and methods of three major categories of approaches to the contemporary study of decision making (decision theory, decision support systems, and psychological decision making) are described. The major emphasis of the chapter is a presentation of research from the psychological decision-making approach, focusing on the cognitive processes involved in decision making rather than on the decision or choice itself. This research is organized according to a cognitive model that describes the process of decision making.

In stage 1, of the five-stage cognitive processing model of decision making, the decision maker must recognize that a problem exists (that is, that a decision needs to be made). In stage 2, the decision maker must clearly define the decision problem. Next, the decision maker generates alternative methods for solving the decision problem. In the fourth stage, the decision maker implements the chosen method of solution. In the final stage, the decision maker evaluates the entire decision process. The cognitive processes involved in each of the five stages are discussed as well as the deficiencies or errors that are associated with the processes.

We propose that emphasizing the cognitive processes involved in decision making has considerable practical value for practitioners and systems designers seeking to improve the quality of decision making. A case study is presented to illustrate how the cognitive processing model of decision making can be adapted to improve real-world decisions. We hope that the material presented in this chapter will aid practitioners and systems designers in their attempts to improve the quality of individual decision making in their organizations.

NOTES

1. There are several excellent sources that describe the various approaches to investigating decision making (for example, Hammond, McClelland, & Mumpower, 1980). There are also many recent reviews of the decision-making literature (for example, Pitz & Sachs, 1984; Einhorn & Hogarth 1981) and discussions of current research issues in this area (Hogarth, 1980; Wallsten, 1980).

2. Many of the cognitive biases discussed in the literature affect all five stages of the decision-making process outlined in Figure 7.1. We discuss particular biases with specific stages for the sake of clarity, but the reader should keep in mind that most of these biases affect all aspects of decision-making behavior.

3. This step differs radically from other stage models of decision making. Typically, such models would prescribe at this point to select among alternatives:

Do I buy the Ford or the Chevy? The goal of this step is to generate a *method* to conduct the selection or "decision" process.

4. Although only the most robust research findings have been selected for this chapter, this topic has received so much recent attention that it is worth discussing. Recently there have been a number of papers discussing how decision makers' "cognitive style" affects their preference for different methods for solving decision problems (Bariff & Lusk, 1977; Benbasat & Taylor, 1982). "Cognitive style refers to the process behavior that individuals exhibit in the formulation or acquisition, analysis, and interpretation of information or data of presumed value for decision making" (Sage, 1981a, p. 642). People are thought to differ according to cognitive style characteristics, such as cognitive complexity, field dependence/independence, and systematic/heuristic styles (Bariff & Lusk, 1977). Proponents of cognitive style contend that some decision makers are "cognitively complex" and prefer very detailed and complex types of information, whereas other decision makers prefer simpler types of information; some decision makers are "field-dependent" and therefore make use of external referents, whereas others are "field-independent" and use internal referents; some decision makers are thought to prefer systematic, analytic methods of problem solution, whereas others prefer intuitive methods. It is not surprising that the large research literature on cognitive style is full of inconsistent findings. Personality psychologists have repeatedly demonstrated the lack of cross-situation generalizability of people's "personalities" (Mischel, 1980). Similarly, decision makers' cognitive styles will vary as a function of the particular decision problem they are faced with and the particular environmental constraints prevailing at the time they are making the decision. Huber's (1983) conclusion is a reasonable one: "(1) that the literature on cognitive styles is weak and inclusive, and (2) that to date the preponderance of evidence indicates that the practical significance of cognitive styles is relatively small, suggest that the currently available literature is not a satisfactory basis from which to derive operations DSS design guidelines" (p. 569).

5. At a minimum, decision-analytic aids such as Bayesian and MAUT procedures could provide a framework for understanding and organizing the mass of information. Expert systems based on artificial intelligence techniques could be incorporated into the system either to take over some of both the higher and lower level decision making or to act as a consultant or adviser to the decision maker. The decision maker and expert system could have a dialectic interchange to facilitate logical, accurate, and efficient processing. Problem-solving procedures and techniques could be either actively or passively available to aid the decision maker in defining and structuring the problem/decision at hand, generating reasonable alternatives, conducting cost-benefit analyses, and the like.

REFERENCES

Bariff, M. L., & Lusk, E. J. (1977). Cognitive and personality tests for the design of management information systems. *Management Science, 23*, 820–829.

Benbasat, I. B., & Taylor, R. N. (1982). Behavior aspects of information processing for systems. *IEEE Transactions on Systems, Man, and Cybernetics, 12*, 439-450.

Billings, R. S., & Marcus, S. A. (1983). Measures of compensatory and noncompensatory models of decision behavior: Process tracing versus policy capturing. *Organization Behavior and Human Performance, 31*, 331-352.

Borgida, E., & Brekke, N. (1981). The base-rate fallacy in attribution and prediction. In J. H. Harvey, W. J. Ickes, & R. G. Kidd (Eds.), *New directions in attribution research* (Vol 3). Hillsdale, NJ: Erlbaum Associates.

Bower, G. H. (1972). Mental imagery and associative learning. In L. Gregg (Ed.), *Cognition in learning and memory*. New York: Wiley.

Brunswick, E. (1955). Representative design and probabilistic theory in a functional psychology. *Psychology Review, 62*, 193-217.

Casey, J. T., Gettys, C. F., Pliske, R. M., & Mehle, T. (1984). A partition of small group predecision processes in informational and social components. *Organizational Behavior and Human Performance, 34*, 112-139.

Corbin, R. M. (1980). Decisions that might not get made. In T. S. Wallsten (Ed.), *Cognitive processes in choice and decision behavior*. Hillsdale, NJ: Erlbaum Associates.

Davidson, D., Suppes, P., & Siegel, S. (1957). *Decision making: An experimental approach*. Stanford, CA: Stanford University Press.

Dawes, R. M., & Corrigan, B. (1974). Linear models in decision making. *Psychological Bulletin, 81*, 95-106.

Doherty, M. E., Mynatt, C. R., Tweney, R. D., & Schiavo, M. D. (1979). Pseudodiagnosticity. *Acta Psychologica, 43*, 111-121.

Edwards, W. (1965). Optimal strategies for seeking information: Models for statistics, choice reaction times, and human information processing. *Journal of Mathematical Psychology, 2*, 312-329.

Einhorn, H. J. (1970). The use of nonlinear, noncompensatory models in decision making. *Psychological Bulletin, 73*, 221-230.

Einhorn, H. J. (1971). Use of nonlinear, noncompensatory models as a function of task and amount of information. *Organizational Behavior and Human Performance, 6*, 11-27.

Einhorn, H. J. (1980). Learning from experience and suboptimal rules in decision making. In T. S. Wallsten (Ed.), *Cognitive processes in choice and decision behavior.* Hillsdale, NJ: Erlbaum Associates.

Einhorn, H. J., & Hogarth, R. M. (1981). Behavioral decision theory: Processes of judgment and choice. *Annual Review of Psychology, 32*, 53-88.

Fischoff, B. (1975). Hindsight foresight: The effect of outcome knowledge on judgment under uncertainty. *Journal of Experimental Psychology: Human Perception and Performance, 1*, 228-299.

Gentner, D. (1982). *A structural-mapping theory of analogy.* Paper presented at 23rd annual meeting of the Psychonomics Society, Minneapolis, MN.

Gentner, D., & Stevens, A. (1983). *Mental models.* Hillsdale, NJ: Erlbaum Associates.

Gettys, C. F. (1983). *Research and theory on predecision processes* (Rep. No. 11-30-83). Norman: University of Oklahoma, Decision Processes Laboratory.

Gettys, C. F., Kelley, M., Pliske, R. M., & Beckstead, J. (1983). *Problem analysis and definition in act generation* (Rep. No. 8-8-83). Norman: University of Oklahoma, Decision Processes Laboratory.

Gettys, C. F., Manning, C., & Casey, J. T. (1981). An evaluation of human act generation performance (Rep. No. 15-8-81). Norman: University of Oklahoma, Decision Processes Laboratory.

Gick, M. E., & Holyoak, K. (1979). Problem solving and creativity. In A. L. Glass, K. J. Holyoak, & J. L. Santa (Eds.), *Cognition.* Reading, MA: Addison-Wesley.

Hammond, K., McClelland, G., & Mumpower, J. (1980). *Human judgment and decision making.* New York: Praeger.

Heider, F. (1958). *The psychology of interpersonal relations.* New York: Wiley.

Hogarth, R. M. (1980). *Judgment and choice: The psychology of decision.* New York: Wiley.

Huber, S. P. (1983). Cognitive style as a basis for MIS and DSS designs: Much ado about nothing? *Management Science, 29*, 567–582.

Irwin, F. W., & Smith, W. A. S. (1957). Value, cost, and information as determiners of decision. *Journal of Experimental Psychology, 54*, 229-232.

Janis, I. L. (1972). *Victims of groupthink.* Boston: Houghton Mifflin.

Janis, I. L., & Mann, L. (1977). *Decision making.* New York: Free Press.

Kahneman, D. (1973). *Attention and effort.* Englewood Cliffs, NJ: Prentice-Hall.

Kahneman, D., Slovic, P., & Tversky, A. (1982). *Judgment under uncertainty: Heuristics and biases.* Cambridge: Cambridge University Press.

Kahneman, D., & Tversky, A. (1972). Subjective probability: A judgment of representativeness. *Cognitive Psychology, 3*, 430–454.

Kahneman, D., & Tversky, A. (1973). On the psychology of predictions. *Psychological Review, 80*, 237-251.

Keeney, R. L., & Raiffa, H. (1976). *Decisions with multiple objectives: Performance and value trade-offs.* New York: Wiley.

Kern, L., & Doherty, M. E. (1983). *"Pseudodiagnosticity" in an idealized medical problem-solving environment.* Unpublished manuscript. Bowling Green, OH: Bowling Green State University.

Lanzetta, J. T., & Driscoll, J. N. (1966). Preference for information about an uncertain but unavoidable outcome. *Journal of Personality Psychology and Social Psychology, 3*, 96–102.

Lichtenstein, S., Earle, T. C., & Solvic, P. (1975). Cue utilization in a numerical prediction task. *Journal of Experimental Psychology: Human Perception and Performance, 104*, 77-85.

Loftus, E. F., & Palmer, J. C. (1974). Reconstruction of automobile destruction: An example of the interaction between language and memory. *Journal of Verbal Learning and Verbal Behavior, 13*, 585-589.

Lord, C. Lepper, M. R., & Ross, L. (1979). Biased assimilation and attitude polarization: The effects of prior theories on subsequently considered evidence. *Journal of Personality and Social Psychology, 37*, 2098-2110.

Mehle, T. (1982). Hypothesis generation in an automobile malfunction inference task. *Acta Psychologica, 52*, 87–106.

Mischel, W. (1980). *Personality assessment.* New York: Wiley.

Mitchell, A., Dodge, B. H., Kruzic, P. G., Miller, D. C., Swartz, P., & Suta, B. E. (1975). *Handbook of forecasting techniques* (IWR Contract Rep. 75-7). Fort Belvoir, VA: Army Engineer Institute for Water Resources.

Mitroff, I. (1974). *The subjective side of science.* Amsterdam: Elsevier.

Montgomery, C. A., Thompson, J. R., and Katter, R. V. (1979). *Human processes in intelligence analysis: Phase I overview.* (Research Rep. 1237). Alexandria, VA: U.S. Army Research Institute.

Mostellar, F., & Nogee, P. (1951). An experimental measurement of utility. *Journal of Political Economy, 59*, 371–404.

Mynatt, C. R., Doherty, M. E., & Tweney, R. D. (1978). Consequences of confirmation and disconfirmation in a simulated research environment. *Quarterly Journal of Experimental Psychology, 30*, 395–406.

Newell, A., & Simon, H. (1972). *Human problem solving.* Englewood Cliffs, NJ: Prentice-Hall.

Nisbett, R., & Ross, L. (1980). *Human inference: Strategies and shortcomings of social judgment.* Englewood Cliffs, NJ: Prentice-Hall.

Norman, D. A., & Bobrow, D. G. (1975). On data-limited and resource-limited process. *Cognitive Psychology, 7*, 44–64.

Ortony, A. (1979). Beyond literal similarity. *Psychological Review, 86*, 161–180.

Phelps, R., Englert, J., & Mutter, S. (1984). *Application of a cognitive model to Army training: Handbook for strategic intelligence analysis* (Technical Rep. 654). Alexandria, VA: U.S. Army Research Institute.

Pitz, G., & Sachs, N. (1984). Judgment and decision: Theory and application. *Annual Review of Psychology, 35*, 139–163.

Pitz, G., Sachs, N., & Heerboth, J. (1980). Procedures for eliciting choices in the analysis of individual decisions. *Organizational Behavior and Human Performance, 26*, 396–408.

Pliske, R., & Gettys, F. C. (1983). *The role of casual explanation in outcome generation* (Rep. No. 8-2-83). Norman: University of Oklahoma, Decision Processes Laboratory.

Reed, R. K., Ernst, G., & Baneji, R. (1974). The role of analogy in transfer between similar problem states. *Cognitive Psychology, 6*, 436-450.

Sage, A. P. (1981). Behavioral and organizational considerations in the design of information systems and processes for planning and decision support. *IEEE Transactions on Systems, Man and Cybernetics, 2*, 640-678.

Simon, H. A. (1960). *The new science of management decision.* New York: Harper & Row.

Simon, H. A. (1976). *Administrative behavior* (3rd ed.). New York: Free Press.

Simon, H. A., & Hayes, J. R. (1976). The understanding process: Problem isomorphs. *Cognitive Psychology, 8*, 165-190.

Slovic, P., Fischoff, B., & Lichtenstein, S. (1982). Facts versus fears: Understanding perceived risk. In D. Kahneman, P. Slovic, & A. Tversky (Eds.), *Judgment under uncertainty: Heuristics and biases.* Cambridge: Cambridge University Press.

Thompson, J. R., Hopf-Weichel, R., & Geiselman, R. E. (1984). *Cognitive bases of intelligence analysis* (ARI Research Rep. 1362). Alexandria, VA: U.S. Army Research Institute.

Thurstone, L. L. (1927). A law of comparative judgment. *Psychological Review, 34*, 273-286.

Tolbert, C., & Phelps, R. (1984, October). *Predecision processes: Human hypothesis testing abilities.* Paper presented at IEEE International Conference on Systems, Man, and Society, Halifax, Nova Scotia.

Troutman, C. M., & Shanteau, J. (1977). Inferences based on nondiagnostic information. *Organizational Behavior and Human Performance, 19*, 43-55.

Tversky, A. (1967). Additivity, utility, and subjective probability. *Journal of Mathematical Psychology, 4*, 175-201.

Tversky, A. (1972). Elimination by aspects: A theory of choice. *Psychological Review, 79*, 218-299.

Tversky, A., & Kahneman, D. (1973). Availability: A heuristic for judging frequency and probability. *Cognitive Psychology, 5*, 207–232.

Tversky, A., & Kahneman, D. (1974). Judgment under uncertainty: Heuristics and biases. *Science, 185*, 1124–1131.

Tversky, A., & Kahneman, D. (1981). The framing of decisions and the psychology of choice. *Science, 211*, 453–458.

Tversky, A., & Kahneman, D. (1982). Evidential impact of base rates. In D. Kahneman, P. Slovic, & A. Tversky (Eds.), *Judgment under uncertainty: Heuristics and biases.* Cambridge: Cambridge University Press.

Van Gundy, A. B. (1981). *Techniques of structured problem solving.* New York: Van Nostrand Reinhold.

Von Neuman, T., & Morganstern, O. (1947). *Theory of games and economic behavior* (2nd ed.). Princeton, NJ: Princeton University Press.

Wallsten, T. S. (1980). *Cognitive processes in choice and decision behavior.* Hillsdale, NJ: Erlbaum Associates.

Wason, P. C. (1960). On the failure to eliminate hypotheses in a conceptual task. *Quarterly Journal of Experimental Psychology, 12*, 129–140.

Winkler, R. (1982). Research directions for decision making under uncertainty. *Decision Sciences, 13*, 517–533.

Wood, G. (1978). The knew-it-all-along effect. *Journal of Experimental Psychology: Human Perception and Performance, 4*, 345–353.

III PERSONNEL SELECTION AND UTILIZATION

One of the more enduring effects of the World War I personnel selection program must be the impetus it gave to mental testing. The Army Alpha tests were the first written tests of mental ability to gain respect and they still serve as the model of scientific testing today. Because tests were administered to groups, they represented a convenient means of ranking everyone for nearly every purpose. Employers were quick to utilize tests as one means of increasing productivity, especially since the tests were perceived as being objective and predictive of later performance. Over the decades numerous validation studies attested to their effectiveness as predictors of training and job success.

However, in recent decades there has been much social and scientific controversy surrounding testing. Critics have focused on tests' fairness and their adverse impact, the limited predictive powers of tests for long-term job performance, and the often narrow range of skills covered by tests. In short, tests are criticized as inadequate for the purposes they were designed to serve. At the same time, scientific critics began to question the theoretical bases of measuring individual differences in cognitive skills, the inability of researchers to break the asymptomatic barrier of job validities (the ".3 problem"), and the limited advancements in theory and practice.

There has been a continuing concern that selection tests deny qualified applicants access to jobs. Title VII of the Civil Rights Act of 1964 has been the primary legal basis for protecting individuals against employment discrimination. The Tower amendment to the act, however, expressly permits the use of professionally developed ability tests in selecting employees. The Supreme Court laid down a series of rulings on test usage that together with the Equal Employment Opportunity Commission Uniform Guidelines define acceptable practices, particularly for demonstrating job-relatedness and equal effectiveness in prediction for minorities and nonminorities.

The legal challenge to testing stimulated an interest in evaluating differential prediction in academia, industry, and the military through comparison of regressive systems for different groups. In general, results show that there are no differences in predictors based on minority or majority group data.

Case law also awakened a long-dormant interest in validity generalization or transportability of tests. The prevailing view through the years was that employment test validations were situation-specific and that empirical data were needed for each new situation. Recent work, correcting for various sources of artifactual, between-study variance, strongly supported the utility of validity generalization and thus makes it possible to develop general principles for linking ability tests to classes of jobs.

However, a long-standing aspiration of researchers was to use something more comprehensive and relevant than training indicators or ratings of job performance as criteria for evaluating selection tests. Again, because of the legal emphasis on empirical measures of test validity against job performance, researchers turned their attention to the difficult, time-consuming, and expensive task of measuring job performance through a combination of objective hands-on measures of performance, job knowledge measures, and behaviorally anchored rating scales.

Although research on "tailored testing" started several decades ago, the everyday application of computerized adaptive testing (CAT) only became possible with advances in microcomputer technology and refinement in Item Response Theory. CAT permits automated testing using a display screen and a light pen (or other device) for responding. Test questions are tailored by the response to the previous question and computer-scored after each response. The terminal used by the examinee is designed expressly for testing purposes. The sequencing of items in tailored testing has as its principal goal equal precision of estimating ability for the total distribution of examinees, not just at the middle or at a given cut-score. Other CAT advantages are test security, simplicity of test revision, scoring accuracy, and efficient use of time. The Department of Defense has an ongoing large-scale implementation program designed to replace traditional paper-and-pencil tests with CAT.

Until recent times, the theory of cognitive abilities in differential psychology depended on factor-analytic techniques. Thurstone's primary mental ability structure (or variations of it), with its seven relatively independent factors, served as the theoretical basis for selection and classification batteries for a half-century. Many cognitive psychologists, however, were looking for a deeper understanding of individual differences in information processing based on an experimental rather than on a correlational approach. In the cognitive approach, stimulus variation is examined more closely than the variation of individuals, which is the focus of the differential approach.

Research is now underway to see to what extent the two approaches can form a common basis for testing abilities for selection and training. The hope is that psychometric testing can be supplemented by information processing procedures. While computer technology now makes this possible, the critical question that remains to be demonstrated is if there is improved validity.

The three chapters of this section deal with the current issues just described in addition to several others, such as job matching and utility or cost-effectiveness of testing. These issues are addressed through an analysis of a common selection and classification battery, the Armed Services Vocational Aptitude Battery (ASVAB), which is administered to 1 million military applicants each year in all four services. A version of the ASVAB also is given to about the same number of high school students for vocational counseling and recruiting purposes. Although the ASVAB is a direct lineal descendant of the Army Alpha of 1917, the services are now more active than ever before in seeking improvements in the ASVAB. This can be attributed to a number of factors, including significant developments in cognitive theories and computer technologies, congressional directives that the ASVAB be shown to be valid against job performance (rather than training performance), and social concerns surrounding testing.

Chapter 8, by Patrick C. Kyllonen, focuses on the theoretical foundations of measuring individual differences. Testing technology has traditionally characterized individuals in terms of a small number of relatively independent and stable abilities or traits. Kyllonen describes the new information processing approach to mental abilities and predicts that there will be a convergence of the "two disciplines of scientific psychology"—the experimental and the correlational. He believes that the experimental cognitive approach to individual difference will lead to a wholly new psychometrics of measurement. Kyllonen critically reviews some of the recent literature evaluating feasibility of new measurement methods. Computerized testing can assess both traditional abilities and previously unmeasured abilities related to learning, attention, and psychomotor skills. A consolidation of cognitive measurement techniques might lead to increased predictive validity of aptitude batteries. He concludes that the new cognitive ability testing techniques will require much more research effort before they are ready for use in operational settings. Even then, significant improvements in test utility await further developments in establishing adequate criterion measures. One approach is to use computerized instructional environments to serve as test beds in validation research. Another approach is that being taken to develop truly comprehensive job performance measures, which is the focus of the next chapter in this section.

Chapter 9, authored by Newell K. Eaton, Lawrence M. Hauser, and Joyce L. Shields, deals with a remarkably ambitious, large-scale, longitudinal Army research effort designed to address many of the current key scientific issues in the selection and classification area. The authors provide details of the research design, along with preliminary empirical findings based on the first three years of effort of about 50 scientists. At this point, a comprehensive set of predictor and performance measures has been developed for 15 representative Army occupations, most with civilian job counterparts. A concurrent validation study is well underway. One feature of the research, especially worthy of comment, concerns the development of criterion measures. A central aim of the research was to validate tests against job performance measures and to ensure that these measures were the best that the state of the art permitted. Consequently, a significant amount of effort was spent on the development of such measures. Because of the multidimensionality of job performance, many different performance measures are not only possible but considered desirable. After careful selection of a cross section of occupations, behavioral job analyses were done on each occupation. The strategy adopted in measuring job performance was to use a combination of measures based on hands-on performance tests, job knowledge tests, and behaviorally anchored ratings. Hands-on performance tests were considered to be the best in terms of job relevance, fairness, and for jobs having a significant psychomotor component. Knowledge tests, linked to knowledge-based task elements, were considered to have wide applicability and feasibility. Performance ratings permitted measurement of dimensions not tapped effectively by other means.

In the last chapter of this section (Chapter 10), Edward J. Schmitz and Betty W. Holz review the state of the art in the remaining significant activity in the utilization of selection and classification data—a person-job matching (PJM) system to inventory available abilities for jobs and to develop a strategy for allocating those abilities to meet organizational goals. The development of a PJM system is an interdisciplinary process using performance criteria and predictor information, models for planning, executing and evaluating person-job decisions, and decision support systems such as data bases, communication interfaces, and control modules to achieve management objectives. The authors describe the components of PJM systems once demand, supply, and differential performance data are available. Such a system can employ a direct assignment approach using either optimization or differential assignment techniques for a planning phase or for an execution phase where situation-specific information may be required. Schmitz and Holz review the utility of PJM systems and find productivity gains measured in dollars to be considerable. They also indicate an interesting application of PJM in the design of jobs and organizational structure. Active research issues include utility analysis, performance assessment of teams, and decision simulation techniques to evaluate personnel policies.

8

THEORY-BASED COGNITIVE ASSESSMENT

Patrick C. Kyllonen

In many large organizations psychological tests are routinely administered to job applicants to obtain information about their likelihood of succeeding on the job or in prerequisite training. For historical and economic reasons, such tests typically consist of a variety of multiple-choice items administered in a paper-and-pencil format. Items are designed to probe the applicant's technical knowledge, knowledge of the English language, ability to reason logically, to think quantitatively, and so forth. Traditionally, these abilities and other skills have been called "aptitudes," reflecting the philosophical stance that such skills are properly characterized as personal traits, relatively impervious to training.

In recent years many psychologists concerned with individual differences have begun to question the foundations of this kind of testing technology. In particular, the model of intellectual functioning that characterizes individuals in terms of a small, finite set of relatively stable traits, or aptitudes, is fast giving way to a whole new conception of intellectual functioning based on the view of the person as an information processor. This reorientation has given rise to a "new look" in ability measurement that promises to overhaul the conventional way we administer psychological tests, as well as the ways we interpret performance on such tests. The new look substantially builds upon traditional factor-analytic–based accounts of individual differences and borrows heavily from the discipline of experimental cognitive psychology. As such, the new research approach to individual differences represents the beginnings of a convergence between what Cronbach (1957) called the "two disciplines of scientific psychology"—the experimental and the correlational. It seems quite likely at this time that the experimental cognitive approach to individual differences will lead to the generation of a whole new psychometrics, based on experimentally studied process models instead of the traditional trait models. A detailed account of what the new information processing approach is likely to bring in the way of new psychological tests and new ways of using test score data is the subject of this chapter.

Before launching into a review of new approaches to cognitive assessment, it is useful to review the role and status of a psychological testing program in a typical organization. Human ability assessment can play a broad and critical role in enhancing human productivity and thereby increasing organizational effectiveness.

Consider four obvious ways any large organization can enhance the productivity of its work force. The first and often most expensive is training. It has been estimated that organizations spend up to 10 percent of their total payroll on training (Gilbert, 1976), which can amount to a substantial sum. Training and assessment are integrally intertwined. An organization trains those most likely to benefit from training, and day-to-day decisions about what to train next depend on an assessment of what the student or trainee knows right now. The second, and in many ways the most elusive, means of productivity enhancement is to increase the employee's motivation levels. The capability for assessing an individual's current motivation level is an obvious prerequisite to evaluating any policy designed to enhance motivation. The third method for productivity enhancement is to design systems so that the way operators interact with them optimizes the efficiency of the human-machine interaction. Following the public attention given to the conditions faced by air traffic control operators, many follow-up studies have been concerned with redesigning these systems to incorporate human factors (see, for example, Hopkin, 1982). In turn, improved human factoring of the work place depends to a large degree on adequate assessment methods. Finally, organizational productivity can be enhanced by establishing an appropriate selection and classification system.

Many managers do not fully appreciate the importance of initial personnel selection and classification decisions. Numerous research studies attest to the wide variation in the learning and performance capabilities of individuals (Rimland & Larson, in press). The data produced by numerous studies have shown that some individuals can acquire skills and knowledge 10 to 20 times faster than others (Payne & Tirre, 1984). Managers often incorrectly conclude that on-the-job performance deficiencies are due to motivation and training deficiencies when an equally plausible case could be made for identifying the source of the problem as a selection and classification error. It is highly unlikely that training can always overcome a serious talent deficiency; in fact, in high demand areas, individual differences more often than not are magnified by training and experience (Cronbach & Snow, 1977) rather than reduced.

Unfortunately, present personnel measurement tests are not highly accurate in identifying before the fact who will be the fast and slow learners. Present tests do not measure many of the abilities required for acquiring skills demanded by diverse occupations. The importance of more accurate measurement of learning abilities is underscored by the forecasts of personnel problems that will emerge in the next decade. The number of 18- to 21-year-olds in the national labor pool will decrease by about 20 percent in the near future and will remain at this low level through the 1990s. At the same time, competition between the military and civilian sectors for these scarce labor resources is expected to increase as a function of an improving and expanding economy. Clearly, the importance of selecting the best people as a means of productivity enhancement will become increasingly important.

Although the most obvious role for assessment methods is in the area of personnel selection and classification, it can be argued that improved techniques can serve all four areas—training motivation, human engineering, and selection and classification. The first section of this chapter begins with a brief review of the history of aptitude testing, with particular emphasis on the evolution of the testing program within the military services. The section concludes by pointing out that in recent years conventional notions of aptitude have come under attack from both within and outside the field, but that recent theoretical developments in cognitive psychology, coupled with the now almost ubiquitous microcomputer, promise to change the nature of ability testing and provide it with a firmer theoretical foundation.

It is important, in discussing a new theory-based approach to assessment, to provide at least the glimmerings of the theory that serves as the base. Thus, in the second section, a description of the human as an information processing system is outlined, and how such a view might serve useful as a foundation for new cognitive-based testing research is discussed. This is followed with a description of new assessment techniques rooted in cognitive theory, and some of the studies that have attempted to determine the utility of these new measurement methods and approaches are also reviewed. The studies can naturally be divided into clusters based on the focus of the investigation. One set of studies is concerned with the question of whether elementary cognitive tasks can supplement or even replace conventional tests. A second set of studies is concerned with how the ability to learn can be measured. A third set addresses the issue of whether complex cognitive skills, such as reading, can be broken down into more elementary skills. In these study review sections, particular attention is given to studies that have been conducted as part of the Air Force Human Resources Laboratory's Learning Abilities Measurement Program (Project LAMP).

Throughout the chapter, numerous possible applications of new methods for cognitive assessment are presented going beyond the obvious ones in the selection and classification contexts. These include applications in remedial diagnosis, the development of training systems, and the design of systems to accommodate human factors. Finally, the chapter summary is a review of these developments and presents the cost-effectiveness of some of the new forms of cognitive assessment.

HISTORY OF COGNITIVE ASSESSMENT

Until the mid-1970s, the predominant form of theorizing about cognitive abilities employed factor-analytic concepts and methods. Perhaps the first theory of cognitive ability was the two-factor theory proposed by Spearman (1905), who noted that correlation matrices of cognitive test scores exhibited what he termed "positive manifold," a condition characterized by the absence of zero or negative correlations. That is, if a person outperforms others on one cognitive test, that person is likely to do better than others on any other cognitive test. Spearman attempted to explain this phenomenon by proposing the concept of "general ability," which itself was defined as the level of "mental energy" available to the person. Spearman assumed that differences in mental energy level were responsible both for differences in success in schooling and success on his cognitive tests.

Later, Thurstone (1938) modified the Spearman proposal by postulating seven relatively independent primary mental abilities, such as verbal, spatial, deductive reasoning, and memory abilities. Thurstone contended that to predict a person's score on any cognitive test, it was not sufficient to know simply that person's general ability level because different kinds of abilities played different roles on various tests. Rather, and more formally, Thurstone proposed that relative standing on one test could be predicted by utilizing the relative standing on other tests by the common factor equation

$$y_{ij} = w_{i1}F_{1j} + w_{i2}F_{2j} + w_{i3}F_{3j} + \ldots + w_{ik}F_{kj} + S_{ij} + e_{ij}$$

In this equation, y_{ij} is the relative standing of the ith person on the jth test; the F's represent the relative level of ability of the person on the $1 \ldots k$ abilities, and the w_i's represent the relative importance of each ability in predicting relative standing on the jth test.

In effect, Thurstone was advancing a kind of "mental chemistry" theory of learning and cognition, in which any learning or performance activity could be characterized by an ability requirements (or importance) profile, and any person could be characterized by an ability level profile. The importance of Thurstone's system for classifying people and tasks was realized by military psychologists, and it might not be too unfair to assert that the form of even present-day selection and classification systems in industry and education as well as in the military services is a fairly direct result of Spearman's and Thurstone's contributions.

Consider, for example, Guilford and Lacey's (1946) monumental work, *Printed Classification Tests*, which is widely credited with establishing the groundwork for virtually all subsequent military selection and classification testing (Weeks, Mullins, & Vitola, 1975). In that report, the authors divide the presentation into a more or less subjective task analysis of aircrew operators' jobs, followed by an evaluation of tests of a number of general and specific abilities. According to Guilford, in his preface, one of the key features of the work was "the inclusion of analysis of job criteria by the factorial methods. It is believed that in this direction lies an economical, systematic, and dependable procedure for coverage of aptitudes and for fitting tests to vocations" (p. iii). That is, the utility of personnel classification tests was made obvious by the inclusion in the basic factor equation of both abilities tapped by tests and abilities demonstrated in training or in jobs.

In one of the earliest validation studies following Guilford and Lacey's report, Dailey (1948) emphasized the Thurstonian underpinnings of military testing by declaring that "a fundamental postulate has been that each airman specialty requires a different combination of specific aptitudes for success. A further postulate is that basic airmen entering the Air Force have greatly different patterns of the specific aptitudes essential to success in various specialties," and further stating that in developing tests "heavy emphasis is placed upon the techniques of factor analysis" (p. 1). Since that time a similar theoretical rationale is routinely stated in the introductory remarks of validation studies (for example, Gragg & Gordon, 1951, p. 3). As evidence that even today Spearman's and Thurstone's influence is felt in classification battery development efforts, consider the following quotation from Weeks et al. (1975):

> The fundamental postulate, which has served as the basis for the development of the classification batteries, is that each Air Force job specialty requires a specific pattern of aptitudes for success. If the major aptitudes common to the various specialties can be separately measured, it would be possible to predict each applicant's probable success in any job specialty by means of an empirically weighted composite score based on those tests measuring aptitudes necessary for that specialty. (p. 7)

It is useful at this point to review the success such a testing philosophy has produced. Despite widespread public attention and some confusion over the matter (Nairn 1980; Gould, 1982), it is the case that relatively short (less than three hours total administration time) batteries of psychological tests are remarkably accurate at predicting future learning and performance criteria. As many have pointed out, one of the problems in some of the public criticisms is the failure to take into account the range-restriction phenomenon. An inspection of the validity coefficients of the College Entrance Examination Board's Graduate Record Exam, for example, leaves a depressing picture of the utility of psychological tests. Wilson (1982, p. 16) found a validity coefficient of .27 using the GRE-V to predict first-year graduate grade point average (GPA) in verbal fields

(N = 620) and a coefficient of .28 using the GRE-Q to predict GPA in quantitative fields (N = 529). At first glance, neither coefficient seems large enough to place a great deal of confidence in the tests' abilities to select candidates for graduate study. However, it is highly likely that the reason for the apparent modesty in the magnitude of the coefficients is to be found in the severely restricted range of ability characteristics of samples of students engaged in graduate study. Samples of military enlistees, on the other hand, offer a much greater, though still not completely representative, degree of heterogeneity, and countless validity studies conducted in military settings over the past 40 years attest to the utility of psychological tests.

Table 8.1 summarizes results of a number of validity studies conducted using evolving versions of military selection and classification tests over the last 40 years. The validities shown in the table are correlations between weighted composites of test scores from the par-

TABLE 8.1. Validity Coefficients of Air Force Test Battery

Test Battery Name	Year	Number of Courses	Range of Validities	Median Validity	Median Sample Size
AC1-A	1951	29	.32–.77	.61	264
AC1-B	1956	21	.34–.77	.60	402
AC2-A	1959	46	.11–.80	.57	124
AQE-D	1958	3	.46–.50[a]	.47	182
AQE-F	1963	41	.29–.90	.63	433
AQE-62	1962	4	.75–.81[a]	.79	1,493
AQE-64	1968	57	.38–.87	.64	410
AQE-66	1973	46	.18–.90	.68	115
AQE-J	1971	4	.69–.84[a]	.82	3,396
ASVAB-3	1968	46	.29–.87[a]	.68	–[c]
AQE/AFQT (1)	1974	42	.16–.63[b]	.42	1,000
AQE/AFQT (2)	1974	43	.16–.65[b]	.44	823
AQE/AFQT (3)	1974	57	.22–.68[b]	.53	890

[a]Inferred validities from test relationships with previous batteries for which actual validity studies were conducted.

[b]Not corrected for restriction of range.

[c]Unknown.

Source: The first ten rows are adapted from Weeks, Mullins, and Vitola (1975); the last three rows are adapted from Christal (1976).

ticular test battery with final technical school grade point average. Across a wide variety of courses and a wide variety of batteries, validity coefficients are consistently high.

One of the problems with the data in Table 8.1, as well as data from most validity studies, is with the criterion of final technical school GPA. Weeks et al. (1975) realized that the lack of an empirical job performance criterion was a critical limitation in these studies, but until recently the problem has been in the lack of any large-scale efforts to develop satisfactory criteria. It seems likely now, with pressure being applied both by the U.S. Congress and the military services, that valid job performance measures are on the horizon (Eaton & Shields, 1985; Gould & Hedges, 1983). Christal (1976) viewed the problem not only in terms of the lack of good performance measures but also in the inherent difficulty of "selling" the utility of aptitude tests when using only the grade point average criterion. He suggested considering other criterion variables, such as time to acquire skills, rate of skills decay, and time for skills reacquisition. He also reported data from a number of studies that showed that such criteria are as predictable by aptitude test scores as is the usual GPA. Nevertheless, there is an obvious need for validation studies to include criteria that are both more valid in their relationship to the target performance and that can be translated more easily to dollars and cents utility.

If indeed it can be recognized that theoretical developments paved the way for subsequent selection and classification applications, it is useful to consider the directions that ability theory has moved since the days of Thurstone. In this way a forecast of future possible changes in actual selection and classification systems can be made.

One avenue of theoretical advance has been in what might be called factor theory. Much of this work may, for the most part, be viewed either as extensions or syntheses of the Spearman and Thurstone proposals. Thus, for example, Vernon (1961) and Burt (1940) have combined the two-factor and primary abilities models by proposing hierarchical models of ability organization, placing general ability at the top and more specific abilities arranged in orderly fashion beneath. A currently popular variation on this scheme is that there are two general abiliites: general fluid-analytic (Gf) and general crystallized (Gc) (Cattell, 1971; Horn, 1968). Gf is believed to be close, if not identical, to Spearman's g (Gustafsson, 1984) and is said to drive the development of Gc, which represents the product of accumulated learning experiences. Some developmental data would appear to support the distinction: Gf level peaks during early adulthood, while Gc level rises continuously with age (Cattell, 1971; Snow & Lohman, 1981).

Work on extending Thurstone's proposal is exemplified by Guilford's structure-of-the-intellect model, which proposes 120 abilities, but more importantly specifies the dimensions of product, operation, and content along which mental tests can be classified. However, even Guilford (1982) admits that these specific abilities may be correlated, and, as Gustafsson (1984) points out, this opens the door to a unifying hierarchical theory of ability organization. In fact, Gustafsson has proposed such a theory, the HILI model (hierarchical, LISREL-based model), which takes advantage of recent developments in linear structural equation modeling techniques. Gustafsson proposes a unifying synthesis of the Thurstonian primary factor model with the Cattell-Horn fluid-crystallized model. It is likely that such a unifying hierarchical model brings with it advantages for practical application. For the most general decisions about an individual's cognitive status, a test or battery of tests designed to tap the highest order factor could be administered. With more subtle requirements for classification decisions, coupled with the luxury of more available testing time, samples from the lower strata of ability levels can be drawn.

Despite these potentially important recent developments in factor theories and methods, much of the theoretical interest in individual differences in learning and intelligence for the most part waned during the 1960s. This lack of interest was due primarily to disaffection for the method of factor analysis and its associated theories of learning and intelligence. Applied psychologists noted a stagnation in in the field from a utility standpoint. Despite increases in the mathematical sophistication of factoring methods, a concomitant increase in occupational and academic validities was not demonstrated (Christal, 1981), which is apparent from the absence of any upward trend in the magnitude of coefficients in Table 8.1 over the years. At the same time, others expressed a renewed dissatisfaction due to not understanding what it was that intelligence tests measured (Hunt, Frost, & Lunneborg, 1973; Sternberg, 1977). An important change in perspective occurred with the development of a psychology of cognition, starting in the late 1960s (see especially Neisser, 1967) and flourishing in the 1970s. The new cognitive psychology provided a set of methodological tools for exploring mental processes within an experimental approach. Beginning in the mid-1970s, the study of individual differences in mental processes was once again an active area of investigation.

With the shift from the traditional differential and correlational methods of investigating cognition to experimental methods came a shift in emphasis. While it is always true that individual differences research is concerned with the ways in which people differ and the underlying sources that lead to those differences, the newer approaches are at least equally concerned with specifying the necessary prerequisite knowledge and cognitive skills that allow any intelligent act, including learning, to occur. Thus, compared to the factor-analytic approach, the experimental approach is characterized to a considerably greater degree by the method of testing competing models of intelligent performance and only then examining individual differences in the parameters of the appropriate model. This general approach actually has taken two forms, labeled by Pellegrino and Glaser (1979) as the "cognitive correlates" and "cognitive components" approaches. The goal of investigations conducted within the cognitive correlates framework is to determine the cognitive skills and knowledge structures underlying observed differences between high- and low-skilled individuals in broad ability (verbal, spatial, numerical) or skill domains (physics, chess, electronics troubleshooting, geometry, computer programming). In this research, high- and low-ability individuals (or experts and novices) are first identified, then administered a series of cognitive tasks, each of which is presumed to be well understood in its cognitive requirements. Tasks are typically selected so as to tap specific cognitive mechanisms, which enables the researcher to test competing hypotheses about the sources of be-tween-skills-group differences.

The goal of research conducted within the cognitive components framework is similar in that it too seeks to explain the cognitive mechanisms underlying broad ability differences. The difference is that this approach directly investigates the usually more complex tasks on which the ability differences are observed, an approach originally suggested by Estes (1974). In the typical cognitive components investigations, individuals attempt tasks that bear a strong resemblance to intelligence test items. By systematically varying features of the task, the researcher allows various mathematical models to be fit to individual subjects' latency or error data. Each model is normally an embodiment of a particular theory of the tasks performed. Parameters of the models usually represent various psychological processes, and thus an individual's process execution times or probabilities are estimated directly in the parameters.

In the last ten years, a considerable amount of individual differences work has used these two approaches or variations, and this has led to the crystallization of different views on the nature of individual differences in intelligence and learning ability. The remainder of this chapter is devoted to consideration of this recent work.

THEORETICAL FOUNDATIONS

When determining what kinds of tests to include in a battery to be used for selection and classification decisions, two criteria are typically employed. The first, which might be designated the "job sample criterion," rests on the evaluation of the content validity of the candidate test. If a secretary must be selected, for example, a battery that includes tests of typing skill and samples other typical secretarial duties would satisfy this criterion. A second criterion, which might be labeled simply the "empirical criterion," is satisfied to the degree that performance on candidate tests correlate positively with performance on the target job.

There are problems with both of these criteria. A logistics problem with the job sample criterion is that there may be too many jobs from which to extract work samples. If the test battery is to be used for classification decisions, and there are many possible jobs into which an applicant might be classified (as is the case in large organizations such as the U.S. Air Force), then the amount of testing time that would be required to sample all possible jobs is prohibitive. However, an even more devastating problem with the job sample criterion is that job requirements are constantly changing. For example, it is likely that the skills involved in successful manuscript production on a mechanical typewriter are different from those employed in using a powerful word processing system.

There are also problems with the empirical criterion. First, the criterion can only be applied after a decision about what test to use has been made. We can determine whether the currently existing battery of secretarial tests does an adequate job, but some other means for selecting those tests in the first place is required. Second, the empirical criterion does not provide an absolute standard against which to measure a test's success; if we find a validity coefficient of .30, does that mean that a test is a good one? The empirical criterion, applied after the fact, never provides information about whether some other test might prove to be more valid than the existing one. Finally, a third problem is that validity studies themselves can be quite expensive.

These problems may be alleviated through the application of a technology of psychological testing derived from cognitive theory, in what might generically be called the cognitive skills assessment approach. Such an approach, in principle, would require (1) the determination of what cognitive skills are required in training and in the work place, (2) the determination of what cognitive skills are involved in taking psychological tests, and (3) matching training/job skills with cognitive task skills and thereby logically deriving training/job skills requirements. This would amount to a kind of decomposition analysis in which aptitudes would be redefined as sets of cognitive skills, and jobs would be defined as sets of cognitive requirements. Such an approach provides a different perspective on the person-job-match system (Schmitz & Holz, 1985) and serves as a flexible, adaptive system for specifying job skills and person skills for all kinds of training situations—computer-assisted instruction, on-the-job training, and even lockstep classroom instruction. Also, such a system offers promise as a test construction tool. It would be possible to specify in advance what cognitive skills will be measured when various facets of a complex cognitive task are systematically manipulated.

A system such as the one outlined above, however, requires the foundation of a solid theory of individual differences in cognition. Unfortunately, such a theory does not yet exist, and much of the remainder of this chapter will be devoted to an assessment of the current status in developing such a theory. We begin by first considering what such a theory should do.

1. A theory of individual differences in cognition should specify the cognitive processes and knowledge structures that underlie individual differences in the ability to acquire and apply knowledge and skills in a broad variety of contexts. Call the underlying attributes the *sources* of individual differences.
2. The theory should specify how these sources can be assessed at the level of the individual.

3. The assessment techniques should yield quantifiable indicators that both provide an account of how well the theory fits the data (that is, how well the source measurements predict performance in learning and intelligent performance contexts) and can be used in principle as ability measurements in an operational context.

In the last few years a number of theoreticians have applied some of the ideas emanating from cognitive psychology in speculating on the form a theory of individual differences in cognition might take. Snow (1978, 1980) has proposed that individuals might differ either in the efficiency with which they are able to execute elementary information processes or in their approach to or their general strategy for attacking problems. Hunt (1978) has suggested that differences in cognitive abilities might be reduced to differences in knowledge, strategies, or mechanistic processes. And Sternberg (1977, 1980) has proposed an elaborate component hierarchy in which individuals differ in meta-components, performance components, acquisition components, retention components, and transfer components. All these proposals must be viewed as somewhat speculative at the present, but, nevertheless they may be useful in proposing research directions.

It can be helpful to adopt a slightly different framework not only as a heuristic for guiding research but also as a way of organizing and classifying the existing and now burgeoning literature on individual differences in cognitive abilities. One useful framework is derived from a critical review of the existing cognitive-differential literature (Kyllonen, 1985a). From the review, three general conclusions can be drawn. First, whatever it is that underlies intelligent performance also underlies the ability to learn. This is consistent with both the empirical evidence and theoretical considerations derived from analyses of current cognitive theory. Second, four sources can be tentatively identified as underlying the ability to learn and to perform intelligently: working memory capacity, information processing speed, the declarative or factual knowledge base, and the procedural or strategic knowledge base. Currently, these sources are merely taxonomic categories for variables that in principle could be measured on individual subjects. Nevertheless, such a taxonomic delineation is a useful first step. The third conclusion to be drawn is that the sources do not contribute additively to proficiency in learning and intelligent behavior—they interact. In particular, the extent of an individual's declarative and procedural knowledge base in a particular domain affects both the individual's effective working memory capacity and his or her speed of processing information related to that domain. These relationships are depicted graphically in Figure 8.1 in what is termed here the "interactive common sources framework."

According to the framework, an individual's experienced success in classroom learning activities, on-the-job training, and on-the-job performance is determined by the individual's level of cognitive and learning proficiency. Cognitive proficiency refers here to an individual's ability to remember, make decisions and choices, and solve problems. Learning proficiency refers to the individual's ability to acquire new facts and cognitive skills. This distinction is meant to align roughly with the classical distinction between learning and performance. In being guided by this framework, a tentative assumption is made that differences between people in learning and cognitive proficiency levels result from differences in the more fundamental sources of processing speed, memory capacity, declarative (factual), and procedural (rule-based) knowledge. The common sources view is that these components are what underlie both learning and cognitive

FIGURE 8.1. Interactive Common Sources Framework.

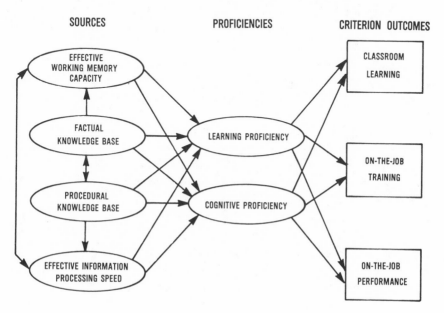

differences. The interactive view is that the sources interact with each other in determining proficiency levels. For example, extensive factual knowledge in a particular domain (for example, chess) can enlarge an individual's effective memory capacity (for example, to memorize a complex board configuration) and effective processing speed (for example, to select the best next move). The following sections present techniques for measuring these variables.

ISSUES AND TECHNIQUES FOR COGNITIVE ASSESSMENT

Although the interactive common sources framework can serve as a useful guide for research, important details have been left unspecified. Before the framework can evolve into a model or theory of individual differences in cognition, three classes of issues must be dealt with. These have to do with assessment methodology, the analysis of complex cognitive skills, and the analysis of learning.

Methods for Cognitive Assessment

It is critical to address the issue of how the underlying sources of knowledge and the information porcessing parameters can be assessed. More precisely, the questions to be asked are, How can processing speed be measured? How can an individual's working memory capacity be determined? How can the extent and quality of an individual's knowledge base be assessed? In each case, the obvious questions must be answered: Can the target source (processing speed, memory capacity, knowledge) be measured reliably? Is it already measured by conventional tests, or are new techniques required? Can the source be considered a unidimensional construct, or is there more than one dimension involved? Finally, does source capability change with practice, and if so, by how much?

We may consider these issues in the context of a number of cognitive correlates studies that have been conducted in the last few years. Much of this work has been driven by the general consideration of whether elementary cognitive tasks might someday supplement or even replace conventional tests as aptitude and performance measures. Cognitive psychologists have been remarkably successful in developing mathematical models that account for patterns of error and latency data across a large number of tasks by positing various mental processes and knowledge structures. It has occurred to a number of individual researchers that to the degree that such models are valid representations of psychological processing, the parameters of such models can serve as direct indicators of the speed or accuracy with which an individual can execute a particular psychological process.

In one of the first large-scale efforts constructed with this general philosophy in mind, Rose and Fernandez (1977) described:

> a program of research dealing with the development and validation of a comprehensive standardized test battery that can be used as an assessment device for the evaluation of performance in a wide variety of situations.... Equally important, the battery is being designed to include tests that possess construct validity: there will be a firm theoretical and empirical base for inferring the information processing structures and functions that the tests purport to measure. It is expected that such a battery will permit improved personnel management decisions to be made for a wider variety of Navy-relevant jobs than is currently possible using existing techniques. (from the abstract)

With equal enthusiasm, Carroll (1980), after an extensive review of the literature, proclaimed that the new approach of investigating individual differences with elementary cognitive tasks offered considerable promise not only by supplementing conventional tests but also as a means for assessing the effects of physiological changes and of aging. Of particular interest to Carroll was the possibility that the absolute measurement afforded by the analysis of cognitive tasks, as contrasted with relative measurement given by conventional correlational methods, might ultimately result in a "Systeme Internationale" of experimental psychology.

Individual Differences on Cognitive Tasks

It is instructive to consider just how promising is the approach of supplementing traditional ability measures with scores from elementary cognitive tasks. The first issue concerns whether there are reliable individual differences in various scores that can be computed from such tasks. If the scores or parameters are not reliable, it does not necessarily follow that such scores are imprecise (Rogosa & Willett, 1983), but it does mean that there are no individual differences to speak of in the task or parameter of interest. Thus, establishing reliability can be viewed as a central issue in determining whether a particular score is a good measure of individual differences.

In the Rose & Fernandez (1977) study, 54 college students were administered a battery of nine cognitive tasks, each presented on a computer. Between 36 and 38 subjects (depending on the task) were readministered the tasks on a second day, thereby allowing the computation of test-retest reliabilities. Tasks were selected to represent the domains of memory, psycholinguistics, and visual information processing. Further, tasks selected had a history of published support, had an adequate theoretical rationale, and were adaptable to paper-and-pencil or computerized administration; also, there was indication that reliable individual differences were present on the task. Table 8.2 presents descriptive statistics on various scores computed from the tasks.

It is beyond the space limitations of this chapter to describe the various parameters for each of the tasks, but the interested reader may consult Rose and Fernandez (1977) for the original references. It may nevertheless be useful to consider the top listed task, Posner and Mitchell's (1967) letter classification task, in more detail, both to provide a sense for the scores that are derived from a single task and because this task in particular has received considerable attention in the individual differences literature.

In this task, the subject is shown two letters side by side. The task is to determine whether the two letters are physically identical (A-A), identical in name (A-a), or the same in terms of vowel-consonant category (A-E). If the letters matched according to task instructions, the subject was to respond by pressing one of two keys on a panel, but if the letters were not the same, the subject was instructed to press the other key. In addition to the mean response times for each of these three tasks (for "same" trials), three other scores could be computed. A "different" score was computed from response times on trials for which the letters did not match. A name identity minus physical identity response time score was computed to reflect the speed with which an individual could access information from long-term memory. The rationale behind this computation is that to make the physical identity judgment, an individual can respond on

TABLE 8.2. Descriptive Statistics from the Rose-Fernandez Study

	M1	M2	SD1	SD2	$r_{xx'}$
Posner and Mitchell Letter Classification Task (response latencies)					
Physical match (PI)	585	547	64	57	.57
Name match (NI)	684	629	100	71	.58
Category match (CI)	849	771	173	121	.78
Different	761	693	104	83	.81
NI–PI	99	81	62	45	.29
CI–NI	164	137	131	102	.69
Meyer Lexical Decision Task (response latencies)					
Word recognition	736	647	112	74	.66
NonWord recognition	916	756	252	113	.53
Encoding facilitation	975	958	78	75	.42
Baron Graphemic/Phonemic Analysis Task (response latencies)					
Sense-nonsense	1,205	1,193	246	197	.83
Homophone-sense	1,289	1,187	300	241	.90
Homophone-nonsense	1,579	1,423	306	235	.47
SH/HN	81	.83	.09	.09	.37
Sternberg Digit Scanning Task (response latencies)					
(Slope, positive)	75	49	32	21	.60
(Intercept, positive)	442	425	88	78	.52
(Slope, negative)	48	47	28	15	.45
(Intercept, negative)	536	464	98	59	.51
Joula Word Scanning Task (response latencies)					
(Slope positive)	56	52	32	24	.19
(Intercept, positive)	483	446	102	89	.46
(Slope, negative)	47	53	32	31	.00
(Intercept, negative)	544	446	145	67	.40
Joula Category Scanning Task (response latencies					
(Slope, positive)	122	93	85	65	.31
(Intercept, positive)	611	637	245	216	.68
(Slope, negative)	214	140	96	56	.32
(Intercept, negative)	575	595	238	176	.36
Clark Sentence-Picture Verification Task (response latencies)					
"Below"	136	110	155	149	-.06
"Negate"	829	685	354	319	.81
"Comparison"	200	146	183	200	.28
"Encode"	1,735	1,489	404	330	.59
Collins and Quillian Fact Verification Task (response latencies)					
Slope, superset relation	63	42	57	77	.21
Intercept, superset relation	1,035	1,017	205	220	.69
Slope, property relation	67	53	89	75	.16
Intercept, property relation	1,118	1,121	257	248	.73
Shepard and Teghtsoonian Recognition Memory Task (probability correct)					
Proportion correct	.73	.73	.07	.07	.56
Exponent on decay function (lag)	-.07	-.10	.19	.08	.31
Intercept on decay function (lag)	.86	.93	.15	.12	.21
Probability (hit)	.73	.77	.11	.12	.56
Probability (false alarm)	.28	.31	.12	.12	.67
d' (sensitivity)	1.28	1.34	.41	.45	.62
Beta (bias)	1.09	.93	.62	.50	.38

Note: Response latencies are in milliseconds. M1: mean on day 1; M2: mean on day 2. SD1: standard deviation over subjects on day 1; SD2: standard deviation on day 2. $r_{xx'}$: day 1, day 2 correlation.

Source: Adapted from data presented by Rose and Fernandez (1977).

the basis of the displayed physical information, but to make a name identity judgment, the individual must retrieve the name of both letters from long-term memory before these abstract name codes can be compared to one another.

Table 8.2 presents means and standard deviations, in milliseconds, for the day 1 and day 2 statistics from the Rose and Fernandez study, in the columns marked M1, M2, SD1, and SD2. Also, the test-retest correlations are displayed as reliability indices in the column marked $r_{xx'}$. Note that in all but a very few cases, there was a considerable decrement in response latency over days, as well as a corresponding decrement in variability. The test-retest reliability data show that in many cases the ordering of individuals changed substantially from one day to the next. This can be interpreted in one of two ways. The conventional wisdom is that this indicates that such scores are unstable and therefore not good candidates for a performance test battery. Alternatively, if both days 1 and 2 internal reliabilities are high but the test-retest reliability is low, it can mean that some individuals are benefiting from practice and others are not, which itself could be an important individual difference variable. Unfortunately, Rose and Fernandez did not provide internal consistency data.

In any event, caution should be applied before taking any of Rose and Fernandez reliabilities too seriously, because they are based on an extremely small sample. Yet the pattern of reliabilities may still be informative, and one pattern result apparent from Table 8.2 is that derived scores are generally less reliable than scores that represent the duration of performing a complete task, which is consistent with many other studies in the literature. For example, while both the name identity (NI) and physical identity (PI) match scores are highly reliable, the NI-PI difference score is not.

Carter and Krause (1983) reported data on some of the tasks in Table 8.2 along with some others, and found that in all cases slope scores (a kind of difference score) were less reliable than the mean response times from which the slopes were computed. From this result they argued that slope scores should not be used as performance measures, but rather the mean response times by themselves are sufficient for answering most questions the applied researcher might be interested in asking. However, the Carter and Krause argument is at odds with the stated philosophy of Rose and Fernandez, who argued that total scores are often less meaningful than scores derived from total scores insofar as they reflect combinations of psychological processes rather than a single process, such as "memory comparison." What is to be made of this discrepancy?

The topic of difference scores has been highly controversial in the psychological literature for at least the last 25 years, but a recent analysis of the topic by Rogosa and his colleagues (Rogosa, Brandt, & Zimowski, 1982; Rogosa & Willett, 1983) is clarifying. Rogosa et al. argued that considering the statistical as well as psychometric properties of change measures leads to an evaluation of the reliability of the difference score that is at odds with widely accepted notions. In particular, they showed that the difference score is unreliable when individual differences in change do not exist, but that it can be highly reliable if in fact individual differences in change do exist. In many of the tasks inspected by Carter and Krause and others, there is a high correlation between one of the scores from which the slope is computed and another one. Also, in many of the reported studies there is an extremely high correlation between response time on the name and physical identity match tasks. What these high correlations indicate is that there is very little in the way of individual differences in the change between performance on the two tasks. Thus, it is not merely a statistical artifact that produces low change score reliabilities. Rather, the low reliabilities (or conversely, high task1-task2 correlations) are interesting empirical results that establish the lack of individual differences in the change variable.

It should be pointed out here that Carroll (1980) has presented analyses of data on many studies similar to the Rose and Fernandez study (1977) that have appeared in the literature. Unfortunately, the vast majority of those studies, like that of Rose and Fernandez, also suffer from a small sample size. More recently, the Naval Biodynamics Laboratory has supported a number of studies that have investigated the psychometric properties of a large number of cognitive tasks (Kennedy, Bittner, Harbeson, & Jones, 1981; Kennedy, Bittner, Carter, Krause, Harbeson, McCafferty, Pepper, & Wiker, 1981; Carter & Krause, 1983). Once again, these studies suffer from small sample sizes.

Do Cognitive Tasks Measure Unique Abilities?

If it turns out that there are reliable individual differences on many elementary cognitive tasks, then the question of whether these scores represent previously unidentified abilities can be addressed. A recently completed study in our laboratory approached this question by comparing cognitive task scores to aptitude test scores. Fairbank, Tirre, and Anderson (1984) administered 30 different cognitive tasks, divided into six task batteries, to six independent samples of Air Force enlistees. Tasks were selected from a taxonomy to reflect verbal, spatial, and quantitative processing and to yield meaningful error and latency scores. That is, not all the tasks were designed solely to measure some form of processing speed. For each task, standard mathematical models of errors and solution latency were fit to the data, then certain parameters of these models were extracted as indicators of various aspects of processing efficiency. It is beyond the scope of this discussion to detail the rationale behind the different models on a task-by-task basis, but the rationale was similar to that given by Rose and Fernandez. However, Fairbank et al. also reported some total task score data (mean over all items). With reference to the previous discussion, such scores are useful to the extent that individual differences on scores derived from total scores do not exist.

One key result from the Fairbank et al. (1984) data was that reliabilities tended to be high, indicating stable individual differences on most of these tasks. When considering average scores, reliabilities for all the elementary reaction time tasks exceeded .90. On the other hand, derived score reliabilities presented a mixed picture. Some of the derived scores such as the NI-PI difference had low reliability (less than .50), while others, such as the slope from memory scanning tasks (Sternberg, 1969), had high reliabilities (greater than .80). Pellegrino (1984) has also found high reliabilities among memory scanning tasks. Fairbank et al. also computed correlations between the information processing scores and standardized test score composites taken from the Armed Services Vocational Aptitude Battery (ASVAB; Department of Defense, 1984). The General (G), Administrative (A), Electronic (E), and Mechanical (M) Composites are those used by the Air Force for personnel classification purposes. Thus, such correlations reflect the degree to which cognitive task data overlap conventional test score data as such data are used operationally in the Air Force.

The pattern of correlations with ASVAB composites showed that despite the fact that the cognitive task scores were fairly reliable, correlations with conventional measures tended to be fairly low—no correlation exceeded .50. This indicates that conventional tests do not tap, at least in a factorially pure sense, the processing skills tapped by the cognitive tasks. Thus, although cognitive tasks are not likely to replace conventional tests, there might very well be room to supplement them. Elsewhere, Kyllonen (1985b), reported data consistent with Fairbank et al.'s finding on this matter. In a factor-analytic investigation, using 17 cognitive tasks tapping verbal, quantitative, and reasoning abilities, along with ASVAB tests, it was found that of eight cognitive factors identified by the conventional and cognitive tests, three (reasoning speed, verbal speed, and quantitative level) were not measured by the ASVAB tests.

There are a number of other interesting trends in the Fairbank et al. data. First, while most of the response time measures correlated highest with the A composite (which bears considerable resemblance to the clerical or perceptual speed factor in the differential literature), the percentage of correct measures computed on the more complex reasoning and memory tasks correlated higher with the G composite (the general ability measure). This suggests that error and latency data may reveal different aspects of performance, a finding consistent with the Kyllonen (1985b) results. It also was found that the intercept in the scanning tasks correlated highest with the A composite, while the slope showed no strong or consistent differential correlation pattern. The intercept is presumed to reflect time for encoding and response, and the slope is presumed to reflect the time it takes to perform a single memory comparison step. Also, Fairbank et al. found that with very few exceptions, scores from cognitive tasks correlated higher with either the A or G composite than they did with the M or E composite, presumably because these latter two scores reflect primarily the extent of specialized knowledge bases in either the mechanical or electronics domains.

Two other results are worthy of mention. One is that mean and standard deviation were highly correlated on almost all of the response time measures, suggesting that increasing variability is associated with slower responding. Finally, on two tasks, sentence verification and three-term series (both linguistic transformation tasks), Fairbank et al. computed percentage of correct scores separately for the first and final blocks of items. In both cases, the correlation between percent correct and G was significantly higher on the first than on the final block, perhaps reflecting the fact that general cognitive demands are greater early on in a test. This is consistent with Fleishman and Hemple's (1954) classic demonstration of changing cognitive demands on a psychomotor task as a function of practice.

Fairbank et al. are currently engaged in further analysis of their extensive data set to explore the degree to which parameters measured on one set of tasks correspond to parameters on various other sets. The purpose of the analysis is to explore the generality of the various processing parameters. Although similar kinds of analyses have been conducted by others (Rose & Fernandez, 1977; Carroll, 1980), as was mentioned previously, most of these have suffered from inadequate sample size. With cognitive task data collected on more than 2,500 Air Force trainees, it should now prove possible to examine various hypotheses beyond the reach of others who have attempted with smaller subject pools.

Analysis of Changes in Processing Efficiency

The final major issue related to assessment methodology concerns how much subjects improve with practice. Rose and Fernandez (1977) showed large improvements on the second day, and these findings are consistent with many published reports of performance on cognitive tasks that have not examined individual differences. It is a fairly well-established finding across many diverse cognitive tasks that response time decreases in accordance with a power law (Newell & Rosenbloom, 1981; Lewis, 1980), as $RT(N) = aN^b$, where $RT(N)$ is response time for an item at trial N, a is response time for the item on trial 1, and b is the parameter governing the rate of change. Recently, researchers have begun to examine whether rate of improvement is an important source of individual difference variation that deserves special consideration.

In one noteworthy study, conducted as part of the LAMP program, Pellegrino (1984) investigated individual differences in changes in information processing efficiency on fairly simple cognitive tasks. In his study, 60 young adults were administered three cognitive tasks in four to eight successive sessions. Tasks were designed to sample visual, verbal, and quantitative abilities. The visual processing task was a perceptual matching task in which subjects were required to compare matrices of varying size with one another for physical identity. The semantic processing task was a version of the Posner and Mitchell's (1967) task in which subjects were instructed to match by letter category, but letters could be either physically, name, or category same (or different). The quantitative task presented elementary number facts involving either addition, subtraction, multiplication, or division, and the subject indicated whether the given answer was true or not. Analyses centered on determining the adequacy of various mathematical models proposed that posited elementary operations such as encoding, comparison, decision, and response; determining the relationships between information processing parameters and standard aptitude test scores; and determining the relationships between standard test scores and slope and intercept parameters derived from a power law analysis of practice effects.

Initial analyses indicated that the models fit the data quite well, and parameters from the models were generally reliable. Also, Pellegrino found that individuals performed all the tasks faster as a function of practice, in accordance with the power law characterization of rate of change. The processing parameter-aptitude correlations were generally low, except in the case of the perceptual speed factor, which was modestly related to the intercept parameter in some of the models (where the intercept reflected time for encoding and responding), consistent with the Fairbank et al. (1984) results. The analysis of starting point (intercept) and rate of change (slope) parameters showed that starting point in many cases was significantly related to perceptual speed and also was related across tasks (median $r = .48$). However, change rate was unrelated to any of the aptitude measures. Further, change rates across tasks were unrelated to each other (median $r = .08$). This result suggests that there is not a general learning ability, at least as this particular type of change is regarded as a form of learning. Rather, learning of this type seems to be task-specific.

Recently, Ackerman and Schneider (1984) reviewed a number of studies that showed data consistent with Pellegrino's results. The authors observed that correlations between initial performance and final performance on a wide variety of psychomotor and cognitive tasks have typically been quite low, which is to say that individual differences early in training do not map very neatly onto individual differences later in training. Considering that the purpose of ability tests when used as aptitude measures is to predict individual differences at the end of training, this is a lamentable finding. It also clashes with the view that intelligence is related to the ability to learn.

With these observations as an impetus, Ackerman and Schneider attempted to provide a comprehensive account of individual differences in changes in information processing efficiency by synthesizing current ideas on the structure of human abilities with considerations of automatic/controlled processing theory (Shiffrin & Schneider, 1977). The ability model they adopted is of the hierarchical variety, reviewed earlier (along the lines of Gustafsson's, 1984, HILI model). The processing model assumed that there are two distinct forms of processing: controlled and automatic. Automatic processing is fast, can be done simultaneously (that is, in parallel) along with other processing activities, and does not draw attentional resources. Controlled processing is slow, is performed in serial, and draws heavily on attention. It has been shown that processing can become more automatic with extensive practice, so long as processing requirements remain consistent from trial to trial. However, if requirements vary, processing will remain in a controlled state (Fisk & Schneider, 1983).

The authors proposed a mapping between the concept of general attentional resources (Kahneman, 1973) and general intellectual ability, from which can be derived the prediction that general ability and broad-domain abilities should be related to success on tasks requiring substantial amounts of controlled processing (where controlled processing, by definition, requires a heavy investment of general or broad-domain attentional resources). Conversely, the authors also proposed a mapping of automatic processing and lower order, highly specific abilities, which leads to the prediction that general ability will not be related to success (for example, speed) during automatic processing, but some low-order factor might be. Ackerman and Schneider (see also Ackerman, 1984) reported data that lent some support to their proposal. They showed that on a task that prevented the development of process automaticity (by varying the processing requirements over trials), general ability and verbal ability (that is, a broad-domain ability) were highly related to response time. The relationship between these broad abilities and performance on a task that enabled the development of process automaticity (by maintaining consistent processing requirements) was lower. It also was found that the relationship between perceptual/motor ability and task performance did not differ between the two tasks.

The Pellegrino and Ackerman and Schneider studies represent important initial steps in the investigation of individual differences in a particular kind of learning, which Rumelhart and Norman (1978) have called "tuning." These researchers have gone beyond considering individual differences in initial performance and are moving toward a characterization of differences in performance changes as a function of practice. Given that such changes are so extremely commonplace on cognitive tasks, and also that the purpose of using cognitive tasks for selection and classification is to predict the endpoint of often extensive training, it is likely that this topic and the general approaches employed by these researchers will become important cornerstones in future individual differences research. Applications may be particularly appropriate in endeavors that apply such methods to predict success in high-speed decision-making activities, such as required by the air traffic controller and aircraft pilot. Although Ackerman and Schneider's call for a change in assessment procedures based on automatic/controlled processing theory may be a bit premature (and impractical in that as much as 20 hours of testing may be required), it is not premature to propose a continuation of research along these lines.

ANALYSIS OF LEARNING

As Ackerman and Schneider (1984) rightfully point out, the purpose of ability testing is often to predict who will do best after extensive training. That being the case, it would seem appropriate to direct ability testing toward the analysis of learning ability. That is, we desire that our ability assessment devices yield information about who learns best in a particular situation, and therefore who will end up as the best performer after training. But just what is learning ability? Is it a unitary individual differences construct, or are there multiple varieties of learning ability?

Rumelhart and Norman (1978) have distinguished three types of learning, which they call accretion, tuning, and restructuring. Accretion refers to the accumulation of facts, restructuring to the development of new cognitive procedures, and tuning to the process of making existing cognitive procedures more efficient. Viewed along these lines, the previous section reviewed studies on individual differences in tuning processes. The present section is concerned with individual differences in the other forms of learning, particularly accretion.

Why is the examination of accretion processes important? In the conventional test setting, the assessment procedures yield data that reflect the current skills level of an examinee. These data certainly must reflect to some degree the amount of prior exposure an individual has had to problems of the type administered. Yet it is possible that individuals reliably differ in their learning rate and thus initial level-final level relations might be attenuated as a result. This attenuation would manifest itself in validity coefficients lower than might be obtained if learning rate were considered along with initial level. With this possibility as a motivation, a number of studies have been conducted in the last few years that have been concerned with determining whether learning rate is likely to be an important variable for consideration in future assessment batteries. In the past, it has been difficult to conduct studies of this nature because of the difficulty of exercising sufficient control over stimulus presentation and response feedback, both of which may be important in investigating dynamic learning processes, but the current widespread availability of microcomputers alleviates this problem.

Two recent studies by Allen and Morgan and colleagues were concerned with the relationship between initial level and learning rate and with the relationship between learning rate and conventional ability measures. In the first study (Allen, Secundo, Salas, & Morgan, 1983), 70 college students were administered three learning tasks (a fourth task was administered, but data were not analyzed due to a computer malfunction). In a coded messages task, subjects studied 12 word-symbol pairs, then made a series of same-different judgments on the equivalence of sentences and symbol strings. For example, an examinee might be questioned about whether the sentence "Enemy aircraft approaching from the North" was equivalent to the string "* I @ -." In an emergency procedures task, subjects studied a set of procedures on how to handle emergencies and then were tested for their knowledge on the serial order of procedures. In a security checking task, subjects studied a map of landmarks on a hypothetical Air Force base, where each landmark had an associated security level (high, medium, or low). In the test, subjects were asked questions such as "What is the security level of the second low security location after the tower?"

Allen et al. computed three scores for each subject. An initial learning level score was the sum of correct responses during the first third (17 minutes of the task); a final level score was the sum of correct responses during the final third of the task; and a rate score was the difference between the two level scores. The important findings were that, first, initial learning level, by itself, did not predict final level accurately; the rate variable added to the prediction significantly. Second, initial learning level was related across the different learning tasks, but rate and final level scores were not. Recall that Pellegrino (1984) found much the same result in his simpler classification and matching tasks.

In a follow-on study (Allen, Salas, Pitts, Terranova, & Morgan, 1984), the investigators readministered the same four learning tasks and three additional learning tasks to separate groups of 63 and 60 students, respectively, along with a battery of conventional aptitude tests. The purpose of this study was to determine whether final levels of performance could be predicted solely by conventional test scores or whether scores from learning tasks would account for additional variance. They found that factor scores derived from an analysis of conventional ability tests were significantly related to final performance on four of the seven learning tasks (with r^2 ranging from .29 to .38) but that on all but one task, goodness of prediction of the final level was significantly enhanced by the inclusion of learning rate variables in the prediction equation (increment in r^2 ranging from .07 to .24). This result suggests that learning rate may be a reliable and somewhat generalizable individual difference variable that is not currently measured by conventional tests. A more compelling demonstration of the utility of learning rate measures, however, would show that such measures predict final performance levels in a long-term learning environment such as that found in standard two-month technical training courses in industry or the military.

Thus, in a third study in the series, Allen, Pitts, Jones, and Morgan (1985) explored the utility of their learning rate measures in predicting final performance levels (course grade) in technical college courses (computer science, $N = 90$; bacteriology, $N = 66$; and engineering, $N = 48$). The major hypothesis tested was that learning task parameters (slope and intercept) would add to the utility of the standard measures (high school grade point average and Scholastic Aptitude Test scores) in predicting final course grade. The intercept of the learning function in the Allen et al. study reflected the amount learned during the pre-performance instructional phase of the task; the slope reflected the average amount of performance improvement during each minute of the task. Thus, both parameters were in some way reflective of learning rate.

Analyses showed that the learning rate measures were significant predictors of final grade in all three courses when considered separately, and that in some cases the rate measures accounted for additional variance in final grade beyond that accounted for by either high school GPA or SAT scores. However, the rate measures did not contribute to the predictive efficiency of the equation that included both GPA and SAT scores. Setting aside the issue of statistical power, this result could be interpreted as indicating that learning rate is already reflected to some degree in either or both the GPA and SAT scores.

Nevertheless, the Allen and Morgan studies taken together demonstrate that even a fairly rough approach to the analysis of learning may be profitable in providing assessment measures with practical utility. Yet there is a need to consider at a somewhat more basic level what it is that contributes to differences between people in such variables as learning rate. The theoretical framework outlined earlier in this chapter, for example, could be read to imply that differences in more fundamental source variables were responsible for differences in general acquisition proficiency. If so, then findings such as some of those emerging from the Allen and Morgan studies need themselves to be explained in more detail. Recall the earlier argument that the reason such detailed analysis is sought, apart from general scientific pursuits, is to provide potentially greater adaptability and flexibility in a system of assessment.

A recent study (Kyllonen, Tirre, & Christal, 1984) addressed directly the question of how processing speed and efficiency, along with factual and procedural knowledge, can play a central role in learning. The logic employed ran as follows. In typical paired associates learning, a person's likelihood of recalling the response term given the stimulus cue depends on the density of the memory structure that was created at the time of study. That is, if a person can create a highly elaborated, interactive structure that connects the stimulus and response terms during study, then it is more likely that the pair will be successfully retrieved (or recognized) when tested. Alternatively, if the learner fails to create any structure that links items together at study time, then the probability of retrieval is reduced. This is essentially the finding of the utility of mnemonic devices. A richer long-term memory structure allows greater opportunity for retrieval because it allows more entry points to access that portion of the structure that is relevant to the memory task.

Our hypothesis was that subjects with high verbal knowledge, that is, those who score well on standard vocabulary tests, come to the experimental session with an already well-developed declarative memory structure for words and associated concepts. If given plenty of time for study, these subjects will have a distinct advantage over their low verbal knowledge counterparts in their ability to integrate stimulus and response terms and thus will more successfully retrieve pairs when tested. The reason for this is that the concepts activated during study should be more highly integrated and thus serve as good cues, or entry points, at test. The paucity of structure characterizing low verbal subjects leads to the activation of fewer and perhaps less distinctive concepts, thus leading to more retrieval difficulties at test.

If study time is short, on the other hand, this advantage for high verbal subjects might not be as great. Although by the logic above, there should still be some advantage, the most critical variable in establishing a connected structure to facilitate recall should be the rate at which relevant concepts can be retrieved. In sum, we predicted that with liberal study time the high verbal knowledge individual should have a distinct advantage; with limited study time the fast verbal processor should have the distinct advantage.

To test these hypotheses, we presented a series of cognitive tasks to Air Force enlistees designed to assess both their breadth of verbal knowledge and the speed with which they were able to access verbal concepts. We also administered a paired associates learning task to subjects. In the task, pairs were presented for study at one of five rates ranging from 0.5 second to 8 seconds.

We tested two hypotheses related to our notions about learning ability. First, an individual's likelihood of correctly responding on items in which pairs were presented at the slow rate (8 seconds) would be more highly related to the breadth of an individual's verbal knowledge than would be the likelihood of correctly responding on items presented at the fast rate (0.5 second). In both cases we expected to find some relationship, but we expected the relationship to be greater at the 8-second condition. Our second hypothesis was that the reverse relationship should hold when the variable of interest was verbal processing speed. That is, probability correct at the 0.5-second level should be more highly related to processing speed than probability correct at the 8-second rate. Indeed, we had no compelling reason to believe that processing speed should have any effect on probability correct at the 8-second rate.

Although the analysis is fairly complex, we did find that under certain conditions the expected relationships did hold. The relationship between learning success and word knowledge was higher in the 8-second condition than in the 0.5-second condition. And the relationship between learning success and verbal processing speed was higher in the high-speed 0.5-second study condition than in the leisurely 8-second condition. Because we included a number of measures of processing speed, each designed to tap a different configuration of psychological processes, we were able to isolate the source of processing speed differences operating in the paired associates task. Our analysis showed that simple motor speed differences, or even simple comparison speed differences, could be ruled out. The critical speed seemed to have been how quickly an individual was able to search memory to retrieve a relevant concept.

One of the implications to be drawn from this study is related to the use to which verbal (or, more generally, semantic) processing speed tasks might be put in application efforts. Much attention has been given in recent years to the letter classification task as a useful index of verbal ability (Hunt, 1978). This results from the modest but apparently reliable relationship found between response time measures on the task and composite verbal aptitude measures. The original interest in the finding was related entirely to the theoretical issue of understanding a cognitive component that might have a causal linkage to the development of verbal knowledge. But there might also have been the implicit belief that the task, along with other similar tasks, might somehow serve as replacement for knowledge-dependent verbal aptitude tests. Our study suggests a more appropriate use for verbal processing speed tests. That is, under conditions of high information flow, such as experienced in the cockpit or a variety of similar kinds of situations, such a measure of processing efficiency might predict who will remember information most effectively as it flows through in real time (see Christal, Tirre, & Kyllonen, 1984, for further discussion along these lines).

Although the studies reviewed in this section present provocative findings, the limitations of this research should be emphasized. In both the Allen et al. and the Kyllonen et al. studies, the criterion tasks were fairly simple fact acquisition tasks. Understanding the relationships between parameters on such tasks, and understanding the cognitive determinants of performance on such tasks, are only useful first steps toward understanding what it is that causes some to learn faster than others. What is needed to make true progress in understanding learning ability is the analysis of how skills develop in the context of more realistic and long-term learning environments. The typical validity studies that identify correlates of final GPA after weeks of technical training are not the solution. Indeed, they present a whole class of new problems, mostly related to the lack of control over the conditions of learning and the failure in yielding dynamic learning progress indices.

There is one new development that does seem promising at the present, however. That is the analysis of learning in the computerized intelligent tutoring system environment where a great deal of information about what progress a student is making could be computed (in principle), and full control over the conditions of learning are possible. One study conducted along these lines compared a variety of aptitude and motivation test scores to a host of dynamic learning variables (Snow, Wescourt, & Collins, 1983). The study, even though only a small number of students were available for analysis, showed great potential for integrating cognitive assessment methods with computerized instruction in an effort to discover the underlying sources of the ability to learn. It is likely that similar efforts will be pursued in the future.

ANALYSIS OF COGNITIVE SKILL

One of the more exciting recent developments in cognitive assessment comes from the analysis of complex cognitive skills, such as reading, electronic troubleshooting, typing, mathematics problem solving, and computer programming. Much of this research employs many of the same techniques and methods used by researchers investigating learning and more elementary cognitive skills, but the goals of the research tend to center on the nature of basic skills for potential training applications rather than selection and classification applications. The general idea is that if the underlying cognitive constituents of complex behavior are understood, it might be possible to be more effective in diagnosing particular learning and performance disabilities and thereby in prescribing more effective remedial training.

One particularly effective application of this strategy can be found in a systematic program of research studies conducted by Fredericksen and colleagues in the area of general reading skills (Fredericksen, Weaver, Warren, Gillotte, Rosebery, Freeman, & Goodman, 1983). Initial work on this project concerned the identification of the components of reading (Fredericksen, 1981, 1982) through the use of differential assessment techniques of the type discussed throughout this chapter. The research strategy administered cognitive tasks, such as letter matching, word recognition, and anagram encoding, tested various models that accounted for the pattern of relationships among measures derived from the tasks. This analysis then resulted in an identification of component skills, individual estimates of which in turn were correlated with scores on standard reading tests to determine the skills that differentiated good from poor readers. Fredericksen et al. (1983) then selected three of the components as particularly critical for reading and developed specific computerized remedial training of the components. The training proved successful on a series of reading tasks, but even more interesting was the fact that Fredericksen et al. identified which training had an effect on which particular set of skills by administering a variety of cognitive criterion measures.

The Fredericksen study is only one of a number of similar (if not as wide-scoped and systematic) studies that have compared experts in a particular subject matter domain with novices in an attempt to define the underlying component skills of expertise. Thus far research has tended toward the analysis of more academic expertise such as physics (Larkin, McDermott, Simon, and Simon, 1980; Chi, Glaser, & Rees, 1981), but it is not too substantial a leap to imagine the analysis of perhaps slightly less esoteric but nevertheless critical areas of technical training.

Recently, the Air Force has become convinced that new cognitive methods of analysis hold the key to a redefinition of what it is that constitutes a "basic skill." Gott and Davis (1983) have related this reconceptualization as a switch in focus from what they call a power-based strategy for assessing general facility to a knowledge-based approach that recognizes the narrow, domain-specific nature of cognitive skill. Traditionally, both within and outside the military system, basic skills have been defined as the three Rs of reading, writing, and arithmetic. However, there is a growing realization that skills defined at this level of generality do not lead easily to prescriptions for how remediation of skills deficiencies can be accomplished. There is the hope that a more fundamental domain-specific characterization of skill might more naturally suggest techniques for overcoming particular deficiencies.

In the first large-scale effort of this kind, two occupational specialties in the Air Force, Jet Engine Mechanics and Avionics Troubleshooting, have been examined (Bond, Eastman, Gitomer, Glaser, & Lesgold, 1983). In an extensive dissertation, Gitomer (1984) has documented a number of studies concerned with identifying the basic skills involved in troubleshooting electronic aircraft equipment. The study was motivated by the observation that there are tremendous differences between first-term Airmen in their ability to perform troubleshooting effectively, despite the fact that the Airmen considered had all completed extensive technical training. Based on ratings by supervisors, Gitomer divided 16 airmen into two groups (of $N = 7$ high-skilled and $N = 9$ low-skilled), and proceeded to administer a series of tasks to the two groups to isolate the source of the skill difference.

Tasks ranged in complexity from a complex troubleshooting simulation to simple picture-name classification tasks. Some of these tasks were variants on standard cognitive tasks discussed elsewhere in this chapter, such as a task that required examinees to identify the name of a pictured component, which bears a resemblance to Posner's name identity task. Others, such as a series of component clustering tasks, and some open interview tasks (for example, "Tell me all you know about *azimuth hydraulic actuators*.") have been used in connection with studies on physics expertise (Chi, Feltovich, & Glaser, 1981). Still others were fairly domain-specific cognitive tasks that resulted from a careful task analysis of troubleshooting activities. An example is the logic gate computation task in which an examinee is required to fill in a blank given a partially complete logic gate truth table (Given the relationship, "NAND," and the input values, high, high, and low, what is the output value?).

From the pattern of differences found over the 13 tasks administered, Gitomer was able to establish the constitution of troubleshooting skill. He found that the more skilled performers differed from the less skilled in that they were driven by better specified goals more consistent with task demands, they had more methods available to them for attacking a problem, they were able to execute such methods more efficiently, and they were better able to select appropriate problem-solving methods across different situations. Some of the areas in which differences were not found may be as revealing as areas of difference. Gitomer found no effect for time in training, and he found (surprisingly) no differences between the two groups on their Electronics Aptitude score. He also found that both groups had poor knowledge of general electronics principles, presumably because after the first few weeks of formal training, such general principles played no part in job task activities.

One of the important issues related to studies along the lines of this one is determining how general basic skills are. Although the generality issue cannot be addressed systematically on the basis of a single study, there is some evidence from Gitomer's work that not all the differences were narrow domain-specific differences. The truth table task, although directly a part of avionics troubleshooting activities, is actually quite general in that it plays a role in a broad variety of complex cognitive activities such as logical analysis and computer programming. And the task revealed substantial differences between high- and low-skilled performers. Although Gitomer did not completely spell out the reasons why the difference might have shown up so clearly, it is possible that the cause may have been related to differences in general working memory capacity, one of the sources identified in our framework (see Figure 8.1).

The important point to draw from this work, which is really only in its preliminary stages, is that through the administration of carefully constructed cognitive tasks it should prove possible to isolate the sources of differences between people who perform complex activities with different degrees of proficiency. The results of such analyses should be prescriptive statements about how the less skilled individuals might be tutored to overcome specific deficits. In this regard, Gitomer has shown how the lack of differences in many of the tasks he administered is actually a quite encouraging sign in that it demonstrates that the poor troubleshooters are not simply worse at all cognitive skills, but rather they suffer particular and isolatable deficiencies. Powerful prescriptions for training are much more likely to result from considerations of these specific deficiencies than from global recommendations to train people to "read better."

SUMMARY

The purpose of cognitive assessment is to apply current understanding of how people think, learn, and remember to the measurement of an individual's proficiency level in these activities. The most obvious way a new technology for cognitive assessment might have an impact is in improving present selection and classification systems. This chapter has reviewed some of the most recent attempts to explore issues related to the feasibility of new measurement methods. It has shown that individual differences on elementary cognitive tasks are generally substantial, and there is evidence that such differences are not being captured by conventional ability tests. This suggests a role for cognitive tasks as supplements to conventional tests, and it may be that they will be particularly valid performance predictors for specialized occupations that require particular kinds of psychological processing. A second possible way current selection and classification systems might be supplemented is with measures that directly assess changes in processing efficiency as a function of practice. Because the form of such changes determines an examinee's expected performance level at the end of training or practice, it is reasonable to expect that current test batteries, which assess an examinee's current state of knowledge, can be profitably augmented by including measures of changes in processing efficiency.

There has been much discussion recently about what possibilities microcomputers hold for changing the way assessment is accomplished. Much of this discussion centers on adaptive testing technology and computerized versions of existing aptitude tests (Moreno, Wetzel, McBride, & Weiss, 1983; Weiss, 1983); but more recently attention has increasingly turned toward the issue of whether new abilities can now be measured (Hunt, 1982; Belmont, 1983). In a thoughtful review, Hunt and Pellegrino (1984) have discussed changes that computerized testing can bring in assessment of both the traditional spatial, verbal, and reasoning abilities and also in the previously unmeasured abilities related to learning, attention, and psychomotor skills. Thus their report might be read as a supplement to the views expressed in this chapter.

Hunt (1982) concluded, in his earlier paper, that although it is not yet practically feasible, a concerted five-year research program that aimed to consolidate cognitive measurement techniques and explore their utility as intelligence tests might have important long-term benefits in leading to increased predictive validity of aptitude batteries. This seems to sum up the current state of the art in ability measurement: The new cognitive assessment techniques show promise, but considerable extra research effort will be required before such tests will be feasible for personnel decision-making purposes in operational settings. Further, truly significant strides in ability measurement applications await further developments in establishing adequate criterion measures. One particularly promising area in this regard is the use of computerized instructional environments to serve as test beds in validation research.

An area that potentially may more quickly benefit from new forms of cognitive assessment has to do with the identification of basic skills. Two studies were reviewed that demonstrated how a careful task analysis followed by a comparison of performers at various skill levels can lead to the identification of component skills. Skills identified in such a fashion tend to be less general than the traditional skills of reading, writing, and arithmetic; and by virtue of their specificity, cognitive diagnosis is more easily accomplished and prescriptions for training specific deficits more naturally result. Here, again, the general approach is only beginning to be explored, but given the tremendous cost of training, the benefits of such an approach are likely to be realized in the near future, and diverse application efforts are likely to be seen.

In sum, cognitive assessment of the type that has been the main focus of this chapter is a promising technology, but one that is not yet ready to be applied in the work place. As the cost of already fairly inexpensive microcomputers comes down even further, while at the same time applied research programs provide more and more demonstrations of the utility of new and diverse forms of cognitive assessment, we are likely to see a transfer of some of the best ideas in this field to practical applications. Such a move will significantly expand current ideas on where, how, and for what purpose people's cognitive capabilities should be measured.

REFERENCES

Ackerman, P. L. (1984). A theoretical and empirical investigation of individual differences in learning: A synthesis of cognitive ability and information processing perspectives (Doctoral dissertation, University of Illinois, 1983). *Dissertation Abstracts International, 45*, 381B.

Ackerman, P. L., & Schneider, W. (1984, August). *Individual differences in automatic and controlled processes* (Tech. Rep. No. HARL-ONR-8401). Champaign: University of Illinois, Department of Psychology.

Allen, G. A., Pitts, E. W., Jones, R. J., & Morgan, B. B., Jr. (1985). *Measures of learning rate, level of learning, and scholastic aptitude as predictors of performance in training-oriented academic courses* (Tech. Rep. No. ITR-85-32). Norfolk, VA: Old Dominion University, Center for Applied Psychological Studies.

Allen, G. A., Salas, E., Pitts, E. W., Terranova, M., & Morgan, B. B., Jr. (1984). *A comparison of cognitive ability factors, learning level measures, and learning rate measures as predictors of learning performance* (Tech. Rep. No. ITR-84-31). Norfolk, VA: Old Dominion University, Center for Applied Psychological Studies.

Allen, G. A., Secundo, M. D., Salas, E., & Morgan, B. B., Jr. (1983). *Evaluation of rate parameters as predictors of the acquisition, decay, and reacquisition of complex cognitive skills* (Tech. Rep. No. ITR-82-27). Norfolk, VA: Old Dominion University, Center for Applied Psychological Studies.

Belmont, J. M. (1983). Concerning Hunt's new ways of assessing intelligence. *Intelligence, 7*, 1-7.

Bond, L., Eastman, R., Gitomer, D., Glaser, R., & Lesgold, A. (1983, December). *Cognitive task analysis of technical skills: Rationale and approach* (unpublished manuscript). Pittsburgh: University of Pittsburgh, Learning Research and Development Center.

Burt, C. (1940). *The factors of the mind.* London: University of London Press.

Carroll, J. B. (1980). *Individual difference relations in psychometric and experimental cognitive tasks* (Tech. Rep. No. 163). Chapel Hill: University of North Carolina, L. L. Thurstone Psychometric Laboratory.

Carter, R. C., & Krause, M. (1983). *Unreliability of slope scores* (unpublished manuscript). New Orleans: Naval Biodynamics Laboratory.

Cattell, R. B. (1971). *Abilities: Their structure growth and action.* Boston: Houghton Mifflin.

Chi, M. T. H., Feltovich, P. J., & Glaser, R. (1981). Categorization and representation of physics problems by experts and novices. *Cognitive Science, 5*, 121-152.

Chi, M. C., Glaser, R., & Rees, E. (1981). Expertise in problem solving. In R. J. Sternberg (Ed.), *Advances in the psychology of human intelligence* (Vol. 1, pp. 7-76). Hillsdale, NJ: Erlbaum Associates.

Christal, R. E. (1976). *What is the value of aptitude tests?* Paper presented at 18th Annual Conference of the Military Testing Association, Gulf Shores, AL.

Christal, R. E. (1981). *The need for laboratory research to improve the state-of-the-art in ability testing.* Paper presented at National Security Industrial Association-DoD Conference on Personnel and Training Factors in Systems Effectiveness, San Diego, CA.

Cristal, R. E., Tiree, W. E., & Kyllonen, P. C. (1984, April). *Two for the money: Speed and level scores from a computerized vocabulary test.* Paper presented at Ninth Psychology in the DoD Symposium. Colorado Springs, CO: U.S. Air Force Academy.

Cronbach, L. J. (1957). The two disciplines of scientific psychology. *American Psychologist, 12*, 671–684.

Cronbach, L. J., & Snow, R. E. (1977). *Aptitudes and instructional methods: A handbook for research on interactions.* New York: Irvington.

Dailey, J. (1948, November). *Development of the Airmen Classification Test Battery* (Research Bulletin 48-4). Brooks Air Force Base, TX: Air Training Command Research Development Program.

Department of Defense (1984). *Test Manual for the Armed Services Vocational Aptitude Battery* (DoD 1340.12AA). North Chicago, IL: U.S. Military Entrance Processing Command.

Eaton, N. K., & Shields, J. (1985). Validating selection tests for job performance. In J. Zeidner (Ed.), *Human productivity enhancement: Vol. 2. Acquisition and development of personnel.* New York: Praeger.

Estes, W. K. (1974). Learning theory and intelligence. *American Psychologist, 29*, 740–749.

Fairbank, B., Tirre, W., & Anderson, N. A. (1984, December). *The selection, administration, and analysis of 30 cognitive tests of individual differences.* Paper presented at NATO Conference on Learning and Cognition, Athens, Greece.

Fisk, A. D., & Schneider, W. (1983). Category and word search: Generalizing search principles to complex processing. *Journal of Experimental Psychogy: Learning, Memory, and Cognition, 9*, 177–195.

Fleishman, E. A., & Hempel, W. E. (1954). Changes in factor structure of a complex psychomotor task as a function of practice. *Psychometrika, 19*, 232-252.

Fredericksen, J. R. (1981). Sources of process interaction in reading. In A. M. Lesgold & C. A. Perfetti (Eds.), *Interactive processes in reading.* Hillsdale, NJ: Erlbaum Associates.

Fredericksen, J. R. (1982). A componential theory of reading skills and their interactions. In R. J. Sternberg (Ed.), *Advances in the psychology of human intelligence* (Vol. 1, pp. 125-180). Hillsdale, NJ: Erlbaum Associates.

Fredericksen, J. R., Weaver, P. A., Warren, B. M., Gillotte, H. P., Rosebery, A. S., Freeman, B., & Goodman, L. (1983, March). *A componential approach to training reading skills: Final report* (Tech. Rep. No. 5295). Cambridge, MA: Bolt, Baranek, and Newman, Inc.

Gilbert, T. F. (1976). The high cost of knowledge. *Personnel, 53* (2), 11-23.

Gitomer, T. (1984). *A cognitive analysis of a complex troubleshooting task.* Unpublished doctoral dissertation, University of Pittsburgh.

Gott, S., & Davis, T. (1983, November). *Introducing specific knowledge domains into basic skills instruction: From generalized powers to specified knowledge.* Paper presented at National Adult Education Conference, Philadelphia.

Gould, S. J. (1982). *The mismeasure of man.* New York: Norton.

Gould, R. B., & Hedges, J. (1983, August). *Air Force job performance criterion development.* Paper presented at American Psychological Association Annual Convention, Anaheim, CA.

Gragg, D. B., & Gordon, M. A. (1951). *Validity of the Airman Classification Battery AC-1* (Research Bulletin 50-3, 2nd ed.). Brooks Air Force Base, TX: Air Training Command, Human Resources Research Center.

Guilford, J. P. (1982). Cognitive psychology's ambiguities: Some suggested remedies. *Psychological Review, 89*, 48-59.

Guilford, J. P., & Lacey, J. I. (Eds.). (1946). *Printed Classification Tests: Army Air Forces Aviation Psychology Research Program* (Rep. No. 5). Washington, DC: U.S. Government Printing Office.

Gustaffson, J. E. (1984). A unifying model for the structure of intellectual abilities. *Intelligence, 8*, 179–203.

Hopkin, V. D. (1982). *Human factors in air traffic control* (North Atlantic Treaty Organization, Advisory Group for Aerospace Research and Development, AGARD-AG-275). Farnborough, Hampshire, England: Royal Air Force Institute of Aviation Medicine.

Horn, J. L. (1968). Organization of abilities and the development of intelligence. *Psychological Review, 75*, 242–259.

Hunt, E. B. (1978). Mechanics of verbal ability. *Psychological Review, 85*, 109–130.

Hunt, E. B. (1982). Toward new ways of assessing intelligence. *Intelligence, 6*, 231–240.

Hunt, E. B., Frost, N., & Lunneborg, C. E. (1973). Individual differences in cognition: A new approach to intelligence. In G. Bower (Ed.), *The psychology of learning and motivation: Advances in research and theory* (Vol. 7). New York: Academic Press.

Hunt, E. B., & Pellegrino, J. W. (1984). *Using interactive computing to expand intelligence testing: A critique and prospectus* (Tech. Rep. No. 84-2). Seattle: University of Washington, Department of Psychology.

Kahneman, D. (1973). *Attention and effort*. Englewood Cliffs, NJ: Prentice-Hall.

Kennedy, R. S., Bittner, A. C., Carter, R. C., Krause, M., Harbeson, N. M., McCafferty, D. B., Pepper, R. L., & Wiker, S. F. (1981). *Performance evaluation tests for environmental research (PETER): Collected papers* (Tech. Rep. No. NBDL-80R008). New Orleans, LA: Naval Biodynamics Laboratory.

Kennedy, R. S., Bittner, A. C., Harbeson, N. M., & Jones, M. I. (1981). *Perspectives in performance evaluation tests for environmental research (PETER): Collected papers* (Tech. Rep. No. NBDL-80R004). New Orleans, LA: Naval Biodynamics Laboratory.

Kyllonen, P. C. (1985a). *Individual differences in learning and cognition: The four-source proposal*. Unpublished manuscript. Brooks Air Force Base: TX: Air Force Human Resources Laboratory.

Kyllonen, P. C. (1985b). Dimensions of information processing speed (Tech. paper no 84-56). Brooks Air Force Base, TX: Air Force Human Resources Laboratory.

Kyllonen, P. C., Tirre, W. E., & Christal, R. E. (1984). *Processing determinants of associative learning.* Paper presented at Psychomomic Society, San Antonio, TX.

Larkin, J. H., McDermott, J., Simon, D. P. & Simon, H. A. (1980). Models of competence in solving physics problems. *Cognitive Science, 4*, 317-345.

Lewis, C. H. (1980). *Speed and practice.* Unpublished manuscript. Pittsburgh: Carnegie Mellon University, Department of Psychology.

Moreno, K. E., Wetzel, C. D., McBride, J. R., & Weiss, D. J. (1983, August). *Relationship between corresponding Armed Services Vocational Aptitude Battery (ASVAB) and Computerized Adaptive Testing (CAT) subtests* (Tech. Rep. No. NPRDC-TR-83-27). San Diego, CA: Navy Personnel Research and Development Center.

Nairn, A., and associates. (1980). *The reign of ETS: The corporation that makes up minds.* Ralph Nader Report on the Educational Testing Service. Washington, DC: Ralph Nader.

Neisser, U. (1967). *Cognitive psychology.* New York: Appleton.

Newell, A., & Rosenbloom, P. (1981). Mechanisms of skill acquisition and the law of practice. In J. R. Anderson (Ed.), *Cognitive skills and their acquisition* (pp. 1-55). Hillsdale, NJ: Erlbaum Associates.

Payne, D., & Tirre, W. E. (1984). Individual differences in learning rate. Paper presented at Ninth Psychology in the DoD Symposium. Colorado Springs, CO: U.S. Air Force Academy.

Pellegrino, J. W. (1984). Individual differences in information processing efficiency. Paper presented at American Psychological Association Annual Convention, Toronto.

Pellegrino, J. W., & Glaser, R. (1979). Cognitive correlates and components in the analysis of individual differences. *Intelligence, 3*, 187-214.

Posner, M. I., & Mitchell, R. E. (1967). Chronometric analysis of classification. *Psychological Review, 74*, 392-409.

Rimland, B., & Larson, G. E. (in press). Individual differences: An undeveloped opportunity for military psychology. *Military Psychology.*

Rogosa, D., Brandt, D., & Zimowski, M. (1982). A growth curve approach to the measurement of change. *Psychological Bulletin, 90,* 726-748.

Rogosa, D., & Willett, J. (1983). Demonstrating the reliability of the difference score in the measurement of change. *Journal of Educational Measurement, 20,* 335-343.

Rose, A. M., & Fernandez, K. (1977, November). *An information processing approach to performance assessment. I. Experimental investigation of an information processing performance battery* (Tech. Rep. No. AIR-58500-TR). Washington, DC: American Institutes for Research.

Rumelhart, D., & Norman, D. (1978). Accretion, tuning, and restructuring: Three modes of learning. In J. W. Cotton & R. Klatzky (Eds.), *Semantic factors in cognition.* Hillsdale, NJ: Erlbaum Associates.

Schmitz, E., & Holz, B. (1985). Technology for person-job matching. In J. Zeidner (Ed.), *Human productivity enhancement: Vol. 2. Acquisition and development of personnel.* New York: Praeger.

Shiffrin, R. M., & Schneider, W. (1977). Controlled and automatic human information processing. II. Perceptual learning, automatic attending, and a general theory. *Psychological Review, 84,* 127-190.

Snow, R. E. (1978). Theory and method for research on aptitude processes. *Intelligence, 2,* 225-278.

Snow, R. E. (1980). Aptitude processes. In R. E. Snow, P. A. Federico, & W. E. Montague (Eds.), *Aptitude, learning, and instruction: Vol. 1: Cognitive process analyses of aptitude.* Hillsdale, NJ: Erlbaum Associates.

Snow, R. E., & Lohman, D. F. (1981). *Cognition and learning in young adults* (Tech. Rep. No. 13). Stanford, CA: Stanford University, Aptitude Research Project, School of Education.

Snow, R. E., Wescourt, K., & Collins, J. C. (1983). *Individual differences in aptitude and learning from interactive computer-based instruction* (Tech. Rep. No. 10). Stanford, CA: Stanford University, Aptitude Research Project, School of Education.

Spearman, C. (1905). General intelligence objectively determined and measured. *American Journal of Psychology, 15*, 201-293.

Sternberg, R. J. (1977). *Intelligence, information processing, and analogical reasoning: The componential analysis of human abilities.* Hillsdale, NJ: Erlbaum Associates.

Sternberg, R. J. (1980). Nothing fails like success: The search for an intelligent paradigm for studying intelligence. *Journal of Educational Psychology, 73*, 142-155.

Sternberg, S. (1969). Memory-scanning: Mental processes revealed by reaction-time experiments. *American Scientist, 57*, 421-457.

Thurstone, L. L. (1938). *Primary mental abilities.* Chicago: University of Chicago Press.

Vernon, P. E. (1961). *The structure of human abilities.* (2nd ed.). London: Methuen.

Weeks, J. L., Mullins, C. J., & Vitola, B. M. (1975, December). *Airmen Classification Batteries from 1948 to 1975: A review and evaluation* (Tech. Rep. No. AFHRL-TR-75-78). Brooks Air Force Base, TX: Air Force Human Resources Laboratory, Air Force Systems Command.

Weiss, D. J. (Ed.). (1983). *New horizons in testing: Latent trait test theory and computerized adaptive testing.* New York: Academic Press.

Wilson, K. M. (1982, October). *A study of the validity of the restructured GRE aptitude test for predicting first-year performance in graduate study* (GRE Board Research Rep. GREB No. 78-6R, ETS Research Rep. 82-34). Princeton, NJ: Educational Testing Service.

9

VALIDATING SELECTION TESTS AGAINST JOB PERFORMANCE

Newell K. Eaton, Lawrence M. Hanser,
and Joyce L. Shields

The major objective of selection and classification procedures is to enhance organizational performance through selection of job applicants who are potentially high performers. The value of a selection/classification system lies in its ability to predict how individuals will perform in specific work, training, or treatment environments (cf. Cronbach & Gleser, 1965). To the extent that these predictions are accurate, productivity is increased, training is more efficient, or treatment is more effective. But prediction is really only part of the process. Social concerns for fairness have raised the complex issue of test bias. Further, legal requirements to set minimum entrance, competency, or certification standards for job applicants, students, teachers, and others challenge our theories and methods. Finally, competition for scarce resources—whether public or private—requires that selection and classification systems be proven to be cost-effective decision-making tools.

When faced with these and other critical issues, we soon discover that determining whether a test is valid for predicting performance is generally only the beginning. We also must ask whether the relationship between a set of predictors and performance measures is essentially the same for all races and both sexes. If not, would a different predictor set serve better? Is the criterion measure really a measure of performance? Can a minimum acceptable level of performance be rigorously defined so that minimum entry standards can be set? Are the benefits of improved performance greater than the costs associated with the selection and classification system?

Most organizations are unable to conduct simple test validation research with sufficient statistical power, let alone engage in the research necessary to address these more complex questions (Cascio, Valenzi, & Silbey, 1978, 1980; Schmidt, Hunter, & Urry, 1976; Trattner & O'Leary, 1980). However, with the resources of a large, complex, and highly visible organization such as the U.S. Army applied to these questions, it should be possible to address them. This is being done in a personnel selection and classification project conducted by the U.S. Army Research Institute (ARI) in conjunction with the Human Resources Research Organization (HumRRO), the American Institutes for Research (AIR), and the Personnel Decisions Research Institute (PDRI).

This research project is unique in scope, size, duration, and design. Nineteen key Army occupations were selected to represent most of the several hundred entry level Army occupations. Those selected include carpenters, clerks, combat soldiers, cooks, drivers, electronic repairers, mechanics, medics, and military police. Most have direct civilian counterparts. The size of the Army and the design of the research permit samples of several hundred in each occupation. And the project is designed to follow these soldiers through their first and second three-year tours. The research is designed to explore the relationships between a broad array of entry measures, training measures, and first and second tour measures using both concurrent and predictive validation paradigms.

CURRENT ISSUES IN SELECTION AND CLASSIFICATION

Validity generalization. A major problem facing the great majority of employers is that they do not employ sufficient numbers of individuals on whom to conduct validation research. This makes it difficult for them to determine to what degree their employment tests are valid. As a consequence, their employment decisions are often based on tests shown to be valid for a similar job but in a different organization.

In a number of published reports, Schmidt and his colleagues (cf. Pearlman, Schmidt, & Hunter, 1980; Schmidt, Gast-Rosenberg, & Hunter, 1980; Schmidt & Hunter, 1977) have demonstrated that the variability in validities of a test across situations is largely artifactual. They have shown, in a series of meta-analyses, that some tests are valid predictors of performance across a wide variety of jobs. However, in the literature they examined, the tests have been largely paper-and-pencil cognitive tests, and the performance criteria have been questionable (Tenopyr, 1981). Perhaps examination of a broader range of predictors and criteria would have resulted in evidence for specificity rather than generalizability. Nonetheless, the basic issue remains: Which types of predictor tests generalize to which kinds of criteria in which types of tasks/jobs/occupations?

Predictive versus concurrent validity. "Predictive validity is the cornerstone of individual differences measurement" (Cascio 1982, p. 150). One of the primary problems with using concurrent validity to estimate predictive validity is that job applicants may differ in many ways from job incumbents (Guion & Cranny, 1982). Applicants scoring poorly on an existing predictor test may have been excluded from employment, leaving only higher scorers to become job incumbents. This preselection results in restriction in range in the incumbent groups. Very low or very high scoring applicants may be more likely to leave the job. They may either fail or be promoted at a higher rate than more average applicants. Also, the scores of incumbents on predictor tests may vary from the scores they would have obtained as applicants. Their training or experience on the job could improve their test performance, or their motivation, morale, or attitude could affect their scores. Further, some individuals may be more affected than others, impacting on their ordering and the validity obtained from the validation procedures.

The purpose of undertaking validity research in employment settings is to test the hypothesis that the performance of applicants on an employment test will predict subsequent performance on the job. But the population of job applicants often differs substantially from a sample of job incumbents for the reasons described above. Although statistical methods exist for correcting range restriction (cf. Lord & Novick, 1968), it is seldom possible to specify accurately the entire set of variables on which selection has occurred. There remains the issue of the degree to which concurrent validation, with common statistical corrections, provides meaningful information about predictive validity.

Diffferential prediction. If two individuals from two different subgroups (for example, racial or sexual) have the same score on an employment test but their predicted scores based on subgroup regression lines are different, differential prediction is said to have occurred. Much of the original research in this area focused on differences between subgroup correlations as an indicator of either single-group or differential validity (Bartlett, Bobko, & Pine, 1977; Bobko & Bartlett, 1978; Boehm, 1977, 1978; Hunter & Schmidt, 1978; Katzell & Dyer, 1977, 1978; Linn, 1978).

Current methods of detecting differential prediction include examining subgroup regression lines for differences in slope, intercept, and/or standard error. The change in emphasis from validity coefficients to regression parameters is at least partly due to Bobko and Bartlett (1978) and Linn (1978). However, most often available sample sizes do not provide sufficient power for detecting reliable subgroup differences. Despite the years of research, procedures for the evaluation of and methods for dealing with differential prediction, this topic remains an issue.

Utility. While several authors (cf. Brogden, 1949; Cronbach & Gleser, 1965; Eaton, Wing, & Mitchell, 1985; Sadacca & Campbell, 1985; Schmidt, et al. 1979) have suggested different strategies for calculating the utility of a set of selection and classification decisions, several problems remain to be resolved. For example, to what degree are dollar utility estimates credible and representative of anticipated dollar savings or payoff?

Classification efficiency. A problem that arises most often in larger organizations is classification efficiency, or differential validity in the traditional sense (cf. Dwyer, 1954; Lord, 1952; Horst, 1960; Votaw, 1952; see also the chapter in this text by Schmitz and Holz). At issue is not whether tests predict performance on one job. Instead, given several jobs for which an applicant is qualified, in which will he or she be expected to contribute the most to the organization?

Setting standards. Most organizations have the liberty of developing lists of applicants and hiring from the top of the list until available positions are filled. The question of whether an applicant meets minimum qualifications seldom arises, and hence, minimum qualifications are seldom rigorously set. This is not the case for all large organizations, and it is definitely not the case for most state, federal, and municipal agencies. Unfortunately, there is little consensus about the best way to set standards in employment settings.

Comprehensive measurement of abilities and performance. Current practice in personnel research generally results in a less than comprehensive set of preemployment tests being correlated with any readily available criterion measure. There are, however, some examples of the successful comprehensive measurement of both abilities and performance (cf. Gael, Grant, & Ritchie, 1975a, b). These authors found relatively sizable validities ranging from .16 to .64 in predicting the performance of telephone operators and clerks. These studies are important because they describe the validity of a range of standardized cognitive tests for predicting carefully developed, credible measures of job performance. There remains the issue of what degree of coverage of the predictor and performance criterion space provides adequate coverage in validity research.

Old Dogs, Old Tricks

Each of the above issues, in one form or another, has been addressed by personnel psychology. These larger questions have been embedded in selection and classification work, but there have frequently been supplied only limited answers. Preference has been to reduce an issue to a manageable size that can be answered in a relatively short time in a controlled environment. While this approach has its virtues, it also incorporates important drawbacks. Chief among them is simply that large and complex problems, like those discussed above, often require longitudinal designs and vast amounts of data. However, as we become more involved in organizational policy, we find that the typical approach fails to meet the expectations or requirements of our sponsors or clients.

Project A: Old Dogs, New Tricks

To tackle complex issues requires a comprehensive plan and a major programmatic effort. The U.S. Army's project "Development and Validation of Army Selection and Classification Measures (Project A)" is just such an effort. In the context of conducting research to revise the Army's selection and classification system, each of the issues noted above were addressed.

1. The Army is a large organization with more than 250 entry level occupations. Since it is not economically feasible to include all of these occupations in the research, validity generalization or synthetic validity will be required to extend the results to the remaining occupations.

2. The organization changes. Is it necessary to engage in an expensive longitudinal validation effort again in the future, or would validity generalization or a concurrent validity effort provide an acceptable substitute?
3. Women and other minorities apply to enter the Army in large numbers. Do entry tests predict equitably for all applicants?
4. More than 150,000 individuals enter the Army every year. What is the best way to assign them to occupations to maximize overall performance? Is there more than one valid general factor in the current or proposed test batteries? Is there basis in these batteries for a system of classification rather than just selection?
5. Many occupations in the Army have large psychomotor and perceptual components. What are the most efficient ways to predict performance in these kinds of occupations? What are acceptable performance criteria? Are computer-administered psychomotor/perceptual tests cost-effective?
6. Finally, how should entry standards be set so they will provide the Army with the quantity and quality of personnel it requires and yet minimize recruiting, training, and adverse discharge costs?

While each of these questions has a specific meaning for the U.S. Army, each also represents a critical problem for the field of personnel psychology as a whole. The next section describes the fundamental design of a single, large, and complex project designed to provide answers to some of these questions and shed substantial light on the others.

The Project A Research Plan

Sample. A total of 19 military occupational specialties (MOS) were selected for inclusion in this project. These occupations were selected to provide broad coverage of the kinds of work performed by Army personnel, as well as to represent a large proportion of the organization itself. Approximately 44 percent of all enlistees in the Army in a given year are slated for training in one of these occupations.

Examination of present validity. The overall research plan for Project A is depicted in Figure 9.1. As can be seen, the research has been planned to take place in several stages. As a first step, existing

FIGURE 9.1. Project A Research Flow.

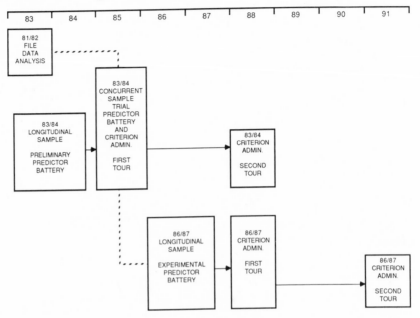

Source: From a paper by Eaton, Goer, & Zook. In *Introduction to Current Army Selection and Classification Research*, Eaton, Goer, Harris, and Zook, ed, 1984.

data on individuals who entered the Army between October 1980 and September 1982 were examined to evaluate the validity of the present enlistment test battery, the Armed Services Vocational Aptitude Battery (ASVAB). The ASVAB contains ten subtests—four are cognitive, four are vocational/technical, and two are speeded. A minimum score on the Armed Forces Qualification Test (AFQT—a composite of four of the ASVAB subtests) qualifies an applicant for enlistment. Scores on one of the ten Aptitude Area Composites (composed of ASVAB subtests) are used for classification in specific occupations. Available criteria are primarily paper-and-pencil tests of job knowledge. The results of the analysis of the current ASVAB are discussed later in this chapter.

Development of measures. The second stage of the project consists of extensive development and iterative field tests of additional potential enlistment and job performance measures. Several of these measures were developed to be computer-administered. Decisions about the types of predictor and criterion measures to be developed were based on a construct validation strategy (Rosse, et al., 1983; Wing, Peterson, & Hoffman, 1984). This strategy was chosen to provide a basis for extending the results to occupations not included in the research.

Validation strategy. The third stage of the project consists of data collection and validation. In the past, most military enlistment tests have been validated against measures of success in training. In this project, however, a full range of predictor tests will be validated against a full range of criteria of training for first and second tour performance. Because of the classification of individuals based on entry scores and the extensive initial training given soldiers, there are good reasons to believe that incumbents are quite different from applicants. This raises the question of the comparability of results from concurrent and predictive strategies. Project A is designed to include both concurrent and predictive strategies and will thus provide the opportunity to make direct comparisons between them over a variety of occupations, predictors, and criteria.

In 1985 a massive concurrent validation effort, involving about 10,000 first tour soldiers, was conducted. The performance of those who reenlist will be measured again in 1988. A modified predictive validity design began in 1986 with another large group of soldiers. In this design, the complete set of predictors is being collected immediately after soldiers arrive at their basic training sites. Measures of performance in training will be collected on these same soldiers at the end of their advanced training. Their first tour job performance will be measured after they have been working in their assigned occupation for a minimum of one year. For those who reenlist, their second tour performance will be measured after an additional three years. The analysis plans provide for sequentially validating each piece of information as well as combining all current information to predict future performance.

Because it is virtually impossible to conduct a true predictive study—to accept all applicants and measure their performance on the job—the modified predictive validity design described above is being followed. It is clear that this design approaches a predictive design, but there are some key differences. First of all, applicants are screened on ASVAB prior to entry, resulting in explicit selection on ASVAB and implicit restriction in performance scores. Second, normal attrition will be allowed to occur during training and assignment at a duty station. This may result in restriction in the range of performance. Nevertheless, this design is longitudinal and has all the attendant advantages. Scores on the predictors will be unaffected by training, and scores in training will be unaffected by job experience. The remainder of this chapter shall refer to this longitudinal design as a predictive validity design.

The longitudinal research data base. One of Project A's principal resources is the longitudinal research data base (LRDB), containing data on more than 600,000 Army applicants, including 300,000 accessions, beginning in October 1980. Predictor information consists of operational applicants' accessions records data: ASVAB and the Military Applicant Profile (MAP—a biodata instrument given male nongraduates). Performance data consist of end-of-course training data reported by the schools (fiscal year 1981 only), job knowledge as indexed by Skill Qualification Test (SQT) scores, and data from the enlisted master file: attrition, promotion, disciplinary actions, awards, and so on.

It also includes test data on every soldier to whom specialized predictor or performance measures are administered. The importance of the LRDB is based on the rapid systematic access it offers to many kinds of data. It can provide, for many MOS, rapid answers to Army questions because new data do not have to be collected. Further, it is a prototype of the kind of data system that could be a powerful personnel management tool. Last, it provides a wealth of real data for use in addressing many of the statistical issues associated with the most appropriate validation models, correction strategies, and the like. A complete description of the LRDB can be found in Wise, Wang, and Rossmeissl (1983).

TESTS FOR PREDICTION OF PERFORMANCE

From the plethora of research data available, Project A researchers attempted to determine the best set of predictor tests that could be used in addition to ASVAB and MAP. There were several useful sources of data to address this issue. One source was an extensive review of the literature, including meta-analyses (Glass, McGaw, & Smith, 1981; Hunter, Schmidt, & Jackson, 1982) and large-scale studies of employment test validities. A second source was the work on the development of task taxonomies. One basis of this work has been the underlying ability requirement for task performance (Fleishman, 1966, 1975; Harman, 1975; McCormick, 1979). A third source of data was an effort to acquire "expert judgments" of ability requirements (Peterson & Bownas, 1982; Schmidt, et al., 1983; Wing, Peterson, & Hoffman, 1984). Together these provided a rich source of information on which to select tests for empirical validation. Based on the analyses of preliminary test batteries derived from these sources, a battery was chosen for use in the concurrent validation in 1985.

Predictor Development

Literature Review

While the literature review documented many different human attributes associated with different types of performance, much of the meta-analytic work has stressed the contribution of a few attributes to many kinds of performance. Based on a review of recent literature, Hunter and Schmidt (1983) concluded that cognitive abilities predict performance in all jobs. The most encompassing reference deals with an evaluation of 515 validity studies by the U.S. Employment Service (Hunter, 1980). Cognitive ability, measured by the General Abilities Test Battery (GATB), had a mean validity of .53 across all jobs.

The validity of cognitive ability found with GATB is consistent with the Project A research on 70,000 soldiers in 81 Army enlisted occupational specialties (McLaughlin, et al., 1984). In that effort, a general cognitive ability composite of four verbal and math subtests of the ASVAB was used as the predictor. This general ability composite had a mean corrected validity of .39 for training performance, and .44 for performance on job knowledge tests administered approximately one year after training. The addition of vocational/technical and speeded subtests dealing with general science, auto/shop information, mechanical comprehension, coding speed, numerical operations, and electronics information produced only minor gains in validity. With the additional tests, the median validity for training was .41, and for job knowledge it was .48. In many occupational groups, the best possible composite from all ten

ASVAB subtests fared little better than the general ability composite. These results are summarized in Table 9.1 for nine clusters of Army enlisted occupations.

Even though the vocational/technical and speeded ASVAB subtests added little empirical validity over that obtained with only general ability subtests (replicating Hunter, 1980), it seemed appropriate to expand the predictor space in Project A beyond general cognitive ability. The strong relationship between general ability and training success or job performance may have been an artifact of the performance criteria. The paper-and-pencil nature of most training and job performance measures adds a general requirement that may not be typical of the job. Further, the high motivational demand of formal training/testing settings leads to measurements of maximum rather than typical performance. Performance evaluations by supervisors and peers would provide better information on typical performance, as well as useful additions to hands-on or job knowledge performance measures. Hands-on performance tests would also add a stronger psychomotor component to the criterion. A last but extremely important consideration supporting broadening the predictor space past general ability involves differential classification of applicants for various Army MOS. To provide for optimal allocation of personnel, predictors must be identified that predict differentially for particular MOS rather than for all MOS.

Task Taxonomies

The task taxonomy literature provides results that stress the differential attribute requirements of tasks. Since the early years of psychology, the development and understanding of measures of human attributes have been intertwined with their relationships to task performance. In 1927, Spearman provided a two-factor theory of intelligence, composed of one general cognitive ability factor and many other components specific to certain tasks or situations. Since then there has been continuous development in the theoretical and empirical bases of the structure of human attributes and task performance. Recent work by Guilford (1977) provides a "structure of intellect" model: a matrix of five kinds of contents, six kinds of products, and five kinds of operations. Tests have been identified to evaluate each of the 150 content X operations X products cells, and empirical data exist for most cells.

TABLE 9.1. Validities of General Ability Composite and Best Composite for Nine Clusters of Army Enlisted Occupations

Clusters of Occupations	Training Performance			Job Knowledge		
	N	General Composite	Best Composite	N	General Composite	Best Composite
Clerical/administrative	5,300	.47	.47	8,000	.58	.58
Combat	2,900	.33	.35	16,000	.43	.45
Electronic repair	2,600	.40	.41	6,000	.43	.46
Field artillery	1,800	.31	.36	7,000	.44	.48
General maintenance	1,900	.48	.52	1,300	.39	.42
Mechanical maintenance	5,400	.39	.44	4,300	.41	.46
Operators/food	4,600	.34	.36	7,700	.49	.53
Surveillance/communications	1,500	.37	.37	3,600	.50	.53
Skilled technical	3,200	.52	.54	6,900	.56	.56

Source: Adapted from McLaughlin, et al., 1984, p. 41.

Concurrent with the work by Guilford, several others have worked to develop taxonomies of cognitive attributes (Dunnette, 1976; Ekstrom, French, & Harman, 1976; French, Ekstrom, & Price, 1963; Harman, 1975), noncognitive attributes (Browne & Howaith, 1977; French, 1973; Harman, 1975), vocational interests (Holland, 1976), and perceptual-motor attributes (Fleishman, 1966, 1972, 1975; Fleishman & Quaintance, 1984). Fortunately, these have been integrated and summarized admirably by Fleishman and Quaintance (1984) and by Peterson and Bownas (1982). Fleishman and Quaintance (1984) proposed a 52-construct taxonomy, including 19 cognitive factors and 33 perceptual-motor factors. They did not consider explicitly personality and interest factors. Peterson and Bownas proposed a 51-construct taxonomy of human characteristics, with 12 cognitive factors, 18 psychomotor and physical abilities, 15 personality factors, and 6 vocational interest factors. This previous work in task taxonomies provided a basis for selecting predictor tests that would span the wide range of human abilities.

Expert Judgments

Several recent strategies illustrate ways information may be obtained on the relationship between human attributes and various aspects of performance using expert judgments. In one effort, the task elements of the widely used Position Analysis Questionnaire were reliably linked to a comprehensive list of human attributes (Marguardt & McCormick, 1972; Mecham & McCormick, 1969). Fleishman and his colleagues have also been successful in evaluating the requirements of various jobs in terms of their taxonomy of abilities (Fleishman, 1975; Fleishman & Hogan, 1978; Theologus & Fleishman, 1973). In this work, subject matter experts (SME) were asked to rate the requirement of the job in terms of the abilities in the taxonomy, using specially constructed scales.

Work in this area has been continued in Project A by Smith and Rossmeissl (1985). However, their research was not used directly as a basis for test battery selection. Instead, the validities of constructs judged to be valid MOS performance predictors from their research will be compared to actual empirical validities of the constructs obtained during Project A concurrent validation efforts. If successful, this work may provide the basis for synthetic validity, one avenue of generalizing empirical test validation findings to occupations for which empirical validation cannot be readily accomplished.

Peterson and his colleagues have used a formal judgment process involving not job experts but testing experts to estimate the likely relationship between a matrix of human attributes and performance. Their initial work was with the jobs of firefighter and correctional officer (Bownas & Heckman, 1976; Peterson & Houston, 1980; Peterson, Houston, Bosshardt, & Dunnette, 1977). This technique has been shown to be as accurate in obtaining validity estimates as moderately sized empirical validity research efforts (Schmidt, et al., 1983).

To identify likely predictor tests for use in Project A, Wing, Peterson, and Hoffman (1984) applied the expert judgment procedure to a taxonomy of 72 criterion constructs. The criterion constructs included 53 job-oriented criterion categories representing the population of first-tour Army enlisted occupations, four categories of training performance, and 15 general soldier effectiveness constructs. The effort resulted in a matrix containing the judged correlations between 53 predictor constructs and 72 criterion constructs. Factor analyses were used to reduce these to a smaller 21 × 16 matrix of predictor and performance cluster correlations and an 8 × 5 matrix of predictor and performance factor correlations. These provided a number of "best bet" constructs for empirical validation as predictors of a wide variety of task clusters.

Preliminary Predictor Battery

Development

Based on the sources described above, and a good deal of judgment, Project A scientists developed several initial test batteries. Their purpose was to cover as much of the predictor space as possible. Their administration was used to learn enough about their properties to estimate the best constructs for Project A use. Further tests or scales could be written specifically for Project A use once the constructs were selected. The first test administration involved only group-administered paper-and-pencil measures, using off-the-shelf tests. These were administered to more than 9,000 soldiers in four MOS. In the second test administration, specially designed paper-

and-pencil, as well as computer-administered, tests were given to about 275 soldiers.

The first test battery administration included a battery of eight paper-and-pencil tests. Five were timed perceptual-cognitive tests from the Educational Testing Service (ETS) "French Kit" (Ekstrom, French, & Harman, 1976), two from the Employee Aptitude Survey (EAS; Ruch & Ruch, 1980), and one from the Flanagan Industrial Tests (FIT; Flanagan, 1965). Also included were four personality scales, two from the Differential Personality Questionnaire (Tellegen, 1982), one from the California Psychological Inventory (Gough, 1975), and Rotter's Locus of Control Scale (Rotter, 1966). Last were Owens' biographical questionnaire (Owens & Schoenfeldt, 1979) and the U.S. Air Force Vocational Interest Career Examination (VOICE) (Alley & Matthews, 1982). In addition, ASVAB scores were available for all soldiers in the sample.

Test Results

Results from the first 1,800 soldiers taking the battery were reported by Hough et al. (1984). The intercorrelations between the eight preliminary battery perceptual-cognitive tests and the ten ASVAB subtests ranged from $-.07$ to $+.57$, with a median of .27. The highest correlations were between ETS following directions and the ASVAB general science (GS), arithmetic reasoning (AR), and word knowledge (WK) subtests (r's = .41, .48, and .43), between FIT assembly and the ASVAB GS, AR, auto/shop (AS) and math knowledge (MK) subtests (r's = .41, .43, .43, and .40), and between EAS numerical reasoning and ASVAB AR and MK subtests (r's = .55 and .50). A principal components factor analysis with varimax rotation yielded five interpretable factors. Most of the eight perceptual-cognitive tests loaded on the first factor, while the ten ASVAB tests loaded on the second through fifth factors: verbal, technical knowledge, speeded performance, and quantitative. These followed the pattern of four factors for ASVAB found by Kass et al. (1983).

Factor analyses were also conducted on the biographical questionnaire items, yielding 15 factors; the VOICE, yielding 17 factors; and the personality items, yielding five factors. In addition, all items from the biographical questionnaire, the VOICE, and the personality instruments were factor-analyzed, yielding a five-factor solution. The results of this analysis, with the factors named and the scales included in each factor, are shown in Table 9.2.

TABLE 9.2. Five-Factor Solution of the Interest, Biographical, and Temperament Scales

	Variance Accounted For	Percent of Common Variance Accounted For
Factor I: Nonrealistic Interests	4.93	24.2
(I) Teacher/counselor (.74)		
(I) Office administration (.74)		
(I) Medical services (.72)		
(I) Food service (.67)		
(I) Aesthetics (.67)		
(I) Craftsman (.66)		
(I) Audiographics (.59)		
(I) Mathematics (.53)		
(I) Automated data processing (.50)		
(I) Drafting (.37)		
Factor II: Realistic Interests	4.34	21.3
(I) Mechanics (.82)		
(I) Heavy construction (.80)		
(I) Marksman (.78)		
(I) Electronics (.73)		
(I) Outdoors (.67)		
(B) Vocational/technical activities (.59)		
(I) Agriculture (.55)		
(I) Law enforcement (.42)		
Factor III: Scientific/Intellectual Orientation	3.46	17.0
(B) Scientific interest (.74)		
(B) Academic confidence (.69)		
(I) Science (.60)		
(B) Academic achievement (.56)		
(B) Positive academic attitude (.41)		
(B) Reading/intellectual interests (.41)		
(B) Effort (.41)		
Factor IV: Potency Athletic and Social	2.84	13.9
(B) Athletic/sports participation (.76)		
(B) Athletic interests (.60)		
(B) Social activity (.58)		
(B) Leadership (.56)		
(B) Physical condition (.55)		
(P) Social potency (.40)		
(B) Independence (.31)		
Factor V: Personal Well-Being	2.39	11.7
(B) Antecedents of self-esteem (.73)		
(P) Socialization (.66)		
(B) Self-control (.61)		
(B) Parental closeness (.60)		
(P) Stress reaction (.43)		
(B) Social confidence (.35)		
(B) Sibling harmony (.27)		
(P) Internal-external locus of control (.15)		
Total	18.0	88.1

Note: I signifies Interest scale; B signifies Biographical scale; P signifies Personality scale; Factor loading shown in parentheses.

Source: Hough, et al., 1984, p. 64.

The intercorrelations between the 40 scales associated with these factors, and the set of perceptual cognitive measures including the eight ETS/EAS/FIT tests and the four ASVAB factors, were quite low. Hough et al. (1984) computed the median correlation between the scales in each noncognitive factor and each of the 12 perceptual-cognitive measures. The range was .02 to .32, and a median of these medians was .06. Only with the noncognitive "realistic interests" factor did correlations above .20 emerge with the perceptual-cognitive tests: It correlated with ASVAB technical knowledge and speeded performance factors and with EAS spatial visualization (r's = .31, .21, and .21).

Later analyses of the complete set of 9,000 soldiers (Hough, et al., 1985) revealed high reliabilities for two of the five personality factors, stress reaction, and social potency (Alpha's .91 and .86), but lower reliabilities for the remaining three (Alpha's .55-.62). However, they remained highly independent of the ASVAB factors (adjusted R^2s .01-.04). Reliabilities for the VOICE were uniformly high, with Alpha's ranging from .75 to .95 with a median of .89, for the 18 scales. These scales remained moderately independent of the ASVAB factors (adjusted R^2s .03-.31, median = .10), while the biographical scale scores were highly independent of the ASVAB factors (adjusted R^2s .00-.15, median = .03). Only R^2s for the scientific interest and academic achievement scales exceeded .10.

Pilot Trial Battery

A second, more comprehensive battery was developed and administered to about 275 soldiers. It included ten computerized measures chosen for development based on expert judgments and literature review. Also included were paper-and-pencil cognitive, biodata, interest, and personality scales. Most were similar to the off-the-shelf measures described above. All of the measures in this battery were created especially for Project A use. McHenry, Rosse, Peterson, Toquam, McGue, Russell, and Corpe (1985) provide a description of the computer-administered measures and the results of the second battery administration.

McHenry et al. (1985) conducted several analyses of these data, including factor analysis for nine of the ten computerized measures (simple reaction time means were unavailable). Five factors, shown in Table 9.3, were identified: psychomotor ability, processing speed,

TABLE 9.3. Five-Factor Solution to Computer-Administered Tests

Computerized Measures	Factor 1 Psychomotor Ability	Factor 2 Processing Speed	Factor 3 Perceptual Speed and Accuracy	Factor 4 Processing Accuracy	Factor 5 Number Facility	Number of Scored Items	Split Half Reliability	Test-Retest Reliability	R^2 with ASVAB	Gain After Practice
Simple reaction time						10	.90	.37	.07	
Two-choice reaction time		.47				15	.89	.56	.09	-.43
Perceptual speed and accuracy						48				
% correct			.49	.53			.83	.59	.14	
Mean time		.40	.66				.96	.65	.06	
Slope time			.99				.88	.67	.09	
Intercept time		.35	-.60				.74	.55	.11	
One-hand tracking	.87					27	.97	.68	.23	.33
Two-hand tracking	.84					27	.97	.77	.17	.21
Target identification						48				
% correct			.31	.38			.84	.19	.05	
Mean time	.49	.41					.96	.67	.16	
Short-term memory						48				
% correct				.62			.72	.34	.10	
Mean time		.80					.94	.78	.06	
Slope time				.62			.52	.47	.01	
Intercept time		.95					.84	.74	.11	
Cannon shoot-time	.35					48	.88	.66	.02	-.11
Number memory						27				
% correct					.75		.63	.53	.40	
Time					-.60		.95	.88	.33	
Target shoot						35				
Time	.30						.91	.48	.06	
Error distance	.50						.86	.58	.11	.26

Source: Adapted from McHenry, et al., 1985, pp. 21, 24, and 29.

perceptual speed and accuracy, processing accuracy, and number facility. Also shown is the number of items, the split half reliability, the test-retest (two-week) reliability, and the gain, in standard deviations, after two weeks and about an hour's practice on five of the tests (using similar, but not identical, items). It was particularly rewarding to see the relatively high reliabilities of these tests when used in a field-test environment, and the relatively small gain scores for the five tests deemed most susceptible to practice. Further, self-reported experience with video games had only a minimal relationship with test performance (r's = .00–.27, median r = .10). Last, no significant differences among our six test stations was observed, indicating a high level of uniformity for the test equipment.

When the computer-administered tests and the paper-and-pencil perceptual-cognitive tests were factor-analyzed together, a six-factor solution emerged. The first was predominantly the paper-and-pencil tests, but included the number memory computer-administered test. The second through sixth factors were essentially the same as observed in the factor analysis of computer-administered tests only, described above. Last, the ten ASVAB subtests were combined in an overall factor analysis with the perceptual-cognitive paper-and-pencil tests and the computer-administered tests. A seven-factor solution was the most sensible. The first factor consisted of the eight ASVAB power subtests, the number memory computer-administered test, and the paper-and-pencil orientation tests. The second factor comprised the paper-and-pencil perceptual-cognitive tests, while the remaining five factors replicated the five for the computer-administered tests, with one exception: The ASVAB speeded tests, numerical operations and coding speed, loaded heavily on the number facility factor.

Trial Battery

From the results of these analyses, a final "trial battery" of predictor measures was developed for concurrent validation on about 10,000 soldiers in 19 MOS during the summer and fall of 1985. These measures, combined with existing ASVAB scores for each soldier, will provide the most comprehensive evaluation of the predictor space ever obtained on U.S. Army soldiers. The scales of the final battery are shown in Table 9.4, as well as the construct being measured, the mode of administration, the factor with which the scale was associated, and the most closely associated published scale.

TABLE 9.4. Project A Final Predictor Battery Constructs and Scales for Summer–Fall Concurrent Validation with 12,000 Soldiers

Construct	Final Battery Scale	Type-Factor	Associated Scale
Verbal	ASVAB	P–R	ASVAB
Memory	Short-term memory	M–S/PA	
	Number memory	M–R/N	
Number facility	ASVAB	P–N	ASVAB
	Number memory	M–N	
Perceptual speed and accuracy	Perceptual speed and accuracy	M–PS	
	Target identification	M–PM/PS	
Reasoning/induction	Reasoning	P–V/R	ETS figure classification
Information processing	Simple reaction time	M	
	Two-choice reaction time	M–3	
Spatial orientation	Orientation	P–V/R	
	Orientation	P–V/R	
Spatial visualization	Object rotation	P–V	EAS visualization
	Assembling objects	P–V	FIT assembly
	Mazes	P–V	ETS map planning
			ETS choosing a path
Technical information	ASVAB	P–R/S	ASVAB
Multilimb coordination	Target shoot	M–PM	
	One-hand tracking	M–PM	
Precision	Target shoot	M–PM	
	Two-hand tracking	M–PM	
Movement judgement	Cannon shoot	M–PM	
Realistic versus artistic	AVOICE scales	P–NR/RI	VOICE scales
Investigative	AVOICE scales	P–NR	VOICE scales
Enterprising	AVOICE scales	P–?	
Social interaction	AVOICE scales	P–NR	VOICE scales
Conventional	AVOICE scales	P–NR	VOICE scales
Adjustment	Self-esteem	P–W	Owens biodata
	Stability	P–W	DPQ stress reaction
Dependability	Conscientiousness	P–W	Owens biodata
	Traditional values	P–W	CPI socialization
	Nondelinquency	P–W	CPI socialization
Achievement	Work orientation	P–SI	Rotter locus of control
Physical condition	Physical condition	P–AS	Owens biodata
	Energy level	P–AS	
Leadership	Dominance	P–AS	DPQ social potency
Locus of control	Internal control	P–W	Rotter locus of control
Sociability	Cooperativeness	P–W	Owens biodata

	Factors	
Type of Administration	Cognitive/Perceptual/Motor	Interest/Biodata/Personality
M–Microcomputer administration	R–Reasoning/verbal	NR–Nonrealistic interests
P–Paper-and-pencil administration	V–Spatial ability/visualization	RI–Realistic interests
	PM–Psychomotor ability	SI–Scientific/intellectual
	S–Processing speed	AS–Athletic/social potency
	PS–Perceptual speed/accuracy	W–Personal well-being
	N–Number facility	
	PA–Processing accuracy	

JOB PERFORMANCE MEASUREMENT

The major objective of the Army's Project A is to enhance organizational performance through selection of applicants who are potentially high performing soldiers. The Army would like to predict not only individual performance but how an individual will impact on organizational performance relative to other available applicants and possible assignments. Reality, however, has indicated that most test validation in the military has been far removed from such issues as organizational success. Instead, individual performance in training and ratings of job performance have served as the most frequently used criteria (Uhlaner & Drucker, 1980).

Defining the Criterion Space

The design of Project A has been driven by the desire to measure job performance comprehensively and to assess the utility of differences in individual job performance to the organization. Because of the dimensionality of job performance, many different performance measures are not only possible but desirable. The problem is to identify the fundamental factors contributing to successful performance in a specific job and then to develop appropriate measures. The selection of the appropriate measures is a matter of judgment and analysis. Therefore, the first step in developing Project A performance measures after careful selection of the 19 MOS chosen to represent a cross section of Army occupations was a job analysis of each of these MOS. Job analysis methodologies describe jobs in terms of tasks and activities that must be performed or in terms of the behaviors required to perform them (McCormick, 1979). For Project A both types of analyses were completed.

An extensive task inventory for each of the 19 key MOS was developed, based on Soldiers Manuals, official occupational surveys, and data from SME. Efforts were made to standardize the generality of task descriptions and to determine the variability of performance, importance, and frequency for each task. This detailed analysis provided a firm basis for test development.

To complete the behavioral analyses for each MOS, critical incident workshops were conducted with noncommissioned officers (NCOs) and officers. They generated examples of effective and ineffective job performance. In another series of workshops, junior officers and NCOs generated behavioral examples that represented those general aspects of soldier effectiveness that contribute to organizational effectiveness, such as following orders and regulations. The target criterion space for these scales went beyond job performance to include aspects of socialization and commitment to the organization. Using the critical incidents generated in these workshops, job-specific and Army-wide performance dimensions were identified and defined.

Developing the Measures

After completing the definition of the domain of job performance for each MOS, decisions on how to measure that performance became critical. The most important consideration in choosing methods by which to measure performance was relevance to the conceptual criterion. However, the questions of cost and feasibility of administering the measure were also important concerns.

Methods of measuring job performance fall into three basic categories: objective measures of performance, tests of job knowledge, and ratings. In a meta-analysis of 14 validity studies, Hunter (1983) showed that these methods tap different aspects of job performance and cannot be substituted for one another without losing some unique information. He found that the corrected correlation between job performance tests and supervisory ratings was .35, while that between two job ratings was .40, and the correlation between job knowledge and job performance tests was .67. These findings strengthen the conclusion of Landy and Farr (1980, p. 72), who suggested that "in some ideal sense, complete performance measurement would include the combination of objective, personnel, and judgmental indices."

Objective hands-on performance tests measure both skill and knowledge components of the job; written job knowledge tests measure knowledge only; and ratings measure motivation and job performance over time. The hands-on measures are the most costly to collect in terms of time and cost to administer, whereas ratings are the most economical method. The final choice of the method or methods to measure job performance is generally a function of the trade-offs between the relevance of the measure, the costs of obtaining the measure, and the quality of the measure.

Administrative Measures

Objective measures of performance can be obtained from such information as personnel data and production data or from specially constructed hands-on performance measures. The personnel data measures include number of unexcused absences, number of accidents, tardiness, and so on. Generally, these types of measures are applicable to only a small percentage of employees and are, therefore, of very limited usefulness. For example, it may be that less than 8 percent of all employees have more than one unexcused absence per year, that 5 percent of the employees have almost all of the accidents, and that tardiness records have not been kept (Landy & Farr, 1980). Objective measures are intuitively attractive, but often have practical limitations that make them unusable.

Hands-on Measures

Hands-on job performance tests are generally viewed as the most relevant method of performance evaluation (Osborn, 1983). Hands-on job performance tests simulate the job and call for application of knowledge, as well as the demonstration of skills equivalent to, or nearly equivalent to, the behaviors required on the job. For this reason some believe that these measures should become the yardstick for all other performance measures. However, a specially constructed hands-on test only measures how well an incumbent can perform a task under standardized, idealized circumstances; it is not a test of how well the individual actually performs (Guion, 1983).

Hands-on performance testing is most appropriate for jobs that involve psychomotor or skilled components, such as flying a plane or firing a weapon. There is an increasing interest in this type of testing in the military (Uhlaner & Drucker, 1980; Vineberg & Joyner, 1983). One of the most widely used measures of proficiency involving hands-on tests was the type of SQT used by the U.S. Army prior to 1983. However, the hands-on portion of the SQT was discarded, partially due to the cost of administration. Other types of hands-on tests include simulations, such as the Multiple Integrated Laser Engagement Simulation (Medlin, et al., 1979).

Job Knowledge Measures

Because of the difficulties and costs associated with administering hands-on performance tests, job knowledge tests are often used instead, and have been widely used in the military. In spite of their appeal, questions remain concerning the usefulness of job knowledge tests in measuring job performance. Job knowledge tests presuppose that the test taker has minimal literacy, which may not in itself be a requirement for the job.

Correlations between hands-on job performance tests and job knowledge tests have been found to vary greatly, depending on the job. For example, for general vehicle repairmen (Engel & Rehden, 1970), the correlation is relatively low, whereas for personnel specialists, in which cognitive skills predominate, the relationship is relatively high (Vineberg & Taylor, 1972). In a recent study conducted by Osborn and Ford (1977), relatively high correlations (.70) were obtained between job knowledge tests and hands-on performance tests. These high correlations were obtained in a situation in which the skill aspect of the job tests consisted of recalling functions but not manual performance, and in which job knowledge items were tied to critical steps in performance. Vineberg and Joyner (1983) argue that it seems that a great deal of benefit would accrue by spending as much effort on developing knowledge tests as has been spent on developing behaviorally anchored rating scales. However, job knowledge tests do not tap the more global and motivational aspects of performance. For this purpose, ratings are more appropriate.

Ratings

Ratings are the most widely used measures of performance (Landy & Farr, 1980). Despite their widespread use, there is considerable dissatisfaction with ratings as performance measures due to the potential for bias. As in all measures of performance, variability in ratings is a function of both true differences in performance and errors in rating. Probably the most often cited rating error is the halo error, initially pointed out by Thorndike (1920). This kind of error is especially difficult to detect because dimensions of performance are often highly correlated. As a measurement issue in ratings, halo has received a tremendous amount of attention and research through the years. Yet the issue continues to be problematic (Borman, 1983; Landy & Farr, 1980).

Many suggestions have been made for how to minimize rater error. Some of these suggestions have concerned how to improve the rating instrument itself. While several rating methods and formats are available, the behaviorally anchored rating scale is often the method of choice (Smith & Kendall, 1963). Behavior can be directly tied to aspects of performance indicated by job analyses. Further, while results tend to be mixed, such measures have often been shown to be less vulnerable to measurement problems (cf. Borman & Dunnette, 1974).

In summary, each of these methods for measuring job performance tap different dimensions and have different advantages and disadvantages. In a paper describing the issues and strategies of measuring performance in Army jobs, Osborn (1983, p. 7) summarized by saying:

> Despite their cost, hands-on performance tests, correctly developed and administered, cannot be equalled in job relevance, fairness or acceptability to examinees. . . ; nor is there a known substitute for a performance test in measuring proficiency on tasks involving psychomotor skill. Knowledge tests if used for the right kinds of job tasks and linked methodically to knowledge-based task elements have wide applicability, acceptable validity, and administrative feasibility. Performance ratings are the most feasible but the most indirect measure of job proficiency, yet they permit the measurement of effective dimensions that cannot be efficiently tapped by other means.

For these reasons the strategy adopted by Project A was to measure job performance using hands-on, job knowledge, and rating methods and through field tests to evaluate the psychometric properties and determine the optimal mix of the criterion measures. The objective in criterion development was to develop state-of-the-art criteria against which the predictor measures could be validated.

Sampling of Tasks and Behaviors and Assignment to Measurement Methods

The final selection of tasks for hands-on and job knowledge testing was based on task importance, task difficulty, and intertask similarity judgments from SME. Tasks were clustered based on intertask similarity. Tasks were selected on the basis of importance and difficulty to represent each cluster. On this basis, 30 tasks were selected for each MOS for development of job knowledge measures and a subset of 15 of these 30 for hands-on measures. Tasks judged to require a high level of physical skill, a series of prescribed steps, and speed of performance were designated for hands-on measurement. Using a similar procedure, a 150-item job knowledge test was developed as an end-of-training criterion measure for each MOS.

Analyses of data from the behavioral workshops formed the basis for development of 11 Army-wide behaviorally anchored rating scales and 6 to 9 behaviorally anchored MOS-specific ratings for each MOS. In addition, scales were developed to rate overall performance, individual potential, performance on 14 common Army tasks, and performance on specific MOS tasks selected for hands-on measurement. Table 9.5 shows the criterion measures developed for the nine MOS with complete criterion measures, as well as the ten MOS with partial criterion measures. Table 9.6 shows the task clusters and rating scale dimensions for the occupation of mechanic (MOS 63B).

An analysis of personnel records was also conducted to determine if administrative data on information such as letters of commendation, disciplinary records, or awards could serve as criteria. A total of 14 items of information were identified as relevant. However, centralized files appeared to be incomplete, and collecting the information from individual files proved cumbersome and expensive.

To help ensure the content validity and representativeness of the performance measures, the Army training and doctrine proponent responsible for each MOS was heavily involved in the total developmental process. At the end of the development process, proponent approval of the total set of measures was obtained. Proponent review and approval were again obtained after field testing and will be sought prior to the concurrent validation.

Field Tests

The final step in the development of each criterion measure for the concurrent validation was a field test designed to assess the administrative feasibility, reliability, and acceptability of the measure. Field tests were conducted with approximately 150 soldiers in each MOS. Information obtained from the field tests formed the basis for

TABLE 9.5. Criterion Measures

MOS-Specific	Army-Wide
15 hands-on tasks	11 behaviorally anchored performance ratings (P&S)
30 job knowledge tasks	14 common task ratings (P&S)
15 task ratings (P&S)	Environmental questionnaire
6-9 behaviorally anchored ratings (P&S)	Personnel file information
Job history questionnaire	Combat prediction scales (P&S)
Item-based job knowledge measures	
Item-based job knowledge measures	11 behaviorally anchored performance ratings (P&S)
	14 common task ratings (P&S)
	Environmental questionnaire
	Personnel file information
	Combat prediction scales (P&S)

P—peer rating; S—supervisory rating.

TABLE 9.6. Task Clusters and Rating Scale Dimensions for Mechanic (MOS 63B)

Task Cluster	Multimethod Testing[1]	Knowledge-only Testing[2]	Occupation-Specific Rating Dimensions
Routine maintenance	1	2	Inspecting/testing
Disabled vehicles	0	2	Troubleshooting
Brakes	3	1	Routine maintenance
Carburetor, radiator	2	2	Repair
Clutch, powertrain	1	1	Technical documents
Electrical system	2	1	Tools and test equipment
Steering, drive components	1	1	Vehicle operation
Personal weapons	1	1	Safety
Individual tactics	0	2	Administration
First aid	1	1	Planning/organizing job
Chemical/biological hazards	1	1	Vehicle recovery
General soldier skills	2	0	Overall performance

[1] Number of tasks tested by hands-on, knowledge, and rating methods.
[2] Number of additional tasks tested by knowledge test only.

determining which criterion measures can be eliminated on the basis of poor psychometric quality or redundancy.

At this time, data are available on the first four MOS. Table 9.7 represents the reliability coefficients and the correlations among job (task-based) knowledge, school (item-based) knowledge, hands-on, and supervisor measures for each of the first four MOS. These initial data corroborate Hunter's (1983) findings that each measure taps a different aspect of performance. For 15 tasks, parallel job knowledge, hands-on, supevisor, and peer rating measures were developed. The reliability coefficients and correlations for these data are also shown in Table 9.7. Despite the high reliability of the measures, their inter-correlations are only moderate. These data indicate that the multi-method measurement approach may yield the most comprehensive measurement of the major factors of job performance. There still remains the difficult question of how best to use multiple criterion measures.

Multiple Versus Composite Criterion Measures

The issue of the use of multiple criteria versus composite criteria has received a great deal of attention over the years. Advocates of multiple criteria (Dunnette, 1963; Ghiselli, 1960; Roach & Wherry, 1970) argue that when various criteria are clearly independent, they should not be combined. They point to examples such as salesmen who have excellent sales records but are poor at paperwork, or secretaries who may be excellent on the telephone but have poor filing and organizational skills. They argue that two individuals can be rated as equally effective on the job while accomplishing the job in very different ways. By combining criteria, one may lose information and have an inaccurate measure. Advocates of composite criterion measures (cf. Brogden & Taylor, 1950) argue that the criterion measure should provide an estimate of an individual's utility to the organization.

For research purposes and for understanding behavior, multiple criteria are most appropriate. For making personnel decisions, however, a composite criterion is needed, whether it be a series of hurdles or a single linear composite that defines performance. From a practical point of view, if the intent is to select individuals for a given job, a way to order candidates relative to their predicted value to the organization must be found.

TABLE 9.7. Field Test Results with Complete Criterion Measures and Measures of 15 Tasks with Parallel Hands-on, Knowledge, and Rating Measures

Complete Criterion Measures

Occupation	Reliability				Uncorrected Correlation					
	$r_{K.K}$	$r_{SK.SK}$	$r_{H.H}$	$r_{S.S}$	$r_{K.H}$	$r_{K.S}$	$r_{H.S}$	$r_{SK.H}$	$r_{SK.K}$	$r_{SK.S}$
Cannon crewman	.87	.89	.82	.85	.33	.33	.33	.20	.62	.25
Motor transport operator	.78	.84	.59	.76	.52	.31	.29	.31	.73	.23
Administration specialist	.79	.84	.66	.85	.52	.21	.25	.54	.62	.27
Military police	.77	.74	.30	.88	.18	.25	.24	.13	.55	.19

15 Tasks with Parallel Measures

	$r_{K.K}$	$r_{H.H}$	$r_{S.S}$	$r_{P.P}$	$r_{K.H}$	$r_{K.S}$	$r_{H.S}$	$r_{K.P}$	$r_{H.P}$	$r_{S.P}$
Cannon crewman	.83	.82	.67	.67	.41	.24	.34	.18	.47	.46
Motor transport operator	.61	.59	.69	.70	.59	.23	.32	.10	.22	.70
Administration specialist	.63	.66	.75	.60	.43	.08	.23	-.05	.16	.17
Military police	.72	.30	.64	.82	.21	.15	.27	.08	.31	.65

K–knowledge, task-based measures. SK–knowledge, item-based measures. H–hands-on, task-based measures. S–supervisory rating. P–peer rating.

All N's = 100–130 except those with peer ratings, where N = 60–65.

USING TESTS: VALIDITY AND THE LAW,
STANDARDS, AND UTILITY

Developing predictor tests with known relationships to job performance is only the first step in determining their appropriate use in personnel decision making. For both legal and practical reasons, the test must be fair. Second, to be most useful in large organizations, entrance standards must be set based on predictor test scores. Finally, the cost-benefit trade-offs, or utility, of using the test must be evaluated.

Validity and the Law

Since the 1964 Civil Rights Act, there has been a marked increase in the awareness of possible unlawful discrimination caused by test usage and a concomitant increase in our knowledge of the degree to which actual unfair discrimination exists. Bersoff (1983, p. 66) described the three sections of Title VII of the Civil Rights Act most pertinent to this issue:

> In Section 703(a)(1), Congress made it "an unlawful employment practice for an employer . . . to fail or refuse to hire . . . any individual, or otherwise to discriminate against any individual, with respect to his compensation, terms, conditions or privileges of employment because of . . . race, color, religion, sex, or national origin." Section 703(a)(2) bans employment practices that would invidiously "limit, segregate, or classify employees or applicants for employment in any way which would deprive or tend to deprive any individual of employment opportunities, or otherwise adversely effect his status as an employee." Despite these prohibitions Section 703(h) does permit the use of employment testing. The act applies to almost all medium and large private employers and since its amendment in 1972, to municipal, state, and federal employers.

Since 1964, there have been a number of legal cases and testing guidelines that have helped shape the interpretation of Title VII. In *Griggs* v. *Duke Power Co.* (1971), the Supreme Court required that professionally developed tests must be job-related, that employment requirements must have a "manifest relationship to the employment in question," and that "the touchstone is business necessity." In reaching these conclusions, the Supreme Court gave "great deference" to the then current Equal Employment Opportunity Commission Guidelines on Employment Selection (EEOC, 1966).

Many cases have followed. In *United States* v. *Georgia Power Co.* (1973), the Fifth Circuit Court of Appeals provided the interpretation that the personnel decision process must use the same combination of test scores for which the test-criterion relationship was demonstrated, not some subset or composite of those scores. In a case related to the use of intelligence tests for educational placement (*Larry P.* v. *Riles*), a 1973 judgment addressed the issue of differential validity. In finding that the validity of test scores was lower for blacks than whites, the Court concluded that more placement errors would be made for blacks, which would be unacceptable (Bersoff, 1983). In *Albermarle Paper Co.* v. *Moody* (1975), the Supreme Court again stressed the need to show test-performance relationships and focused on the need for the performance measures to be based on job analyses of significant job requirements at the level of employment at which the personnel decisions will be made. In this case, the Court referred to both the EEOC guidelines and the standards for Educational and Psychological Tests (APA, 1966, 1974).

In *Washington* v. *Davis* (1976), the Supreme Court ruled in a case based on the Constitution, not Title VII, that training performance in a formal training program required for new police officers was an adequate criterion. It also affirmed the legitimacy of construct and content validity approaches in addition to empirical validity. In *Guardians Association of New York City* v. *Civil Service Commission* (1981), the appropriateness of content and construct validation procedures was again confirmed. Nevertheless, empirical validation appears to provide the firmest ground for a legal defense of test use. In *United States* v. *City of St. Louis* (1981), the Eighth Circuit Court of Appeals ruled that a paper-and-pencil selection test of job knowledge, although developed by subject matter experts, was deficient because no empirical evidence was provided linking test performance and job performance.

From these cases and guidelines it can be concluded that an empirical validation of the test scores used in personnel decision making, against a job relevant criterion showing common and race-sex subgroup validity, is usually sufficient. Where adverse impact exists such that one racial or gender group consistently scores at a lower level than other groups, one should continue to search for equally valid tests with reduced adverse impact. Interestingly, this is the same evidence dictated by good business practice. It "simply" requires that one make personnel decisions based on merit using tests applicable to the widest applicant pool possible.

To evaluate differential validity, regression equations can be developed for the pooled sample of employees, as well as each race-sex group separately. Test scores are then evaluated to determine the degree to which a score from the common regression line would be associated with a performance level substantially different from that obtained from any of the race-sex regression lines. One step in this process is to compare the validity coefficients of each subgroup. Adjustment for restriction in range is appropriate following the methods given in Lord and Novick (1968, p. 146). Next, one may compare the predicted performance of subgroup members based on their separate regression lines over the range of predictor scores of interest—the area above and below proposed cut scores. In doing so, the difference between subgroup predicted scores through subtraction can be computed and the standard error of the difference can be computed through a procedure given by Rogosa (1980). Finally, one may inspect plots of the common and subgroup regression lines for evidence of over- or underprediction. These methods were utilized in the evaluation of the current ASVAB-based selection/classification system.

Validity Analyses

To assess the potential value of any changes to the current predictor battery, ASVAB, two strategies were followed. First, several analyses were conducted using the newly developed set of predictors to estimate the unique, reliable variance that each might potentially add to ASVAB. These analyses have been discussed in detail in the section on the development of new predictor measures. Second, the validity of the present battery was examined to provide a baseline of validity against which to judge improvements.

Hanser and Grafton (1983) examined the validity of the current ASVAB composites for five MOS and obtained validities, corrected for range restriction, of .50 to .73. The criteria used in their analyses were scores on SQT, which at that time included written, hands-on, and supervisory rating components. Minor differences between subgroup regression lines were found, but generally did not occur over the score intervals used in selection. Their subgroup sample sizes ranged from just over 200 to almost 11,000.

McLaughlin et al. (1984) analyzed data on approximately 70,000 soldiers in 81 MOS who had enlisted between October 1980 and September 1982. The average corrected validities of the current ASVAB composites ranged from .36 to .58. They examined the impact of differential prediction on black and white racial subgroups by calculating mean subgroup regression line differences at five-point intervals, from 80 to 110, along the ASVAB composite scales. This range includes all operational cutoff scores currently in use for classifying applicants to Army MOS.

While some of these subgroup differences were significant, they were relatively small compared to the standard deviation of the criterion. The average differences in predicted criterion scores ranged from less than 1 to almost 6 points, while the criterion standard deviation was 20 points. Only for relatively high values of the predictor did the differences between subgroups become large. For all the current composites, the prediction errors would result in overprediction for blacks. Similar results were obtained for male/female subgroup analyses, except that there were very few significant differences. Also, performance for females is neither over- nor underpredicted consistently.

Validity Extension

A major problem for personnel psychologists is determining the validity of employment tests for jobs where traditional methods of establishing validity are not feasible. Schmidt and his colleagues (cf. Schmidt & Hunter, 1977) have been responsible for tremendous advances in this area with the use of validity generalization and meta-analytic techniques. However, these analyses are dependent on the quality of the data on which they are based, and as a result a number of questions remain with regard to their limits. In an article on "The Realities of Employment Testing," Tenopyr (1981, p. 1122) states that a relevant question "concerns the nature of criteria in studies showing validity to generalize so widely." Supervisors' ratings are the main criteria used in many validity generalization studies, and these criteria are well known to measure largely a general factor. Under these circumstances, the extent to which validity has been shown to generalize should not be surprising.

Even though the U.S. Army is one of the largest organizations in the United States, it faces many of the same problems as smaller public and private organizations with regard to feasibility of performing validity research. Many highly critical occupations contain too few incumbents to perform meaningful analyses. Even in the larger occupations, incumbents are spread so widely around the world that it is often extremely expensive to collect data on a sufficient number of them. For these as well as other similar reasons, the Army must rely on some form of validity extension to establish the validity of its entrance tests for all Army occupations.

Assume that we can determine, using meta-analytic techniques, that the differences in validity of a given test for predicting success in clerical jobs are artifactual. The question that then immediately confronts us is, how similar does another job have to be to the set of jobs in our meta-analysis before we would be willing to say that the test is also valid for this new job? While it would be possible to determine empirically the jobs to which one can extend validity, this is certainly not practical. The important question then revolves around the limits of generalization and hence around how we can best determine the similarities or differences of jobs.

Researchers have generally applied two major techniques of placing jobs into similar groups: clustering and ANOVA or MANOVA. Legal issues related to Equal Employment Opportunity and comparable pay have dictated a search for a technique that could be used to determine when two or more jobs are statistically different. Attempts at this have met with a fair amount of controversy (cf. Arvey & Mossholder, 1977; Hanser, Mendel, & Wolins, 1979).

Project A Plans and Initial Results

Project A provides a unique opportunity to test the limits of validity generalization theory as well as to learn a great deal about techniques for determining job similarity. In suggesting a resolution to potential problems with the validity generalization literature, Tenopyr (1981, p. 1122) recommended "the only answer to the dilemma thus posed is carefully designed research involving performance measurement instrumentation that will allow general, group, or specific factors to manifest."

Because of the comprehensive measurement of performance in Project A, the concern expressed by Tenopyr (1981) can be directly addressed. For nine of the occupations included in Project A, performance is being measured by general and task-specific supervisory ratings, paper-and-pencil job knowledge tests, and hands-on performance tests. For the remaining ten occupations, all of the above measures, except hands-on performance tests, are being used. Because of this design, the generalizability of validities based on each of these kinds of criteria can be examined.

At the base of our intentions to examine validity generalization lies the plan for sampling occupations. The project is developing a system for a population of jobs, but only a sample of occupations could be included. Hence, occupations are the primary sampling units. The 19 occupations to be included were chosen on the basis of number of incumbents, representation of aptitudes measured by ASVAB, high priority for the Army, coverage of Army Career Management Fields, and representation of jobs crucial to the Army's mission.

While the method described for sampling occupations ensured broad coverage of Army occupations, as well as inclusion of critical occupations, it was necessary to lay the groundwork for future extension of validity to other occupations. Toward that end, 111 MOS were selected to be clustered. These 111 were chosen to represent proportionately each of the Army's Career Management Fields. All of Army MOS were not included in order to keep the sorting task manageable.

Job descriptions were typed on index cards, and 17 psychologists and 8 Army officers each independently sorted the jobs into similar groups. The reliability of this sorting technique across all 25 sorters was estimated to be .94. The similarity matrix that resulted from the sorting was subjected to orthogonal and then oblique factor analysis. The resulting solution suggested 23 relatively oblique clusters. A complete description of this work can be found in Rosse et al. (1983). Further clustering research is planned to encompass the remaining Army occupations. The results of the research in clustering Army occupations will provide a useful beginning for extending validity to those occupations not included in the project.

Standard Setting

As in most organizations, the U.S. military services have minimum entrance standards based on selection/classification tests (Eitelberg, et al., 1984). Setting these standards has been an issue within the Army for some time, and in the last decade has also attracted the attention of Congress. In the process of implementing the ASVAB in 1976, a mistake was made in the norming tables for the test (Sims, 1978). This error resulted in a substantial, though unknown at that time, lowering of both enlistment standards and soldier performance. This has led to substantially increasing emphasis on the appropriateness of enlistment standards and the methods by which the standards are set.

One result has been increased pressure to set standards empirically. Unfortunately, this is easier said than done. According to *Principles for the Validating and Use of Personnel Selection Procedures* (Society for Industrial and Organizational Psychology, 1980, p. 18–19), "Selection standards may be set as high or as low as the purposes of the organization require, if they are based on valid predictors. . . . It is to be pointed out that judgment is necessary in all critical score establishment. A fully dependable numerical basis for a critical score is seldom, if ever, available."

Standard Setting and Cutoff Scores

The goal of any organization is to fill vacancies with the best people available, while at the same time not underutilizing overqualified individuals. For example, it is not wise to hire either an unskilled laborer or an electrical engineer to fill an electrician's position. This is as true in the military as in any other organization. Entrance standards and cutoff scores are used to minimize hiring of the underqualified. Under most economic conditions, social and economic considerations minimize the hiring of the overqualified.

Cutoff scores are often confused with entrance standards. However, they have somewhat different functions. Entrance standards are minimum scores predictive of adequate performance. Cutoff scores are based on the minimum score an applicant must have to be accepted for employment, but are usually set so that all vacancies can be filled. Thus, if there are more than a sufficient number of applicants who meet the entrance standard, the cutoff score may be set higher than the entrance standard.

Cascio (1978) describes a method for setting cutoff scores based on Thorndike's predicted yield method (1949). This method uses information on the number of expected vacancies, number of applicants, and expected distribution of predictor scores to set the cutoff. The result is a cutoff score that will select enough individuals to fill all vacancies and yet select them from the top of the performance distribution. However, depending on the overall quality of applicants, this procedure may or may not result in qualified hires in the sense of minimum competency; it does not provide a means for determining minimum skills required for entry into a job.

While there have been some notable exceptions (cf. Cronbach & Gleser, 1965), the personnel psychology literature contains few published works dealing with the setting of standards, preferring instead to focus on the question of the validity of various selection measures and the utility of their application (cf. Taylor & Russell, 1939). One must look instead to the educational testing literature to find indepth discussions of standard setting.

Standard Setting in Education

In recent years, educators have struggled with the issues related to setting minimum competency standards for both students and teachers. The problems of setting employee selection standards and minimum job performance standards are identical to the problems of setting minimum competency standards. If we consider two major uses of standards in education, minimum scores on entrance exams for admission to higher education and minimum scores on competency exams for student graduation or teacher certification, these standards correspond to minimum scores on employment tests for selection and minimum levels of job performance for compensation or promotion decisions.

Listings of available methods for setting standards may be found in numerous sources (cf. Hambleton & Eignor, 1979). Glass (1978) categorizes standard-setting methods into six groups: performance of others (Frankel & McWilliams (1981), counting backwards from 100 percent, bootstrapping on other criterion measures, judging minimal competence (Arngoff, 1971; Ebel, 1972; Nedelsky, 1954), decision-theoretic approaches (Cronbach & Gleser, 1965), and operations research methods (Black, 1972). Several researchers have examined the comparability of methods for setting standards (cf. Koffler, 1980;

Poggio, Glasnapp, & Eros, 1981) and have gotten mixed results. In some cases standard-setting methods converge, and in others they do not. Rowley (1982, p. 94) makes an important point with regard to these various standard-setting methods. He notes that all standard-setting methods are based on the judgments of experts, but these methods do not create the judgments, they only provide a means for processing judgments. This serves to highlight the fact that "setting a cutting score is inevitably judgmental."

Burton (1978, p. 263) reviewed three widely accepted methods for setting performance standards and concluded that "no practical performance standards technology exists (despite the growing amount of legislation that depends on such a technology), that the potential for such a technology is extremely limited, and that, therefore, the use of performance standards is not a promising vehicle for social decisionmaking." Glass (1978), writing in the same special volume of the *Journal of Educational Measurement*, states that criterion levels or standards cannot be determined "other than arbitrarily" (p. 237). He went on to say, "With respect to setting criterion scores on criterion-referenced tests, nothing may be safer and better than something" (p. 258). Others (cf. Scriven, 1978) are more optimistic, although they still admit that standards are based on judgment.

Standard Setting in the U.S. Army

Unlike most organizations, the military services permit virtually no lateral entry. Almost every sergeant major entered as a private and almost every general as a lieutenant. As a consequence of this policy, among the soldiers who begin their Army careers in a given year, there must be sufficient potential to fill high-level management positions 20 years later. A single minimum entry score is not sufficient to meet this requirement. If every entrant barely passed the standard, future personnel needs would not be met. If the standard were raised to accommodate future needs, the cost of recruiting would be unnecessarily high, and many overqualified individuals would be selected. Instead of a single entrance standard, a projected distribution of scores must be developed, so that through maturation and attrition privates will grow into sergeants and lieutenants and captains will grow into generals.

Recently, the Army attempted to generate such a distribution of required entry scores. The final distribution of required entry scores was developed in three steps. First, correlations and expectancy tables displaying the relationships between entrance scores (ASVAB) and various criteria were calculated. A wide range of criteria representing different facets of performance were used. These included attrition, reenlistment and promotion data, scores on job knowledge tests, and scores on relevant hands-on performance, such as tank gunnery scores. In some cases these data were available longitudinally and in others across cohorts. Second, these data were passed to job experts for judgments regarding minimum acceptable performance for a new soldier as well as for experienced soldiers. Based on judged requirements for experienced soldiers and known attrition and reenlistment rates, the required entry-level distribution was developed for each occupation and aggregated across the entire Army. The data were also examined to determine relative increments in performance associated with increments in entry scores.

Finally, cost data were examined to estimate the cost-effectiveness of the judged requirements compared to other slightly higher or lower requirements. Cost analyses included recruiting, training, pay, and retirement costs. The cost data provided a new and more objective means of judging the appropriateness of our standards. Cost analyses indicated that the judged-required distribution of ability could be raised slightly and still be cost-effective. The expert judges estimated that 59 percent of all entrants would need to be in the fiftieth to ninety-ninth AFQT percentiles, but cost analyses indicated that could cost-effectively be raised to 63 percent.

This research was based largely on expert judgment and, therefore, the results are open to discussion. However, it serves as one example of how an organization can effectively apply both the principles of personnel selection and those of cost analyses in reaching personnel selection standards.

Utility

Although selection and classification testing is common, cost-benefit analyses such as those mentioned above are not frequently conducted. Test implementation costs are usually couched in real dollar terms: salaries, space, computer time, personnel for scoring, and the like. The costs of implementing a new test battery will be especially relevant in Project A, where much of the testing will be by microcomputer. The acquisition of testing equipment for 500,000 applicants per year will be costly indeed! But the benefits of improved performance are not usually measured in comparable terms. Consequently, judgments of the net impact of test implementation would be difficult to make. This had led to a systematic evaluation of the dollar utility of selection testing.

Brogden (1949) and Cronbach and Gleser (1965) provided the first systematic descriptions of the utility of testing programs indexed in dollars. They linked normally distributed performance levels to the dollar values estimated for those performance levels. Their formula for the dollar value of the gain in productivity, or utility ($U\$$), obtained by using valid selection procedures includes Ns, the number of individuals selected; $SD\$$, the standard deviation of performance, scaled in a utility metric such as dollars; and the average performance expected on the criterion by the selected group as estimated from a valid predictor, given by $Rxy\ Zx$:

$$U\$ = Ns\ SD\$\ Rxy\ Zx$$

While the values of most of the variables on the right-hand side of the Brogden-Cronbach-Gleser formula can readily be determined (and corrections made for test administration costs), the estimation of $SD\$$ is problematic. A recent review by Hunter and Schmidt (1982) reports that only two published efforts have attempted the computation of $SD\$$ using cost accounting methods. One common alternative to the cost accounting methods is to estimate the dollar values to the organization of performance at the 50th percentile level (V50), the 85th percentile level (V85, one standard deviation above the mean), and sometimes the 15th percentile level (V15, one standard deviation below the mean). The dollar difference between 15 percent, 50 percent, and 85 percent provides an estimate of $SD\$$ (that is, $SD\$ = V85–V50$ or $V50–V15$).

This "$SD\$$ estimation technique" was used by Cascio and Silbey (1979) with second-level managers in food and beverages sales (mean = $30,000, $SD\$$ = 9,000); by Schmidt, et al. (1979) with computer programmers ($SD\$ = \$10,413$); by Hunter and Schmidt (1982) with budget analysts ($SD\$ = \$11,327$); by Bobko, Karren, and Parkington (1983) with insurance counselors (mean = $16,000, $SD\$ = \$5,550$); and by Burke and Frederick (1984) with district sales managers (mean = $75,000, $SD\$ = \$32,284$).

The *SD$* estimations reported above were derived in contexts where dollar values were relatively easy to assess. Managers were instructed to "consider the cost of having an outside firm provide these products and services" (Schmidt, et al., 1979, for computer programmers), or to "consider what the cost would be of having an outside consulting firm produce these products and services" (Hunter & Schmidt, 1982, for budget analysts).

In Project A, two additional methods have been developed by Eaton, Wing, and Mitchell (1985). These are more appropriate for occupations where supervisors are more accustomed to considering the relative productivity of employees or where employees operate very complex, expensive equipment, or where they are focal to the productivity of a costly system. Such conditions are typical in the Army, as well as in many government and private sector organizations.

The first method is somewhat like the *SD$* estimation technique. Instead of using estimates of the dollar value of 85th percentile performance, however, the technique uses estimates of how many superior (85th percentile) performers (*N*85) would be needed to produce the output of a fixed number of average (50th percentile) performers (*N*50). This estimate, combined with an estimate of the dollar value of average performance (V50), provides an estimate of *SD$*, and is the basis for the name "superior equivalents technique." Their formula follows:

$$SD\$ = V50 \left[\frac{N50}{N85} - 1 \right]$$

The second "systems effectiveness" technique is an extension of the Brogden-Cronbach-Gleser formula and is based on changes in aggregate system performance. In a system composed of many units, total aggregate performance may be improved by increasing the number of units (such as tanks) or improving the performance of each unit. The value of any aggregate performance improvement due to increased performance of a fixed number of units may be indexed by the cost of the increased number of units required to yield comparable increases in aggregate systems performance. That is, if five high performing tanks equal the aggregate effectiveness of six average tanks, the value of the improved performance can be indexed by the cost of the additional tank and crew. Such cost estimates can and frequently are made in accounting departments.

When the superior equivalents technique was applied to collect data from two groups of 50 tank commanders, $SD\$$ data in the $27,000–$31,000 range were obtained. When the systems effectiveness technique was applied, the $SD\$$ estimate was $60,000. The utility per tank ($N = 1$) and utility per system ($N = 2,500$) calculations for both techniques were based on an assumed selection ratio of .5 and a test validity of .30. They yielded per tank and per system utilities of about $7,000 and $17,000,000 per year with superior equivalents and about $14,000 and $36,000,000 with superior effectiveness techniques. Eaton et al. (1985) suggested that these two methods provide estimates that bracket the true utility values. The superior equivalents technique may underestimate the value of average performance due to the absence of pay comparability data, while the systems effectiveness technique may overestimate the contribution of a key individual, such as a tank commander, to the overall effectiveness of the tank and crew.

In addition to serving to illustrate the benefits of improved performance associated with the cost of selection testing, utility indices play an important role in classification decision. The relative importance of performance at several levels is needed for each occupation for which classification decisions are to be applied. This is certainly no small task for an organization like the Army with more than 250 entry-level occupations. Yet, in addition to considering the individual's desires, one must ask whether he or she can contribute more in any particular occupation at the same or a different predicted performance level. Fortunately, the relative value of each performance level in each MOS does *not* have to be expressed in dollars for classification algorithms to operate.

Sadacca and Campbell (1985) have undertaken an ambitious scaling effort in Project A to provide estimates of the relative utility of five levels of performance in each of 250 MOS. In this endeavor, midlevel Army officers worked with subsets of the 1,250 performance level/MOS combinations. Their efforts included rank ordering, paired-comparison, subjective estimation scaling, and conjoint scaling with six performance factors. Both wartime and peacetime scenarios were used. Preliminary results indicated high intercorrelations, in the .80–.90 range, between ranking and subjective estimation scaling of utility values averaged across judges. Average interjudge correlations were .60–.80. Typical results of two workshops are shown in Table 9.8. Utility values were based on subjective estimation scaling by eight officers using a wartime scenario. The ratio scale values were transformed so that the utility of an average (50th percentile) infantryman was set equal to a scale value of 1.0. In later workshops, with a peacetime scenario, the judged utility of performance in combat arms occupations was somewhat lower, while that in support and administrative occupations was higher.

Overall one expects the implementation of a selection and classification program to result in improved employee performance and a savings to the organization. The utility methods described differ greatly in their specific focus and assumptions. Ultimately, the desire

TABLE 9.8. Relative Value of Performance at Three Different Levels in 19 Selected MOS

MOS	Percentile		
	10	50	90
Administrative specialist (71L)	.10	.23	.46
Ammunition specialist (55B)	.17	.49	1.01
Carpentry and masonry specialist (51B)	.09	.21	.43
Chemical operations specialist (54E)	.26	.70	1.51
Food service specialist (94B)	.10	.23	.53
Light wheel veh./power gen. mech. (63B).	.16	.43	.75
Medical specialist (91B)	.21	.58	1.29
Military police (95B)	.17	.34	.66
Motor transport operator (64C)	.12	.37	.68
Petrol. supply specialist (76W)	.13	.31	.71
Radio teletype operator (05C)	.15	.41	.91
TOW/Dragon repairer (27E)	.23	.64	1.26
Unit supply specialist (76Y)	.08	.23	.45
Util. heli. repairer (67N)	.17	.52	1.06
Infantryman (11B)	.34	1.00	2.01
Armor crewman (19E/K)	.42	1.28	2.71
Cannon crewman (13B)	.29	.75	1.53
Manpads crewman (16S)	.27	.72	1.26
Combat engineer (12B)	.26	.72	1.46

Source: Sadacca & Campbell (1985), p. 58.

is not for *the* answer to selection and classification utility but converging data that illuminate the benefits. Benefits should be stated in dollar terms compared to research and implementation costs. Of equal importance are observations and quantitative descriptions of significant return in terms of increased individual and system performance. Together, these data should support the decision making associated with the implementation of a new personnel system for the Army.

SUMMARY

The state of the art in empirical test validation has advanced markedly since the early days of employment testing, providing the benefits derived from countless ad hoc test validation efforts, numerous systematic efforts to organize the structure of the predictor and criterion space, as well as highly sophisticated technology to permit advanced statistical treatment of results. Our society has also matured in its association with testing to ask, and demand answers to, many appropriate questions concerning test content, validity, and fairness.

Project A was conceived as a large-scale research project to take advantage of these developments. In addition to serving its primary function of significantly improving Army selection and classification, it was intended to provide a focus for advancing the solution to many issues of scientific interest. Three years' research by 50 scientists on this project has produced many of the empirical findings and research designs described in this chapter. Most are documented in Eaton and Goer (1983) or Eaton et al. (1984). It is hoped the research will prove fruitful during the coming years and be applicable to future research and practice in human resources management.

In this brief chapter, an attempt has been made to describe this extremely large and ambitious research project. In doing so, inevitably, a number of details associated with its design, execution, and results to date have been ignored or inadequately addressed. The focus instead was on a limited number of critical issues facing personnel psychologists and how this research project approaches them. An outline of these issues and an attempt to weave them into the discussions throughout the chapter was made. The scope, size, duration, and design of the project should provide data pertinent to each of these issues.

At this point, a comprehensive set of predictor and performance measures have been developed for 19 representative Army occupations, most with counterparts in the civilian work force and the other services. The large-scale concurrent validation that will illuminate the relationships among these variables is well on its way. The ultimate success of the project, however, will depend on the nature of the results obtained, the optimism they generate for the initiation of the longitudinal validation, and the wisdom, commitment, and diligence of its scientists, managers, and leaders.

While there are few opportunities for large-scale programmatic research like Project A, such efforts have several significant advantages. Long-term research support and advocacy are easier to maintain when potential organizational payoffs are large. Large projects also provide the opportunity to address issues of scientific interest that are either "too hard" or too resource-intensive for smaller projects. Our ability to collect and responsibly maintain massive data sets from integrated research projects provides the keystone to the answers to many exciting scientific issues: the parameters underlying discriminant and differential validity, validity generalization, the mapping of a comprehensive predictor space onto a comprehensive performance space, the utility of selection/classification trade-offs, and many others.

In conclusion, it appears that the future holds many opportunities to improve organizations through selection and classification research. The scientific basis of this discipline is advancing rapidly. Many questions that have challenged scientists and managers for years are within sight of resolution. Large-scale research projects like Project A offer one technique for efficiently addressing these questions. It is hoped that the lessons learned and the benefits obtained from Project A will be useful in achieving the best that selection and classification psychology can offer employees and organizations.

REFERENCES

Albermarle Paper Co. v. *Moody.* (1975). 422, U.S. 405 (1975).

Alley, W. E., & Matthews, M. D. (1982). The Vocational Interest Career Examination. *Journal of Psychology, 112,* 169–193.

Angoff, W. H. (1971). Scales, norms, and equivalent scores. In R. L. Thorndick (Ed.), *Educational measurement.* Washington, DC: American Council on Education.

APA (1966). American Psychological Association, American Educational Research Association, and National Council on Measurement in Education. *Standards for educational and psychological tests.* Washington, DC: American Psychological Association.

APA (1974). American Psychological Association, American Educational Association, and National Council on Measurement in Education. *Standards for educational and psychological tests.* Washington, DC: American Psychological Association.

Arvey, R. D., & Mossholder, K. M. (1977). A proposed methodology for determining similarities and differences among jobs. *Personnel Psychology, 30,* 363-374.

Bartlett, C. J., Bobko, P., & Pine, S. M. (1977). Single-group validity: Fallacy or the facts? *Journal of Applied Psychology, 62,* 155-157.

Bersoff, D. N. (1983). Regarding psychologists testily: The legal regulation of psychological assessment. In C. J. Sheirer & B. L. Hammonds (Eds.), *Psychology and the law.* Washington, DC: American Psychological Association.

Black, J. H. (1972, April). *Student evaluation: Toward the setting of mastery performance standards.* Paper presented at the annual meeting of the American Educational Research Association, Chicago.

Bobko, P., & Bartlett, C. J. (1978). Subgroup validities: Differential definitions and differential prediction. *Journal of Applied Psychology, 63,* 12-14.

Bobko, P., Karren, R., & Parkington, J. J. (1983). The estimation of standard deviations in utility analyses: An empirical test. *Journal of Applied Psychology, 68,* 170-176.

Boehm, V. R. (1977). Differential prediction: A methodological artifact. *Journal of Applied Psychology, 62,* 146-154.

Boehm, V. R. (1978). Populations, preselection, and practicalities: A reply to Hunter and Schmidt. *Journal of Applied Psychology, 63,* 15-18.

Borman, W. C. (1983). Implications of personality theory and research for the rating of work performance in organizations. In F. Landy, S. Zedeck, & J. Cleveland (Eds.), *Performance measurement and theory* (pp. 127-165). Hillsdale, NJ: Erlbaum Associates.

Borman, W. C., & Dunnette, M. D. (1974). *Selection of components to comprise a Naval Personnel Status Index (NPSI) and a strategy for investigating their relative importance.* Minneapolis, MN: Personnel Decisions, Inc.

Bownas, D. A., & Heckman, R. W. (1976). *Job analysis of the entry-level firefighter position.* Minneapolis, MN: Personnel Decisions, Inc.

Brogden, H. E. (1949). When testing pays off. *Personnel Psychology, 2*, 171-183.

Brogden, H. E., & Taylor, E. K. (1950). The dollar criterion: Applying the cost accounting concept to criterion construction. *Personnel Psychology*, 3, 133-154.

Browne, J. A., & Howaith, E. A. (1977). A comprehensive factor analysis of personality questionnaire items: A test of 20 positive hypotheses. *Multivariate Behavioral Research, 12*, 399-427.

Burke, M. J., & Frederick, J. T. (1984). Two modified procedures for estimating standard deviations in utility analyses. *Journal of Applied Psychology, 69*, 482-489.

Burton, N. (1978). Societal standards. *Journal of Educational Measurement, 15*, 263-271.

Cascio, W. (1982). *Applied psychology in personnel management.* 2nd ed. Reston, VA: Reston.

Cascio, W. F., & Silbey, V. (1979). Utility of the assessment center as a selection device. *Journal of Applied Psychology, 64*, 107-118.

Cascio, W. F., Valenzi, E. R., & Silbey, V. (1978). Validation and statistical power: Implications for applied research. *Journal of Applied Psychology, 63*, 589-595.

Cascio, W. F., Valenzi, E. R., & Silbey, V. (1980). More on validation and statistical power. *Journal of Applied Psychology, 65*, 135-138.

Cronbach, L. J., & Gleser, G. C. (1965). *Psychological tests and personnel decisions* (2nd ed.). Urbana: University of Illinois Press.

Dunnette, M. D. (1963). A note on *the* criterion. *Journal of Applied Psychology, 47*, 251–254.

Dunnette, M. D. (1976). Basic attributes of individuals in relation to behavior in organizations. In M. D. Dunnette (Ed.), *Handbook of industrial and organizational psychology*. Chicago: Rand McNally.

Dwyer, P. S. (1954). Solution of the personnel classification problem with the method of optimal regions. *Psychometrikas, 18*, 11–26.

Eaton, N. K., & Goer, M. H. (Eds.). (1983). *Improving the selection, classification, and utilization of Army enlisted personnel: Technical appendix to the annual report* (Research Note 83-37). Alexandria, VA: U.S. Army Research Institute for the Behavioral and Social Sciences.

Eaton, N. K., Goer, M. H., Harris, J. H., & Zook, L. M. (Eds.). (1984). *Improving the selection, classification, and utilization of Army enlisted personnel: Annual report 1984 fiscal year* (Technical Rep. 660). Alexandria, VA: U.S. Army Research Institute for the Behavioral and Social Sciences.

Eaton, N. K., Wing, H., & Mitchell, K. J. (1985). Alternate methods of estimating the dollar value of performance. *Personnel Psychology, 38*, 27–40.

Ebel, R. L. (1972). *Essentials of educational measurement.* Englewood Cliffs, NJ: Prentice-Hall.

Eitelberg, M. J., Laurence, J. H., Waters, B. K., & Perelman, L. S. (1984). *Screening for service: Aptitude and education criteria for military entry.* Washington, DC: Office of Assistant Secretary of Defense, Manpower, Installations, & Logistics.

Ekstrom, R. B., French, J. W., & Harman, H. H. (1976). *Manual for kit of factor-referenced cognitive tests.* Princeton, NJ: Educational Testing Service.

Engel, J. D., & Rehden, R. J. (1970). *A comparison of correlated job and work sample measures for general vehicle repairmen* (HumRRO Technical Rep. 70-16). Alexandria, VA: Human Resources Research Organization.

Equal Employment Opportunity Commission. (1966, August). *Guidelines on employee selection procedures* (29 C.F.R.-1607). Washington, DC: Equal Employment Opportunity Commission.

Flanagan, J. C. (1965). *Flanagan industrial test manual.* Chicago: Science Research Associates.

Fleishman, E. A. (1966). Human abilities and the acquisition of skill. In E. A. Bilodeau (Ed.), *Acquisition of skill.* New York: Academic Press.

Fleishman, E. A. (1972). Structure and measurement of psychomotor abilities. In R. N. Singer (Ed.), *The psychomotor domain: Movement behavior.* Philadelphia: Lea & Febiger.

Fleishman, E. A. (1975). Toward a taxonomy of human performance. *American Psychologist, 30,* 1127–1149.

Fleishman, E. A., & Hogan, J. C. (1978, June). *A taxonomic method for assessing the physical requirements of job: The physical abilities approach* (ARRO Technical Rep. 3012/R78-6). Washington, D.C.: Advanced Research Resources Organization.

Fleishman, E. A., & Quaintance, M. K. (1984). *Taxonomics of human performance.* New York: Academic Press.

Frankel, M. R., & McWilliams, H. A. (1981). *The profile of American youth: Technical sampling report.* Chicago: National Opinion Research Center, University of Chicago.

French, J. W. (1973). *Toward the establishment of noncognitive factors through literature search and interpretation.* Princeton, NJ: Educational Testing Service.

French, J. W., Ekstrom, R. B., & Price, L. A. (1963). *Manual for kit of reference tests for cognitive factors.* Princeton, N.J.: Educational Testing Service.

Gael, S., Grant, D. L., & Ritchie, R. J. (1975a). Employment test validation for minority and nonminority telephone operators. *Journal of Applied Psychology, 60,* 411–419.

Gael, S., Grant, D. L., & Ritchie, R. J. (1975b). Employment test validation for minority and nonminority clerks with work sample criteria. *Journal of Applied Psychology, 60,* 420–426.

Ghiselli, E. E. (1960). Differentiation of tests in terms of the accuracy with which they predict for a given individual. *Educational and Psychological Measurement, 20,* 675–684.

Glass, G. V. (1978). Standards and criteria. *Journal of Educational Measurement, 15,* 237–261.

Glass, G. V., McGaw, B., & Smith, M. L. (1981). *Meta-analysis in social research.* Beverly Hills, CA: Sage Publications.

Gough, H. G. (1975). *Manual for the California Psychological Inventory.* Palo Alto, CA: Consulting Psychologists Press.

Griggs v. *Duke Power Co.* (1971). 401 U.S. 424.

Gross, L. J. (1982). Standards and criteria: A response to Glass' criticism of the Nedelsky technique. *Journal of Educational Measurement, 19*, 159-162.

Guardians Association of New York City v. *Civil Service Commission.* (1981). 630 F.2d 79 (2d Cir., 1980), cert. denied 452 U.S. 939.

Guion, R. M. (1983). Comments on Hunter. In F. Landy, S. Zedeck, J. Cleveland (Ed.), *Performance Measurement and Theory.* Hillsdale, NJ: Erlbaum.

Guion, R. M., & Cranny, C. J. (1982). A note on concurrent and predictive validity designs: A critical reanalysis. *Journal of Applied Psychology, 67*, 239-244.

Guilford, J. P. (1977). *Way beyond the IQ.* Buffalo, NY: Creative Education Foundation.

Hambleton, R. K., & Eignor, D. (1979). *A practitioner's guide to criterion-referenced test development, validation and test score usage* (Laboratory of Psychometric and Evaluative Research Rep. No. 70). Amherst: University of Massachusetts.

Hanser, L. M., & Grafton, F. C. (1983). *Predicting job proficiency in the Army: Race, sex, and education* (Personnel Utilization Working Paper 82-1). Alexandria, VA: U.S. Army Research Institute for the Behavioral and Social Sciences.

Hanser, L. M., Mendel, R. M., & Wolins, L. (1979). Three flies in the ointment: A reply to Arvey and Mossholder. *Personnel Psychology, 32*, 511-516.

Harman, H. H. (1975). *Final report of research on assessing human abilities* (PR-75-20). Princeton, NJ: Educational Testing Service.

Holland, T. L. (1976). Vocational preferences. In M. D. Dunnette (Ed.), *Handbook of industrial and organizational psychology.* Chicago: Rand McNally.

Horst, P. (1960). Optimal estimates of multiple criteria with restrictions on the covariance matrix of estimated criteria. *Psychological Reports.* Monograph Supplement 6-V6.

Hough, L., Dunnette, M. D., Wing, H., Houston, J. S., & Peterson, N. G. (1984). Covariance analyses of cognitive and noncognitive measures of Army recruits: An initial sample of preliminary battery data. In N. K. Eaton, M. H. Goer, J. H. Harris, & L. M. Zook (Eds.), *Improving the selection, classification and utilization of Army enlisted personnel: Annual report 1984 fiscal year* (Technical Rep. 660). Alexandria, VA: U.S. Army Research Institute for the Behavioral and Social Sciences.

Hough, L., Houston, J. S., McGue, M., & Barge, B. (1985, March). *Non cognitive area.* Paper presented at IPR meeting, Minneapolis.

Hunter, J. E. (1980). *Validity generalization for 12,000 jobs: An application of synthetic validity and validity generalization to the General Aptitude Test Battery (GATB).* Washington, DC: U.S. Employment Service.

Hunter, J. E. (1983). A causal analysis of cognitive ability, job knowledge, job performance and supervisor ratings. In F. Landy, S. Zedeck, & J. Cleveland (Eds.), *Performance measurement and theory.* Hillsdale, NJ: Erlbaum Associates.

Hunter, J. E., & Schmidt, F. L. (1978). Differential and single-group validity of employment tests by race: A critical analysis of three recent studies. *Journal of Applied Psychology, 63*, 1-11.

Hunter, J. E., & Schmidt, F. L. (1982). Fitting people to jobs: The impact of personnel selection on national productivity. In E. A. Fleishman & M. D. Dunnette (Eds.), *Human performance and productivity: Vol. 1. Human capability assessment.* Hillsdale, NJ: Erlbaum Associates.

Hunter, J. E., & Schmidt, F. L. (1983). Quantifying the effects of psychological interventions on employee job performance and work force productivity. *American Psychologist, 78*, 473-478.

Hunter, J. E., Schmidt, F. L., & Jackson, G. B. (1982). *Meta-analysis: Cumulating research findings across studies.* Beverly Hills, CA: Sage Publications.

Kass, R. A., Mitchell, K. J., Grafton, F. C., & Wing, H. (1983). Factor structure of the Armed Services Vocational Aptitude Battery (ASVAB) Forms 8, 9, and 10: 1981 Army applicant sample. *Educational and Psychological Measurement, 43*, 1077-1088.

Katzell, R. A., & Dyer, F. J. (1977). Differential validity revived. *Journal of Applied Psychology, 62*, 137-145.

Katzell, R. A., & Dyer, F. J. (1978). On differential validity and bias. *Journal of Applied Psychology, 63*, 19-21.

Koffler, S. L. (1980). A comparison of approaches for setting proficiency standards. *Journal of Educational Measurement, 17*, 167-178.

Landy, F. J., & Farr, J. L. (1980). Performance ratings. *Psychological Bulletin, 87*, 72-107.

Larry P. v. *Riles.* (1980). 343 F. Supp. 1306 (N.D. Cal. 1972) (Order granting preliminary injunction) aff'd 502 F.2d 963 (9th Cir., 1974); 495 F. Supp. 926 (N.D. Cal. 1979) appeal docketed, No. 80-4027 (9th Cir., Jan 17, 1980).

Linn, R. L. (1978). Single-group validity, differential validity, and differential prediction. *Journal of Applied Psychology, 63*, 507-512.

Lord, F. M. (1952). Notes on a problem of multiple classification. *Psychometrika, 17*, 297-304.

Lord, F. M., & Novick, M. R. (1968). *Statistical theories of mental test scores.* Reading, MA: Addison-Wesley.

McCormick, E. J. (1979). *Job analysis: Methods and applications.* New York: AMACOM.

McHenry, J., Rosse, R., Peterson, N. G., Toquam, T., McGue, M., Russell, T., & Corpe, V. (1985). *Presentation of results and recommendation for pilot trial battery computer tests, March 1985.* Paper presented at IPR meeting, Minneapolis.

McLaughlin, D. H., Rossmeissl, P. G., Wise, L. L., Brandt, D. A., & Wang, M. M. (1984). *Validation of current and alternate ASVAB area composites, based on training and SQT information of FY81 and FY82 enlisted accessions* (U.S. Army Research Institute Technical Rep. 651). Alexandria, VA: U.S. Army Research Institute.

Marguardt, L. D., & McCormick, E. J. (1972). *Attribute ratings and profiles of job elements of the Position Analysis Questionnaire (PAQ).* Lafayette, IN: Occupational Research Center, Purdue University.

Mecham, R. C., & McCormick, E. J. (1969). *The rated attribute requirements of job elements in the Position Analysis Questionnaire.* Lafayette, IN: Occupational Research Center, Purdue University.

Medlin, S. M., Epstein, K. I., Wanschura, R. G., Mirabella, A., & Boycan, G. G. (1979, September). *Multiple Integrated Laser Engagement Simulation (MILES) Training and Evaluation Test (TET) evaluator guidebook.*

Nedelsky, L. (1954). Absolute grading standards for objective tests. *Educational and Psychological Measurement, 14,* 3–19.

Osborn, W. (1983). *Issues and strategies in measuring performance in Army jobs.* Paper presented at American Psychological Association Convention, Anaheim, CA.

Osborn, W. C., & Ford, J. P. (1977). *Research on methods of synthetic performance testing* (HumRRO Final Rep. FR-CD (L)-76-1). Alexandria, VA: Human Resources Research Organization.

Owens, W. A., & Schoenfeldt, L. F. (1979). Toward a classification of persons. *Journal of Applied Psychology Monographs, 64,* 569–607.

Pearlman, K., Schmidt, F. L., & Hunter, J. E. (1980). Validity generalization results for tests used to predict job proficiency and training success in clerical occupations. *Journal of Applied Psychology, 65,* 373–406.

Peterson, N. G., & Bownas, D. A. (1982). Task structure and performance acquisition. In M. D. Dunnette & E. A. Fleishman (Eds.), *Human capability assessment.* Hillsdale, NJ: Erlbaum Associates.

Peterson, N. G., & Houston, J. S. (1980). *The prediction of correctional officer job performance: Construct validation in an employment setting.* Minneapolis, MN: Personnel Decisions Research Institute.

Peterson, N. G., Houston, J. S., Bosshardt, M. D., & Dunnette, M. D. (1977). *A study of correctional officer job at Marion Correctional Institution, Ohio: Development of selection procedures, training recommendations, and an exit information program.* Minneapolis, MN: Personnel Decisions Research Institute.

Poggio, J. P., Glasnapp, D. R., & Eros, D. S. (1981, April). *An empirical investigation of the Angoff, Ebel, and Nedelsky standard setting methods.* Paper presented at the annual meeting of the American Educational Research Association, Los Angeles.

Roach, D. E., & Wherry, R. J. (1970). Performance dimensions of multi-line insurance agents. *Personnel Psychology, 23,* 239–250.

Rogosa, D. R. (1980). Comparing nonparallel regression lines. *Psychological Bulletin*, 88, 307–321.

Rosse, R. L., Borman, W. C., Campbell, C. H., & Osborn, W. C. (1983, October). *Grouping Army occupational specialties by judged similarity.* Paper presented at the Annual Conference of the Military Testing Association, Gulf Shores, AL.

Rotter, J. B. (1966). Generalized expectancies for internal versus external control of reinforcement. *Psychological Monographs, 80* (1, Whole No. 609).

Rowley, G. L. (1982). Historical antecedents of the standard-setting debate: An inside account of the minimal-beardedness controversy. *Journal of Educational Measurement, 19*, 87–95.

Ruch, F. L., & Ruch, W. W. (1980). *Employee aptitude survey: Technical report.* Los Angeles: Psychological Services.

Sadacca, R., & Campbell, J. P. (1985, March). *Assessing the utility of a personnel/classification system.* Paper presented at the annual convention of the Southeastern Psychological Association, Atlanta.

Schmidt, F. L., Gast-Rosenberg, I., & Hunter, J. E. (1980). Validity generalization results for computer programmers. *Journal of Applied Psychology, 65*, 643–661.

Schmidt, F. L., & Hunter, J. E. (1977). Development of a general solution to the problem of validity generalization. *Journal of Applied Psychology, 62*, 529–540.

Schmidt, F. L., Hunter, J. E., Croll, P. R., & McKenzie, R. C. (1983). Estimation of employment test validities by expert judgment. *Journal of Applied Psychology, 68*, 590–601.

Schmidt, F. L., Hunter, J. E., McKenzie, R., & Muldrow, T. (1979). The impact of valid selection procedures on workforce productivity. *Journal of Applied Psychology, 64*, 609–626.

Schmidt, F. L., Hunter, J. E., & Urry, V. W. (1976). Statistical power in criterion-related validity studies. *Journal of Applied Psychology, 61*, 473–485.

Scriven, M. (1978). How to anchor standards. *Journal of Educational Measurement, 15*, 273–275.

Sims, W. H. (1978). *An analysis of the normalization of the Armed Services Vocational Aptitude Battery (ASVAB) Forms 6 and 7* (CNS 1115). Arlington, VA: Center for Naval Analysis.

Smith, E. P., & Rossmeissl, P. G. (1985). *Attribute assessment.* Unpublished manuscript.

Smith, P. C., & Kendall, L. M. (1963). Retranslation of expectations. An approach to the construction of unambiguous anchors for rating scales. *Journal of Applied Psychology, 39*, 330-333.

Society for Industrial and Organizational Psychology. (1980). *Principles for the validation and use of personnel selection procedures* (2nd ed.). Arlington, VA: Society for Industrial and Organizational Psychology, Division 14 of the American Psychological Association.

Spearman, C. (1927). *The abilities of man.* New York: Macmillan.

Taylor, H. C., & Russell, J. T. (1939). The relationship of validity coefficients to the practical effectiveness of tests in selection. *Journal of Applied Psychology, 23*, 565-578.

Tellegen, A. (1982). *Brief manual for the Differential Personality Questionnaire.* Unpublished manuscript, University of Minnesota.

Tenopyr, M. L. (1981). The realities of employment testing. *American Psychologist, 36*, 1120-1127.

Theologus, G. C., & Fleishman, E. A. (1973). Development of a taxonomy of human performance: Validation study of ability scales for classifying human tasks. *JSAS Catalogue of Selected Documents in Psychology, 3*, 29 (Ms. No. 326).

Thorndike, E. L. (1920). A constant error in psychological ratings. *Journal of Applied Psychology, 4*, 25-29.

Thorndike, R. L. (1949). *Personnel selection: Test and measurement techniques.* New York: Wiley.

Trattner, M. H., & O'Leary, B. S. (1980). Sample sizes for specified statistical power in testing for differential validity. *Journal of Applied Psychology, 65*, 127-134.

Uhlaner, J. E., & Drucker, A. J. (1980). Military research on performance criteria: A change of emphasis. *Human Factors, 22*, 131–139.

U.S. Army Research Institute. (1983). *Improving the selection, classification and utilization of Army enlisted personnel. Project A: research plan* (Research Rep. 1332). Alexandria, VA.

United States v. *City of St. Louis*. (1981). 616 F.2d 350 (8th Cir., 1980), cert denied 452 U.S. 938.

United States v. *Georgia Power Co*. (1973). *Federal Reporter*, 474, 906.

Vineberg, R., & Joyner, J. N. (1983). Performance measurement in the military services. In F. Landy, S. Zedick, & J. Cleveland (Eds.), *Performance measurement and theory* (pp. 233–250). Hillsdale, NJ: Erlbaum Associates.

Vineberg, R., & Taylor, E. (1972). *Performance in four Army jobs by men at different aptitude (AFQT) levels 24. Relationships between performance criteria.* (HumRRO Tech. Rep. 72–73). Alexandria, VA: Human Resources Research Office.

Votaw, D. F. (1952). Methods of solving some personnel classification problems. *Psychometrika, 17*, 255–266.

Washington v. *Davis*. (1976). 426 U.S. 229.

Wing, H., Peterson, N. G., & Hoffman, R. G. (1984). Expert judgments for predictor-criterion validity relationships. In N. K. Eaton, M. H. Goer, J. H. Harris, & L. M. Zook (Eds.), *Improving the selection, classification, and utilization of enlisted personnel: Annual report 1984 fiscal year* (Technical Rep. 660). Alexandria, VA: U.S. Army Research Institute for the Behavioral and Social Sciences.

Wise, L. L., Wang, M. M., & Rossmeissl, P. G. (1983). *Development and validation of Army selection and classification measures, Project A: Longitudinal research data base plan* (Research Rep. 1356). Alexandria, VA: U.S. Army Research Institute.

10

TECHNOLOGIES FOR PERSON-JOB MATCHING

Edward J. Schmitz and Betty W. Holz

Matching people with jobs is a key human resources decision for any organization. Person-job matching plays a major role in determining the effectiveness of an organization because people are the greatest productive resource in most organizations. Most successful organizations view personnel development as a key strategic area.

Person-job matching is an interdisciplinary process involving personnel psychologists, operations research analysts, and computer scientists, all working with management. Personnel psychologists provide information on performance criteria and predictors. Operations researchers develop models for planning, executing, and evaluating person-job decisions. Computer scientists develop data bases, communications interfaces, and processing systems to support decisions. Management establishes organizational goals and objectives and provides feedback on the extent to which decisions support these goals.

This chapter focuses on the operations research and computer science technologies presently available to support person-job matching. The second section provides an overview of the personnel assignment problem including its general characteristics, historical development, and mathematical formulation. The third section describes the general systems approach to person-job matching. Along with detailed discussion of methodologies and examples of the major systems functions, the fourth section discusses the application of information derived from these functions to real organizational problems, including examples from military and civilian sectors of government and private industry, and directions for future research. The chapter concludes with a summary.

WHAT MAKES PERSON-JOB MATCHING IMPORTANT?

Person-job matching (PJM) is a significant activity for any organization. While the costs and benefits of PJM may be hidden in many organizations, their value can be detected throughout all sectors of the economy. Midsize and large organizations are willing to pay headhunters substantial fees to locate the right persons to fill key positions. Sports teams operate extensive scouting systems and maintain minor league teams for player development. Universities may take many months searching and evaluating hundreds of candidates to fill academic positions. Local governments go through considerable effort and expense to develop tests for selecting firefighters and police officers.

This section describes what makes PJM important, how different organizational or environmental settings may affect the process, and how various disciplines, notably psychology and operations research, have contributed to the development of PJM technology.

Characteristics of the Assignment Problem

The person-job matching process makes use of several concepts in personnel psychology: selection, differential classification, and differential assignment.

Selection focuses on the differences among individuals, generally using a single scale of value or utility. Applicants are classified into two categories: those satisfactory for employment and those not. Most organizations make selection decisions when matching people to jobs. Applications are usually made for a specific job, and a decision is made whether to accept or reject a candidate based on his or her expected utility in one job.

Differential classification deals with differences within an individual with respect to various skills. A particular individual may have a high aptitude for mathematics but poor writing skills. Another may have considerable talent for electronics jobs but poor communication ability. Classification requires the use of two or more different performance predictors. Its use implies that each candidate can be considered for more than one job. Pure classification assumes that all candidates must be assigned to some job. The military has been one of the major users of classification data. Many large companies undergoing major reorganizations, relocations, or retraining programs may use classification tests.

Classification data are the raw material for the person-job matching system. While it is useful to know the kind(s) of job(s) for which individuals are well qualified, these capabilities may not match the needs of the organization. The person-job matching system must inventory the aptitudes available and develop a strategy for allocating these aptitudes so that organizational objectives are met. What are the objectives of the organization? Increased labor productivity is the goal of a person-job matching system. Whether it is increased output, improved product or service quality, or reduced cost, the objectives of the system for placing candidates into jobs should reflect the criterion of achieving job performance goals.

The way one maximizes organizational productivity depends on the type of job. Thompson (1967) and Cascio (1982) discuss three kinds of jobs: independent, sequential, and interdependent. Independent jobs, such as selling, are those where the performance of the worker is largely independent of the actions of others. Sequential jobs can be found in assembly lines, where productivity is a function of successive sets of activities. Interdependent jobs are those requiring a great deal of coordination or interaction. This kind of job can be found in the activities of a basketball team, a tank crew, or a group engaged in a research project.

Most job assignment systems have been developed for independent jobs (Dunnette, 1982). This simplifies the placement problem because the value of each potential assignment can be assessed individually and aggregated directly to assess the overall productivity impact. Sequential and interrelated jobs depend on the interaction of several people. While most of this chapter deals with achieving increased organizational productivity through raising individual performance, one should be aware of group effects that may be present in many situations.

Figure 10.1a illustrates a typical person-job assignment problem of assigning three people to three jobs. (Expected job performance has been scaled from 1 to 10 in this example.) Each individual must take one job, and each job must be filled. For example, if person 1 is given job A, then person 2 can take only job B or C. The best possible allocation, in terms of maximizing total job performance, is given by the circled combination of assignments. Note that individuals are not

FIGURE 10.1. Examples of Person-Job Trade-off Matrices.

		JOB		
		A	B	C
	1	10	(8)	9
PERSON	2	(7)	2	5
	3	5	3	(8)

Figure 1(a). Person-Job Tradeoff Matrix

		JOB		
		A	B	C
	1	10	10	10
PERSON	2	7	7	7
	3	5	5	5

Figure 1(b). Example of a Person-Job Tradeoff Matrix Without Differential Classification.

		JOB		
		A	B	C
	1	10	5	7
PERSON	2	10	5	7
	3	10	5	7

Figure 1(c). Example of a Person-Job Tradeoff Matrix Without Differential Job Performance

necessarily assigned to their highest rated job (for example, person 1 to job B).

There can be situations when person-job match technology would not be appropriate. Often, positions are filled one at a time, with candidates being considered only for a single position. It may not be possible to classify differentially people against jobs. If job performance cannot be predicted, then a person-job matching system would not provide any benefits.

For example, Figure 10.1b provides a case where there is no differential performance of individuals across jobs. Person 1 always performs at level 10; similarly, person 2 performs at level 7 regardless of the job assigned. While individuals differ in their ability to perform (person 1 is always preferred to person 2 or 3), once the selection of people has been made, it does not matter which jobs they take. (In this discussion, it is assumed that there are no priorities reflecting the relative importance of the different jobs.)

Figure 10.1c provides an example where differential job performance does not exist. Here there is no difference in job performance due to the individual. No matter who is assigned to job A, its performance is the same. It may be there is no predictor of job performance, or the job is engineered so that individual differences are negligible (for example, assembly line work).

In most cases there is variability that can take advantage of PJM technologies. There will usually be some kind of classification measure that can differentiate—probability of job success, hiring costs, training costs, or job tenure. It is not necessary for all jobs or persons to be differentiable, merely that some variability exists in the person-job trade-off matrix. However, it is important that classification measures be scaled so that the utility of assignments across jobs can be assessed.

This person-job assignment problem has existed formally for more than 40 years. Brogden (1946) developed an algorithm for assigning individuals to multiple job categories. The years immediately following World War II also saw the development of two other sciences that would change person-job matching technology: operations research and computer science.

The assignment of a batch of individuals to jobs has been known as an area of management science application. The problem of assigning n individuals to n jobs can be formulated as

$$\text{Maximize:} \quad Z \equiv \sum_{i=1}^{n} \sum_{j=1}^{n} c_{ij} X_{ij}$$

$$\text{Subject to:} \quad \sum_{i=1}^{n} X_{ij} = 1$$

$$\sum_{j=1}^{n} X_{ij} = 1$$

The objective is to maximize the weighted assignment of a group of i individuals to j jobs, subject to the constraints, that each individual is assigned and each job is filled. The weight, c_{ij}, represents the utility of assigning individual i to job type j.

Operations research provides a variety of mathematical techniques for solving complex resource allocation problems. In 1947, George Dantzig developed the technique of linear programming (LP). LP was initially developed to solve complicated resource allocation problems for scheduling training and distributing supplies (Dantzig, 1982). LP became one of the most widely applied mathematical techniques for solving a large number of practical decision problems, with personnel assignment receiving early recognition as a type of problem that could be solved by means of this technique. Votaw showed in 1952 how the LP approach could be applied to job assignments. In 1955 Kuhn developed an efficient mathematical algorithm for solving personnel assignment problems.

Complexities Introduced in Organizations

The ideal situation of batch solution to the problem rarely exists. Variations to the assignment problem that are likely to occur include

- Assignment of individuals to jobs one at a time (sequentially) rather than in a batch
- Consideration of multiple types of measures, or figures of merit, for each assignment, such as level of performance versus cost of recruiting, training, and compensation
- Changes in requirements over time—for example, growth or contraction of the organization, or changes in the types or mix of positions resulting from modernization or changes in mission/ objectives
- Changes in the supply of personnel due to shifts in economic conditions, compensation, recruiting effort, and/or population/ demographic distributions
- Seasonal patterns for the recruitment of personnel
- Varying lead time for training as a function of job type and personnel qualifications
- Varying turnover rates, or expected service life, as a function of personnel attributes, organization policies, and other factors

While operations research provided a methodology for assigning batches of individuals to jobs, the computer processing and data base limitations of the 1950s and early 1960s made such approaches infeasible to implement. For example, the computer systems of 1952 could only assign 30 people to jobs with several hours of computer time (Votaw, 1952). Consequently, Dwyer (1954), Ward (1959a), and Horst and Sorenson (1976) developed assignment algorithms that approximated the theoretical optimal with various decision rules.

By the mid-1960s, computer technology and operations research computational algorithms had improved to the point where larger assignment batches were possible (Hatch, 1971). Decision makers then sought to make assignments based on multiple criteria. This topic was pursued from an optimization standpoint using goal programming to achieve objectives where trade-offs were not explicitly made (Charnes, et al., 1972). This procedure allowed for the exclusion of certain kinds of persons from certain jobs (for example, women from combat duty), while simultaneously attempting to meet performance and cost goals.

A separate but related topic in personnel problems is the assessment of the objectives of the problem. Initially, decision makers were faced with explicit trade-offs of costs and quotas for job assignment. However, as mathematical sophistication increased, management became concerned with how goals were elicited and measured. Keeney and Raiffa (1976) provided a discussion of methods for evaluating such complex decisions. Ward et al. (1978) provided an approach to capture the decision makers' willingness to make various trade-offs in personnel assignment problems.

By the early 1970s, problems arose that made it necessary to relax the assumption that the jobs needing to be filled were known. For example, as the Vietnam War was winding down, the Army found it was faced with costly uncertainties in forecasting and planning for job requirements. Thus person-job matching systems were extended to include requirement projections (Holz & Wroth, 1980).

In the mid-1970s, with the initiation of the All-Volunteer forces, the military was faced with a new organizational variable, uncertainty of personnel supply. Thus, supply forecasting was added to personel assignment systems (Huck & Allen, 1977).

Large organizations do not make personnel assignments independent of the rest of the organization or their external environment. For example, recruiters would like to bring 120,000 new soldiers into the Army every summer when they graduate from high school. Trainers would like to train 10,000 per month year-round. This situation, coupled with the fact that different training programs have different training times, led to new systems to support person-job planning (Holz & Wroth, 1980).

These illustrations point out how the person-job matching system has evolved over the years. The problem has expanded to make use of such expertise as personnel psychology, operations research, computer science, econometrics, multiattribute utility theory, and systems analysis. The next section describes a comprehensive systems approach to the person-job assignment decision and key technological factors that should be considered in designing person-job matching systems.

SYSTEMS APPROACH

Modern person-job match technology involves a variety of disciplines to bring together the right kinds of information for personnel assignment decisions. A systems approach is needed to integrate the assignment process within the organization. The traditional static job assignment problem does not exist in practice. Within organizations there is the need for dynamic systems that respond quickly to changing personnel demands, supplies, costs, and objectives.

Figure 10.2 depicts the modules of a personnel management system: projection of personnel requirements; forecasting the supply of candidates; planning, including the establishment of selection standards; making individual selection and job assignment decisions; and evaluating organization performance and alternative policies and procedures. The objective remains the same as in the original problem: to compare candidates against job requirements so that the "best" decisions can be made. The systems approach extends this process to include not only this decision but the determination of requirements and supply and execution and evaluation of the decision. While not all aspects of the system are equally important for all organizations, they are usually present and should be considered by the developer and implementer of PJM systems.

The remainder of the section describes the characteristics of each module, including the technological features for its design.

FIGURE 10.2. Personnel Management System.

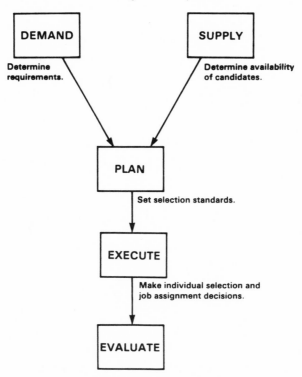

Determination of requirements is the essential first step in personnel planning. Personnel requirements are specified in terms of the numbers and types of positions that are associated with plans for the organization's size and structure. These in turn are based, at least in principle, on projections of the requirements/demand for the organization's output of products or services.

For organizations in both the public and private sectors, these projections are made with considerable difficulty and uncertainty, since they must be embedded in assumptions concerning the environment in which the organization will function. However, in spite of the difficulty and uncertainty, these projections serve a key function in providing the basis for the PJM process.

In addition to specification of the numbers and types of personnel spaces (positions), the PJM system requires projections of recruiting requirements—that is, the numbers and types of jobs to be filled from external sources. The total number of recruits can be estimated as the difference between total positions and the number of employees projected to remain in the organization at each specified point in the planning horizon. To provide input to the PJM process, this projection must be refined to specify the numbers of positions to be filled by type and level (grade or rank). The latter determination depends on projections of promotions, position transfers, terminations, and retirements. These projections can be derived from analyses of historical time series data, with provision for evaluating the impact of changes in exogenous factors—for example, economic conditions and organizational policy. Examples of procedures in current use by the U.S. Army for recruiting requirements determination are discussed in Holz & Wroth (1980) and Holz et al., 1983).

Personnel Supply

An organization needs to plan for the acquisition of personnel in advance of their actual arrival. It is important for an organization to understand the factors that affect its supply of personnel. These include both exogenous factors, such as economic conditions and demography, and factors controllable by management, such as compensation, recruiting, and advertising.

Two types of forecasts are likely to be available: individual specific forecasts and aggregate categorical forecasts. Individual forecasts provide the most detailed information for job assignment. This kind of information is obtained when a company places a newspaper advertisement or a college recruits students. Specific data are gathered on the persons available for jobs, including specific predictions of their "worth" in various assignments. Frequently such data do not exist. It may be that hiring is carried out in such a manner that hiring and assignment decisions must be made as people apply. Or it may be that a new project or division is being planned and only aggregate forecasts of the numbers and types of people likely to apply are available.

In such cases, aggregate categorical data can be used to develop forecasts. Data must be categorized in a manner that is relevant for differential job assignment. For example, it would do no good to forecast only the numbers of high school and college graduates likely to apply for jobs if information is needed on typing ability or computer programming experience.

Furthermore, forecasts need only be made for critical or scarce kinds of people. Projecting that a particular advertisement for computer programmers will generate 100 applicants for 10 vacancies may not be as useful as projecting the number who will be experienced in PL/1, FORTRAN, or COBOL computer languages.

A variety of techniques are available for making forecasts. These can range from experienced judgment to complex mathematical techniques. Experienced judgment is usually the most useful approach for small firms or unique situations where there are highly specialized attributes to be forecast. For larger organizations where there are frequently recurring vacancies, it may be beneficial to develop a mathematical model. Such a model would make estimates of the numbers and types of candidates as a function of other variables. There are three main types of such models: empirical, econometric, and programming.

An empirical model simply provides the best predictor of applicants as a function of other known variables. A common example of this is exponential smoothing, which projects the number of applicants tomorrow, based on the number of applicants today, the previous forecast, and the accuracy of the previous forecast (Moskowitz & Wright, 1979). These models are most useful for short-term estimates. For a more detailed discussion of a variety of empirical models, see Box & Jenkins (1976) and Makridakis et al. (1982).

Often there is additional information known about the kinds of candidates likely to be available. For example, it may be that the number of high school graduates, the unemployment rate, the overall wage rate, and the organization's wage rate are all known to have an impact on job applicants. In such a case, an econometric forecasting model can be constructed. Such models are usually more reliable for longer term planning and permit the user to assess the sensitivity of supply to projected changes in key variables like wage and unemployment rates. An example of such an application can be found in Dale and Gilroy (1983). A discussion on how to develop such models is provided in Pindyck and Rubinfeld (1981).

Finally, it may be that the organization does not wish simply to make forecasts but to affect forecasts to achieve desired personnel goals. In this case, a model is needed that relates the available programs to their ability to accomplish various recruiting goals. For example, different means such as advertising, personnel agencies, increased recruiting trips, or increased compensation can be evaluated with respect to their impact on hiring various kinds of personnel. For an example of this methodology, see Charnes and Cooper (1961).

Planning Module

The solution of PJM problems is known. Operations research techniques provide methodologies for assigning people to jobs so that the "best" possible performance is achieved. The size of the problem is no longer a concern, as today's computer systems can easily handle the simultaneous assignment of 10,000 or more people.

However, the ideal solution is seldom achieved. To accomplish optimal assignment policy, the personnel planner must have accurate predictions of individual performance across all feasible job possibilities, be able to assign many people simultaneously, and constrain people to accept the planners' matching decisions. These assumptions are unrealistic at the individual level. Performance predictors are usually not relied on for fine levels of differentiation. People do not have to accept recommended person-job matches. Also, assignments are usually made individually or in small batches.

For these reasons, we distinguish between the planning and execution modes of person-job matching. The optimization techniques are most useful when applied to personnel planning. The assumptions necessary to evaluate optimal assignment strategies are usually appropriate for PJM planning with aggregate data. Accordingly, the development of assignment policies is presented here as a two-stage process: first, aggregate planning coupled with an individual execution stage, and second, operational solutions. This section discusses the kinds of models available for aggregate planning or when the theoretical conditions can be met. The following section discusses operational solutions.

Given projections of personnel supply and demand, a planning model can be formulated for many organizations. Such a model, using operations research technologies, determines the pairings of personnel types to job categories, where the personnel types are defined in terms of attributes that have been found to be significant for predicting performance.

There are a variety of techniques available for solving optimization problems of the kind described above. These include network programming, linear programming, and goal programming.

Network programming problems are a special class of LP problems with a special structure that lends itself to fast and efficient solution. Personnel assignment problems frequently contain this type of structure. Figure 10.3 presents a simple example of a personnel assignment problem in a network structure. There are three supply categories (people) available for assignment to three demand points (jobs). Each possible assignment defines an arc with a particular value associated with it. The goal in this case is to maximize total performance. The special structure is provided by the constraints in such a problem. Each arc involves only one demand and one supply constraint. Problems with this kind of structure can be solved very efficiently with current computer algorithms (see Klingman & Mote, 1983).

Frequently, there are additional restrictions on the person-job match that fundamentally change the problem. For example, if there are budget constraints and different salaries associated with each assignment possibility, then the requirements of network program-

FIGURE 10.3. Example of a Person-Job Network Programming Problem.

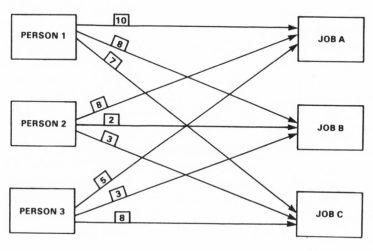

ming no longer hold. LP techniques exist that can solve such problems. Examples of the formulation and solution of LP problems can be found in such texts as Charnes and Cooper (1961), Hadley (1963), Moskowitz and Wright (1979), and Hillier and Lieberman (1980). The complexity of additional constraints such as budgets will, in principle, either reduce the size of problem that can be solved or add to solution times. However, use of a combination of network and LP formulations has made it feasible to solve some large problems of this type (Holz, et al., 1983).

Other times the personnel planner will want to evaluate more complicated assignment policies. Personnel assignment policies frequently need to consider multiple time periods. The assignment decisions made today will affect the pool of individuals available for promotion a year from now, for example. There may be several objectives that are being pursued simultaneously, such as maximizing performance, minimizing job turnover, and minimizing salary costs. Or the planner may not want to achieve extreme solutions but simply achieve a solution within some acceptable range.

Goal programming provides an approach to dealing with such complexities as multiple objectives, conflicting constraints, and satisficing (instead of maximizing) behavior. Goal programming approaches to the personnel assignment problem are provided in Charnes et al. (1972), Niehaus (1977), and Steuer & Wallace (1978). The general approach and formulation of such problems can be found in Charnes and Cooper (1961), Moskowitz and Wright (1979), and Hillier and Lieberman (1980).

Figure 10.4 provides examples of how the above methodologies can be used to solve personnel planning problems. In this example, two personnel categories (graduates and nongraduates) are to be assigned to two jobs (technical and nontechnical). Nontechnical training costs are the same for both groups. However, graduates cost only $5,000 to train for technical jobs compared to $8,000 for nongraduates.

The first solution is the minimum training cost solution. In this example, all 300 graduates and only 50 of the nongraduates are assigned to technical jobs. This problem can be solved with network optimization, since each person-job assignment affects only one goal or constraint on the problem (cost). Now suppose a personnel goal concerning retention is imposed. The organization desires a 50 percent retention of personnel in each occupation so that there will be

FIGURE 10.4. Examples of Personnel Allocation Problems.

	INPUT DATA		
Type	Item	Value	
Job requirements	Technical (T)	350	
	Nontechnical (NT)	350	
Personnel available	Graduates (G)	300	
	Nongraduates (NG)	400	

Training Costs ($1000)

	T	NT
G	5	3
NG	8	3

Retention rates (%)

G	35
NG	65

SOLUTIONS

I. Minimize training costs

	T	NT
G	300	0
NG	50	350

Training cost: $2950

II. a. First, meet goal of at least 50% retention
b. Second, minimize training costs

	T	NT
G	177	123
NG	173	227
Retention	50%	54%

Training cost $3319

sufficient experienced personnel in each job category. Nongraduates have a higher retention rate than graduates. Solution 2 illustrates the result when the retention goal is imposed over the cost goal. The number of nongraduates in technical jobs has increased. Total costs have increased from $2,950 to $3,319, but the retention rate for each occupation is now 50 percent or greater.

This problem requires a linear or goal programming approach. The conflicting objectives of cost and retention cannot be solved using a network code. Each assignment decision affects both goals. In practice, the three techniques for solving personnel assignment problems can frequently be combined. For example, some problems can be structured to combine related linear programming and network programming problems. The personnel planner has to assess carefully the nature of the problems, available resources, and solution objectives in the structuring of any planning model.

Execution Module

In most organizations it will be impractical to implement directly the theoretically optimal solution. Decisions need to be made in real time concerning the individuals to be selected and their job assignments. The participants will have a say in determining whether they accept such decisions. Situational-specific information may be brought to bear.

The kind of solution technique used will depend on the nature of the problem. Two general methodologies are decision rules and expert systems. If the problem is well structured, decision rules are most effective. If they are not well defined or routine, expert systems may be appropriate. A discussion of the different decision-making techniques can be found in Simon (1977).

Decision rules have long been applied to personnel assignment. In fact, organizations frequently reduce the assignment problem to a selection problem by restricting individuals to apply for only one job. Work by Brogden (1946) in classification and assignment used decision rules for assignment.

Decision rules use a payoff function that generates a value for a candidate against each possible assignment. A person is assigned where the greatest payoff is computed (subject to meeting minimum standards). The development of a payoff function involves identification of the factors to be included in the function and assigning weights to different factors. Discussions of approaches to such decision problems can be found in Keeney and Raiffa (1976) and Starr and Zeleny (1977).

Usually, the values important to personnel assignment should be apparent. These may include job classification scores, education, job importance, time available to fill the job, personnel retention or turnover rates, and training costs. It should be emphasized that differentiation in these measures across people and jobs is important. Otherwise, situations such as described in Figure 10.1b or 10.1c will exist.

Once the factors have been identified, they must be combined into scores for decision making. A payoff function can be created either by determining the decision maker's value preferences in advance or analyzing a set of decisions made previously. The first approach has been referred to as the method of "policy specifying" (Ward, 1977). The second approach can be solved using a variety of statistical analysis procedures, such as regression analysis, if an assessment has been made of which classification decisions were "good" or "bad."

If person-job matching data are not standardized, yet it is possible to differentiate between "good" and "bad" decisions, the problem may lend itself to an expert systems approach. In this case, a knowledge base of detailed decision guidance would be structured, tested, and validated. A discussion on development of expert systems can be found in Hayes-Roth, Waterman, & Lenat (1983). Usually, specific computer software is needed to perform this kind of modeling.

Evaluation Module

This module provides tools for monitoring progress against goals; evaluation of policy, program, and budget alternatives; and measurement of the accuracy of forecasts made by the PJM system. A key feature of the PJM system is its dynamic capability to adapt to organizational needs. To achieve this effect, feedback mechanisms are needed to identify problems, trade-offs, and opportunities within the system. Such evaluations include the extent to which requirements will be met, whether recruiting efforts are sufficient, whether retention and promotion are at acceptable levels, and whether decisions made are in agreement with organizational goals. The PJM system not only performs the basic distribution of people to activities but also supports myriad related management tasks. In fact, investigating the impact on an organization of different courses of action is a major function of the system. This section discusses the uses of an evaluation module within such a system.

One of the earliest roles of computer systems was to monitor the personnel process. As employees move through organizations, they are promoted, switch jobs, leave, or retire. All of these actions produce changes in personnel records. These can be analyzed at a later time to determine the impact of policies and to provide data to examine relationships between personnel characteristics and outcomes.

The modern PJM system may operate as part of a decision support system (DSS) for human resource planners. DSSs possess much broader capabilities for processing information than the older management information systems. While both collect and process information, DSSs provide powerful abilities for analysis and modeling. For example, if retention is an important organizational objective, the DSS can provide not only data on retention but also a variety of models for estimating retention, relating models to policies and programs, and implementing policies concerning retention. A useful reference on DSS characteristics is provided by Bonczek et al. (1981).

One important outcome of the evaluation is to modify the system itself. For example, if certain jobs are difficult to fill, examination can be made of the possibility of redesigning the jobs. If people with certain skills are difficult to recruit, plans can be made to develop them internally.

Computer Science Technology

Current systems are designed to take advantage of the capabilities of both micro- or minicomputers and large mainframes, with associated communications networks. The former are used in an interactive mode for all forms of user interface—from DSS functions to input of user-furnished data and control of system runs—whereas the latter are used for batch processes, including the maintenance of large data bases and solution of large-scale optimization models.

An area of special interest is the design of graphical and tabular displays in a way that is easy for nonprogrammers to use and that provides, in a form that is readily assimilated, access to a vast amount of data with complex interrelationships. An example of a very comprehensive, integrated family of automated systems for use in personnel planning, policy development, and management is the U.S. Army's FORECAST system (see U.S. Army, 1983). Figure 10.5 is an example of the graphical displays available from the FORECAST manage-

FIGURE 10.5. Example of Graphical Display from the Army FORECAST System.

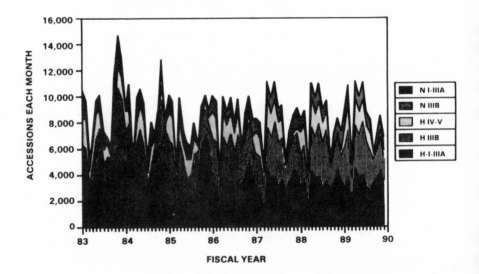

ACTIVE ARMY MILITARY MANPOWER PROGRAM
MALE RECRUITING TERMS 3, 4
ACCESSIONS BY EDUCATION AND MENTAL CATEGORY

ment information system. The figure shows historical and projected recruits broken out by whether high school graduate (N or H) and "mental category" (I-IIIA, IIIB, or IV), where the latter is based on the scores from the Armed Forces Qualification Test, given to recruiting applicants for all the military services. The projections shown in the figure are output from a goal programming model that considers projected supply, strength targets or goals, losses due to separations and retirement, and policy constraints—for example, on the acceptable profile of recruits by the previously referenced characteristics (Holz & Wroth, 1980).

IMPLEMENTING PERSON-JOB MATCHING TECHNOLOGIES

This section discusses the application of PJM technology. Included in the discussion are the benefits and costs of a PJM system and examples of PJM applications, including specific organizational characteristics that make particular features desirable.

The Utility of Person-Job Matching

A key issue in person-job matching systems is the estimation of the benefits and costs of these activities. Considerable effort on the part of personnel psychologists, management analysts, and computer scientists may be required to establish and maintain the systems. Naturally, management will only be willing to devote resources to improve person-job matching if there is a strong likelihood it will benefit the organization. This section discusses approaches for evaluating the benefits and costs of PJM systems.

The costs of PJM technology are usually easier to estimate than the benefits. However, even the costs cannot often be projected with precision. Development and operating costs often include some portion of existing personnel processing, telecommunications, and data processing expenses. When new systems are simply modifications or enhancements of existing systems, only incremental costs should be considered. However, these may be difficult to separate from existing operating costs.

While costs may be difficult to estimate, benefits are likely to be even more intractable to assess. Since most PJM systems involve some increased costs over existing processes, it is necessary that they show some value to the organization. Further, the value of these decisions reflects not only the value of the PJM technology but of many related personnel management activities as well. The value of the PJM decision also reflects the usefulness of selection, classification, recruiting, and personnel planning activities. If these functions do not improve the matching of personnel resources with organization requirements, then their value is also questionable.

The value of PJM systems should be reflected in both improvement in productivity and reduction of management uncertainty. Some approaches to identifying each of these benefits are provided below.

The maximization of productivity or utility of job assignment decisions is a principal goal of PJM systems. If classification systems can identify the characteristics associated with good job performance, and personnel recruiters can find candidates with these attributes, then the PJM system can optimally assign people to jobs and the value of increased performance can be directly computed. However, the marginal value of individual job assignments is difficult to estimate. Most organizations produce an aggregate output where the contribution of specific jobs to output cannot be measured directly. Many of these difficulties in assessing the productivity of individual workers in organizational settings have been described in Thompson (1967), Thurow (1975), and Cascio (1982).

Brogden (1959) showed that the theoretical utility of classification data depended on predictor validity, the intercorrelation of predictors, the number of different jobs, and the standard deviation of job performance in dollars. Even with highly correlated predictors and no rejection (pure classification), the utility of optimal assignment procedures can be substantial. Hunter and Schmidt (1982) estimated that a job classification system for the U.S. economy could be worth $169 billion.

What are some ways of assessing labor productivity? Three principal methods have been identified: direct utility measurement, subjective utility measurement, and substitution cost measurement.

Cronbach & Gleser (1965), Dunnette (1966), and Cascio (1980) discuss the measurement of utility from differential assignment. Both direct and subjective measurement rely on Brogden's utility formula. They differ in their approach to estimating the standard deviation of performance. Direct productivity measurement involves the direct valuation of the output produced by workers with different attributes. For example, if salespersons with certain characteristics sell twice the products of salespersons with other characteristics, then the former are twice as productive as the latter. However, it is not usually easy to collect the data necessary for this kind of assessment.

Subjective assessment typically involves asking experts, such as supervisors, to estimate the relative value of excellent, average, and poor performers in specific jobs. Hunter and Schmidt (1983) have used this method to estimate the impact of personnel selection and provided examples of its application. Using this method they have found the standard deviation of job performance to range from 42 to 60 percent of the annual wage.

Subjective assessment has many desirable features. It provides the kind of information needed to estimate the utility of job performance. However, there are a number of potential weaknesses. The situation or scenario under which utility is evaluated is often not specified with sufficient detail or directly related to actual organizational objectives. Also, stringent assumptions are required to permit the use of average values (see Keeney & Raiffa, 1976). For additional discussion of the use of subjective utility theory in personnel assignment, see Keeney (1980). An application of subjective utility theory that attempts to correct for these inherent limitations is provided by Charnes et al. (1982).

Another approach to evaluating the benefits of job performance is to determine what the organization would have been willing to pay to achieve a given performance level through other means. For example, if the organization is willing to pay an additional $200 in recruiting costs to achieve performance gains made through person-job matching, then this would be an estimate of the value of PJM technology. This is the concept of consumer's surplus used by economists in performing benefit-cost analysis. Examples of its measurement are provided in Baumol (1977), Armor et al. (1982), Schmitz et al. (1984), and Fernandez (1985).

One of the major reasons for implementing PJM technology is for strategic planning. Such systems should enable an organization to forecast personnel problems and develop alternatives prior to their occurrence. Thus, a major function of PJM systems is to reduce organizational uncertainties. Accordingly, one area where there may be significant PJM payoffs is in reducing work force demand and supply uncertainties. Given the magnitude of personnel costs in most organizations, small improvements should provide substantial payoffs. One example of these benefits was provided by Holz and Wroth (1980) in their system for forecasting Army enlisted strength, gains, and losses. Their accurate system enabled the Army to save $100 million annually in its military personnel budget.

Applications of Person-Job Matching Technology

Any organization large enough to be continually recruiting people needs some system for evaluating and assigning candidates to jobs. This section reports on some of the applications of PJM technology that have been made in both the public and private sectors.

The military has been the leader in development of person-job matching technologies, for two reasons: First, during wartime, the military has been faced with the task of quickly classifying and assigning literally millions of people to jobs. The magnitude of these mobilization problems has led to the development of efficient algorithms for job assignment. However, even in peacetime, each service recruits many thousands of individuals who must be evaluated against hundreds of different jobs. This fact, the constant arrival of applicants with different abilities who must simultaneously be assessed against jobs with different expected payoffs, creates the classic assignment problem.

However, there is a second reason why the military has been involved in the broader aspects of person-job matching technology, notably demand and supply forecasting and evaluation and control systems. Except for the lowest levels of the organization, the military acquires people only internally. During peacetime, there is minimal capability to acquire experienced soldiers, sailors, and airmen in the civilian labor market. (During periods of mobilization, the activation of personnel from the reserve components of the services does provide such a capability, while during peacetime there is a very limited capability through the reenlistment of individuals who have had a break in prior service.) Thus, the military has been forced to take human resources planning seriously. In fact, a historical analysis of personnel management finds that the military has traditionally been a leader in personnel planning systems and that the private sector has frequently adopted methods developed for the military (Hayes, 1978).

The U.S. military PJM systems represent some of the most sophisticated attempts to incorporate social science concerns, management science technology, and computer science for personnel decision making. The Air Force (Ward, et al., 1978) and Navy (Kroeker & Rafacz, 1983) systems rely on multiobjective utility theory to assess dynamically the relative importance of both job and person characteristics. Other examples of military assignment systems can be found in Moore & Sholtz (1974), Abellera, Mullins, & Earles (1975), Niehaus (1977), Eastman (1978), and Gray (1978). Such systems have been shown to improve the value of job assignments both to the services (in terms of job performance and retention) and to the individual (in terms of his or her job satisfaction and performance).

The U.S. Army is presently implementing the kind of PJM technology outlined here. (See Schmitz, et al., 1984, for a detailed description of this system.) The Army recruits 140,000 new soldiers annually to fill 5,000 training classes in more than 250 different kinds of jobs. Two general criteria available for evaluating candidates are predicted job performance and training cost. The job performance predictor data are available from the Armed Services Vocational Aptitude Battery (ASVAB) taken by applicants prior to enlistment. Jobs are classified into one of nine different aptitude composites. Attrition can serve as a cost measure, using the probability that a person will not complete his or her enlistment tour. This attrition probability can be predicted as a function of applicant and job characteristics, including education, gender, and test scores (Buddin, 1984).

The PJM problem is further complicated by management policies. A decision concerning the type of job training an applicant will receive is made prior to enlistment. Further, since an applicant can wait as long as a year before starting training, the Army must manage not only the applicant-job match but the amount of delay prior to entry into the service. Failure to maintain the proper flow of recruits into job training can lead to wasted training resources, unfilled jobs, and higher training costs (Manganaris & Schmitz, 1985).

The Enlisted Personnel Allocation System solves the PJM problem using the systems approach outlined earlier:

- Aggregate job demands and applicant forecasts are analyzed using optimization techniques.
- Individual job assignments are made on the basis of a job payoff equation using guidance from the optimization results in real time.

- Job vacancies and applicant forecasts are updated as applicants reserve training seats, and the optimization model is periodically recomputed to adjust job assignment guidance.

The optimization model works with job and applicant data in some creative ways to achieve organizational performance objectives. Jobs are aggregated into about 40 clusters that are similar in terms of their performance characteristics. These include such characteristics as the predictor, level of difficulty, performance level desired, and gender restrictions.

Total applicant forecasts are disaggregated into groups of applicants that facilitate prediction of differential job performance. The applicant clustering is done on the basis of gender, education, selection test score, and combinations of classification test scores. (For example, it is important to know not just how many people have a high aptitude for electronics jobs but also the number of those who have high aptitudes for other jobs as well.) Approximately .60 differential aptitude groups are used in the optimization.

The optimization module ensures that the job demands are filled by the appropriate supply of candidates. For example, if there is a strong requirement to fill electronics jobs, individuals with talents in both electronics and communications will be steered into electronics. The real-time decisions are made by using a job utility equation that adjusts the aggregate guidance by taking into account more detailed information available for individual applicants. The real-time utility equation takes account of specific test scores, job training seats, and applicant preferences. For example, if a candidate is well qualified for both electronics and communications jobs, but best qualified in communications, the system could recommend the candidate take a communications job, even if guidance favors filling electronics jobs first.

What kind of impact can such a PJM system have on organization performance? First of all, EPAS is an enhancement to an existing system that has been shown to have considerable value (Schmitz & Nelson, 1984). Even so, considerable performance gains are expected. The present system attempts to achieve both minimum individual performance levels and aggregate job performance levels. However, it has been meeting job performance goals in only two-thirds of the jobs. EPAS will

- Achieve minimum individual performance levels.

- Achieve job performance goals in all jobs.
- Increase total job performance through differential classification by .2 standard score unit.
- Reduce total job attrition by more than 5 percent.

What is the utility of the performance gains created by EPAS? Attrition reductions can save the Army $60 million annually in training costs. Performance gains are more difficult to measure, since there is no market mechanism for determining the value of the Army's performance. However, it is estimated job performance gains would cost from $126 million (Schmitz & Nelson, 1984) to $200 million (Fernandez, 1985) to achieve through additional recruiting effort and higher enlistment standards. Thus, for an annual investment of less than $1 million, the Army can achieve benefits worth $186 to $260 million through an improved person-job matching system.

Figure 10.6 provides an example of the impact of EPAS according to the nine major job groupings. In this example, all job categories achieved equal or better performance using EPAS. This is a desirable objective for a PJM system, for a system that achieves total gains through substantial decrements in performance in some jobs may be difficult to implement.

Compared to the military, civilian organizations tend to place less emphasis on the execution phase of person-job matching. This function is usually decentralized. Also, while classification devices are frequently used, the problem is usually simplified by permitting individuals to select the specific occupation for which they want to be considered. This reduces the problem from a complicated assignment problem to a more simple selection problem.

However, for several reasons, PJM technologies are expanding, particularly in aggregate planning and evaluation. First of all, new forms of organization and management structure have created the need for better information on personnel abilities. For example, the matrix form of project management has led to the need for personnel data bases with information on individual skills (see Hemsley, 1978).

Also, government programs such as Equal Employment Opportunity (EEO) have produced the need for organizations to monitor and plan for the development of their personnel by demographic and other attributes. An example of this kind of system developed for AT&T is provided in Niehaus (1979). Sears, Bank of America, and

FIGURE 10.6. Comparison of Existing System to EPAS's Impact on Performance by Job Grouping.

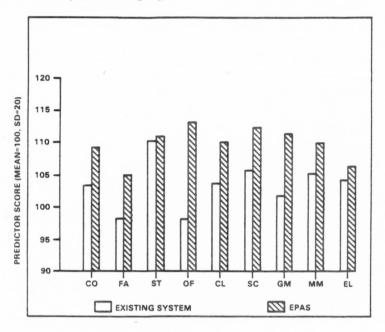

Source: Schmitz et al. (1984), p. 59.

General Motors have also developed advanced career management techniques because of EEO and affirmative action concerns (Walker, 1979).

Private organizations have developed extensive PJM systems for managing scarce human resources—technical personnel and managers. An example of an application to the petroleum industry is given by Bright (1976). Here the Union Oil Company was primarily concerned with its engineers and key managers. Forecasting and developing systems for internal transfer, promotion, and succession were two of the most frequently cited duties in a survey of corporate human resource planners (Walker & Wolfe, 1982).

Thus, while detailed PJM modules may not be used as frequently in nonmilitary settings, many organizations are developing systems for monitoring, analyzing, and planning for the development of personnel within the organization. These kinds of systems have been developed in many countries (Zolzer, 1978), in activities as diverse as health care (West 1978) and research (Childs & Wolfe, 1972), and many large private companies (Casson, 1978).

Directions for Future Research

Person-job matching problems will be a concern for most large organizations for years to come. Several aspects of the problem should show considerable research activity in the near term. These include performance assessment and utility analysis, decision simulation systems, and organizational design.

The key value of PJM systems is increasing the productivity of an organization through better personnel decisions. Most productivity gains are based on subjective or indirect estimates of utility. If direct and physically measurable output gains from job assignment systems can be identified, the use of such systems will undoubtedly expand.

Group or team productivity presents a particularly perplexing set of problems. The utility of a particular job assignment could be either much greater or smaller than one would estimate for an individual. Very limited utility work has been done in this area. Different operations research techniques would also be required to implement any findings in this area.

As computer data bases and flexible software proliferate, it is likely that personnel assignment policies will be incorporated into strategic planning models. Managers can then examine recruiting, training, compensation, and promotion policies and their impact on personnel performance and organizational productivity.

A final area for further research is organizational design. The present PJM systems have assumed that job requirements are specified. In the future, feedback from the PJM system can assist in the design of jobs and the structuring of the organization. PJM data will assist human factors experts and industrial engineers in determining which job design alternatives to implement.

SUMMARY

Person-job matching technology can be used to increase organizational productivity. This chapter has shown how the PJM system relates to selection and classification. The development of PJM solution techniques in both personnel psychology and operations research has also been discussed.

A systems approach to PJM was developed. Requirements determination and projection of the numbers and kinds of applicants are important inputs to the assignment process, in addition to classification data. Once demand, supply, and differential performance data are available, a plan can be made for matching people to jobs. This may be a straightforward direct assignment approach using either optimization techniques or a differential assignment algorithm. In large organizations there can be a two-stage process with both planning and execution phases.

A discussion of implementing PJM technologies was presented. The problems of quantifying the utility of such systems were described, using both personnel psychology and economic approaches to its measurement. An example of a major PJM system implementation for the Army was also presented. Directions for future research in utility analysis, decision simulation systems, and organizational design have been discussed.

Assessments of the impact of improved PJM appear to be substantial. Both Hunter and Schmidt (1982) and Schmitz and Nelson (1984) have found significant benefit to improved job assignment systems using quite different solution methods. PJM systems have the potential to produce substantial increases in labor productivity. However, there is need for personnel psychologists and operations researchers to work closely with management to identify systems benefits and to see that these are realized.

REFERENCES

Abellera, J. W., Mullins, C. J., & Earles, J. A. (1975, March). *Value of personnel classification information* (TR-75-2). Brooks Air Force Base, TX: Air Force Human Resources Laboratory.

Armor, D. J., Fernandez, R. L., Bers, K., & Schwarzbach, D. (1982, September). *Recruit aptitudes and Army job performance* (R-2874-MRAL). Santa Monica, CA: Rand Corp.

Baumol, W. J. (1977). *Economic theory and operations analysis.* Englewood Cliffs, NJ: Prentice-Hall.

Box, G. E., & Jenkins, G. M. (1976). *Time series analysis: Forecasting and control*. San Francisco: Holden Day.

Bonczek, R. H., Holsapple, C. W., & Whinston, A. B. (1981). *Foundations of decision support systems*. New York: Academic Press.

Bright, W. E. (1976, January). How one company manages its human resources. *Harvard Business Review, 54*, 80-93.

Brogden, H. E. (1946). An approach to the problem of differential prediction. *Psychometrika, 11*, 139-154.

Brogden, H. E. (1959). Efficiency of classification as a function of number of jobs, percent rejected, and the validity and intercorrelation of job performance estimates. *Educational and Psychological Measurement, 19*, 181-190.

Buddin, R. (1984, July). *Analysis of early military attrition behavior* (R-3069-MIL). Santa Monica, CA: Rand Corp.

Cascio, W. F. (1980). Responding to the demand for accountability: A critical analysis of three utility models. *Organizational Behavior and Human Performance, 25*, 32-45.

Cascio, W. F. (1982). *Applied psychology in personnel management*. Reston, VA: Reston.

Casson, R. J. (1978). Re-evaluating company manpower planning in light of some practical experiences. In D. Bryant & R. J. Niehaus (Eds.), *Manpower planning and organization design*. New York: Plenum Press.

Charnes, A., Coleman, R., Cooper, W. W., Kress, M., Lehto, R., & Lewis, K. (1982, July). *An in-context efficiency rating and utility function approach to force structure planning in the U.S. Navy* (CCS Research Rep. 433.) Austin: Center for Cybernetic Studies, University of Texas.

Charnes, A., & Cooper, W. W. (1961). *Management models and industrial applications of linear programming*. New York: Wiley.

Charnes, A., Cooper, W. W., Niehaus, R. J., & Stedry, A. (1972). Static and dynamic assignment models with multiple objectives, and some remarks on organization design. In A. Charnes, W. W. Cooper, & R. J. Niehaus (Eds.), *Studies in manpower planning*. Washington, DC: Department of the Navy.

Childs, M., & Wolfe, H. (1972, February). A decision and value approach to research personnel allocation. *Management Science, 18*, 269–278.

Cramer, J., & Pollatschek, M. A. (1979, May). Candidate to job allocation problem with a lexicographic objective. *Management Science, 23*, 466–473.

Cronbach, L. J., & Gleser, G. (1965). *Psychological Tests & Personnel Decisions.* Urbana, IL: University of Illinois Press.

Dale, C., & Gilroy C. (1983, March). The effect of the business cycle on the size and composition of the US Army. *Atlantic Economic Journal, 11*(1), 42–53.

Dantzig, G. (1982, April). Reminiscences about the origin of linear programming. *Operations Research Letters, 1*, 43–48.

Derman, C., Lieberman, G. J., & Ross, S. M. (1972). A sequential stochastic assignment problem. *Management Science, 18*, 349–355.

Dunnette, M. D. (1982). Critical concepts in the assessment of human capabilities. In M. D. Dunnette and E. A. Fleishman (Eds.), *Human performance and productivity: Human capability assessment.* Hillsdale, NJ: Erlbaum Associates.

Dunnette, M. D. (1966). *Personnel selection and placement.* Belmont, CA: Wadsworth.

Dwyer, P. S. (1954). Solution of the personnel classification problem with the method of optimal regions. *Psychometrika, 19*, 11–25.

Eastman, R. F. (1978, June). *The assignment module: An element of an experimental computer-enhanced career counseling system for Army officers* (Tech. Paper 294). Alexandria, VA: U.S. Army Research Institute.

Fernandez, R. L. (1985, January). *Setting enlistment standards and matching recruits to jobs using job performance criteria* (R-3067-MIL). Santa Monica, CA: Rand Corp.

Gray, N. H. (1978, September). *Canopy over Israel.* San Diego, CA: Personnel Training and Analysis Office (NAVSEACEN PAC).

Hadley, G. (1963). *Linear programming.* Reading, MA: Addison-Wesley.

Hatch, R. S. (1971). Development of optimal allocation algorithms for personnel assignment. In A. R. Smith (Ed.), *Models of manpower systems.* New York: American Elsevier.

Hayes, J. H. (1978, August). *The evolution of military officer personnel management policies: A preliminary study with parallels from industry* (R-2276-AF). Santa Monica, CA: Rand Corp.

Hayes-Roth, F., Waterman, D. A., & Lenat, D. B. (1983). *Building expert systems.* Reading, MA: Addison-Wesley.

Hemsley, J. R., Skragia, R., & Vasconcellos, E. (1978). Matrix organization in an industrializing society: Case studies from Brazil. In D. Bryant & R. J. Niehaus (Eds.), *Manpower planning and organization design.* New York: Plenum Press.

Hillier, F. S., & Lieberman, G. J. (1980). *Introduction to operations research* (3rd. ed.). San Francisco: Holden Day.

Holz, B. W., & Wroth, J. M. (1980). Improving strength forecasts: Support for Army manpower management. *Interfaces, 10,* 37-52.

Holz, B. W., et al. (1983, September). *Military occupational specialty enlisted strength and personnel management data forecasting system (MOSLS):* Executive summary (1244-04-84-CR). McLean, VA: General Research Corp.

Horst, P., & Sorenson, R. C. (1976, December). *Matrix transformation for optimal personnel assignments* (Tech. Note 77-5). San Diego, CA: Navy Personnel Research and Development Center.

Huck, D., & Allen J. (1977, March). *Sustaining volunteer enlistments in the decade ahead: The effect of declining population and unemployment.* McLean, VA: General Research Corp.

Hunter, J. E., & Schmidt, F. L. (1982). Fitting people to jobs: The impact of personnel selection on national productivity. In M. D. Dunnette & E. A. Fleishman (Eds.), *Human performance and productivity: Human capability assessment.* Hillsdale, NJ: Erlbaum Associates.

Hunter, J. E., & Schmidt, F. L. (1983, April). Quantifying the effects of psychological interventions on employee job performance and work-force productivity. *American Psychologist,* 473-478.

Kenney, R. L. (1980, August). *Manpower planning and personnel management models based on utility theory.* San Francisco: Woodward-Clyde Consultants.

Keeney, R. L., & Raiffa, H. (1976). *Decisions with multiple objectives: Preferences and value tradeoffs.* New York: Wiley.

Klingman, D., & Mote, J. (1983, March). *Survey of optimization solution approaches for career path planning models.* Austin, TX: Analysis, Research and Computation.

Kroeker, L. P., & Rafacz, B. A. (1983, November). *Classification and Assignment within PRIDE (CLASP): A recruit assignment model* (TR84-9). San Diego, CA: Navy Personnel Research and Development Center.

Kuhn, H. W. (1955). The Hungarian method for the assignment problem. *Naval Research Logistics Quarterly, 2,* p. 83-97.

Makridakis, S., Anderson, A., Carbone, R., Fildes, R., Hibon, M., Lewandowski, R., Newton, J., Parzen, E., & Winkler, R. (1982, April). The accuracy of extrapolation (time series) methods: Results of a forecasting competition. *Journal of Forecasting, 1,* 111-154.

Manganaris, A., & Schmitz, E. J. (1985, February). *The impact of the delayed entry program on first term attrition* (Tech. Rep.). Alexandria, VA: U.S. Army Research Institute.

Moore, B. E., & Sholtz, D. (1974, October). *Organizational tests of a static multiattribute assignment model.* Washington, DC: Office of Civilian Manpower Management, Navy Department.

Moskowitz, H., & Wright, G. P. (1979). *Operations research techniques for management.* Englewood Cliffs, NJ: Prentice-Hall.

Niehaus, R. J. (1977, July). *Computer-assisted manpower models using goal programming.* Washington, DC: Office of Civilian Personnel, Navy Department.

Niehaus, R. J. (1979). *Computer-assisted human resource planning.* New York: Wiley.

Pindyck, R. S., & Rubinfeld, D. L. (1981). *Econometric models and economic forecasts.* New York: McGraw-Hill.

Schmitz, E. J., & Nelson, A. (1984, June). *The allocation of Army personnel to military occupational specialties* (Tech. Rep.). Alexandria, VA: U.S. Army Research Institute.

Schmitz, E. J., Nord, R. D., McWhite, P. W., Brown, G. N., Gilmore, E. A., Konieczny, F. P., Moore, D. W., Randall, M. J., Paul, G. E., & Smyre, D. A. (1984, August). *Development of the Army's enlisted personnel allocation system* (Tech. Rep.). Alexandria, VA: U.S. Army Research Institute.

Simon, H. A. (1977). *The new science of management decision.* Englewood Cliffs, NJ: Prentice-Hall.

Starr, M. K., and Zeleny, M. (1977). MCDM—State and future of the art. *TIMS Studies in the Management Sciences.* North-Holland, 6.

Steuer, R. E. & Wallace, M. J., Jr. (1978). A linear multiple objective programming model for manpower selection and allocation decisions. In A. Charnes, W. W. Cooper, & R. J. Niehaus (Eds.), *Management science approaches to manpower planning and organization design.* Amsterdam, Netherlands: North-Holland.

Thompson, J. D. (1967). *Organizations in action.* New York: McGraw-Hill.

Thurow, L. C. (1975). *Generating inequality.* New York: Basic Books.

U.S. Army. (1983). *The Forecast System Master Plan.* Washington, D.C.: U.S. Army, Office of the Assistant Secretary (Manpower and Reserve Affairs).

Votaw, D. F. (1952). Methods of solving some personnel classification problems. *Psychometrika, 17,* 255-266.

Walker, J. W. (1979). Human resource planning: An evolution. *Pittsburgh Business Review, 47,* 2-8.

Walker, J. W., & Wolfe, M. N. (1982). Patterns in human resource planning practices. In J. W. Walker & K. F. Price (Eds.), *The challenge of human resource planning: Selected readings.* Human Resource Planning Society.

Ward, J. H. (1959a). The counseling assignment problem. *Psychometrika, 23,* 55-56.

Ward, J. H. (1959, April). *Use of a decision index in assigning air force personnel* (WADC Tech. Note 59-38). Lackland Air Force Base, TX: Personnel Laboratory.

Ward, J. H., Haney, D. L., Hendrix, W. H., & Pina, M. (1978, July). *Assignment procedures in the Air Force procurement management information system* (Tech. Rep. 78-30). Brooks Air Force Base, TX: Air Force Human Resources Laboratory.

Ward, J. H. (1977, August). *Creating mathematical models of judgement processes* (Tech. Report 77-47). Brooks Air Force Base, TX: Air Force Human Resources Laboratory.

West, E. N. (1978). An interactive manpower planning and scheduling system for a health facility. In D. Bryant & R. J. Niehaus (Eds.), *Manpower planning and organization design.* New York: Plenum Press.

Zolger, G. A. (1978). On the application of analytical models in personnel planning in the Bundeswehr. In D. Bryant & R. J. Niehaus (Eds.), *Manpower planning and organization design.* New York: Plenum Press.

NAME INDEX

SUBJECT INDEX

Abductive problem solving, a non-rule-based approach in AI, 280–87
Ability theory, updated, 345–46
Ability measurement, "new look", 338–39
Accretion type of learning, 363–66
Accuracy and reliability in military intelligence analysis, 318
Administrative criterion measure limitations, 404
Aggregate categorical forecasts, 448–49
Alternatives to organizational hierarchy: matrix organizations, 139–40; semi-autonomous work groups, 139–40
Alternative work schedules, 98–100
Analogies in cognitive processing model of decision making, 306
Analysis of cognitive skills: basic skills, 370–72; component skills, 370–71
Anchoring (estimations of probability values), 315
Application of person-job matching technology, 460–64; government, such as EEO, 463; military, 460–61; optimization model, 462–63; private organizations, 464–65
Appraisal and feedback in enhancing productivity, 81–85
Approaches to knowledge representation: conceptual dependency, 183–87; conversation theory, 192–95; human associative memory, 181–83; idealist perspective, 180; knowledge representation language (RRL), 190; semantic net formalism, 177–78; SHRDLU, 187–90

Approaches to studying decision making: decision support systems in dealing with large volumes of information, 299–300; decision theory, 299; psychological decision making models, 300–01
Aristotle, 170
Armed Services Vocational Aptitude Battery (ASVAB), 335
Army Alpha tests, 333
Artificial intelligence, 157, 160, 165; area of computer science, 236ff; in enhancing human productivity, 167; in factory of the future, 143; non-rule-based approaches, 275–78
ASVAB composite, pattern of correlations with, 358–59, 361
Attrition among bank tellers, 78–79
Automated support for decision makers, 300
Automation: as important technological force, 127; in work-systems, 148

Backtracking, types of state-space search strategy, 255
Basic constructs in leader & organizational behavior: environmental complexity by level, 47; issues of information acquisition and use, 46; organizational adaptation requirements, 45–46
Battery development and administration for Project A, Pilot, 398–400
Bayesian classification, a non-rule-based approach in AI, 278–80
Behavior approach to study of leadership, 8, 9–10

ABOUT THE EDITORS AND CONTRIBUTORS

JOSEPH ZEIDNER is research professor of public policy and behavioral sciences and director of the Administrative Sciences Program, Graduate School of Arts and Sciences, The George Washington University. Before joining George Washington University in the fall of 1982, Zeidner was the technical director of the U.S. Army Research Institute and chief psychologist of the U.S. Army. Recently, he co-authored *Behavioral Science in the Army: A Corporate History of the Army Research Institute*, to be published by the U.S. Government Printing Office. His current interests include person-computer interaction, human factors in systems design, cognitive science, personnel selection, and training technology.

T. O. JACOBS and **ELLIOTT JAQUES** ("Leadership in Complex Systems")

OWEN JACOBS is chief of the Executive Development Research Group (EDRG) of the U.S. Army Research Institute. He received B.A. and M.A. degrees from Vanderbilt University and the Ph.D. from the University of Pittsburgh in 1956. He joined the Army Research Institute in 1975. His research interests have centered primarily on leadership and organizational development and now are focused primarily on the executive level with dual objectives of facilitating the growth of executive skills and developing methodology for assessing performance at senior organizational levels.

ELLIOTT JAQUES is professor of sociology and director of the Institute of Organization and Social Studies at Brunel University, England. He holds an M.D. from Johns Hopkins Medical School and a Ph.D. in social relations from Harvard. His work is in the field of social institutions and individual behavior. He is currently engaged on two long-term projects, one with the U.S. Army through the Army Research Institute and the other—an organizational development project—with a large Australian-based international mining corporation.

CYNTHIA M. PAVETT, LAURIE A. BROEDLING, and **KENT H. HUFF** ("Productivity in Organizations")

CYNTHIA M. PAVETT is an associate professor of management in the school of Business Administration at the University of San Diego. Since the receipt of her Ph.D. from the University of Utah in 1978, she has conducted research in the areas of feedback and stress management work, motivation, and productivity. Her current research endeavors are focused on the effects of exercise on organizational attitudes and behaviors. For the past five years, she has been on a part-time faculty appointment at the Navy Personnel Research and Development Center. Pavett is active in the Academy of Management and holds memberships in the American Psychological Association and the American Institute for Decision Sciences.

LAURIE A. BROEDLING is director of the Training Systems Development Division at the Navy Personnel Research and Development Center. She has a B.A. in psychology from Brown University and a Ph.D. in organizational psychology from The George Washington University. Broedling has conducted research in work motivation, productivity, and management practices. Her current interests focus on management training and development.

KENT H. HUFF is a personnel research psychologist with the Navy Personnel Research and Development Center, where he serves as the chief administrative officer to the Human Factors and Organizational Management Systems Laboratory. Before joining NPRDC, Huff was a research scientist with the Human Resources Research Organization, where he directed research in functional literacy and training. He has also served in the Air Force as psychologist assigned to the Air Force Human Resources Laboratory, where he directed and managed a R&D program in literacy training and motivation.

KENYON B. DE GREENE ("Sociotechnical Systems") received his Ph.D. in biological/behavioral sciences (physiological psychology) from UCLA. He held positions at Rand Corporation, System Development Corporation, Northrop Corporation, and Aerospace Corporation. At these corporations De Greene was responsible for the analysis, design, and management of a number of complex aerospace systems, but particularly large-scale computerized command-control-communications-intelligence ($C^3 I$) systems. He is presently a professor of systems management at the University of Southern California, where he teaches graduate courses in organization and environment, organizational and management behavior, systems analysis, and human factors. De Greene is the editor and main contributing author of *Systems Psychology* (McGraw-Hill Series in Management, 1970) and the author of *Sociotechnical Systems: Factors in Analysis, Design, and Management* (Prentice-Hall, 1973) and of *The Adaptive Organization: Anticipation and Management of Crisis* (Wiley, 1981). He is the author of more than 50 articles in *Behavioral Science, Ergonomics, Human Factors, Organizations and Administrative Sciences, IEEE Transactions on Systems, Man, and Cybernetics, Progress in Cybernetics and Systems Research*, and other scholarly journals, books, encyclopedias, and national and international conference proceedings.

DIK GREGORY ("Philosophy and Practice in Knowledge Representation") is a senior psychologist at the Applied Psychology Unit of the Admiralty Research Establishment in Teddington, England. He received a psychology honors degree from Nottingham University in 1978, which included a year spent working on the Royal Navy's manpower selection programs. For the last seven years he has been concerned with developing psychological and cybernetic approaches to the problems of knowledge acquisition and representation for human-machine systems. In May 1983 he began a three-year exchange appointment at the U.S. Army Research Institute, Alexandria, Virginia, working on designs for intelligent computer support systems for job aiding and training and on conversational modeling.

GORDON PASK and **DIK GREGORY** ("Conversational Systems")
GORDON PASK is a research professor at Brunel University, London, Concordia University, Montreal, and the Architectural Association School of Architecture, London. He also is director of research, System Research, Ltd., London. He acquired qualifications in engineering and an M.A. from Cambridge University in 1954, a Ph.D. in psychology from London University in 1966, and a D.Sc. from

Oxford University in 1977. Pask has been a visiting professor at several universities in North America and Mexico and a fellow of NTAS, and has directed research in cybernetics at various nonprofit corporations. He has received a number of honors, including gold medals from cybernetics associations in England and the United States. Current research includes adaptive knowledge systems, conversations theory, and a protologic Lp. He has written more than 200 papers and seven books, and has two books in publication.

DANA S. NAU ("Knowledge-Based Expert Systems") is an associate professor of computer science at the University of Maryland. Nau received a B.S. in applied mathematics from the University of Missouri at Rolla in 1974. He received an A.M. and a Ph.D. in computer science from Duke University in 1976 and 1979, respectively. Nau has published more than 40 papers, mainly on subjects related to artificial intelligence. His current research interests include searching and problem-solving methods in artificial intelligence, expert computer systems, and automated manufacturing. He has recently received a Presidential Young Investigator Award from the National Science Foundation.

RUTH H. PHELPS, **REBECCA M. PLISKE**, and **SHARON A. MUTTER** ("Improving Decision Making: A Cognitive Approach")
RUTH H. PHELPS is chief of the Scientific Coordination Office, Boise, at the U.S. Army Research Institute. She is responsible for managing Army R&D programs in the use of technology to train Army personnel in the Reserve Component. Phelps received her Ph.D. degree from Kansas State University, specializing in the modeling of decision-making and human judgment processes. She has conducted research in the areas of cognition, decision making, memory processes, and technology for the Army.

REBECCA M. PLISKE is a research psychologist in the Personnel Utilization Technical Area of the U.S. Army Research Institute. She received a B.A. in psychology from Miami University and M.A. and Ph.D. degrees in psychology from Bowling Green State University.

Her current research interests include behavioral economic modeling of personnel decisions and the design of decision aids.

SHARON A. MUTTER is a research psychologist at the Army Research Institute for the Behavioral and Social Sciences. She received a Ph.D. in experimental psychology from George Washington University in 1984. Mutter's research interests focus on the areas of attention and memory. Since joining ARI, she has conducted research on the cognitive skills involved in military intelligence analysis, the impact of cognitive and motivational variables in foreign-language acquisition and loss, effect of elaborative encoding processes on retention, and individual differences in memory performance. Mutter is a member of the American Psychological Association and the Eastern Psychological Association.

PATRICK C. KYLLONEN ("Theory-Based Cognitive Assessment") was a personnel research psychologist in the Manpower and Personnel Division of the Air Force Human Resources Laboratory, where he conducted basic research on cognitive assessment as part of the Learning Abilities Measurement Program (LAMP). He received a B.A. in psychology from St. John's University and a Ph.D. in educational psychology from Stanford University in 1984. His interests are in the area of individual differences in learning and cognition with particular focus on development of learner models for use in computerized instruction. Kyllonen is an assistant professor of educational psychology at the University of Georgia.

NEWELL K. EATON, LAWRENCE M. HANSER and **JOYCE L. SHIELDS** ("Validating Selection Tests Against Job Performance")
NEWELL K. EATON is director of the Manpower and Personnel Planning Research Laboratory and associate director of the U.S. Army Research Institute (ARI). His undergraduate and graduate degrees earned at the University of Minnesota, University of Iowa, and University of Oregon Health Services Center. After completing his Ph.D. in 1975, he joined the ARI field office at Fort Knox, where he conducted research on tank crew selection, motivation, training, and turnover. In 1980 he moved to the ARI headquarters in Alexandria, Virginia,

to design and manage research in recruiting and retention. For the past three years he has led the ARI selection and classification research group, and has been the ARI principal scientist on Project A, the large-scale selection and classification project described in his chapter.

LAWRENCE M. HANSER is chief of the Selection and Classification Technical Area at the Army Research Institute, where he manages a program of institutional research to support the Army's operational, selection, and classification system. His professional pursuits have emphasized the application of personnel science to personnel practice. Prior to joining ARI he was an assistant professor of psychology at Western Kentucky University. Hanser received a Ph.D. in industrial psychology from Iowa State University in 1977.

JOYCE L. SHIELDS is a senior principal and manager in the Human-Systems Development Practice of the **HAY** Group, Inc. Before joining HAY, Shields was director of the Manpower and Personnel Research Laboratory and associate director of the U.S. Army Research Institute for the Behavioral and Social Sciences (ARI). Her professional pursuits have emphasized applied R&D to enhance performance of military systems through design of manpower, personnel, and training programs. Her most significant Army project was a massive, multiyear, multi-million-dollar program to improve the selection, classification, and utilization of enlisted personnel. She is a fellow of the American Psychological Association (APA), president of the Division of Military Psychology of the APA, and on the editorial board of the *Journal of Military Psychology.*

EDWARD J. SCHMITZ and **BETTY W. HOLZ** ("Technologies for Person-Job Matching")
EDWARD J. SCHMITZ is team leader for Manpower and Personnel Planning at the Army Research Institute. His research interests include human resources planning, decision support systems, and evaluation research. He is a member of the Institute of Management Science, Military Operations Research Society, American Economic Association, and the Inter-University Seminar on Armed Forces and Society.

BETTY W. HOLZ is director of the Management Sciences Group for General Research Corporation. She has been involved in the design, development, and implementation of major automated systems used, for example, by the Army for personnel management and policy development. Her areas of technological expertise and interest include interactive decision support systems and management information systems, forecasting from historical time series data, large-scale linear optimization, and artificial intelligence.